Get the eBooks FREE!

(PDF, ePub, Kindle, and liveBook all included)

We believe that once you buy a book from us, you should be able to read it in any format we have available. To get electronic versions of this book at no additional cost to you, purchase and then register this book at the Manning website.

Go to https://www.manning.com/freebook and follow the instructions to complete your pBook registration.

That's it!
Thanks from Manning!

JavaScript on Things

JavaScript on Things

HACKING HARDWARE FOR WEB DEVELOPERS

LYZA DANGER GARDNER

MANNING

SHELTER ISLAND

For online information and ordering of this and other Manning books, please visit
www.manning.com. The publisher offers discounts on this book when ordered in quantity.
For more information, please contact

Special Sales Department
Manning Publications Co.
20 Baldwin Road
PO Box 761
Shelter Island, NY 11964
Email: orders@manning.com

Manning Publications Co.   Developmental editor: Susanna Kline
20 Baldwin Road   Review editor: Ivan Martinovic
PO Box 761   Project editor: Kevin Sullivan
Shelter Island, NY 11964   Copyeditor: Andy Carroll
                                             Proofreader: Melody Dolab
                                             Typesetter: Gordan Salinovic
                                         Cover designer: Leslie Haimes
               Cover and interior illustrations: Lyza Danger Gardner

ISBN 9781617293863
Printed in the United States of America
1 2 3 4 5 6 7 8 9 10 – EBM – 23 22 21 20 19 18

brief contents

v

          OTHER ENVIRONMENTS 295

          10 ▪ JavaScript and constrained hardware   297
          11 ▪ Building with Node.js and tiny computers   332
          12 ▪ In the cloud, in the browser, and beyond   375

contents

vii

preface

On a late summer day in 2013, I stood on a stage in a large tent on the grounds of Bletchley Park in England, the site where British codebreakers (famously including Alan Turing) defeated the Enigma machine in World War II. It was one of the better days of my life, as two fundamentally wonderful things had just happened.

First, I'd just somehow managed to win a hacking contest (that's why I was onstage). The National Museum of Computing—also located on the grounds of Bletchley Park—was seeking tech help in creating web-based, interactive timeline exhibits. I'd stayed up through the night, extending an open source JavaScript library and building a prototype: this was my entry, which was, to my great delight, declared best in show. The second wonderful thing was that I'd won a prize—and not just any prize.

The reward I received was one of the original Arduino Uno starter kits—an Arduino board, a collection of electronic components, and an instructional book. It profoundly changed my life. I'd later find that combining my newly learned electronics skills with the stuff I did every day—coding open source, standards-based websites and apps—resulted in one of the most fascinating alchemies I'd ever experienced: JavaScript on Things. That is, I could use the JavaScript I already knew as a turbo boost to electronics hacking and the internet of things (IoT).

That came later, however. Initially, I learned how to construct simple electronic circuits by working through the examples in the kit's book and, later, avidly searching the web to learn more. I learned how to apply logical control to these circuits by programming the Arduino Uno's microcontroller, writing simple sketches (programs) in

Arduino's (very) C/C++–like language, optimized for the board's (very) limited program space and memory.

And then, at the end of 2013, I discovered Johnny-Five. The open source Node.js framework was young at the time, but already powerful. Instead of writing lower-level, constrained Arduino code, I could write higher-level JavaScript programs to control my Uno. I thought, "Wow, if I'd only discovered this earlier."

The combination of JavaScript and microcontrollers isn't just a parlor trick, performed for the sake of coating the entire known world with JavaScript. At first, even I, a Node.js adherent, was skeptical: maybe this is pointless; maybe it will never take root.

Don't worry. It's not, and it did.

Adding JavaScript into the mix perversely *simplified* my experience, and made prototyping little projects much, much faster. I could use development workflows that were more familiar to me as a web developer. I didn't have to concern myself as much with lower-level memory and resource optimization. Johnny-Five's encapsulation of behavior into high-level *component classes* is intuitive: the resulting code can be cleaner and easier to work with than many Arduino libraries. And it allowed me to take advantage of the almost fathomless depths of the worldwide Node.js ecosystem via npm. I could simply import modules, just like any other Node.js script out there. It was wonderful.

I want to be very clear: there's nothing wrong with Arduino or more "traditional" C-based microcontroller programming. There are very good reasons to care about memory management, for example, especially if you're writing firmware or making production devices. And Arduino is rather a miracle: its entire *raison d'être* is to make embedded electronics accessible to novices. Starting from scratch with Arduino and the Arduino programming language is a perfectly reasonable, surmountable approach.

But JavaScript can help web developers get up to speed with electronics faster. For one thing, introductory materials for Arduino (and other platforms) often assume no pre-existing knowledge of programming whatsoever, which means you may end up wading through explanations of what an array is and how loops work. The finicky constraints and particulars of microcontrollers can be distracting when you're just learning how things work. IDEs can be clunky. In some cases, you can end up spending a lot of time getting things configured and not much time making things actually happen. JavaScript has the power to abstract much of this away, letting you focus on the essential new things you need to learn.

From that notion, this book arose: the idea that JavaScript can serve as a gateway to electronics, making it easier for more people to learn how to make cool stuff with a minimum of cognitive pain. JavaScript is the most popular programming language in the world, the de facto language of the web; and the internet of things and maker culture is tantalizing both creatively and commercially. Why not make a happy blend of the two?

At the end of the day, *this stuff is fun*. It's a kick to be able to dream up and make real your own inventions. It's confidence-lifting to have a basic competency with low-voltage electronic circuits, and to understand how embedded systems work in the real world.

Maybe you'll really love this like I do. Maybe you'll help contribute to open source projects. Maybe you'll construct a wildly clever gadget. Maybe you'll teach other people what you've learned.

Perhaps you'll simply have fun. That, on its own, is more than enough.

acknowledgments

My gratitude starts right where my love of hardware hacking began: with the Over the Air conference crew and The National Museum of Computing (UK), whence my initial Arduino Starter Kit originated. None of this would have happened without that serendipitous event. Dan Appelquist, Margaret Gold, and Matthew Cashmore—thank you for creating such a superb conference and inviting me to it, more than once, even!

Rick Waldron achieves more in a day than I do in a month. (Rick, your JavaScript genius is legend.) His involvement with TC-39, the ECMA working group responsible for the JavaScript language itself, means he is literally indispensable. Oh, and he also invented Johnny-Five, the leading open source Node.js framework for robotics and IoT, around which much of this book revolves. I could go on for pages, chapters, about Rick.

Writing a book takes a ridiculously large amount of time. Huge thanks go to leaders and colleagues at Bocoup for giving me the time and support I needed, and for continuously pumping steady amounts of enthusiasm in my direction, as well as to the partners and staff at Cloud Four for their patience.

Great editors are a true gift in a world that sometimes dismisses the value of editorial process and feedback. My editor, Susanna Kline, provided helpful and insightful support through the long haul. Brad Luyster, your technical review feedback was phenomenal; it's hard to say thank you hard enough. Several other reviewers also provided helpful feedback on the manuscript at different stages: Alessandro Campeis, Amit Lamba, Andrew Meredith, Bruno Sonnino, Earl Bingham, and Kevin Liao. I also want to thank Manning's publisher, Marjan Bace, and the rest of the editorial and production teams who worked on the book behind the scenes.

Thanks also to Francis Gulotta for technical input, Kyle Jackson at Manning for fielding my tech support needs, and my pal Chau Doan for sharing his firmware and embedded-electronics wisdom.

The Johnny-Five and related JavaScript-on-Things communities have been just brilliant. Thanks, Derek Runberg of SparkFun! Thanks, Donovan Buck, David Resseguie, Brian Genisio, and all the other Johnny-Five contributors!

Shawn Hymel's Arduino library for the APDS-9960 sensor—a handsome piece of work—served as a springboard for parts of chapter 9. And the rover examples in chapters 6 and 8 are adapted from code written by Rick Waldron. (Again, Rick, thanks!)

Equally important to those who help you on a project itself are those who help you keep your sanity while enduring it: thank you, my splendid family and friends.

I saved this extra-best spot right here to thank my partner (and all-round fantastic person) Bryan Fox: without his joyful and steady presence, this book could not possibly exist.

about this book

"I'm curious about hardware and electronics and IoT, but I have absolutely no idea where to begin." I've heard that notion, in many variations, from many (dozens?—at least—maybe a hundred?) web developers. Yes, it certainly *would* be fun to be able to build robots and clever gadgets. Yes, it *would* be useful to know how to read data from sensors and do interesting things with the data, to be able to construct your own automated, web-connected devices (for feeding your pet on time, detecting rainfall amounts, displaying the latest rugby scores—the mind really does boggle at all the possibilities). But also, yes, it can feel like a daunting, even overwhelming, new landscape if you've never so much as made an LED blink, much less written and flashed optimized firmware to an embedded microcontroller.

Good news! You can take advantage of your understanding of JavaScript and general programming metaphors to frame your learning adventure, and make wrapping your head around this new world a bit less chaotic. JavaScript can lend a sheen of familiarity, providing a touchstone to ease your introduction to electronics, hardware, and the internet of things (IoT).

This book teaches the fundamentals of electronics and embedded systems for folks who are comfortable with basic JavaScript but who may have no experience whatsoever wiring up even the simplest circuit. Emphasis is put on the topics that will be new to software developers: the critical basics of designing and building circuits, hardware components (sensors, motors, resistors, and the like), and the interface between hardware and software.

Over the course of this book, you'll get hands-on with a variety of development boards, hardware components, and software platforms. For the experiments (small projects) in the first two-thirds of the book, we'll use the Johnny-Five open source Node.js framework with the Arduino Uno development board. Johnny-Five's API provides many intuitive component classes that you can use to quickly prototype your gadgets and inventions. The Uno is the most ubiquitous hobbyist board in the world, boasting stability, simplicity, reliability, and a huge community of users and educators. The last third of the book surveys a broader range of platforms, including the Node.js-capable Tessel 2 and the very popular Raspberry Pi.

By the end of the book, you should have a foundational toolkit—both mental and physical—for planning, designing, implementing, and extending your own JavaScript-controlled electronic creations.

Roadmap

The book consists of 12 chapters:

- Chapter 1 defines what embedded systems are and enumerates the physical components from which they're built. It explains the ways in which JavaScript and hardware can work together.
- Chapter 2 introduces the Arduino Uno development board and gets you hands-on, quickly, with some basic blinking LEDs. We'll briefly look at how to control the Uno with the Arduino IDE before jumping into JavaScript and Johnny-Five.
- Chapter 3 zooms way in on the fundamentals of electronics that serve as the foundation for all the circuits you'll ever build. You'll plumb the depths of Ohm's law and build a few different kinds of simple circuits.
- Chapters 4 through 6 are a romp through key electronics and concepts for embedded gadgets, exploring input (sensors), output (actuators), and physical movement (motors and servos). Using the Johnny-Five framework, you'll get a chance to build a bunch of different experiments with an Arduino Uno board.
- Chapter 7 examines serial communication, which is used for exchanging more sophisticated data. You'll try out several serial components, including a compass (magnetometer), an accelerometer, and a GPS, again using Johnny-Five and the Arduino Uno.
- Chapters 8 and 9 introduce the Node.js-capable Tessel 2 development board. In chapter 8, you'll learn how to make projects that aren't tethered by wires. In chapter 9, you'll explore the process of taking an original project from idea to inception.
- Chapters 10 and 11 delve into other I/O-capable embedded hardware and JavaScript. Chapter 10 looks at JavaScript and JavaScript-like environments on constrained platforms like the Espruino Pico. Chapter 11 explores more general-purpose single-board computers (SBCs) like the Raspberry Pi.

- Chapter 12 touches on cloud services and hardware control from the browser, and it looks to the future. You'll learn how to use a cloud service, resin.io, to manage and deploy a Johnny-Five application to a BeagleBone Black, and you'll build an in-browser wireless doorbell with the Puck.js device and the Web Bluetooth API.

Who should read this book?

This is a book for people who have some experience with JavaScript, but who know little or nothing about electronic circuitry and microcontroller programming.

Code examples in this book are not, for the most part, complex. My philosophy is that it's better for code to be readable and understandable than for it to be show-offy and clever. You certainly don't need to have a deep familiarity with every word in the ECMA-262 spec (that's the document that defines the JavaScript language); but if you feel faint at the sight of arrow functions or haven't yet gotten to know Promises, for example, you may want to brush up a bit or keep a friendly companion at your side, such as the very excellent *Secrets of the JavaScript Ninja, Second Edition*, by John Resig, Bear Bibeault, and Josip Maras (Manning, 2016; www.manning.com/books/secrets-of-the-javascript-ninja-second-edition). Code complexity and the use of modern language features increase toward the end of the book.

Although the step-by-step instructions for the experiments provide all the commands you'll need to make your creations go, you should have basic competency in installing, managing, and using Node.js and the npm package manager. You should also be comfortable with executing commands from within a terminal environment.

A working knowledge of HTML and general grasp of CSS is helpful, although not essential. (You could always cut and paste source markup for those components.) Chapter 12 involves the use of Git version control software—prior experience with Git is helpful but not critical.

Code conventions and downloads

This book includes copious examples, which include various resources needed for applications and experiments: JavaScript, HTML, CSS, JSON, and so on. Source code in listings, or in text, is in a fixed-width font to separate it from ordinary text. Additionally, method or class names, variable names, object properties, method parameters, HTML elements, and the like, in text are also presented using a fixed-width font.

Johnny-Five is open source, released under the (liberal) MIT software license. The book makes use of many other open source software projects, including a dozen or so third-party npm modules. Most of the hardware platforms explored are open source as well; an exception is the Raspberry Pi 3, covered in chapter 11. To complete the "weather ball" example in chapter 5, you'll need a (free) API key from Dark Sky (https://darksky.net/dev/register).

Code annotations accompany many of the source code listings, highlighting important concepts.

The source code and assets for all examples in this book are available at https://github.com/lyzadanger/javascript-on-things. Most examples in the book include all the needed code and markup in the text (source code for third-party modules isn't included). But you can find the complete source of a few longer examples toward the end of the book, as well as binary assets for examples (such as the MP3 used in the web-controlled doorbell in chapter 12), in the code repository.

A zip file containing source code at the time of publication will also be available on the publisher's website: www.manning.com/books/javascript-on-things.

Book forum

Purchase of *JavaScript on Things* includes free access to a private web forum run by Manning Publications where you can make comments about the book, ask technical questions, and receive help from the author and from other users. To access the forum, go to https://forums.manning.com/forums/javascript-on-things. You can also learn more about Manning's forums and the rules of conduct at https://forums.manning.com/forums/about.

Manning's commitment to our readers is to provide a venue where a meaningful dialogue between individual readers and between readers and the author can take place. It is not a commitment to any specific amount of participation on the part of the author, whose contribution to the forum remains voluntary (and unpaid). We suggest you try asking the author some challenging questions lest her interest stray! The forum and the archives of previous discussions will be accessible from the publisher's website as long as the book is in print.

About the author

LYZA DANGER GARDNER likes figuring out how to do things. In turn, she likes to teach others how to do new things, too. Lyza cofounded Cloud Four, a web consultancy in Portland, Oregon. She's been building web things for over 20 years, advocating for elegant standards, education, and compassion in pursuit of the best possible future web. You can find her online at www.lyza.com or @lyzadanger on Twitter. As a counterpoint to her futuristic technical vantage, she lives in the forest in Vermont and enjoys anachronistic hobbies. She reads and reads and reads.

Part 1

A JavaScripter's introduction to hardware

This part of the book will introduce you to the fundamentals of embedded systems and electronic circuits. In chapter 1, you'll learn what *embedded systems* are and how to analyze their constituent components. We'll spend some time looking at what it means for JavaScript to "control" hardware, and we'll examine the different ways that JavaScript and electronics can work together.

You'll meet the Arduino Uno R3 development board in chapter 2, which we'll use with all of the experiments through chapter 7. You'll learn what the main parts of development boards do and how they interact with other software and hardware components. You'll try out some basic LED experiments with the Uno using both the Arduino IDE and the Johnny-Five Node.js framework.

Chapter 3 will teach you the key fundamentals of electronic circuitry, diving into Ohm's law and the relationships between voltage, current, and resistance. You'll work on a breadboard, constructing series and parallel circuits that contain multiple LEDs.

When you're finished with this part of the book, you'll have grasp of the basic embedded-system underpinnings and core circuit concepts. You'll be ready to start building small, JavaScript-controlled projects with different kinds of inputs and outputs.

Bringing JavaScript and hardware together

This chapter covers

- Components and hardware involved in hobbyist projects and the "internet of things"
- Common components of embedded systems
- Different methods for using JavaScript with embedded systems
- Tools and supplies you'll need to start building

As a JavaScript-savvy web developer, you make logical alchemy happen every day. But now it's possible to wield your software-development skills in a new way, to program and control things in the real world. In this chapter, you'll learn about the hardware involved in different kinds of projects and devices, and you'll also see how JavaScript and hardware can work together.

We're surrounded by little magical *things* that blend the physical world with the realm of the logical, connected, and virtual (figure 1.1). A keychain that broadcasts its location wirelessly so you can find it with an app on your smartphone. A plant pot that makes whining noises when it needs to be watered, or, better yet, sends you

Figure 1.1 Oh, the magical things in our world!

a petulant text message. Billions of such objects blink, beep, tweet, automatically dim the lights, make customized pots of tea, and otherwise perform their specialized duties across the planet.

It's fun to build this stuff. The creativity involved when crafting with these kinds of physical gadgets, the grassroots charm of inventive homebrew projects—these are the kinds of things that hold appeal for web developers. We're cut out for prototyping, experimenting with new technologies, and blazing our own trails.

But getting started can be intimidating. When we see all the wires and components, hear the jargon, stand on the outside looking in at hardware-hacking communities, the kinds of skills involved can feel formidable, foreign. As a JavaScript developer, you may be faced with some hurdles—perceived complexity, overabundant and scattered information, conflation of hardware and software concepts—as you make your tentative first forays into the world of physical hardware.

We're going to use your JavaScript know-how as an advantage, an aid to learning how to design and build the kinds of *things* that make up the "internet of things" (IoT) and inspire hardware hackers. You'll be able to use your software-development skills to skip past some distractions and get focused, quickly, on the new skills you need to learn.

To get a feel for the journey we're taking, let's first take a look at the kinds of things you'll be learning to build. Let's explore what we mean, exactly, when we say *things* or *hardware*.

1.1   *The anatomy of hardware projects*

We could build a little gadget that would automatically turn a fan on when it gets warm. This miniature, independent climate-control device would continuously monitor the temperature of the surrounding environment. When it gets too hot, the fan comes on. When it's nice and cool again, the fan turns off.

While we wouldn't win any prestigious awards for the invention of this admittedly pedestrian contrivance, its basic ingredients are common to the other—more inspiring—things you'll learn to build.

1.1.1 *Inputs and outputs*

The most important thing—really the only thing—our temperature-triggered device needs to do is turn a fan on when it's too toasty and turn it back off again when the area around it has cooled off. The motor-driven fan is an example of an *output device*.

To get continuous information about the temperature of the immediate environment—so that the device can make decisions about when to turn the fan on or off—we need data from an *input*, in this case a temperature sensor (figure 1.2).

Inputs provide incoming data to the system, and *sensors* are a type of input that provides data about the physical environment. There are all kinds of sensors you can use in projects: sensors for light, heat, noise, vibration, vapors, humidity, smells, motion, flames—you name it. Some, like our fan's temperature sensor, provide simple data—just a single value representing temperature—whereas others, like GPS or accelerometers, produce more elaborate data.

A project's *outputs* represent its net functionality to someone using it. Blinking lights, irritating beeping sounds, status readouts on LCD screens, a robotic arm moving sideways—all these are kinds of outputs. For this project, the fan is the sole output.

Not all inputs and outputs necessarily manifest in the physical world. A customer encountering an error when trying to order a product online (virtual input) might cause a red light to go on (physical output) on a device sitting on a support technician's desk. Conversely, a change in soil humidity (physical sensor input) might cause a plant pot to send a demanding text message (virtual output).

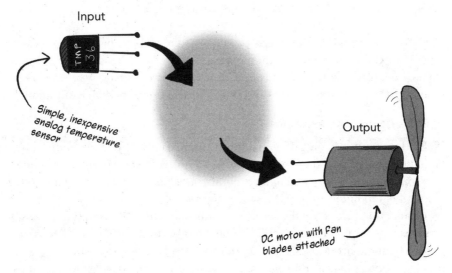

Figure 1.2   The automatic fan system needs to take *input* from a temperature sensor and manage the *output* of a motorized fan.

1.1.2 Processing

Our automatic fan also needs a brain, something that can pay attention to the temperature sensor's readings and turn the fan on when it gets too warm. The kind of brain it needs is in fact a tiny computer: a processor, some memory, and the ability to process inputs and control outputs. When processor, memory, and I/O functionality are contained in a single physical package, we call the resulting chip a *microcontroller* (figure 1.3).

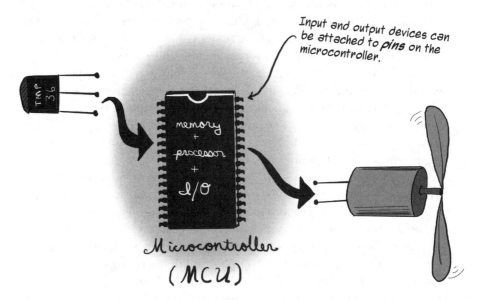

Figure 1.3   The automatic fan needs a brain. A popular option is a microcontroller, which combines a processor, memory, and I/O capabilities in a single package.

Microcontrollers (MCUs) aren't as powerful as the general-purpose processors in laptops. Most can't run a full operating system (most, not all, as you'll see), but they're cheap, reliable, small, and consume minimal power—that's why they're positively ubiquitous in hardware projects and products like our apocryphal automatic fan.

1.1.3 Power, circuits, and systems

We've now got input, output, and a brain—time to pull the bits together into a *system.* We'll need to connect the components using one or more electronic circuits and provide some power. Constructing a system involves both circuit design and the manipulation of components in physical space (figure 1.4).

Connecting wires directly to a microcontroller's tiny *pins* would require solder and a very steady hand. Not to mention that we'd end up with a lot of loose parts awkwardly floating around. To aid hardware developers, microcontrollers are often mounted onto physical *development boards* (figure 1.5). Among other things, boards make it easier to connect I/O devices to the microcontroller.

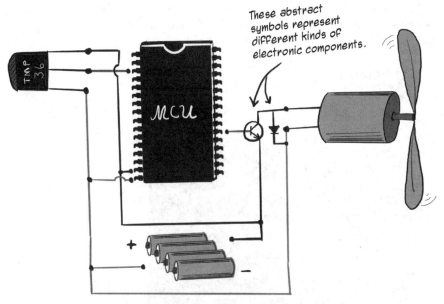

Figure 1.4 A rough schematic drawing showing how the fan's inputs, outputs, and microcontroller are connected in a system with power and circuitry. Don't stress out if the symbols are new to you—you'll be learning about circuitry as we continue our journey.

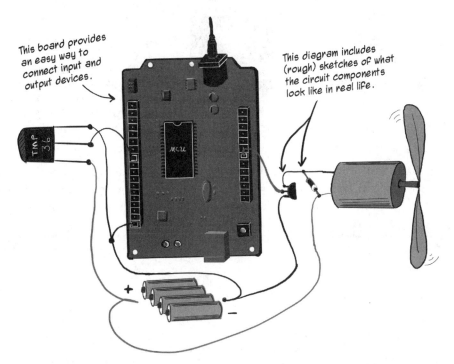

Figure 1.5 Microcontroller-based development boards make it more convenient to connect input and output devices.

A development board helps, but we're still left with a number of loose wires and components. To help corral this, hardware developers use a prototyping tool called a *breadboard* (figure 1.6) to lay out circuits in physical space.

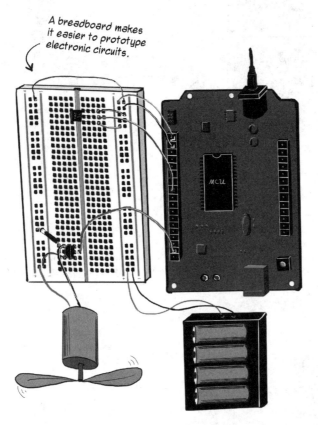

A breadboard makes it easier to prototype electronic circuits.

Figure 1.6 A breadboard provides an electrically connected grid on which to prototype electronic circuits.

1.1.4 *Logic and firmware*

Our hardware design is moving along, but you might be wondering how the microcontroller knows what to do. There's logic involved here, as shown in the following listing: listening to the sensor, making decisions, sending instructions to turn the fan on or off.

Listing 1.1 Pseudo-code for temperature-triggered fan logic

```
initialize temperatureSensor
initialize outputFan
initialize fanThreshold to 30 (celsius temperature)

loop main
    read temperatureSensor value into currentTemp
    if currentTemp is greater than fanThreshold
        if outputFan is off
            turn outputFan on
```

```
else if currentTemp is less than or equal to fanThreshold
    if outputFan is on
        turn outputFan off
```

The dominant language for programming microcontrollers has long been C (or C-like derivatives). Writing C for microcontrollers tends to be platform-specific and can be quite low-level. References to specific memory addresses and bitwise operations are common.

The code is compiled to architecture-specific assembly code. To get the code into the project, it is physically uploaded, or *flashed*, to the microcontroller's *program memory*.

This program memory is usually non-volatile memory—ROM, the kind of memory that lets the microcontroller "remember" the program even if it's powered off (in contrast with RAM, which only retains its contents if it's powered). The space available for programs is constrained, often on the order of a few tens of kilobytes, meaning programs that run on microcontrollers need to be carefully optimized.

Once the program is flashed to the microcontroller, it functions as the microcontroller's *firmware*—when powered, the microcontroller runs the program continuously until it's programmed with something different (or otherwise reset).

For JavaScript developers accustomed to higher-level logic, this lower-level specificity may feel off-putting. Fret not. This is where JavaScript can help us, allowing us to write programs for microcontroller-based hardware without having to use C or tangling ourselves up in the nitty-gritty of hexadecimal register addresses right off the bat.

The process of getting program firmware onto microcontrollers has also become a lot easier thanks both to advances in chip technology and the wide availability of hobbyist-friendly development boards (figure 1.7).

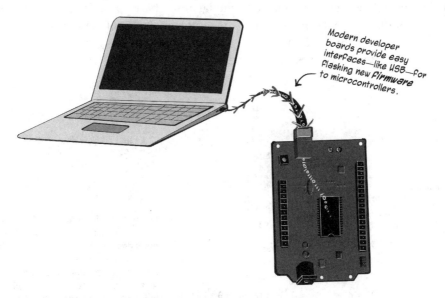

Modern developer boards provide easy interfaces—like USB—for flashing new *firmware* to microcontrollers.

Figure 1.7 Non-volatile program memory (EEPROM and Flash) and user-friendly boards have made it easier to program microcontrollers with firmware.

EEPROM (electrically erasable programmable ROM), exemplified by the well-known *flash memory* medium, is commonly used in microcontrollers. This kind of rewritable memory makes it feasible to reprogram microcontrollers over and over again with different logic.

Development boards, in addition to making I/O connections easier, also aid hardware hackers by providing convenient interfaces for programming the board's microcontroller (USB is quite common). This alleviates the need for specialized hardware programming devices. These days, programming microcontrollers is often as easy as plugging in a USB cable and clicking a button in an IDE.

1.1.5   Enclosures and packaging

Our fan's design is almost done. But we can take it to the next level by packaging the auto-fan inside a nice enclosure—*embedding* our system inside of something, where its wires and circuits will be hidden from view (figure 1.8). Ta-da!

1.1.6   Embedded systems

Though the term *embedded system* can sound a bit formal or forbidding, it's not really too complicated. A tiny computer combining processor, memory, and I/O forms the brain. As you saw with our automatic fan, connecting the inputs, outputs, and microcomputer together and giving them power creates an independent *system*. We say it's *embedded* because it's often squirreled away inside of something—an enclosure, a teddy bear, a washing machine's control panel, an umbrella.

Though an automatic fan, an umbrella that lights up when it rains, and a tweeting teddy bear don't seem immediately similar, they have more in common than you might think. These examples, along with the majority of hardware projects and devices that form the IoT, can be described as *embedded systems*.

Now let's see how JavaScript fits into the picture.

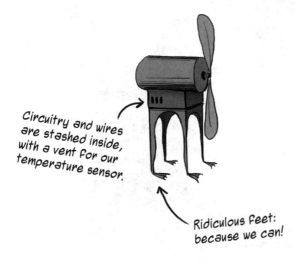

Circuitry and wires are stashed inside, with a vent for our temperature sensor.

Ridiculous feet: because we can!

Figure 1.8   The completed, packaged, automatic fan is an example of an embedded system. Inputs and outputs are processed by a microcontroller-based microcomputer and supported by power and circuitry. And the whole thing is hidden inside a pretty fancy box, because, why not?

1.2 How JavaScript and hardware work together

When combining JavaScript with embedded systems, we still build electronic circuits in the same way as we would for other types of hardware projects. There are still inputs and outputs, wires and components. However, instead of using assembly code or C to define what the project's microcontroller or processor does, we use JavaScript.

There are several ways to do this, different *methods* for using JavaScript to provide the logic for hardware projects. These methods are categorized based on where the JavaScript logic itself executes: on a host computer separate from the embedded system, on the embedded system's microcontroller, or somewhere else entirely.

1.2.1 Host-client method

To get around the constraints of certain microcontrollers, the *host-client method* allows you to execute JavaScript on a more powerful *host* computer. As the host runs the code, it exchanges instructions and data with the embedded hardware, which behaves like a *client* (figure 1.9).

Many microcontrollers have limitations that impact their ability to run JavaScript. Program memory is constrained, meaning that complex programs either won't fit or

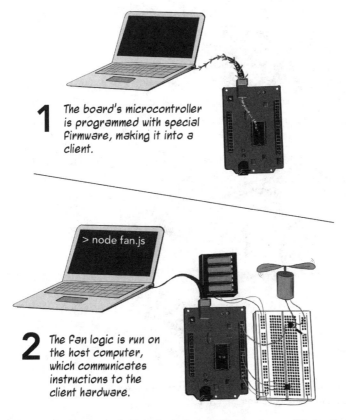

1 The board's microcontroller is programmed with special firmware, making it into a client.

2 The fan logic is run on the host computer, which communicates instructions to the client hardware.

Figure 1.9 The host-client method of controlling hardware with JavaScript

have to be greatly optimized. Also, many inexpensive microcontrollers are built with 8- or 16-bit architectures running at clock speeds that are low relative to, say, desktop computers. Most wouldn't be up to the task of running an operating system, ruling out the ability to run a Node.js or other JavaScript runtime directly on the chip.

Instead, the host-client method involves executing JavaScript logic on a host computer, such as your laptop, which does have the brawn necessary to run a full OS. The host machine is able to run Node.js and can make use of the worldwide JavaScript software ecosystem (including npm and the web).

The trick to getting this setup to work is to make the client hardware (such as the microcontroller) and host system (your laptop) communicate with each other using a mutually intelligible "language"—a common API (figure 1.10).

To configure our automatic fan system to use this method, we'd first need to prepare the embedded hardware by uploading special firmware to the microcontroller's program memory. Instead of a specific, single-purpose program for controlling the fan, this firmware program makes the microcontroller able to communicate back and forth with other sources that speak the same "language" (the API). That is, it turns the microcontroller-based hardware into a client, all ears and ready to do the bidding of the host computer (figure 1.11).

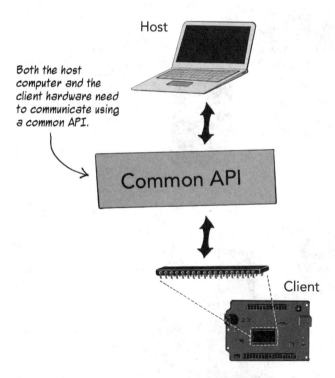

Figure 1.10   For host computer and client hardware to communicate in this method, they both need to use a common API.

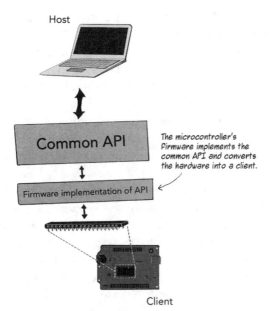

Host

Common API

The microcontroller's firmware implements the common API and converts the hardware into a client.

Firmware implementation of API

Client

Figure 1.11   Specific firmware converts the microcontroller into a client.

The hardware is now ready to communicate—the next step is to write software for the fan, using the host computer. For the hardware and software to understand each other, the host computer needs to bark out instructions in a language the microcontroller can comprehend. To make this happen, we can write code using a library or framework that implements the common API (figure 1.12).

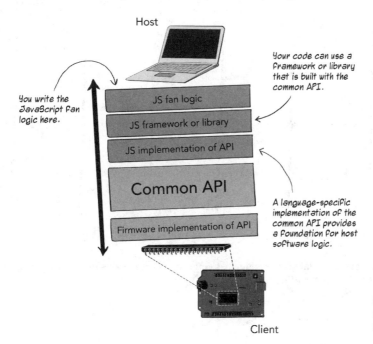

Host

You write the JavaScript fan logic here.

Your code can use a framework or library that is built with the common API.

JS fan logic

JS framework or library

JS implementation of API

Common API

A language-specific implementation of the common API provides a foundation for host software logic.

Firmware implementation of API

Client

Figure 1.12   The host also needs to communicate using the common API.

The host is connected to the client hardware, either with a physical, cabled connection (often USB) or wirelessly (WiFi or Bluetooth).

Then we execute the fan-controlling JavaScript on the host computer. The host continuously communicates instructions for running the fan to the client. The client can also send messages back to the host, such as data from the temperature sensor (figure 1.13).

Don't panic, you won't have to write low-level firmware protocol API software! There are straightforward, open source options for firmware and Node.js frameworks that implement those firmware protocols, so you can write your host-side JavaScript logic with minimal fuss.

The benefits of the host-client approach are that it's easy to set up and it's supported on many platforms. What's more, it gives you access to the entire Node.js ecosystem, while avoiding the performance and memory constraints of inexpensive microcontrollers. The downside is that the client hardware is helpless without the host—it can only do its thing when the host computer is actively running the software.

We'll go wireless eventually, but we'll be starting out with the simplest of host-client options—USB tethering. That means that, for a while, your projects will be physically attached to your computer.

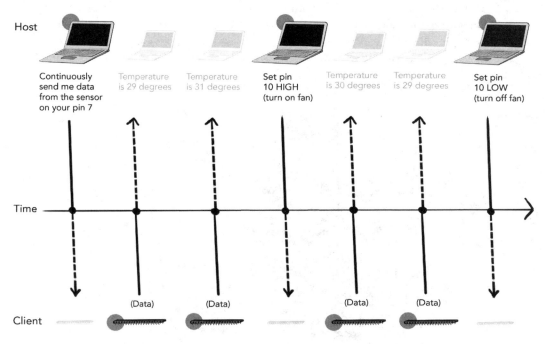

Figure 1.13   As the host executes the JavaScript logic, instructions and data are continuously exchanged between client and host, using a common API.

1.2.2 Embedded JavaScript

With *embedded JavaScript*, the JavaScript logic to control the project runs directly on the hardware's microcontroller.

Many microcontrollers aren't up to running JavaScript natively, but some are. As you'd expect with the march of technology, inexpensive microcontrollers are getting more advanced. It has become possible to run JavaScript, or an optimized variant of JavaScript, directly on certain embedded processors.

Each embedded-JavaScript platform is a combination of hardware and software ingredients working in tandem. On the hardware side, development boards up to the task of running code natively are based on more capable (but still cheap) chips.

Most platforms also provide a suite of software tools to complement their hardware. There may be a library or framework to use for writing compatible JavaScript code and a CLI (command-line interface) or other method for preparing the code and uploading it to the microcontroller.

Espruino (www.espruino.com) is an example of a JavaScript-based embedded platform. Espruino's flavor of JavaScript combines optimized core JavaScript with an API of hardware-relevant features. For example, you write code for the Espruino Pico board in a web-based IDE and upload it to the board via USB (figure 1.14). To adapt our automatic fan for an Espruino board, we'd need to write the logic using Espruino's API.

Another example of embedded JavaScript is the Tessel 2 (https://tessel.io/), a Node.js-based development platform. You can control and deploy code to your Tessel

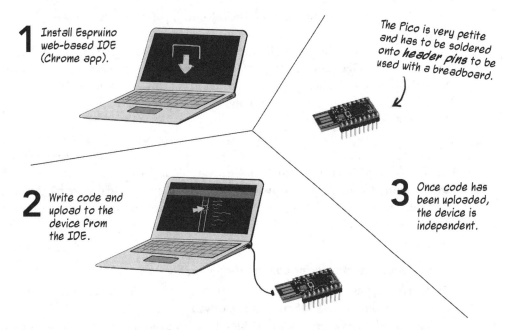

1 Install Espruino web-based IDE (Chrome app).

The Pico is very petite and has to be soldered onto header pins to be used with a breadboard.

2 Write code and upload to the device from the IDE.

3 Once code has been uploaded, the device is independent.

Figure 1.14 The Espruino platform combines small hardware boards with an IDE development environment.

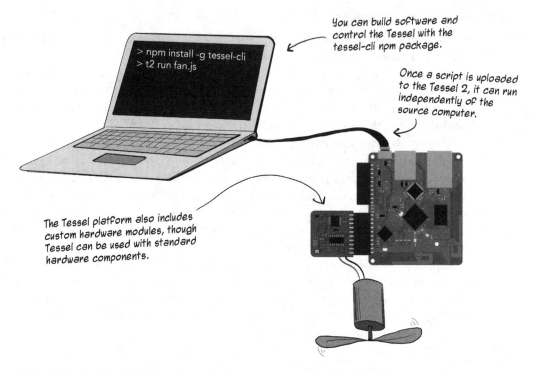

You can build software and control the Tessel with the tessel-cli npm package.

> npm install -g tessel-cli
> t2 run fan.js

Once a script is uploaded to the Tessel 2, it can run independently of the source computer.

The Tessel platform also includes custom hardware modules, though Tessel can be used with standard hardware components.

Figure 1.15   The Tessel 2 is an open source platform that runs Node.js natively.

using the `tessel-cli` npm module—wirelessly, if you like, because Tessel 2 has built-in WiFi (figure 1.15).

Being able to run JavaScript directly on embedded hardware can be power-efficient and self-contained. Projects are independent systems that can run on their own. Unlike the host-client setup, which requires firmware to translate from JavaScript to machine code, there are (usually) fewer layers of abstraction between your JavaScript and the hardware.

This sounds great, and you might wonder why we wouldn't use this approach exclusively. There are a few downsides. For one, there are fewer hardware options at the moment. Also, each platform has its own platform-specific techniques (software, tools, methodology), which can muddy the waters when learning hardware basics. Most also have certain limitations, either in JavaScript language feature support or in the types of inputs and outputs supported. But it's an inspiring method with a very bright future.

1.2.3   *Other hardware-JavaScript combinations*

Aside from the host-client method and running embedded JavaScript, there are a few other ways to combine JavaScript with hardware projects.

Tiny, *single-board computers* (SBCs) blend the host and the client into one unit. Cloud-based services make it possible to write JavaScript code online and deploy it wirelessly to hardware. And emerging, new, and experimental features in web browsers themselves may offer a portal into the world of hardware for millions of web developers.

RUNNING JAVASCRIPT ON TINY COMPUTERS (SBCs)

Single-board computers (SBCs) like the Raspberry Pi family and BeagleBone Black can run full OS environments (typically Linux), and, by extension, Node.js. Instead of an 8- or 16-bit microcontroller, SBCs have higher-performance, general-purpose processors. But many SBCs also have I/O pins and capabilities built right into the same board (figure 1.16).

Using an SBC to control a hardware project blends aspects of both the host-client method and running embedded JavaScript. The processor has to continuously run the JavaScript logic for the project to work (as in the host-client model), but the whole package is contained on one board and feels more like an independent, embedded setup.

Unlike microcontrollers that run embedded JavaScript logic, though, the processor on an SBC doesn't run a single-purpose program—it can simultaneously run other processes.

These single-board computers are getting cheap. At this moment, there's the $5 Raspberry Pi Zero (if you can get your hands on one—they're notoriously out of stock) and the WiFi-enabled Pi Zero W for just a tad more. There's no longer such a large cost differential between low-power microcontroller hardware and legitimate tiny computers with processors that rival tablets and smartphones.

Figure 1.16   Several single-board computers (SBCs): Intel Galileo, Gen 2 (top), Raspberry Pi 2 Model B (bottom left), and Raspberry Pi Zero (bottom right)

Although running JavaScript on single-board computers with GPIO (general-purpose I/O) support gives you lots of options on one piece of packaged hardware, it has a few drawbacks. SBCs aren't as low-power as many microcontroller-based boards—the Raspberry Pi 2 Model B draws 4 watts. The SBCs we'll look at do have GPIO support, but the pin mappings and usage can be confusing and documentation sketchy or technical, which can be challenging if you're just learning about hardware hacking. You'll also need to be ready to face system administration hurdles, as the Linux distributions for SBCs, especially when combined with Node.js, can require some debugging and patience.

CLOUD-BASED SERVICES AND THE BROWSER

This last catch-all category for hardware-JavaScript combinations is admittedly blurry. Stuff's changing. *Fast.* The current growth of commercial, cloud-based services for the IoT has taken on the proverbial hockey-stick shape, and we're just seeing the very vanguard of advances that will let us directly interface with hardware from the browser itself.

Cloud-based services try to ease the complexity of managing fleets of IoT devices at scale. Many of these are targeted at the enterprise. Resin.io (figure 1.17), for example, builds, packages, and deploys containerized application code to provisioned devices, taking care of some of the security and automation headaches for you.

And then there's the browser itself, where many of the most cutting-edge hardware-JavaScript combinations are just starting to emerge. A few browsers already allow you to

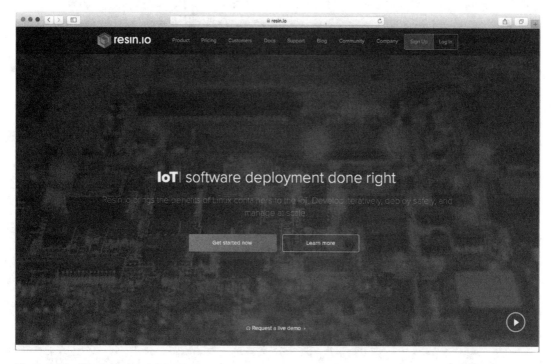

Figure 1.17   The Resin.io service helps to streamline application deployment to and management of Linux-capable SBCs.

experiment with Web Bluetooth, an API that, while not currently on the standards track, may be a harbinger of webby things to come. Web Bluetooth, as its name suggests, lets you connect to and control Bluetooth Low Energy (BLE) hardware, using JavaScript, from within the browser.

Another open project coming out of Google, the Physical Web, proposes an uncomplicated idea: give a small device the ability to broadcast a URL with Bluetooth Low Energy (BLE). A beacon used like this could transform a bus stop sign into a real-time arrivals tracker by broadcasting the URL to a web app with that information (figure 1.18). A simple concept, but flexible.

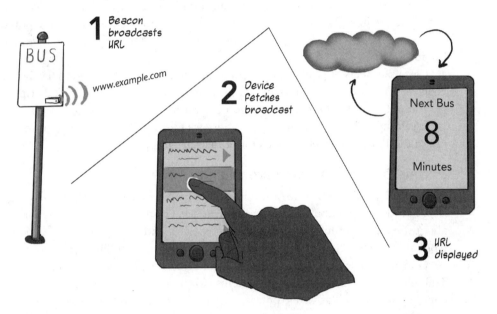

Figure 1.18 In this example application of the Physical Web, a bus stop sign uses a BLE beacon to broadcast a URL once per second (1); a human in the vicinity can scan for available beacons on their device and select the one corresponding to the bus stop (2); the bus-rider's device can now fetch the URL broadcast by the beacon and display it in the browser (3).

Of all the marriages between JavaScript and hardware, this variant—the deeper integration of the web with hardware—is the most volatile. It's simultaneously intriguing and unpredictable. It's likely that the demand for more ways to build IoT products with JavaScript will lead to head-spinning acceleration in this space.

1.3   *Is JavaScript a good fit for hardware?*

So maybe we can use JavaScript to hack on hardware in various ways, but should we? Is there utility here or is it just a self-indulgent parlor trick?

When the idea of using JavaScript with hardware first started surfacing a few years ago, it wasn't met with universal enthusiasm. It was seen by some as arbitrary and misplaced cleverness—a *do we really have to use JavaScript everywhere?* weariness. Others argued that the performance of JavaScript on constrained hardware would never be acceptable for anything but hobby use. A certain amount of old-guard crustiness surfaced, comment threads bogged down with passionate excoriations against anything but C/C++, and naysayers warned that a higher-level language would obscure essential low-level hardware nuances from newcomers.

And yet, there were many who remained open-minded. *Why use JavaScript when C/C++ is good enough?* had a curious echo of an earlier paradigm shift in hardware: *Why use C when assembly language is good enough?*

Whether it's awesome or it sucks—and we're not going to have that argument now—JavaScript is the de facto programming language of the internet. People know it, people use it, and it's everywhere. JavaScript's ubiquity gives it a unique potential to serve as a gateway for millions of web developers who sure would love to get going on the IoT.

Certain aspects of JavaScript programming lend themselves well to hardware, especially its proficiency at event handling and asynchronous processes. JavaScript is also a good tool for prototyping, a boon for fast iteration.

It's going to be fascinating to see where we end up. The JavaScript train is pulling out of the hardware station, and a lot of folks are jumping on for the ride.

1.4   *Putting together a hardware toolkit*

You've had a whirlwind tour of the ingredients that make up embedded systems and the methods of combining hardware with JavaScript. Let's now get more specific about the types of physical hardware, accessories, and tools needed to concoct these types of projects. Then we'll be ready to stock up a basic toolkit to get you started.

Our projects will combine a development board with input and output hardware. To build circuits and connect the systems together, you'll need supporting electronic components, as well as wires, power, and accessories. Throw in a few basic tools and you're ready to go.

1.4.1   *Development boards*

Development boards, also called *prototyping boards* or just *boards*, are physical development platforms that combine a microcontroller or other processing component with useful supporting features (figure 1.19). They're the bread and butter of the hardware-hacking lifestyle. Boards range in cost from just a few bucks to over $100 for high-end SBCs.

Boards are centered around their brain, a combination of processor, memory, and I/O. 8- or 16-bit microcontrollers are at the center of straightforward, entry-level prototyping boards like (most) Arduinos (figure 1.20). Boards with more sophisticated 32-bit microcontrollers may be able to run embedded JavaScript.

Not all boards are microcontroller-based. More powerful SBCs are powered by components you'd normally find on a computer's motherboard. The architecture of these boards is accordingly more complex, involving one or more miniaturized systems on a chip (SoCs) and additional interconnects like HDMI, audio, or Ethernet.

Figure 1.19 Some typical microcontroller-based development boards, clockwise from top left: a Tiva C-Series LaunchPad from Texas Instruments, an Arduino Uno R3, an Adafruit Trinket (5V model), and a Particle Photon

Figure 1.20 This Arduino Uno board is powered by the AVR ATmega 328-P, a 8-bit microcontroller.

Although SBCs may have physical I/O interfaces on-board—Raspberry Pis do, for instance—their general-purpose processors can as easily be put to use to power non-hardware-centric projects.

1.4.2 Input and output components

Oh, my, there are so many sensors and gizmos you can connect to your boards to enhance your projects! This is all sorts of fun, but it can also feel overwhelming at first. Lots of technical terms get thrown around, and there are lots of numbers, values, and specifications to absorb. You'll learn to find your bearings as you go through this book.

Most of the input and output components we'll work with are simple in design and ready to be plugged into a breadboard (that is, they are *breadboard-friendly*). Some are packaged as *breakout boards*. In the same way that development boards make I/O easier

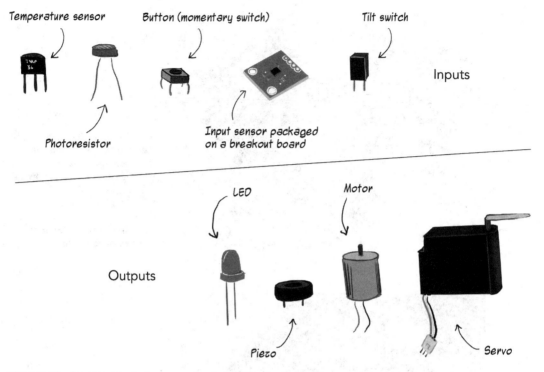

Figure 1.21   An assortment of common input and output components

by wiring a microcontroller's tiny pins to connections that are more convenient, breakout boards make it easier to work with single-purpose sensors or output devices by wiring their pins to more convenient connections (figure 1.21).

1.4.3   Other electronic components

Cobbling together electronic circuits requires a collection of supporting electronic components.

Although it can feel like there are a lot of little pieces, the basic components like resistors, capacitors, diodes, and transistors are inexpensive and can be bought in convenient starter kits (figure 1.22). We'll take our time to get to know these parts—soon they'll feel like old pals.

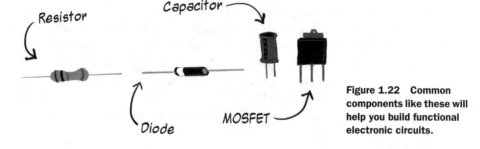

Figure 1.22   Common components like these will help you build functional electronic circuits.

1.4.4 Power, wires, and accessories

One thing you'll soon realize is that there are a whole lot of ways to power a project!

Development boards can be powered over USB or by plugging them into a DC adapter (wall wart). In many cases, other project components can take advantage of that same power source (figure 1.23).

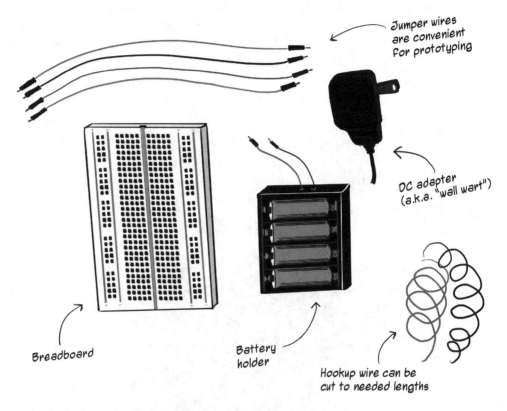

Figure 1.23 A sampling of wires and accessories for power and circuitry

Batteries are useful for making projects wire-free, as well as for providing additional power at different voltages. There are many kinds of battery *snaps* and holders for connecting batteries to projects.

To connect stuff together, you'll need wires. *Jumper wires* are precut wires. One particularly handy variety has pins on each end that slide easily into breadboards and the I/O pins on many boards. Jumper wires are great for quick prototyping. Alternately, *hookup wire* usually comes on a spool and can be cut to specific lengths as needed.

1.4.5 Tools

A pair of needle-nose pliers and a precision screwdriver or two are useful companions when building projects. You'll want a pair of wire strippers—which usually have built-in wire cutters—if you're cutting or stripping hookup wire (precut jumper wires don't need to be cut or stripped). As you progress, you might want to get your hands on a *multimeter*, a tool for measuring voltage, current, and resistance.

STORING YOUR ELECTRONIC COMPONENTS   As you start building projects, you'll end up with a lot of small parts. You can find compartmentalized storage boxes or drawer units at hardware and hobby stores. Boxes and cases designed for fishing lures can make especially handy containers for electronic parts because their compartments are small and their dividers fit snugly (figure 1.24).

It's time to start our journey. Hacking with low-power embedded hardware can be fun, creative, and exciting—and it's increasingly useful in the commercial world. Web

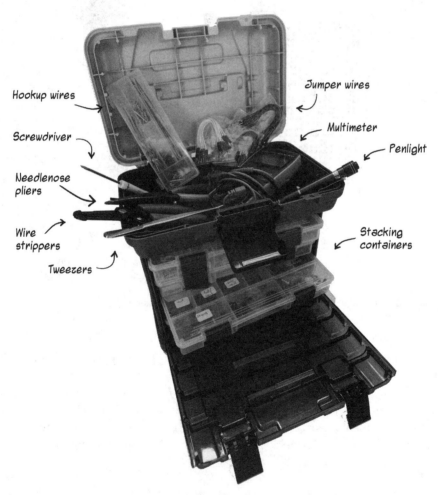

Figure 1.24   This compact tackle box has space in the top for tools, and storage for components in stacking, removable containers.

developers (like you) already have skills that can be great stepping stones on your path. You can use the ubiquitous language of the web, JavaScript, to get you going and reduce roadside distractions.

On our adventure, you'll get a fundamental understanding of the few basic relationships that make electronic circuits work. Not mathy? Don't fret, neither am I. You'll meet some helpful characters on the way: components and modules, different kinds of boards and software. We'll try out different combinations of things and learn how to dust ourselves off and try again when we blow up an LED.

The road goes on forever, the horizons are infinite. We won't be able to visit it all, but by the end of this book you'll be prepared to assess and use future technologies that haven't yet dawned. By the time you're midway through your travels, it's likely the road you set out on will have changed remarkably. But by relying on some constants as your compass—hardware basics, the application of JavaScript, web technologies— you'll be able to find your way.

Summary

- Starting from scratch on an embedded-electronics hobby can feel intimidating, but your existing JavaScript skills can give you a boost.
- Embedded systems combine a brain—a microcontroller or power-efficient processor—with inputs and outputs in a small package.
- A microcontroller combines a processor, memory, and I/O in a single chip. Logic defining the behavior of a microcontroller—the firmware—is typically flashed to the MCU's program memory.
- There are several ways JavaScript can control hardware: host-client, embedded JavaScript, Node.js on SBCs, and even from within a browser.
- In a host-client setup, Node.js executes on a host computer, and instructions and data are exchanged with the microcontroller using a messaging protocol (API). The project can't function without the host computer.
- Some constrained microcontrollers are optimized to run JavaScript (or a subset of JavaScript) directly on the chip (embedded JavaScript).
- Single-board computers (SBCs) have more sophisticated processors and additional features, like USB ports or audio connections. These devices can usually run full-fledged OSs and often behave like tiny computers. Many give you the option of controlling I/O and behavior with higher-level languages like python, C++, or JavaScript.
- Development boards are platforms combining a microcontroller (or other processing component) with handy supporting features. They provide convenient connections to I/O pins, allowing for quick prototyping of projects.
- Building projects involves a certain amount of electronic gear: development boards, input and output components, basic electronic components like resistors and diodes, power connections, and basic tools.

Embarking on hardware with Arduino

2

This chapter covers

- What Arduino is and the features of the Arduino Uno R3 development board
- Connecting components and power to the Arduino Uno
- Coding and uploading a sketch using the Arduino IDE to make an LED blink
- Configuring an Arduino Uno in a host-client setup using Firmata firmware and the Johnny-Five Node.js framework
- Using JavaScript to control an Arduino Uno and make an LED blink

---

Arduino. It's a company. It's a project. It's hardware. It's a user community. Arduino is, well, it's *Arduino*, a broad concept combining open source hardware and software with the goal of making it easy (and inexpensive) for beginners to build interactive devices.

Like most development boards, Arduino boards have a microprocessor, I/O pins, power connections, and other standard features. There are a dozen or so current board models, including the Uno, shown in figure 2.1. Each Arduino board has standardized dimensions and layouts, such that modular *shields* can be used. Shields are manufactured to fit the shape of an Arduino and provide an extra feature—like WiFi or GPS—that isn't provided by the board itself. (Breakout boards are another way to extend the functionality of development boards, but shields are tailored to the Arduino's form factor specifically.)

Figure 2.1 The Arduino Uno is Arduino's most popular board and the one we'll be exploring over the next several chapters.

Arduino: what's in a name?

Although all Arduino hardware (and software) is open source, meaning that you can easily obtain the schematics and even construct your own boards without too much effort, only "official" boards manufactured by the Arduino company are marketed using the name "Arduino."

The term *Arduino-compatible board* describes boards that are manufactured to the same design specifications as official Arduino boards but are not necessarily produced by Arduino (the company).

Genuino is a brand name used for Arduino boards marketed outside of the United States.

Several products, such as the pcDuino and the Netduino, use the *-duino* suffix to hint at their Arduino-like qualities, and both have form factors that allow the use of Arduino-compatible shields. The pcDuino allows you to program using the Arduino programming language if you so desire (though it also supports higher-level languages).

For this chapter, you'll need the following:

- 1 Arduino Uno Revision 3 (R3)
- 1 USB cable (USB A to USB B)
- 1 standard LED (any color)

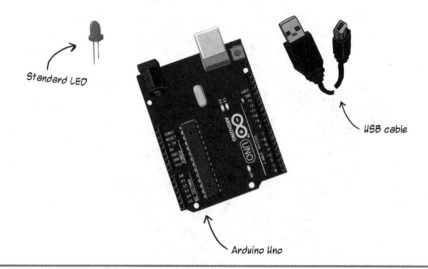

Standard LED

USB cable

Arduino Uno

Typically, programming the Arduino is accomplished by composing *sketches*—bits of code—in Arduino's cross-platform IDE (integrated development environment) and uploading compiled sketches to the board's microcontroller. Code inside of sketches is written in the Arduino programming language, which is similar to C++, but with extra hardware-controlling goodies thrown in. The IDE takes care of compiling sketches and sending them to the board, usually over a USB connection.

Arduino hardware is very popular, inexpensive, and well-tested. It's straightforward to configure an Arduino with the kind of firmware that will let you control it using the Johnny-Five Node.js framework, so it makes an ideal jumping-off place for combining JavaScript and hardware.

2.1 *Getting to know the Arduino Uno*

Of all of the Arduino board models, the Arduino Uno is the most popular. It's been put through its paces all over the world by hardware novices and shouldn't pull any big surprises on us. It's reliable and ubiquitous.

In chapter 1 you saw some of the common features of development boards, like microcontrollers, I/O pins, and connections for power. Figure 2.2 shows these and the other major features of an Arduino Uno board:

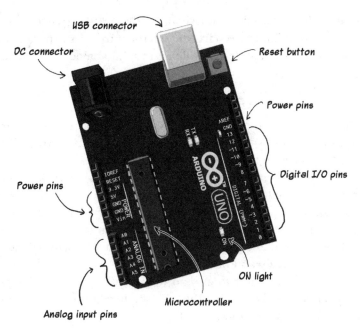

Figure 2.2 Major parts of an Arduino Uno

- *Microcontroller*—The Uno's Atmel ATmega328P microcontroller has an 8-bit processor and 32 KB of flash memory to hold programs. Remember that a microcontroller combines a processor, memory, and I/O processing capabilities into a single package.
- *Connection for programming and communication*—The USB connector lets you connect the Uno to your computer. You can upload programs to the Uno over this connection, and you can also use USB to power the board.
- *Digital I/O pins*—Of the Uno's I/O pins, 14 are *digital pins*, which can be used either as inputs or outputs.
- *Power pins*—Several pins on the Uno give you access to a steady source of power and ground. You can use these to provide power to your projects.
- *Analog input pins*—Six of the Uno's pins are capable of processing *analog input*. Digital pins can only read or produce two states (HIGH or LOW, more on that shortly), but analog input pins use the Uno's onboard *analog-to-digital converter* (ADC) to convert analog input—different voltages—to values between 0 and 1,023. This is useful for obtaining data from sensors. Analog pins can also be used as digital pins.
- *DC (direct current) connector*—If you're not powering the board over USB, the Uno's DC barrel jack lets you plug the board into a DC power adapter or other DC power source.

- *ON light*—The little *ON* LED lights up whenever the board is powered.
- *Reset button*—The reset button restarts the microcontroller's firmware and sets the Uno's pins back to default levels, which is roughly analogous to "rebooting" the board.

2.1.1 Creating your first circuit with an Arduino Uno

In software tradition, Hello World programs are a common first exercise when learning a new language or system—usually these programs do something trivial like make the words "Hello, world" print to the screen.

Basic tricks with LEDs are the Hello World of hardware hacking. Making one light up and blink has been the first foray into electronics for scores of hardware newbies.

To light up an LED, you'll need to construct a *circuit*. A circuit provides an unbroken pathway from power to ground along which electrons can travel. Along this path, the electrons might encounter and travel through components, causing interesting things to happen, like lighting up an LED.

Any gaps in the road from power to ground will ruin the whole thing—no electrons are going to go anywhere. To light up the LED, you need to complete a circuit by filling in the breaks between power and ground.

To build your first circuit, you'll need
- 1 Arduino Uno
- 1 USB cable to connect the Uno to your computer's USB port
- 1 standard LED (any color)

The Arduino board needs to be powered to work. There are several ways to provide power to an Arduino board, but the easiest for right now is to connect it to a USB port on your computer. Go ahead and plug the Arduino into the USB with the cable that was packaged with the board. The ON LED shown in figure 2.3 should light up.

When the board receives power, several of the board's power pins (figure 2.4) become active. When active, they provide a voltage—that is, a steady source of low-voltage power—and you can connect components to them, should you want to (and we do!).

You'll learn more about voltages and power in chapter 3, but figure 2.4 provides a quick look at some of the Uno's basic power pins.

ON LED

Figure 2.3   The ON LED lights up whenever the Uno has power.

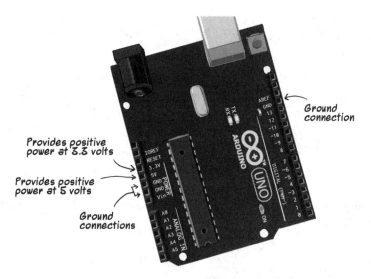

Figure 2.4   Some of the Arduino Uno's power pins. These are powered whenever the board is powered.

CREATING THE LED CIRCUIT

LEDs like the one shown in figure 2.5 are *light-emitting diodes*—a kind of diode that dissipates some energy as light when current moves through them.

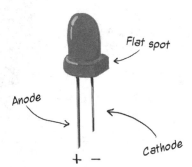

Diodes are electronic components that only allow current to flow through in one direction—a diode won't allow current to go through it backwards. Because of this, it's important to identify the positive (*anode*) and negative (*cathode*) terminals of any kind of diode before trying to plug it in to anything.

The ON light on the Uno, as seen in figure 2.5, is an LED too—a *surface-mount* LED. Surface-mount components are often seen in mass-produced, machine-built boards. They have to be soldered, and their itsy-bitsy dimensions make them tricky to use in projects built by hand. Instead, we'll stick with larger, *through-hole* components (they have

Figure 2.5   Standard LEDs have an anode (positive terminal) and a cathode (negative terminal). Typically, the anode is longer than the cathode, making identification easier. Many LEDs also have a flat spot on the negative (cathode) side.

leads that fit *through* the *holes* of pins, breadboards, or other circuit boards) like the LED in figure 2.5.

> **UNPLUG!** Always make sure to disconnect your development board from power sources before connecting components. If you don't, you risk causing damage to the components or the board.

Now you're ready to build the circuit to light up an LED. Before proceeding, make sure you unplug your Arduino Uno from USB or any other power source. Connect the LED to the Arduino:

1 Locate the cathode (negative terminal) of your LED. See figure 2.5 if you need help finding it. Plug the cathode terminal of the LED into one of the pins marked GND in the POWER section of the board, as in figure 2.6.

2 Locate the anode (positive terminal) of the LED and plug it into the pin marked 3.3 V in the POWER section.

Once the LED is oriented and connected, connect the Uno to your computer with USB so that it has power.

Ta-da! You used the LED's leads to connect power to ground, creating a circuit and lighting up the LED (figure 2.6).

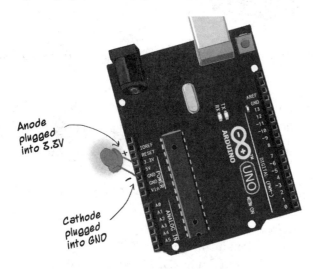

Anode plugged into 3.3V

Cathode plugged into GND

Figure 2.6 Lighting up an LED with an Uno. Connecting power (3.3 V) to ground (GND) with the LED completes the circuit, removing any gaps and allowing electrons to flow through.

Voltages and the Arduino Uno

The typical operating voltage for an Arduino Uno is 5 V, and the projects you'll build in the next several chapters will primarily involve circuits based on this voltage. That may make you curious as to why the LED in this example is connected to 3.3 V power. Plugging this kind of LED straight into the 5 V Arduino power pins gives it a little too much juice—it's not super risky, but you might burn your LED out. You'll learn more of the hows and whys of this kind of stuff as we go, and I'll stop using loose terms like *juice*.

In future projects, we'll use *resistors*, electronic components that resist the flow of electricity, to bring the current in the circuit to a level that's less hard on LEDs and other components. For now, we'll just use 3.3 V, which, at the Uno's current, isn't as rough on your LED.

Having said that, it's never a great idea to power an LED without a current-limiting resistor for long periods of time, so don't leave your Uno-LED arrangement plugged in for longer than a few minutes or so (you may notice your LED getting warm to the touch the longer it's lit).

By connecting power from the 3.3 V pin to ground through an LED, you completed a circuit (figure 2.7). Power is able to flow through this circuit and, as a nice side effect, it makes your LED glow.

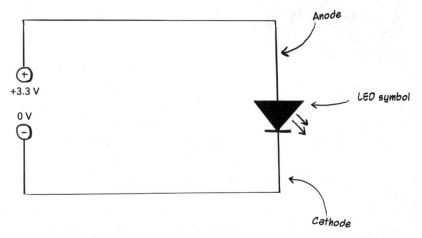

Figure 2.7   A diagram of the basic LED circuit. In the conventional way of representing circuits, power flows from positive to negative. Power flows into the anode (positive) end of the LED and out of the cathode (negative) end.

You could have constructed the basic LED circuit with any low-voltage power source, like batteries. There's no logic involved, so you didn't technically need a development board (though the Uno's steady power source is handy). But things get more interesting when you program the Arduino to do different things—let's try that now.

2.2   *Working with the Arduino workflow*

Before we bring JavaScript into the Arduino mix, let's make your LED blink using the typical Arduino workflow. It's helpful to see how the Arduino works in its stock form before we heap a layer of JavaScript abstraction atop it.

2.2.1   *Arduino Uno's digital pins*

No Hello World LED situation is complete without making it blink.

But you can't make the LED blink using the pins it was connected to in the previous exercise. The 3.3 V power pin will always be powered whenever the board itself is powered—the LED will always be lit because the circuit will always be complete.

Pins 0 through 13 are *digital pins*. These pins can be configured as either input or output.

Figure 2.8   Arduino Uno's digital pins

What we need to do instead is control an LED that's connected to one of the Arduino's programmable digital pins—pins 0 through 13 on the Uno (figure 2.8).

A configured digital pin can have one of two states: HIGH or LOW. This binary logic may feel familiar to you as a programmer—the true/false, 1/0, yep/nope duality is a seminal theme in software development and digital architecture in general.

On a hardware level, HIGH and LOW logic corresponds to voltages. When a digital pin is configured as an output, a HIGH state means the pin is providing voltage, so there's power applied to that pin (in Uno's case, 5 V or near to it)—it is, in effect, *on.* LOW means that the voltage on the pin is at or near 0 V—the pin is effectively *off.*

Programming a digital pin configured as an output to cycle between HIGH and LOW is the ticket to making a connected LED blink.

> **DIGITAL INPUTS** When a digital pin is configured as an input pin, the HIGH and LOW states are also at play, but in a slightly more nuanced way. More about that when we talk about digital sensors in a later chapter.

2.2.2   *Sketches and the Arduino IDE*

To configure and program the digital pins on the Uno, you'll need to write a sketch and upload it to the board using the Arduino IDE.

Head over to the Arduino software page (www.arduino.cc/en/Main/Software) and download the latest version of the Arduino IDE for your OS platform. It's free and it supports Windows, Mac OS, and Linux. After installing the software, launch the IDE. You'll see something similar to figure 2.9.

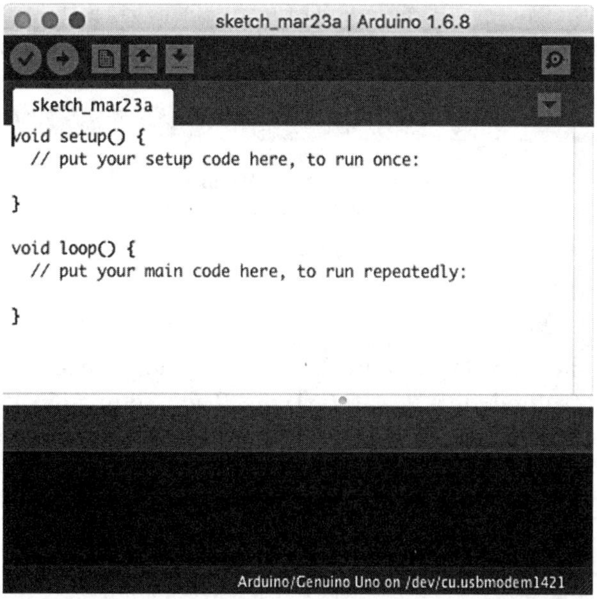

Figure 2.9 The first time you launch the Arduino IDE, it will create a new empty sketch for you.

What's a sketch?

Sketch is simply a fancy word for *code* or *program*. Arduino keeps your sketches in a so-called *sketchbook* (basically a folder). The term *sketch* can be traced back to the *processing* programming language and its IDE, from which the Arduino's IDE is descended.

Hints of Arduino's lineage can also be seen in some of the Arduino programming language's library of hardware-supporting functions, which are derived from the *wiring* development platform, itself an offshoot of processing.

THE ARDUINO PROGRAMMING LANGUAGE

Within the Arduino IDE, you can write sketches for your Arduino Uno (or other Arduino-compatible boards) using the Arduino programming language. Let's look at a few example snippets of code, which look quite different from the JavaScript we'll use later on.

To get a digital pin ready to support an LED, you set it up in an Arduino sketch as an output pin—the LED is, after all, an output component. Configuring a digital pin as an output pin looks like the following in the Arduino programming language.

Listing 2.1 Example of configuring a digital output pin

```
pinMode(12, OUTPUT);
```
◁── **Configures (digital) pin 12 as an output**

To program the output pin, you set it HIGH or LOW by using the digitalWrite function that's built into the Arduino programming language, as shown in the next listing.

Listing 2.2   Setting a digital output pin

```
digitalWrite(12, HIGH);                Setting a pin to HIGH applies
digitalWrite(12, LOW);                 voltage to the pin (turns it "on")
```
Setting a pin to LOW sets the
voltage low (turns it "off")

2.2.3   *Connecting the LED to a digital pin*

It's ostensibly possible to take the LED from the last exercise and connect its anode to pin 12 on the Uno and its cathode to a nearby GND pin. Then, setting pin 12 to HIGH from a sketch would provide voltage and turn the LED on, whereas setting it to LOW would turn the LED off.

But you shouldn't do this. Remember, digital pins' output voltage when set to HIGH is 5 V. We're not using resistors to manage voltage (yet), and the pin's 5 V output could overwhelm the LED and potentially burn it out (figure 2.10).

Figure 2.10   It's hard on your LEDs to plug them directly into a 5V Uno digital I/O pin.

We're in luck, though. Arduino Unos have a built-in LED on pin 13 (figure 2.11). Ever so convenient! Whenever digital pin 13 is set to HIGH, the onboard LED will light up. For this experiment, you don't have to wire anything up—instead, let's concentrate on the programming part.

Figure 2.11 The tiny surface-mount LED next to pin 13 lights up (orange) whenever pin 13 is set to `HIGH`.

2.2.4 Programming the LED to blink

It's time to pull this all together into a sketch to control the Uno.

An Arduino sketch is divided into two parts:

- `setup`—This is where you can—I bet you've already guessed it—put setup code for your sketch. This code executes once at the beginning of the program's execution.

  To set up your LED blinking sketch, the `setup` will need to configure the pin connected to the LED (13). Even though you won't physically connect an external component to this pin, you still need to configure it as a digital OUTPUT pin.

- `loop`—After setup completes, the code in the `loop` will get executed over and over and over again until the Arduino loses power or is reset.

  This is the part of the sketch that needs to alternately set pin 13 `HIGH` (5 V voltage applied) and `LOW` (no voltage) so that the LED will blink.

In the Arduino IDE, create a new sketch to hold the code to blink the onboard LED, as shown in the following listing.

Listing 2.3   A complete sketch to blink an LED

```
void setup() {
    pinMode(13, OUTPUT);      ← Configures pin 13 (with
}                               built-in LED) as an OUTPUT
void loop() {
    digitalWrite(13, HIGH);   ← Sets pin 13 HIGH to
    delay(500);                 turn on the LED
    digitalWrite(13, LOW);    ← Sets pin 13 LOW to
    delay(500);                 turn off the LED
}
```

Waits for 500 ms (half a second)

If the Arduino programming language looks like C/C++ to you, you're right, it basically is, minus a few types and features. The Arduino language also provides a built-in library of hardware-specific functions, including pinMode and digitalWrite.

EXAMPLE SKETCHES   If you don't feel like typing the blinking sketch into the Arduino IDE, or you just want to see more example sketches, you can find a similar blink sketch and many more under File > Examples in the IDE.

UPLOADING THE BLINK SKETCH

Go ahead and connect your Arduino Uno to a USB port on your computer. From the IDE, you can click on the Verify button in the sketch window (figure 2.12) to make sure your code is error-free, or go straight to the Upload button, which will verify, compile, and upload your sketch to the board's microcontroller. If you haven't saved the sketch yet, you will be prompted to do so when you upload it.

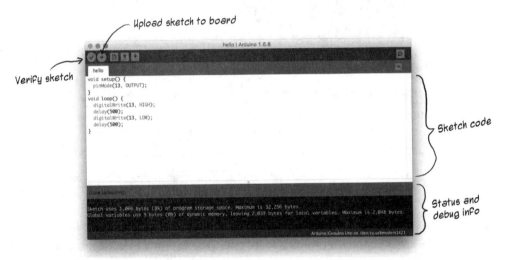

Figure 2.12   Sketch window inside the Arduino IDE

If everything went right, you should see the onboard LED blink every 500 ms (figure 2.13).

Though the Arduino programming language is a lower-level syntax than JavaScript, it's still a high-level language. The contents of your sketch are first compiled into machine code that the microcontroller can execute natively. That compiled code is then written to the non-volatile program memory on the microcontroller. The Uno's microcontroller stores the program in flash memory, the same technology commonly used in memory cards and solid-state drives.

Just like photos don't disappear from a memory card when you remove the card from a digital camera, the sketch will remain in place on the microcontroller even if the microcontroller loses power. Compare this to volatile memory (such as RAM), which loses its contents if not powered. Your successfully uploaded sketch will remain until replaced by something else.

Figure 2.13   The uploaded sketch should make the onboard LED blink every 500 ms.

A program stored indefinitely like this in non-volatile memory is called *firmware*. Each time you upload a new sketch to an Arduino, you're replacing its firmware. The firmware won't "go away" after you unplug the board from its USB tether. If you plug the board back into the USB, or plug it into another power source, the LED will start blinking again because the firmware is still intact.

Resetting the Arduino board

When an Arduino regains power after a disconnection, it will *reset*, bringing its pins back to the default behavior and restarting the microcontroller's firmware. The execution of the firmware in program memory will start from the beginning. From the perspective of an Arduino sketch, that means the `setup` code will run again. Resetting can be a sanity-saving tactic if you have something running amok on a development board.

You don't have to unplug the Arduino Uno board from power to reset it. You can use the handy onboard RESET button—press and hold it for a moment—to accomplish the same thing.

Now you've seen the basic lay of the land of the Arduino Uno and learned the basics of writing and uploading sketches using the IDE. It's time to get to the JavaScript!

2.3   Controlling the Arduino with JavaScript

The workflow for working with an Arduino using JavaScript and a host-client configuration is different from the default Arduino workflow. Instead of authoring and repeatedly uploading sketches using the Arduino IDE, you'll initially upload a single sketch that will stay in place as the board's firmware.

After that, you won't use the Arduino IDE anymore—instead, you'll write JavaScript code using your text editor of choice and execute it with node from within a terminal.

These are the steps for setting up a host-client configuration with the Uno:

1 Upload a sketch containing compatible firmware to the board.
2 Install the Johnny-Five Node.js framework on your computer.

2.3.1 Configuring the Arduino as a client

Recall from chapter 1 that the host-client method involves communicating via a common API between the host and the client. The Node.js framework you'll be using in the next several chapters—Johnny-Five—communicates (by default) with boards using a protocol called Firmata.

Firmata allows hosts (computers) and clients (microcontrollers) to exchange messages back and forth in a format based on MIDI messaging. The Firmata protocol specifies what those command and data messages should look like. The Arduino implementation of Firmata provides the actual firmware you can put on your board to make it "speak" Firmata. It takes the form of an Arduino sketch that you upload to the board (figure 2.14).

Good news: Firmata is popular enough that the Firmata sketches you need come packaged with the Arduino IDE.

Figure 2.14   The first step to configuring the host-client setup with the Uno is to upload a Firmata sketch that will allow the board to communicate using the Firmata protocol.

UPLOADING FIRMATA TO THE UNO

Follow these steps to upload the right flavor of Firmata to your Uno so it can be used as a client in a host-client setup:

1 Connect your Arduino Uno to USB.
2 Launch the Arduino IDE.
3 Access the File > Examples > Firmata menu and select StandardFirmataPlus from the list (figure 2.15).
4 Send the sketch to the Uno by clicking the Upload icon.

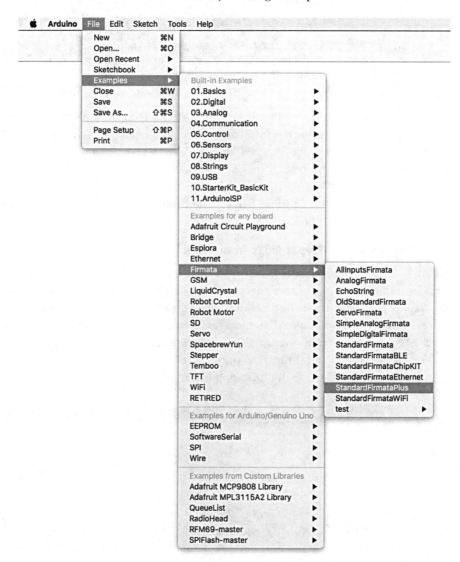

Figure 2.15   Selecting StandardFirmataPlus from available example sketches

> **Why so many Firmatas?**
>
> The Examples > Firmata menu in the Arduino IDE provides quite a banquet of Firmata sketch options.
>
> This is somewhat analogous to optional feature packages for new vehicles. Customers can preorder a car or truck with a certain combination of options—a sunroof, premium sound, floor mats—but you can't combine every option in a single vehicle. There's not room for three kinds of floor mats, and only a few consumers are interested in the most decadent performance suspension.
>
> Likewise, different Firmata sketches implement different assortments of goodies, tailored for different Arduino hardware or use cases. StandardFirmataEthernet adds support for Ethernet shields. AnalogFirmata attempts to maximize the number of analog inputs that can communicate at once. StandardFirmataPlus is a nice balance of all the most popular stuff, and it's what we'll use.

When you made the blinking LED using the Arduino IDE, you uploaded a sketch that became the board's firmware. This firmware was single-purpose—it blinked an LED.

In contrast, the Firmata firmware doesn't have a specific purpose. Instead, it's a program that allows the board to communicate with the Node.js framework you're about to install.

You're done with the Arduino IDE for the time being—you can quit the program after uploading the Firmata sketch.

2.3.2   *Installing the Johnny-Five Node.js framework*

Johnny-Five is an open source Node.js framework created by Bocoup for controlling development boards in a host-client configuration (http://johnny-five.io). Johnny-Five has a special emphasis on robotics, but you can do a lot of different things with the software. It's been around longer than most JavaScript frameworks for hardware and has a clear API and a little bit of maturity—both ideal things for hardware beginners.

To create your first Johnny-Five project, create a directory for it and install the framework npm package, as the following listing shows.

Listing 2.4   First Johnny-Five project preparation

```
$ mkdir hello-world
$ cd hello-world
$ npm install johnny-five
```

> **Installing Johnny-Five: getting help**
>
> Usually Johnny-Five installs happily with just an `npm install` command, but the installation process does compile some native extensions, which can occasionally cause woe.

If you're using Windows and run into trouble, try executing this command:

```
npm install johnny-five --msvs_version=2012
```

Here are a couple of other resources, should you run into trouble:

- The troubleshooting section in Johnny-Five's wiki: http://mng.bz/nW62
- NodeBots Community Forum: http://forums.nodebots.io

2.3.3 Hello World blinking LED with Johnny-Five

You've seen what a blinking-LED script looks like in the Arduino programming language. Now it's time to write a JavaScript version of the Hello World blinking LED to get to know Johnny-Five.

Inside the hello-world directory where you installed Johnny-Five, create a file called hello.js, and open it in the text editor of your choice. Inside this JavaScript file, you can write the code to control your Arduino Uno, shown in the next listing.

Listing 2.5 hello.js

Waits for the board to fire the ready event

Requires the johnny-five package

Initializes a new Board object representing your Uno

Makes the LED blink every 500 ms

Instantiates an LED object on pin 13 (Uno's built-in LED pin)

```
const five = require('johnny-five');
const board = new five.Board();

board.on('ready', () => {
  const led = new five.Led(13);
  led.blink(500);
});
```

Save the file. Plug your Uno into a USB port on your computer if it's not already connected. In a terminal, `cd` to the project directory and run this command:

```
node hello.js
```

You'll see some output like the following in your terminal.

Listing 2.6 Running hello.js in a terminal

```
$ node hello.js
1457806454739 Device(s) /dev/cu.usbmodem1421
1457806454752 Connected /dev/cu.usbmodem1421
1457806458536 Repl Initialized
```

Built-in LED blinking? That's it! You've just controlled an Arduino Uno with JavaScript.

2.3.4   *Firmata, Johnny-Five, and the host-client method*

While the script is running, you'll see the built-in TX (transmit) and RX (receive) LEDs—identified in figure 2.16—flash. This is because the host and the client are exchanging serial messages using the Firmata protocol.

To stop the execution of your Johnny-Five hello.js program, type Ctrl-C twice in the terminal window. Take a look at your Uno. Depending on the moment you quit the program, the pin-13 LED may be off, or it may steadily be on. In either case, it won't be blinking anymore.

That's because the program on the host computer has stopped executing, and as a result it has stopped sending messages to the Firmata firmware. The board is left in a state representing the last successfully communicated messages from the program.

Now that the hello.js script is no longer running, press and hold the Uno's RESET button for a moment. The Uno's pin-13 LED will be off and it will stay off.

Recall that, when reset, the Arduino Uno resets its pins and restarts the firmware program. Earlier, when your firmware was the blinking LED sketch uploaded from the Arduino IDE, the blinking would resume. Now the firmware is Firmata, which doesn't make LEDs blink itself, but instead waits for instructions about what to do. The LED on

Figure 2.16   When the host script is executing, the Uno's TX and RX (transmit and receive) LEDs will blink as communication is exchanged between the host and the client.

pin 13 is turned off by the hardware reset of pins, and nothing has told it to start blinking again.

In the host-client method, the client doesn't do anything on its own—it has to be continually directed by the host. The Uno client is like a puppet in this setup. It needs constant input from a puppeteer—our host-executed JavaScript.

2.3.5 *Structuring scripts with Johnny-Five*

The structure of sketches written in the Arduino programming language with the Arduino IDE differs from the structure of Johnny-Five scripts.

In the Arduino programming language, you split your code into `setup` and `loop`. The code within `loop` gets executed perpetually until the board is reset or the firmware is replaced. To make an LED blink forever, you wrote the following code.

> **Listing 2.7 LED blinking with the Arduino programming language**

```
void loop() {
  digitalWrite(13, HIGH);
  delay(500);
  digitalWrite(13, LOW);
  delay(500);
}
```

Each time the code within the `loop` is executed, it sets pin 13 `HIGH`, waits 500 ms, sets it `LOW`, and waits another 500 ms. Then the `loop` executes again (and again and again and again…). The alternating HIGH and LOW voltages provided to pin 13 with durations of 500 ms makes the LED appear to blink.

However, with Johnny-Five you wrote the following.

> **Listing 2.8 LED blinking with Johnny-Five**

```
board.on('ready', () => {
  const led = new five.Led(13);
  led.blink(500);
});
```

Boards only fire the `ready` event once (don't worry, though; if you bind to the `ready` event after it fires, it'll still invoke the event handler function). That means the function you pass as the handler will also only get executed once—it's not a loop.

Another difference is that Johnny-Five provides a higher-level API. Instead of configuring a pin as a generic digital output, with Johnny-Five you initialize an object representing an LED component, specifically. This gives you access to some handy methods and properties on the `Led` class, which include the methods `blink`, `on`, `off`, and `toggle`, along with more interesting ones you'll meet later.

Instead of manipulating the LED by setting a pin to `HIGH` or `LOW` and invoking `delay` between the two, you can invoke the `blink` method with an argument that defines the blink period in milliseconds. Under the covers, Johnny-Five uses a set-Interval to handle the timing on blinks. An LED will blink until you tell it to stop.

ADAPTING THE BLINKING LED

But how do we tell the LED to stop blinking? This is where JavaScript metaphors start having a role and give you some great options for interacting with your device. In Johnny-Five, the Led's blink method takes an optional second argument, a callback function. Every time the LED blinks on or off, the callback will be invoked.

Listing 2.9   Using LED callbacks in hello.js

```
const five = require('johnny-five');
const board = new five.Board();

board.on('ready', () => {
  const led = new five.Led(13);
  var blinkCount = 0;
  const blinkMax = 10;

  led.blink(500, () => {
    blinkCount++;
    console.log(`I have changed state ${blinkCount} times`);
    if (blinkCount >= blinkMax) {
      console.log('I shall stop blinking now');
      led.stop();
    }
  });
});
```

Configures how many times the LED should blink in total

Keeps track of how many times the LED has blinked on or off

This callback function gets invoked each time the LED turns on or off.

Once blinkCount has hit blinkMax, invokes the stop method

Go ahead and try out hello.js again:

```
$ node hello.js
```

You should see output similar to the following listing.

Listing 2.10   Running the altered hello.js script

```
1457808024073 Device(s) /dev/cu.usbmodem1421
1457808024079 Connected /dev/cu.usbmodem1421
1457808027867 Repl Initialized
>> I have changed state 1 times
I have changed state 2 times
I have changed state 3 times
I have changed state 4 times
I have changed state 5 times
I have changed state 6 times
I have changed state 7 times
I have changed state 8 times
I have changed state 9 times
I have changed state 10 times
I shall stop blinking now
```

This example stops the LED from blinking after a particular number of blinks, but you could do various other things by using a callback on `Led.blink`. For example, you could change the blink frequency, or simply keep track of the total number of blinks over a long period of time.

When you look at Johnny-Five code, it may feel more natural and familiar than the lower-level Arduino sketch code. As a software person, hardware—specifically electronic circuitry—may be a completely new world for you. But there's some basic stuff you need to know. That's where we'll go next.

Summary

- Arduino boards are a common jumping-off point for learning about hardware because they're straightforward, widespread, and well-tested.
- In a typical Arduino workflow, sketches are written in Arduino's cross-platform IDE and uploaded, as firmware, to boards.
- Sketches are written in the Arduino programming language, which is similar to C or C++. Arduino sketches are composed of a `setup` section and a `loop`.
- To control an Arduino board with JavaScript in a host-client setup, the board's microcontroller needs to run firmware that can communicate using the same protocol as the host. Firmata is one such protocol, and it can be uploaded to the board as a sketch.
- The Johnny-Five Node.js framework communicates using the Firmata protocol, but it also exposes a higher-level API. `Led` is an example of a Johnny-Five class for controlling a hardware component.
- Scripts written in Johnny-Five can be executed from the command line, using node. The code on the host must execute and communicate constantly with the client board—the client can't run independently.
- In contrast to the `setup` and `loop` sections in an Arduino sketch, the structure of Johnny-Five scripts is event-driven, a familiar design pattern for JavaScript programmers.

How to build circuits

3

This chapter covers

- Using Ohm's law to manipulate voltage, current, and resistance in a circuit
- Prototyping basic circuits on breadboards
- The difference between parallel and series circuits
- Nitty-gritty details about LEDs and how to wire them up in several useful configurations
- Identifying and selecting the right resistor for different circuits and components
- Calculating the resistance in a series circuit and a parallel circuit

 For this chapter, you'll need

- 1 Arduino Uno
- 4 standard LEDs, red
- 4 220 Ω resistors

- 4 560 Ω resistors
- 1 100 Ω resistor
- 1 push-button switch
- 1 9 V battery
- 1 9 V battery snap
- 5 red and two black jumper wires
- 1 half-size breadboard

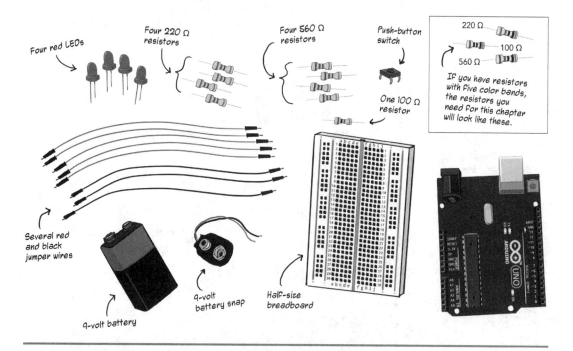

Designing and building circuits may be completely new to you, and may seem intimidating. The good news is that there are just a handful of core concepts to wrap your head around. Once you understand the interplay of voltage, current, and resistance—as formalized in Ohm's law—you're well on your way to being able to understand basic circuits.

There are a couple of metaphors traditionally used to illustrate voltage, current, and resistance. The most common analogy is a hydraulic (water) system involving tanks and pipes. Effective, but not always memorable. Let's try a different adventure.

3.1 Voltage, current, and resistance

High in the mountains, deep in the forest of some place that doesn't exist, a tribe of gnomes found themselves inexplicably in possession of an infinite supply of jellyfish.

The gnomes, being ornery and mischievous, struck out to find a humorous use for the otherwise-inert creatures. They found great fun in dropping jellyfish over cliffs, watching them splash into the lake below or bounce off the roofs of local villages.

The nearby townspeople were initially inconvenienced but soon recognized that the plummeting invertebrates carried energy and could be a free source of power for their cookie factories—but only if the onslaught could be harnessed safely. So they observed, and, over time, came to understand and manipulate the core factors of electrical circuits: voltage, current, and resistance.

Townspeople noticed quickly, for example, that the higher and steeper the cliff, the more energy the tossed jellyfish have when they reach the lake on the valley floor. Lesser drop-offs don't provide as much potential energy for hijinks when the jellyfish splash down (figure 3.1).

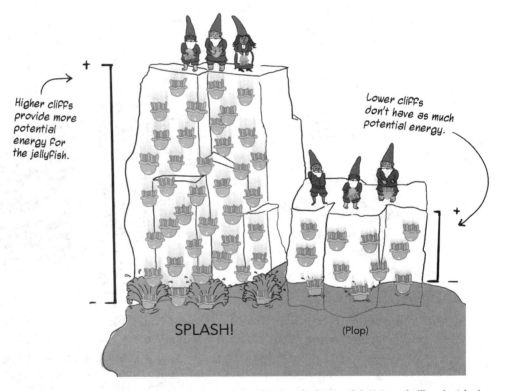

Higher cliffs provide more potential energy for the jellyfish.

Lower cliffs don't have as much potential energy.

SPLASH!   (Plop)

Figure 3.1   Higher cliffs provide more "voltage," that is, electrical potential. *Voltage* is like electrical "pressure," pushing the charges (jellyfish) from high potential energy toward a location of lower potential.

Voltage is a measurement of the difference of potential energy between two points. It's something like pressure or tension or gravitational force, as electricity is always itching to move from higher voltage to lower voltage. Voltage, measured in volts, is *potential* energy, but voltage alone, without moving charged electrons (jellyfish), can't wreak any havoc (figure 3.2).

Until this charge
(jellyfish) moves
through the circuit,
voltage just gives it
potential energy.

**Figure 3.2 Voltage
is potential energy.**

For something interesting to happen, jellyfish need to get actively chucked over the edge of the cliff, a task that the gnomes are more than happy to perform.

The townspeople learned to measure jellyfish *current* by staking out a spot on the cliff and precisely counting the number of jellyfish that passed by, over a precise period of time (figure 3.3). Current, the flow of electric charge, is measured in *amperes*, often abbreviated as *amps*.

The townspeople needed to find a way to manage the current of jellyfish so that it wouldn't overwhelm the delicate cookie presses and ovens. This is the lynchpin of

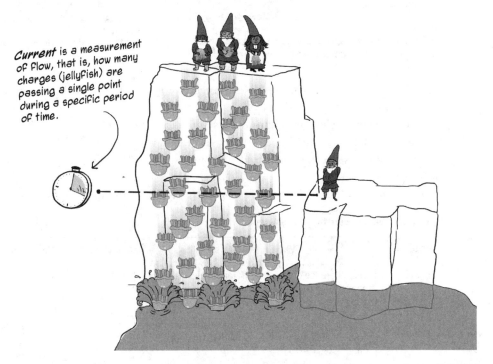

Current is a measurement
of flow, that is, how many
charges (jellyfish) are
passing a single point
during a specific period
of time.

Figure 3.3 Current, the flow of electricity, can be measured by counting how many charges (jellyfish) pass a specific spot on a cliff during a defined period of time.

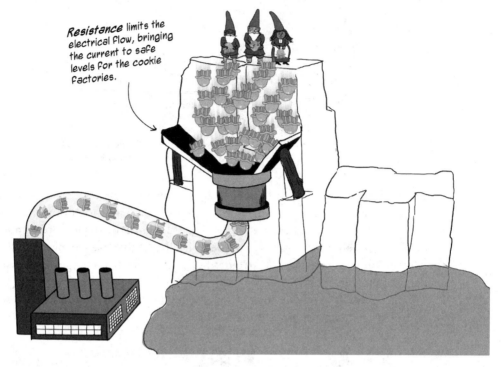

Resistance limits the electrical flow, bringing the current to safe levels for the cookie factories.

Figure 3.4   Townspeople add resistance to the circuit by channeling falling jellyfish through a series of tubes. Increasing resistance lowers the current.

jellyfish circuit control: *resistance*. Resistance is how much a material is able to resist electrical flow. It's measured in *ohms*.

They engineered jellyfish-channeling systems into the cliff faces (figure 3.4), restricting the jellyfish flow to a more reasonable level. For circuits near the higher cliffs (more voltage), these systems had to be more robust because of the immense jellyfish-falling pressure from above.

A summary of the townspeople's discoveries is shown in table 3.1.

Table 3.1   Voltage, current, and resistance

Factor	What it means	Abbreviated as	Measured in units
Voltage	The difference of electrical potential between two points, akin to electrical "pressure." It's what pushes electrical charges through a circuit.	V	Volts
Current	Electrical flow: how many electrical charges are passing a single point during a defined period of time.	I	Amperes (amps)
Resistance	A measurement of a material's ability to resist electrical flow.	R	Ohms (denoted by the Ω symbol)

In the end, the townspeople perfected the circuit and the jellyfish helped to make some of the best cookies around.

There's a power source—troops of gnomes—tossing jellyfish over a cliff. The higher the cliff, the more *voltage* (potential energy) is supplied to the circuit. The *current* (flow) of jellyfish heads toward the factory machinery.

To reduce the jellyfish current to manageable levels, channeling systems and pipes add *resistance*.

Once the jellyfish have given power to the cookie-making machinery and reached the floor of the factory, they reach the point of lowest potential in the circuit. Jet-pack-wearing gnomes act like a pump of sorts, hoisting the weary jellyfish back up the cliff where they can be thrown over again. And again and again... (figure 3.5).

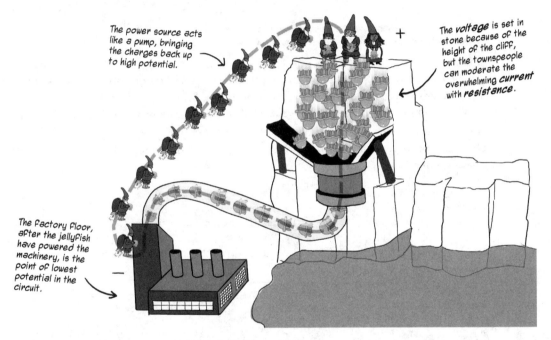

The power source acts like a pump, bringing the charges back up to high potential.

The *voltage* is set in stone because of the height of the cliff, but the townspeople can moderate the overwhelming *current* with *resistance*.

The factory floor, after the jellyfish have powered the machinery, is the point of lowest potential in the circuit.

Figure 3.5 A complete gnome-and-jellyfish "circuit"

Voltage, current, and resistance are vital concepts of basic circuitry. The next step is to understand how these factors relate to each other, and how they apply to real-world circuits.

3.1.1 *Ohm's law*

Voltage, current, and resistance are related to each other in consistent ways. Each of the three factors is like a lever: tweak one and you'll affect the others. These interplays became so central to the town's populace that the factories started producing cookies that illustrated the relationships (figure 3.6).

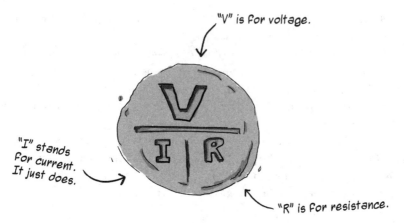

"V" is for voltage.

"I" stands for current. It just does.

"R" is for resistance.

Figure 3.6   The townspeople's new signature cookie shows the relationship between voltage (V), current (I), and resistance (R).

The bearer of the cookie can bite off the factor they wish to determine—then see how it can be derived from the other two factors (figure 3.7).

Georg Ohm figured out these key relationships between voltage, resistance, and current back in the 1820s, well before the clever cookie-townspeople, which is why *Ohm's law* bears his name. If you prefer your math in non-cookie form, these are the relevant equations:

```
V = I x R (voltage equals current times resistance)
I = V / R (current equals voltage divided by resistance)
R = V / I (resistance equals voltage divided by current)
```

"OK," you might be thinking, "but how do I apply this in the real world?"

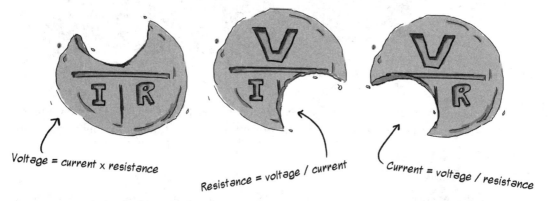

Voltage = current x resistance

Resistance = voltage / current

Current = voltage / resistance

Figure 3.7   By biting off the edge of the cookie imprinted with the factor the cookie-eater wants to figure out, they can quickly see the equation they need to solve. For example, if they want to determine resistance (R), they could bite that off and see that R = voltage (V) divided by current (I).

APPLYING OHM'S LAW TO REAL-WORLD CIRCUITS

Designing and building basic circuits starts with the right balance of the key factors: voltage, current, and resistance.

Table 3.2 outlines a few common examples of how to adjust voltage, current, and resistance in basic circuits. The examples aren't exhaustive (for example, there are additional ways to adjust voltage in a circuit) but they highlight the kinds of things we'll be doing in the short term to make our circuits work correctly.

Table 3.2 Adjusting voltage, current, and resistance in hobby electronics

Factor	Relationship	Example of common way to increase	Example of common way to decrease
Voltage	$V = IR$	Use a power supply with a higher voltage.	Use a power supply with a lower voltage.
Current	$I = V / R$	Remove resistance by removing resistors or using resistors with lower resistance. Current can also be increased by raising the voltage of the power supply.	Add resistance by adding resistors or using resistors with higher resistance. Current can also be decreased by lowering the voltage of the power supply.
Resistance	$R = V / I$	Add resistors or use resistors with higher resistance.	Remove resistors or use resistors with lower resistance.

One of the most common calculation needs that comes up in hobby electronics hacking is "given a supply *voltage*, what *resistor* do I need to use to make sure my component is supplied with a desired *current*" (figure 3.8)?

Voltage is often defined by the power supply for the project—batteries, USB power, DC adapter—and you know you want to provide a particular current to a component in the circuit. Voltage and current are, then, defined, which means you need to solve for R, resistance.

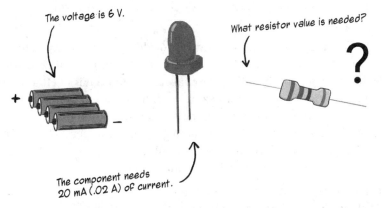

The voltage is 6 V.

What resistor value is needed?

?

+ −

The component needs 20 mA (.02 A) of current.

Figure 3.8   A common real-world Ohm's law problem: what resistor value is needed to provide an LED with 20 mA of current in a circuit with a 6 V supply voltage?

Say you know that your supply voltage is going to be 6 V, and you have a component that needs 20 mA (.02 A, or 20 thousandths of an amp) of current (figure 3.10). Solving for R (resistance in ohms) means dividing .V (voltage in volts) by I (current in amps) because R = V / I:

```
R = 6 V / .02 A
so
R = 300 Ω
```

> **WATCH YOUR UNITS!** Make sure to keep your units consistent when using Ohm's law equations. Current should always be measured in amps (A), voltage in volts (V), and resistance in ohms (Ω). Volts and ohms tend to be straightforward, but when you're dealing with current in hobby-electronics ranges—often tens of milliamps—don't forget to express those values in amps or you'll get the wrong answer:
>
> ```
> 300 (Ω) = 6 (V) / .02 (A)
> ```
>
> but
>
> ```
> 300 (Ω) ≠ 6 (V) / 20 (mA)
> ```

OK! Almost ready. But before we start cobbling together circuits with this new understanding, let's have a grown-up moment and protect ourselves against some potential problems.

3.1.2 *Problems and dangers*

In the kind of electronics hacking we're doing, we're working with voltages that are quite low—5 V or 3.3 V are typical examples—using components that draw current measured in tens of milliamps (mA). These kinds of current and voltage combinations aren't going to throw you across the room (or worse) if you do something slightly daft. But there are a couple of things to be aware of (and avoid).

Avoid too much current

The first of the two problems arises when you provide too much current to a component in a circuit (often by using too low of a resistor value or forgetting to add one to the circuit entirely). Some of that energy is converted into what is likely a desired outcome—light in the case of an LED, for example—but the rest of it has to get used up too. If you provide 100 mA of current to an LED that's rated for a maximum of 20 mA for steady (not blinking) use, that's not going to go well in the long run. The first sign of too much current is often warmth—the LED will start to feel hot to the touch. At a certain point, it'll get overwhelmed and burn out completely.

Avoid creating a short circuit

The second "uh oh" has the potential to be much worse. If there's no *load* in a circuit—that is, no components or resistors to draw or resist current—things get nasty indeed.

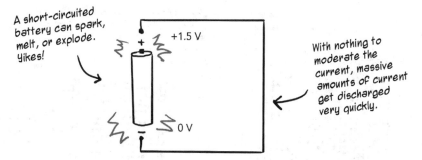

Figure 3.9 **A short circuit has no load to moderate the current. A common illustration of a short circuit is running a wire directly from the positive to the negative terminal of a battery (don't do this in real life).**

If there is, say, a path running directly from the positive to the negative terminal of a battery, there's no resistance to limit the current running through the circuit. This is a *short circuit* (figure 3.9), and it causes immense amounts of current to discharge through the circuit very, very quickly. This energy can cause heat, fire, even explosions.

Development boards can protect you from the worst of this. If you short-circuit the Uno's power to ground (P.S., don't), you won't blow up because the board has *current limiters* on its output pins (your board may be toast, though). The most current you'll ever get out of its 5 V pin is 450 mA; the most out of a single I/O pin is about 40 mA. You get no such protection against outrageous currents if you're working with batteries—you can cause a regrettable festival of sparks, or worse. So be careful.

3.2 *Building circuits*

Now that you've been debriefed, let's experiment! As you start adding components to circuits, you're going to need a way to lay them out without losing your mind. Twisting wire together or trying to hold several components in place in a circuit with your fingers is impractical (and maybe a bit risky).

Instead, *breadboards* make great foundations for laying out circuits. They play a role sort of like a LEGO base, providing a grid to plug components and wires into.

3.2.1 *Using breadboards to prototype circuits*

Breadboards for prototyping circuits are *solderless,* meaning you can stick things right into the board without any need for solder. They come in various shapes and sizes but are consistent in how the board's connections are wired. Figure 3.10 shows the layout of a *half-size* breadboard (*full-size* breadboards are like two half-sized breadboards connected end to end; they're twice as long).

A typical breadboard combines horizontal *terminal rows* (a technical-sounding term that really means "spots to plug components into") with vertical *power rails* (holes meant for connecting power between power sources and components) on both sides.

Terminal rows often have a notch between each set of five holes. A ten-hole terminal row—two sets of five connected holes divided by a notch—is a common layout.

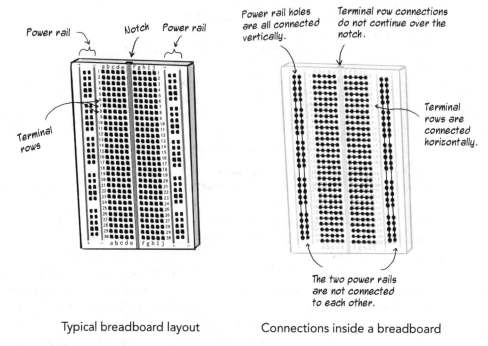

Typical breadboard layout   Connections inside a breadboard

Figure 3.10   A typical breadboard and the connections inside it

Each hole in a five-unit row is electrically connected, but connections do not continue across the notch.

Power rails have two holes per row: one for positive and one for negative. These are usually helpfully marked for you in red (positive) and blue or black (negative). Connections in the power rails run vertically down the length of the board. The power rail on one side of the board isn't connected to the power rail on the other side of the board.

Let's get a feel for how these connections work by using a breadboard to rewire the simple LED circuit from the last chapter.

3.2.2   *Wiring a simple LED circuit on a breadboard*

What you'll need

- 1 Arduino Uno and USB cable
- Jumper wires: two red, one black
- 1 standard red LED
- 1 220 Ω resistor

First, let's check in with Ohm's law to figure out what we'll need to adjust to make the circuit work correctly. Here's what we know:

- The Arduino will provide a 5 V supply voltage.
- The maximum current we should run through the LED is somewhere around 20 mA (0.02 amps)—for most standard LEDs, 20 mA is a general rule of thumb.

SELECTING A RESISTOR FOR THE LED

Because we have a fixed voltage and a target current, the variable value is resistance. What resistor value is needed to create the circuit? Remember,

```
R = V / I
```

so

```
R = 5 V / 0.02 A
R = 250 Ω
```

Resistors come in certain common resistance values, and 250 Ω is not a commonly produced resistor. Calculating a needed resistance value only to find that there is no such resistor happens all the time—not to worry. Typically, the rule of thumb is to round *up* to the next common resistor value (having too much resistance is safer than not enough, ordinarily).

For the moment—trust me, I'll explain shortly—we're going to do the opposite and round *down* a bit to the nearest common resistor: 220 Ω.

Finding the right resistor

Resistors are color-coded in a standard way to aid identification. There are two striping systems out there: four-band resistors and five-band resistors. Four-band resistors are somewhat more common.

Every resistor has bands of color representing *leading digits* in the resistor's value. Four-band resistors have two of these bands, whereas five-band resistors have three.

The last two bands of a resistor are its *multiplier* band and its *tolerance* band, respectively.

The color of the *multiplier band* indicates how many zeros to add after the value indicated by the preceding digit bands. In other words, multiplying the leading digits by this power of ten gives you the resistor's *value*.

The *tolerance band* color indicates how accurate the resistance is guaranteed to be. A tolerance of +/-5% (gold) is common for the types of resistors we're using.

A four-band resistor has two digit bands. The four-band resistor in the following figure is coded as follows:

1 First digit: 2 (red)
2 Second digit: 2 (red)
3 Multiplier: 1 (brown) = 10^1
4 Tolerance: +/- 5% (gold)

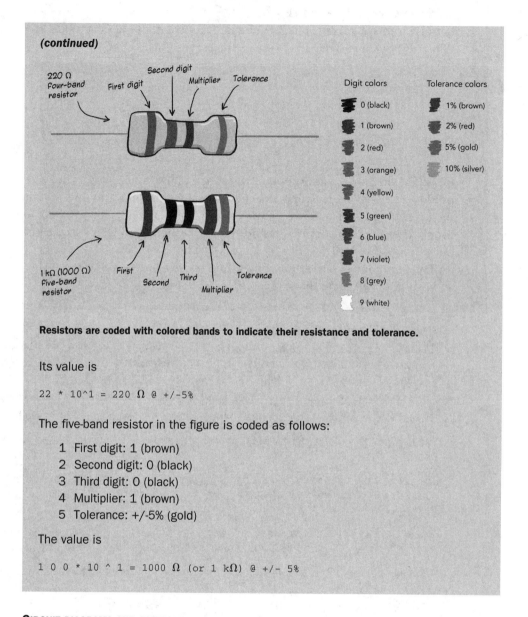

(continued)

Resistors are coded with colored bands to indicate their resistance and tolerance.

Its value is

```
22 * 10^1 = 220 Ω @ +/-5%
```

The five-band resistor in the figure is coded as follows:

1 First digit: 1 (brown)
2 Second digit: 0 (black)
3 Third digit: 0 (black)
4 Multiplier: 1 (brown)
5 Tolerance: +/-5% (gold)

The value is

```
1 0 0 * 10 ^ 1 = 1000 Ω (or 1 kΩ) @ +/- 5%
```

CIRCUIT DIAGRAMS AND SCHEMATICS

There are a couple of ways to represent a circuit visually, to provide other builders with a "map" to recreate the circuit. The most formal way to represent a circuit is through a schematic, as seen in figure 3.11. A *schematic* is a graphical representation of components using standardized notation and symbols. It can be thought of as a sort of visual, abstracted graphic: the position of components in a schematic don't necessarily correspond to their layout in physical space.

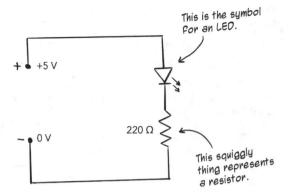

This is the symbol for an LED.

+ • +5 V

220 Ω

This squiggly thing represents a resistor.

− • 0 V

Figure 3.11 Schematic of the simple LED circuit. Schematics are concise and standardized representations of circuits, but they don't show how to position components in physical space.

There are many possible ways to physically implement the schematic in figure 3.11, so a wiring *diagram* can be a helpful tool. Diagrams, like the one in figure 3.12 (created with the open source Fritzing desktop application), show one specific implementation of the circuit and how it could be laid out (in this case, on a breadboard).

Schematics can feel mathy and abstract at first, but they're universally used in the electronics community. You'll get to know more symbols and conventions as we continue our journey, and they'll start feeling more comfortable. To improve your understanding of schematics, make a habit of comparing wiring diagrams back to their source schematics.

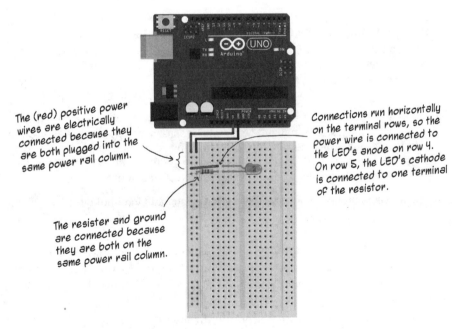

The (red) positive power wires are electrically connected because they are both plugged into the same power rail column.

Connections run horizontally on the terminal rows, so the power wire is connected to the LED's anode on row 4. On row 5, the LED's cathode is connected to one terminal of the resistor.

The resister and ground are connected because they are both on the same power rail column.

Figure 3.12 Wiring diagram of the simple LED circuit, showing a specific physical layout to implement the circuit from its schematic. This diagram was created in the open source Fritzing desktop application.

Plugging things in the right way: polarity

LEDs are *polarized*, meaning they need to be plugged in in a certain way to function correctly. As you learned earlier, the anode is the positive terminal and the cathode is the negative terminal.

Resistors are not polarized, meaning it doesn't matter which direction you plug them in. They work just fine oriented either way.

Another thing to note is that although I'll give you precise row and column breadboard coordinates in this exercise, you could just as successfully plug the components into any row or column as long as the connections work out in the end (terminal rows are connected horizontally; power rails, vertically).

Time to build the circuit. Referring to figure 3.12, begin by connecting components into the terminal rows. Plug the anode of the red LED into hole 5C (row 5, hole C) and its cathode into hole 5D (the next row down). Plug one end of the resistor into hole 5B, next to the LED's cathode.

POWERING THE CIRCUIT

The circuit needs to be connected to power. First, you'll need to connect the components in the terminal rows to the power rail—recall that terminal rows are isolated (for good reason!) from the power rails.

Plugging things in the right way: jumper wire colors

If you have a packet of colored jumper wires, you might be wondering which colors are for what purpose. By convention, power connections are usually made with red (positive) and black (ground) wires. Other colors you may see representing negative power connections include white or other dark colors (brown or purple).

Green and yellow are often used for input and output connections, which will come up in later chapters. Although there is widespread consistency in using red and black/white for power connections, different hackers use different color combinations for various other things. Long story short: there are no hard and fast rules, but try to be consistent in whichever combination you implement.

Jumper wires aren't polarized. They can be connected in either direction.

Use a red jumper wire to connect hole 5B—electrically connected to the anode of the LED—to a hole in the red (positive) column of the power rail. The fourth row down should do nicely if you can't decide on a favorite. Connect the resistor's free end directly into the negative power rail as shown in figure 3.12. Now there's an unbroken path leading from the positive power rail, through the red wire to the LED, out of the LED and through the resistor back to the negative power rail.

The current is flowing... *which* way now?

The kinds of projects we're building with development boards and embedded systems use DC (direct current) circuits. Current flow in a DC circuit is in a single direction, usually rendered as going from positive source (highest potential energy) toward negative, or ground (lowest potential energy).

Technically, this isn't correct—current can be more accurately described as flowing from negative toward positive, and even that's an oversimplification. But the convention of drawing circuits with flow in the positive to negative (+ toward –) direction is deeply entrenched, and there's nothing inherently harmful in representing DC current flow in this traditional way, as long as you're consistent. Fun fact: the practice of envisioning current flow from positive to negative was established by none other than electricity pioneer Benjamin Franklin.

Besides DC, the other type of current flow is AC (alternating current), in which the flow of current reverses directions periodically. Wall-outlet power is AC, oscillating direction 50 or 60 times per second, depending on what part of the world you live in.

UNPLUG THE UNO! As ever, make sure your Uno is unplugged from USB or wall power before connecting it to components or circuits.

The Uno can provide a nice, steady 5 V from its 5 V power pin. Using a red jumper wire, plug one end into the Uno's 5 V pin and the other into the top row of the positive power rail. Run a black jumper wire from the Uno's GND pin to the top row of the negative power rail. This completes the circuit wiring.

Now plug your Uno into USB or wall power. Your LED should light up!

Troubleshooting the circuit

If your LED doesn't light up, there are a few things to check. The most common reason for a circuit like this to fail is that it's an *open circuit*, meaning there's a gap in the path from the positive to negative ends of the circuit. Check the positions of your components and wires, and make sure wires are snugly plugged into breadboard holes. Make sure that none of the exposed metal terminals on the components are touching each other. Also double-check that your Uno's power LED is lit.

If those steps don't do the trick, try swapping out your LED with a fresh one on the off chance that the LED is dead. On occasion, a breadboard's connections can be wonky (though this is more typical for breadboards you've been using for a long time). As a last resort, try wiring the components onto a different part of the breadboard or try with another breadboard.

SERIES AND PARALLEL CIRCUITS

This simple LED circuit (figure 3.13) is a *series circuit*. A series circuit has only one path for electrons—current, those individual flowing jellyfish of the gnome world—to take. Because there's only one possible route, all jellyfish/electrons go through the whole

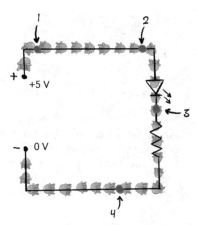

Figure 3.13   A series circuit has only one possible path for the charges (jellyfish) to flow through—there are no branches. The current is the same at any point in a series circuit, meaning that points 1, 2, 3, and 4 all have equal current.

route; they're not able to wander off on some shortcut or side road. That means the current is the same at all points in the circuit (figure 3.13).

When modifying the current of a series circuit with resistors, it doesn't matter whether you use, say, one resistor rated at 200 Ω or two resistors at 100 Ω. The values of the resistors add together and modify the current across the whole circuit (figure 3.14).

VOLTAGE AND SERIES CIRCUITS Although *current* is the same at any point in a series circuit, *voltage* may differ from point to point. We'll talk about this when we build *voltage dividers* in chapter 4.

One detail of these series circuits that might have given you pause is the position of the *current-limiting resistor(s)* (a current-limiting resistor is one that's placed to moderate the current in the circuit).

In figure 3.14, the resistors are connected between the LED and ground; that is, they're positioned "after" the LED. As it turns out, it doesn't matter where the resistors are positioned relative to the LED in a series circuit.

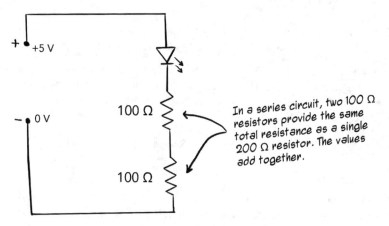

In a series circuit, two 100 Ω resistors provide the same total resistance as a single 200 Ω resistor. The values add together.

Figure 3.14   Resistor values add together in a series circuit.

A current-limiting resistor placed in a series circuit affects current throughout the whole circuit, no matter its position—remember, current is the same at all points in a series circuit.

3.2.3   *Expanding a series circuit with a button*

What you'll need

- 1 Arduino Uno and USB cable
- 1 push button
- 1 standard red LED
- 1 220 Ω resistor
- 3 jumper wires

In the simple LED series circuit you wired, all of the current runs through the LED, then through the resistor, and then to ground (figure 3.14). A single gap in a series circuit will cause the entire circuit to stop working, because it's a gap in the only path through the circuit. That makes it possible to activate and deactivate the whole circuit with one switch.

You can see how this works by adding a button to the circuit. A *button* is a kind of switch that only completes a connection when it's pressed down (sometimes buttons are called *momentary switches*) (figure 3.15).

In figure 3.16, the button is connected to a breadboard, oriented such that the "always-connected" pins span the notch in the middle. That means the top row's high-lighted connections are always connected electrically, as are those highlighted in the bottom row. While the button is inactive (not pressed), the two rows are isolated from each other. When the button is pressed, however, a connection is made between the top and bottom pins on the button's left side, and the top and bottom pins on its right

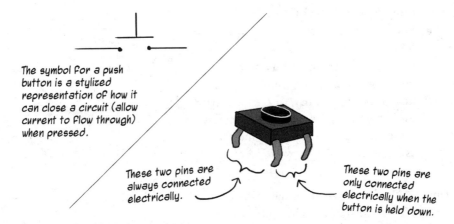

The symbol for a push button is a stylized representation of how it can close a circuit (allow current to flow through) when pressed.

These two pins are always connected electrically.

These two pins are only connected electrically when the button is held down.

Figure 3.15   Pins on opposite sides of the button are always electrically connected, whereas pins sharing a single side are only connected when the button is held down.

side. The effect is that both highlighted rows are electrically connected to each other while the button is pressed.

When a properly connected button is pressed and held, the circuit is *closed*, completing the path and allowing electrons to flow through the circuit. When released, the circuit is *open*—it has a gap and no current flows. The schematic of the circuit you need to construct is shown in figure 3.17.

BUILD THE CIRCUIT: BUTTON AND LED

To build the button circuit in figure 3.18, follow these steps:

1. Disconnect the Uno from power.
2. Remove the LED and the resistor from the breadboard.
3. Using a black jumper wire, connect GND on the Uno to the top row of the negative power rail on the right side of the breadboard.
4. Connect the button to the breadboard. Your button might be a different size and fit more comfortably between different rows, which is fine.
5. Plug the LED's anode (longer leg) into a slot in the same row as the bottom two legs of the button.
6. Plug the LED's cathode in one row down.
7. Connect the resistor from a slot in the same row as the LED's cathode to the negative power rail. You can leave the red wire connecting the left-hand power rail to row 4 in the same place as it was in the previous exercise.
8. Reconnect the Uno's power.

The LED should not be lit initially. Press the button. The LED should light up for as long as you hold the button down.

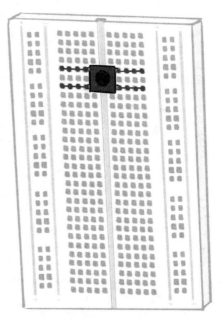

Figure 3.16 A push button connected to a breadboard, spanning the center notch. When not pressed, the pairs of pins at the top and bottom of the button are connected electrically (horizontally). When pressed and held, the pairs of pins on the left and right sides of the button are electrically connected (vertically).

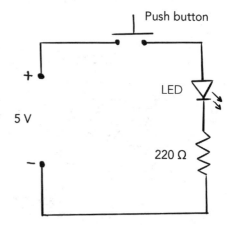

Figure 3.17 Schematic of the updated circuit, integrating a push button

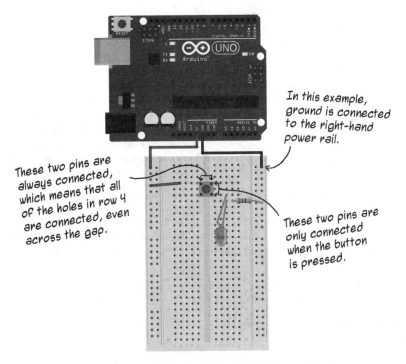

In this example, ground is connected to the right-hand power rail.

These two pins are always connected, which means that all of the holes in row 4 are connected, even across the gap.

These two pins are only connected when the button is pressed.

Figure 3.18 Wiring diagram of adapted LED circuit with a push button

3.2.4   *LEDs in series*

There's one more stop on the series-circuit discovery tour. Let's construct a circuit containing multiple LEDs wired in series—that is, multiple LEDs on a circuit that only has one path. Here's where I can come clean about the detail left out in the LED-resistor calculation we did earlier in the chapter.

To jog your memory, the calculation was aimed at finding the right resistor value for an LED—target current 20 mA—in a 5 V circuit:

```
R = 5 V / .02 A
R = 250 Ω
```

Instead of rounding up to the next common resistor value, we rounded down to 220 Ω.

The reason that a 220 Ω resistor is more than plenty for an LED in a 5 V circuit at 20 mA is that, because of a characteristic of LEDs, we don't need to account for the full 5 V when calculating for the right resistor value. In fact, 220 Ω is slightly high.

There's a relevant law, called Kirchoff's voltage law (*KVL* to those in the know). It states that all of the voltage in the circuit has to be in balance: the amount generated has to be the same as the amount used. Voltage in, voltage out.

In the LED-series circuit, 250 Ω would be the correct approximate resistor to use if the resistor were the only thing in the circuit "using" some voltage. But it's not.

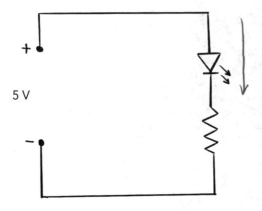

Figure 3.19   As electricity travels across an LED, some voltage is used, or *dropped*. The amount of voltage used is called the LED's *forward voltage*. It ranges between about 1.8 V and 3.5 V, depending on the color of the LED— the higher the frequency of the emitted light, the higher the voltage drop.

LEDs have a metric called *forward voltage drop*. There's a bit of detail to that, but for our purposes it's the approximate amount of voltage the LED will use up in the circuit (figures 3.19 and 3.20).

While most workaday standard LEDs have a consistent *forward current* (for purposes of brevity, you can think of that as "roughly the current it should receive") of 20 mA, forward voltage differs between LEDs, mostly related to the color of the LED.

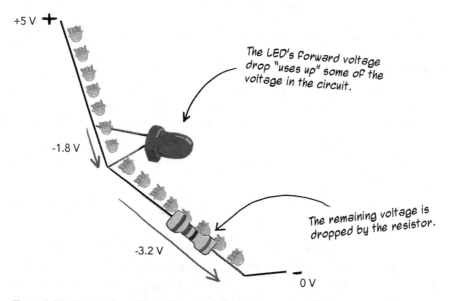

Figure 3.20   Hearkening back to the analogy of voltage as cliff steepness or height, the same series-LED circuit can be seen from a different perspective. As the jellyfish current moves through the LED, 1.8 V is "used up," reducing the remaining voltage to 3.2 V (reducing the steepness). That 3.2 V is then used up by the current-limiting resistor. When the jellyfish reach the point of lowest electrical potential, all of the voltage in the circuit has been accounted for.

Red LEDs have a forward voltage that varies for the most part between 1.8 and 2 V. If the LED in the circuit has a forward voltage drop of 1.8 V, we can subtract that from the system voltage of 5 V, and that is the voltage that the resistor needs to account for:

```
5 V (supply voltage)
- 1.8 V (red LED forward voltage)
-------------------------------
= 3.2 V (remaining voltage)
```

Given that we want to aim for that 20 mA current (0.02 A), the resulting Ohm's law equation is

```
R = 3.2 V / 0.02 A
```

or

```
R = 160 Ω
```

A 220 Ω resistor is close enough in value to be just dandy—rounding up to the next common resistor value as per convention. Now, 220 Ω is more resistance than 160 Ω, so you might wonder what effect using a higher resistance value has on the LED and the circuit. Higher resistance with steady voltage means the current goes down (because, as always, Ohm's law):

```
I = V / R
I = 3.2 / 220 Ω
I = 0.0145 A
```

In the end, the LED gets less current than 20 mA—about 15 mA (.0145 A). The amount of current provided to an LED is directly proportional to its brightness: an LED getting 15 mA will not be as blindingly bright as one receiving 20 mA.

What's the situation if another identical red LED is added into this series circuit? What's the needed resistor? We'll need to account for the voltage drop of both LEDs (figure 3.21).

Fortunately, this is a question of straightforward arithmetic. After subtracting the voltage drop of each LED from the total circuit voltage, we're left with 1.4 V:

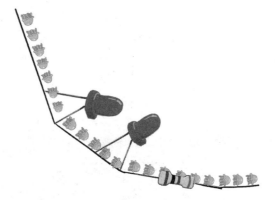

Figure 3.21 Each of the two LEDs drops some of the voltage in the circuit, and, again, the remaining voltage is dropped by the resistor.

```
5 V (supply)
- 1.8 V (LED 1)
- 1.8 V (LED 2)
--------------
= 1.4 V

R = 1.4 V / 0.02 A
R = 70 Ω
```

Rounding up to the next common resistor value, a 100 Ω resistor will do nicely, as shown in the schematic in figure 3.22.

BUILD THE CIRCUIT: TWO LEDs IN SERIES

What you'll need
- 1 Arduino Uno and USB cable
- 1 push button
- 2 standard red LEDs
- 1 100 Ω resistor
- 3 jumper wires

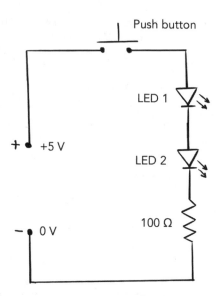

Figure 3.22 The two LEDs are wired in series with a 100 Ω resistor. There's only a single path through this circuit when the button is pressed: through the first LED, through the second LED, through the resistor, and back to ground.

To build the circuit in figure 3.23, follow these steps:

1 Unplug your Uno from power.
2 Unplug the 220 Ω resistor from the breadboard and put it away.
3 Plug the anode of a second LED into the same row as the cathode from the first LED (row 7 in figure 3.23).
4 Connect a 100 Ω resistor from the negative power rail to the row containing the second LED's cathode (row 8).

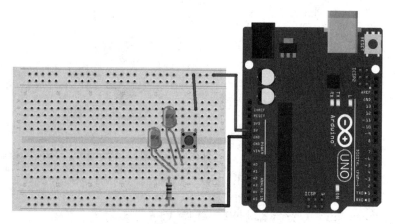

Figure 3.23 Wiring diagram of two LEDs in series

If you plug your Uno into power and then press the button, both LEDs should light up. They're wired in series, which may be easier to visualize by looking at figure 3.22 again.

And what if you add a third LED? Trick question: you can't really. Not if you want to produce reliable and bright light. There's only 1.4 V "left" after the first two LEDs' voltage drops. That's not quite enough to power a third LED—an LED requires at least its voltage drop value to light up. You might be able to get the three LEDs to light up weakly, but they wouldn't be robust.

It is possible to steadily power more than two LEDs with 5 V, but to do so you need a parallel circuit.

3.2.5 *Parallel circuits and current dividers*

In a series circuit, there's only one path for electrons to take, but in a parallel circuit, there are two or more possible paths, or *branches* (figure 3.24).

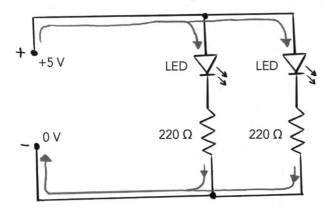

Figure 3.24 **In a parallel circuit, there's more than one path, or branch, current can take. In this example, there are two branches: each has its own LED and resistor.**

As electrons move through the circuit and encounter a fork in the road, they each make a decision about which branch to take. Current prefers a path with less resistance (figure 3.25).

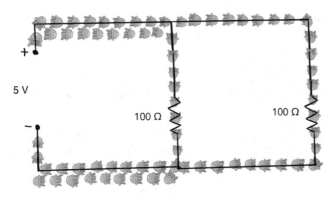

Figure 3.25 **Because the two branches in this parallel circuit have the same resistance (100 Ω), half of the current will take one branch and half will take the other.**

When calculating how much resistance is in the parallel circuit, things get a bit weird and counterintuitive. Look again at the parallel circuit in figure 3.25. What's the total resistance that the two 100 Ω resistors provide?

The total resistance of series circuits is easy to figure out—just add 'em up and voilà! You've got the total resistance. It's tempting to do the same at first with parallel circuits—to assume the total resistance is 200 Ω. Nope. Or maybe you spied that any given charge going through the circuit is only going through one resistor, not both. So that must mean there's a total resistance of 100 Ω? Also, sorry, nope.

The correct answer is 50 Ω.

I know, I know. That doesn't feel right, but it's true: in a parallel circuit, the total resistance will always be *less than* the smallest resistor value. Let's arm ourselves with Ohm's law and a few deep breaths and examine how this can possibly be. Calculating equivalent resistance in parallel circuits is one of the more challenging concepts to novice electronics hackers, so don't pull your hair out just yet.

Let's break it down and put it back together. The 5 V series circuit with a 100 Ω resistor shown in figure 3.26 will draw 50 mA of current (I) because

```
.005 A (I) = 5 V (V) / 100 Ω (R)
```

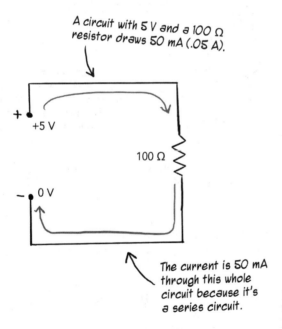

A circuit with 5 V and a 100 Ω resistor draws 50 mA (.05 A).

+5 V

100 Ω

0 V

The current is 50 mA through this whole circuit because it's a series circuit.

Figure 3.26   This series circuit draws 50 mA because 5 V / 100 Ω = .05 A.

Now say you duplicate that same path—5 V and a 100 Ω resistor—and glom it onto the circuit. That second path will also independently draw 50 mA because the supply voltage (5 V) and the resistance (100 Ω) stay the same (figure 3.27).

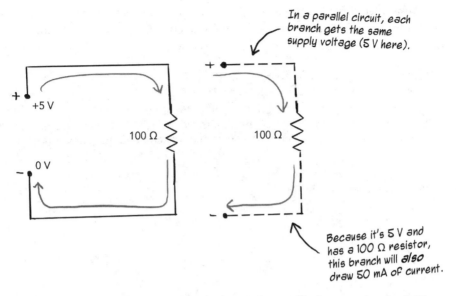

In a parallel circuit, each branch gets the same supply voltage (5 V here).

Because it's 5 V and has a 100 Ω resistor, this branch will *also* draw 50 mA of current.

Figure 3.27 Each branch of a parallel circuit in isolation acts like its own series circuit. We can use Ohm's law to verify that this branch will also draw 50 mA.

Added together, the current drawn by the two branches is 100 mA—the total current draw of the circuit has increased (figure 3.28).

Looking at the circuit as a whole now, its total current is 100 mA (.1 A) and supply voltage is, as ever, 5 V. Plugging that into Ohm's law,

```
Total resistance (R) = 5 V (V) / .1 A (I)

R = 50 Ω
```

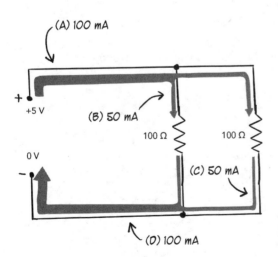

(A) 100 mA

+5 V

(B) 50 mA

100 Ω   100 Ω

0 V

(C) 50 mA

(D) 100 mA

Figure 3.28 The total current going in to the circuit is 100 mA (point A). It splits equally into two branches—each branch gets 50 mA (points B, C). The current rejoins and at point D is again 100 mA. In a parallel circuit, the supplied voltage is constant for each branch but the current varies.

The resistance provided by each resistor in a parallel circuit is reduced because each branch in a parallel circuit increases the total current in the circuit. Current is going up while voltage is constant: resistance goes down.

Current dividers

Any circuit that splits the current coming from the power source into more than one branch is called a *current divider*. The parallel circuit in the following figure is an example of a current divider: some current follows one branch while the rest follows the other.

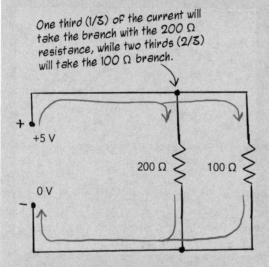

One third (1/3) of the current will take the branch with the 200 Ω resistance, while two thirds (2/3) will take the 100 Ω branch.

+5 V

200 Ω   100 Ω

0 V

If the branches have unequal resistance, current will proportionally flow through each branch.

If a charge finds itself at a fork in the road and both available paths have the same resistance, the charge is equally likely to take either route (like the parallel circuit in figure 3.28). But If the resistance is unequal, more charges will opt for the road with less resistance—that is, more current will take the less-resistant branch.

You can calculate the total resistance in the circuit shown in this figure by looking at each branch in isolation and figuring out the circuit's total current draw:

```
Branch 1:
5 V / 200 Ω = .025 A (25 mA) because I = V / R

Branch 2:
5 V / 100 Ω = .05 A (50 mA) because I = V / R

  .025 A (branch 1)
+ .05 A  (branch 2)
============================
= .075 A (75 mA) total current

R(Total) = 5 V / .075 A because R = V / I
R(Total) = 66.667 Ω
```

> Doing calculations for total resistance in this manner can become cumbersome as the number of branches increases. We won't be architecting complex current dividers with lots of branches with different resistances, but if you're the curious type, there's a formula for calculating equivalent (total) resistance in any parallel circuit:
>
> ```
> 1 / R(Total) = 1 / R1 + 1 / R2 + 1 / R3 ... + 1/Rn
> ```

Some of this parallel-circuit calculation may seem pointlessly convoluted, but it does have useful applications.

Here's the rub: each branch of the parallel circuit is provided with the same voltage. So if we take the series-circuit LED and add more branches to it (turning it into a parallel circuit—figure 3.29), each branch gets "its own" 5 V to work with. This way, we can wire three, four, or even more LEDs on the same circuit and not run out of voltage like we would in a series circuit.

BUILD THE CIRCUIT: LEDS IN PARALLEL

What you'll need

- 1 Arduino Uno and USB cable
- 4 standard red LEDs
- 4 220 Ω resistors
- 6 jumper wires

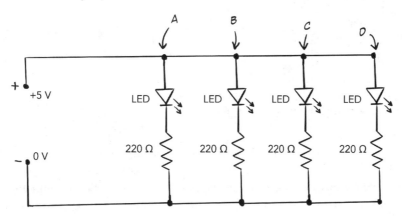

Figure 3.29 In the schematic for the parallel-LED circuit, each of the branches A, B, C, and D is supplied with 5 V. Each branch receives 1/4 of the total current in the circuit.

Figure 3.30 shows a physical layout of the same circuit. To wire four LEDs on the same circuit, start with a fresh, clean breadboard and follow these steps:

1. Connect the anode terminals of four LEDs to a hole in rows 2, 9, 16, and 23.
2. Plug the cathode ends into the same terminal row but on the other side of the gap (such that they aren't electrically connected).

3 Run four red jumper wires from the positive power rail on the left side of the board to the anode row of each LED.

4 Connect a 220 Ω resistor from each LED's cathode row to the negative power rail on the right side of the board.

5 Connect the power rails to the Uno's 5 V and GND pins (using a red and black jumper wire, respectively).

6 Plug the Uno into USB or DC power.

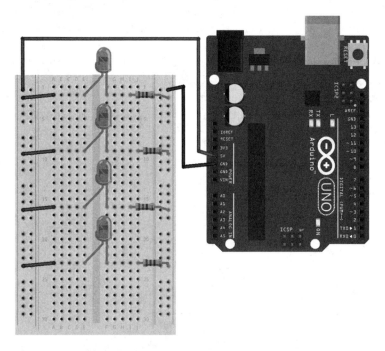

Figure 3.30   Wiring LEDs in parallel allows you to wire more in a single circuit because each branch gets the same voltage (5 V).

If everything goes right, all four LEDs should happily light up.

Parallel circuits have another useful feature. If you were to remove the red wire between the LED in row 2 and the power rail, the other 3 LEDs would still light up. The circuit still has three other complete paths it can use. Contrast this to a series circuit, where a single gap stops current from flowing to any component.

3.2.6 *Powering your project with batteries*

So far, you've been providing power to the breadboard using the Arduino Uno's onboard 5 V power, but there are other ways to provide power to projects. One (obvious) option is to use batteries.

A single, 9 V battery is a convenient power source, and in the case of the LED circuits you've been building, it removes the reliance on a development board.

BUILD THE CIRCUIT: 9 V POWERED LEDs

What you'll need

- 1 breadboard
- 9 V battery and snap, with wires
- 4 standard red LEDs
- 4 jumper wires
- 4 560 Ω resistors

With a 9 V battery, the supply voltage is (obviously) different than the Arduino's 5 V. That means we'll need to use different resistors for the LEDs in the parallel circuit.

Recall that each branch in a parallel circuit "gets" the full 9 V supply voltage to work with, so you can calculate the resistor needed on each branch using Ohm's law:

```
R = 9 V / 20 mA
R = 450 Ω
```

A 560 Ω resistor is the nearest common resistor value, and it will do fine (have you noticed there's a bit of fudge room, as long as you round up?).

Disconnect the breadboard's power rails from the Arduino and swap out each of the 220 Ω resistors in favor of the brawnier 560 Ω resistors. Now plug the battery case's positive and negative wires into the breadboard's power rails (figure 3.31). All done!

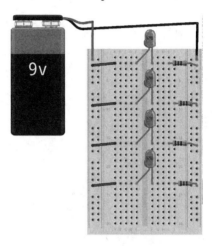

Figure 3.31   Powering the parallel LED circuit with a 9 V battery involves swapping out some resistors and connecting a 9 V battery snap to the power rails.

Summary

- The relationships between voltage, current, and resistance—as formalized in Ohm's law—are the keys to understanding basic circuitry.
- Breadboards provide a tangible and convenient prototyping platform, with standard connection patterns, for trying out circuits.
- A series circuit provides one single path for electrical flow. A parallel circuit has two or more paths.
- LEDs have a characteristic called *forward voltage drop*. When calculating the right resistor for an LED wired in series, first subtract this forward voltage drop from the supply voltage.
- In a series circuit, the current is equal at all points of the circuit, whereas in a parallel circuit, all branches have equal voltages.

- In a series circuit, it's straightforward to calculate total resistance in the circuit: add the resistor values together.
- A circuit with more than one path splits up the current in the circuit and is called a *current divider*. Determining the total resistance in such a parallel circuit can be accomplished using a current-division formula.

Part 2

Project basics: input and output with Johnny-Five

This part of the book is where things really get cooking: you'll learn how to add sensors, outputs, and moving parts to projects, building a whole bunch of small experiments along the way with your Arduino Uno board and Johnny-Five.

In chapter 4, you'll get to know all about inputs (sensors), both analog and digital. You'll try your hand at reading data from a simple temperature sensor and a photosensitive resistor, and you'll learn to detect button presses.

Chapter 5 concerns itself with outputs, building on your earlier experimentations with LEDs. You'll move beyond blinking LEDs to animated LEDs and full-color RGB LEDs. You'll display text on a parallel LCD module and build your own "weather ball" (a simplified weather conditions display).

If you've been waiting for the robots part, chapter 6 is it! This chapter is all about motion: motors and servos. We'll investigate how motors work and how to power and control them. At the end of chapter 6, you'll build a simple roving robot using an inexpensive robot chassis kit.

By the end of this part of the book, you'll have surveyed all of the major types of simple inputs and outputs for small embedded projects. You'll be able to read environmental data from sensors and output light and sound. You'll be ready to build more sophisticated, wires-free projects.

Sensors and input 4

This chapter covers

- The role sensors play in projects as *transducers*, converting physical phenomena to electrical signals
- How microcontrollers use analog-to-digital conversion (ADC) to interpret incoming analog signals
- Building voltage divider circuits to read *resistive sensors* like photoresistors
- Using Johnny-Five's generic `Sensor` class to read sensor data and listen for data and changes
- Taking advantage of Johnny-Five's component-specific `Thermometer` and `Button` classes
- Managing default digital logic levels using pull-down resistors

To build nifty gadgets, whether they're temperature-controlled automatic fans or more interesting inventions, you've got to be able to gather information and input from the real, physical world.

For this chapter, you'll need the following:

- 1 Arduino Uno and USB cable
- 1 photoresistor
- 1 4.7 kΩ resistor
- 1 TMP36 analog temperature sensor
- 1 push button
- 1 10 kΩ resistor
- Black, red, and green jumper wires
- 1 half-size breadboard

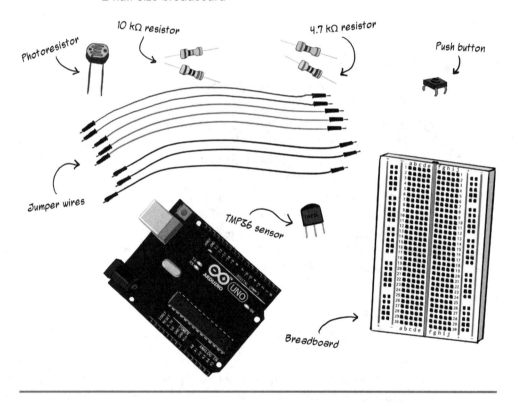

Analog and digital sensors pay attention to a particular phenomenon in the physical environment—temperature, brightness, dampness, pressure, vibration—and they output information about changes in the intensity of that phenomenon as a signal. In the automatic fan example in chapter 1, a temperature sensor translated temperature changes into an electrical signal that the microcontroller's firmware could read and process (figure 4.1).

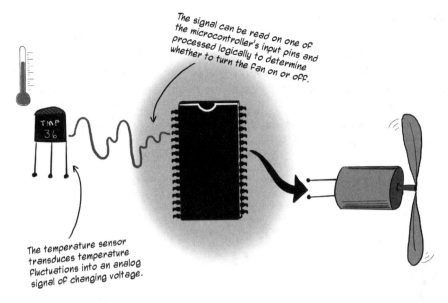

The signal can be read on one of the microcontroller's input pins and processed logically to determine whether to turn the fan on or off.

The temperature sensor transduces temperature fluctuations into an analog signal of changing voltage.

Figure 4.1   The temperature-controlled fan from chapter 1 used an analog temperature sensor to gather information about changing temperatures in the surrounding environment.

That conversion from physical input to electrical output means that sensors are a type of *transducer*, which is any device that converts one form of energy into a signal (or vice versa).

Sensors and inputs are classified based on what kind of signal they produce: analog, a continuous, smooth set of values with no gaps, or digital, consisting of a discrete, finite set of values (figure 4.2).

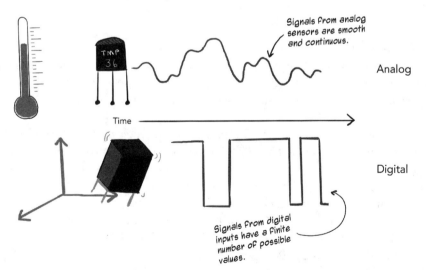

Signals from analog sensors are smooth and continuous.

Analog

Time

Digital

Signals from digital inputs have a finite number of possible values.

Figure 4.2   An analog sensor like a temperature sensor (top) transduces changes in temperature into a smooth, analog signal. A digital input like a tilt switch (bottom) might have as few as two discrete output values: one when oriented normally (off, LOW, 0, or false) and one when inverted (on, HIGH, 1, true).

4.1   *Working with analog sensors*

Our physical reality is analog: we live in a world of the infinite. There are an infinite number of temperatures between 0 and 20 degrees Celsius, an infinite number of colors, an infinite number of sound frequencies. Of course, as humans, we can't discern 280.3984 Hz from 280.3985 Hz, but the two different values exist.

Analog sensors are sensitive to these analog, real-world inputs. Their output is a smooth signal, usually of varying voltage that corresponds to the intensity of the thing they're measuring (figure 4.3).

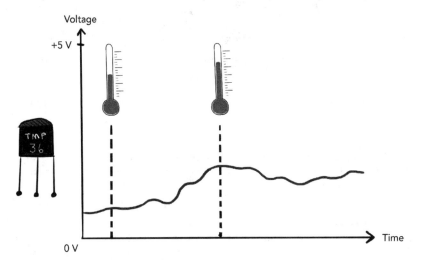

Figure 4.3   The output signal from an analog temperature sensor varies in voltage over time as the temperature changes.

4.1.1   *Analog-to-digital conversion*

Analog sensors like the temperature sensor in the fan provide an analog signal, but our programming world is digital. Analog input signals need to somehow be sampled and normalized—quantized—into discrete digital values so they can be processed with digital logic.

Doing this conversion of signal samples from analog to digital requires a bit of hardware and processing. The Arduino Uno's microcontroller provides built-in *analog-to-digital conversion* (ADC) capability on six of its pins. Analog input pins—those with ADC support—are prefixed with "A" on the Uno (figure 4.4).

The number of possible values that can be derived from an incoming analog signal depends on the *bandwidth* of the ADC hardware on the microcontroller. The ATmega328P on the Uno provides 10-bit ADC for each of its six enabled pins. That means it can resolve 1024 (2^{10}) possible interpreted digital values. An analog input of 0 V will be interpreted as 0, 5 V as 1023, and anything between scaled to the nearest (integer) step value.

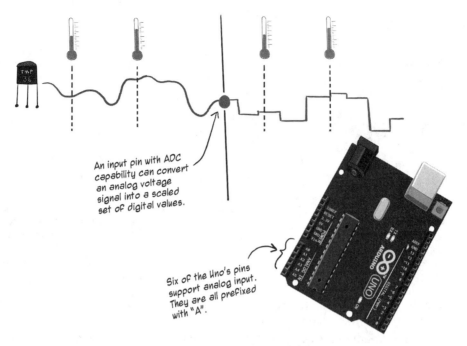

An input pin with ADC capability can convert an analog voltage signal into a scaled set of digital values.

Six of the Uno's pins support analog input. They are all prefixed with "A".

Figure 4.4   ADC is supported by the ATmega328P microcontroller on specific pins (made available as A0-A5 on the Uno). ADCs convert analog signals to discrete digital values.

An analog sensor responds to a physical stimulus to which it is sensitive, transducing that physical energy into an output signal of varying voltage. That signal can be sampled by an analog input pin on a microcontroller and converted to digital values using the MCU's analog-to-digital (ADC) capability. To see how this works in action, let's experiment with a basic analog sensor.

4.1.2   *Working with photoresistors*

A *photoresistor*, also called a *photocell* or *light-dependent resistor* (LDR), is a simple sensor. Its name gives away that it's actually a kind of resistor, but its conductivity changes depending on the brightness of incident light hitting it—it's *photoconductive*.

When things are dim, the photoresistor has higher resistance, topping out at about 10 kΩ when it's totally dark. As the amount of light it's exposed to increases, it becomes more conductive—its resistance decreases—down to about 1 kΩ when things are quite bright (figure 4.5).

VOLTAGES IN A CIRCUIT

Let's say we want to be able to use the Uno's ADC-capable pin A0 to read a signal representing changing ambient light values. We need a circuit that contains the photoresistor and that's connected to power, ground, and pin A0 on the Uno.

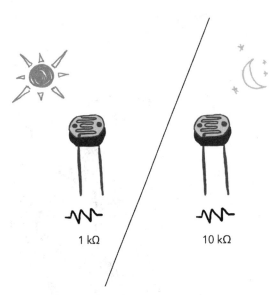

Figure 4.5   As light conditions change, the resistance of the photoresistor changes. It becomes more conductive— that is, less resistive—when more light hits it. When it's darker, the resistance is higher.

But the circuit shown in figure 4.6 isn't going to do the trick. Remember *Kirchoff's voltage law* (KVL) from chapter 3? All of the voltage in a circuit has to get used up. The only component in the circuit in figure 4.6 that "uses up" any voltage is the photoresistor itself.

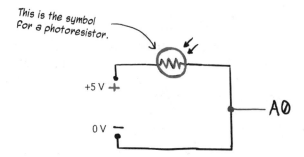

Figure 4.6   With a circuit like this, there won't be any meaningful voltage variance on pin A0.

This means that no matter what the actual resistance value of the photoresistor is at any given moment, it's going to use up all of the voltage in the circuit anyway—meaning that the voltage at A0 won't change.

In chapter 3, you also saw how current is the same at every point in a series circuit. The circuit shown in figure 4.7 assumes a 2 V forward voltage drop across the LED, leaving 3 V for the resistors to take care of. The total resistance in the circuit is 200 Ω (the two 100 Ω resistors add together), so

```
I = V / R
```

thus

```
0.015A = 3 V / 200 Ω
```

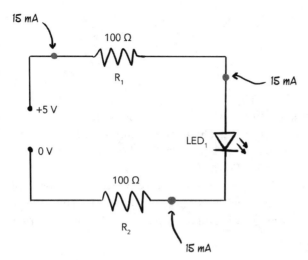

Figure 4.7   In a series circuit, current is the same at all points.

The current at all points in the circuit will measure 15 mA.

The key thing for figuring out our photoresistor problem here is that voltage gets divided up amongst the components in the circuit (figure 4.8) and it's not constant at every point.

Let's tease the circuit in figure 4.7 apart and analyze it to see where the voltage is going.

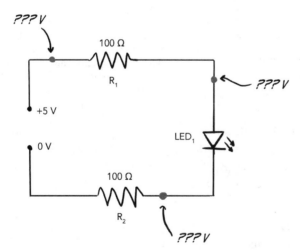

Figure 4.8   In a series circuit, voltage can differ at different points. Each component uses up, or *drops*, its own share of the circuit's available voltage.

2 V of the 5 V supply is getting chewed up by the LED because of its forward voltage drop. That leaves 3 V that needs to go…*somewhere*. It gets divided up amongst the remaining components in the circuit.

The amount of voltage allotted to each remaining resistive component—the two resistors, R_1 and R_2—is a ratio of the given component's resistance to the total resistance in the circuit.

Let's calculate the voltage allotted to R_1:

```
R1 resistance value    =    100 Ω
Total circuit resistance = 200 Ω
Proportional voltage R1  = 100 Ω / 200 Ω = 1/2
Thus, voltage across R1  = (1/2) * 3 V remaining = 1.5 V
```

Because there are two resistors, and they're of equal resistance, the remaining voltage will be distributed 50–50 between them. The results would be different if the resistors had differing values (for example, if R_1 were 300 Ω and R_2 were 100 Ω, their allotted voltages would be 1.125 V and .375 V respectively).

In the circuit depicted in figure 4.9, the two resistors R_1 and R_2 have *equal* resistance—each provides half of the total resistance in the circuit. Thus the remaining voltage (3.0 V) in the circuit will get divided up equally (50–50) between them—1.5 V each.

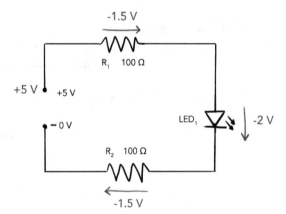

Figure 4.9   Kirchoff's voltage law states that adding up all voltages in a circuit always produces 0. That is, all voltage in the circuit needs to be accounted for (be used up).

A more formal way of saying that "all voltage in a circuit needs to get used up" is that all voltages in a circuit must add up to 0. Traveling around the circuit in figure 4.9, we start at the power supply: +5 V. Then R_1 drops its share, 1.5 V; the LED drops 2.0 V; and R_2 drops 1.5 V. All of this adds up to 0:

```
(+5 V) + (-1.5 V) + (-2 V) + (-1.5 V) = 0 V
```

Because we know how much voltage each component in the circuit is using up, we can derive the voltage at different points in the circuit (figure 4.10).

So when there's only one component in a circuit, it's going to use up all the voltage. If you wired the photoresistor without any other components (figure 4.11), it would provide 100% of the resistance in the circuit (technically, this isn't quite true because of a resistor we'll meet later that's hidden inside the microcontroller, but it's close enough).

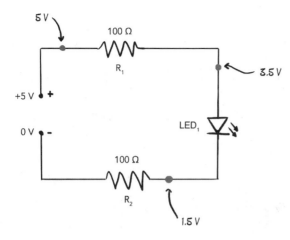

Figure 4.10 Voltages at different points in a series circuit vary based on how much voltage has been dropped by components in the circuit.

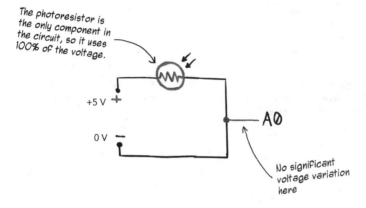

The photoresistor is the only component in the circuit, so it uses 100% of the voltage.

No significant voltage variation here

Figure 4.11 With only the photoresistor in the circuit, there's no point of reference at which to read measurable voltage changes.

We need a way to create a circuit that has a point of reference, a point where voltage does vary in a predictable way and can be read.

4.1.3 Voltage dividers

Voltage dividers to the rescue! A voltage divider circuit makes it possible to read useful values from the photoresistor. To understand how, let's first look at what a voltage divider is and how it works.

A *voltage divider* is a circuit that uses a pair of resistors to convert a higher supply voltage into a lower output voltage. Although the voltage of the circuit as a *whole* is the supply voltage (5 V in our examples), voltage *between* the two resistors is a new output voltage (figure 4.12).

If the two resistors used in the voltage divider have equal resistance and are the only components in the circuit, it's intuitive that the voltage available at V_{out} in figure 4.13 will be half of the original supply voltage—R_1 drops its proportional share of the supply voltage, 50%, as electricity flows across it.

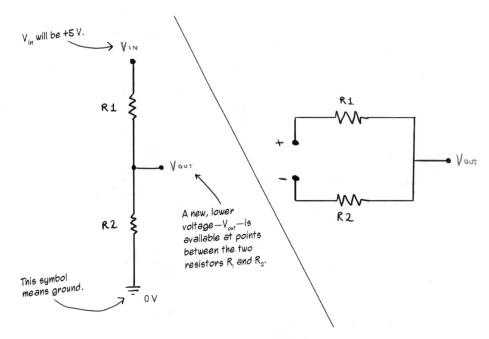

Figure 4.12   A voltage divider provides a new, lower voltage at V_{out}, available at points between two resistors, R₁ and R₂. There are several ways to draw a voltage divider schematic; the two circuits depicted here are functionally identical.

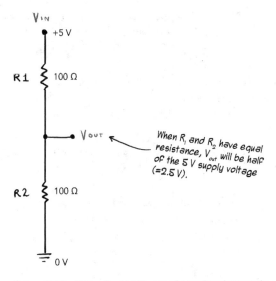

Figure 4.13   When R₁ and R₂ are of equal resistance in a circuit, V_{out} is half of V_{in}, as each resistor drops 50% of the supply voltage.

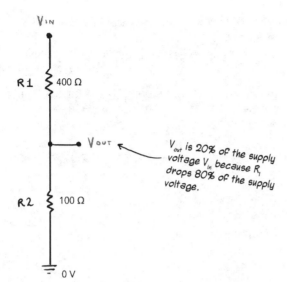

V IN

R1 400 Ω

V OUT

V_out is 20% of the supply voltage V_in because R_1 drops 80% of the supply voltage.

R2 100 Ω

0 V

Figure 4.14 V$_{out}$ is 1/5 (20%) of the supply voltage because R$_1$ provides 80% of the total resistance in the circuit.

On the other hand, if R$_2$ remained at 100 Ω but R$_1$ changed resistance to 400 Ω, 80% of the available voltage would be dropped by R$_1$ (figure 4.14), such that the output voltage at point V$_{out}$ is now 20% of the supply voltage.

Voilà! Changes in the proportion of resistance R$_1$ provides to the circuit are reflected as voltage changes at V$_{out}$. There's the point of reference we need!

VOLTAGE DIVIDER FORMULA

The formula for voltage divider circuits—that is, the method for determining what voltage will be at V$_{out}$ between the two resistors—is as follows:

```
V(out) = V(in) * (R2 / (R1 + R2))
```

V$_{out}$ is what's "left over" of the supply voltage after R$_1$ has dropped its portion of the circuit's voltage.

We'll be using a fixed 4.7 kΩ resistor as R$_2$ (figure 4.15). The photoresistor will play the part of R$_1$. Its resistance ranges between 1 kΩ and 10 kΩ depending on ambient brightness.

As the resistance of R$_1$ (the photoresistor) changes proportionally to the circuit's total resistance, the output voltage on A0 will also vary. We can measure that voltage with the Uno and see how the light levels are fluctuating.

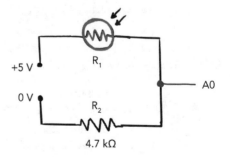

+5 V

R$_1$

0 V

R$_2$

A0

4.7 kΩ

Figure 4.15 The schematic for the photoresistor circuit

Calculating the voltage range of V_{out}

You can calculate the range of possible voltages at V_{out} by using the voltage divider formula.

At the photoresistor's highest resistance, when it's dark, R_1 will have a resistance of 10 kΩ (remember, R_2 is always 4.7 kΩ). This higher-resistance response to darkness will produce the lowest voltage in the range:

```
V(out) = V(in) * (R2 / (R1 + R2))

R1 = 10000 Ω
R2 = 4700 Ω

V(out)
  = 5 V * (4700 / 14700)
  = 5 V * .32
  = 1.6 V
```

When it's bright, R_1's lowest possible resistance is 1 kΩ, resulting in the highest voltage in the range:

```
V(out) = V(in) * (R2 / (R1 + R2))

R1 = 1000 Ω
R2 = 4700 Ω

V(out)
  = 5 V * (4700 / 5400)
  = 5 V * .825
  = 4.125 V
```

By using a voltage divider circuit with the photoresistor, you can create a readable output voltage signal for pin A0 that varies from 1.6 V to 4.125 V.

4.125 – 1.6 V = 2.525 V, or just slightly more than 50% of the total 0–5 V range. That means you'll get a decent spread of values—ranging from (very roughly) about 328 (~1.6 V) to 845 (~4.125 V) of the possible 10-bit (0–1023) range.

4.1.4   *Wiring and using a photoresistor*

What you'll need

- 1 Arduino Uno and USB cable
- 1 photoresistor
- 1 4.7 kΩ resistor (or 10 kΩ will also work)
- Red (2), black (2), and green (1) jumper wires
- 1 half-size breadboard

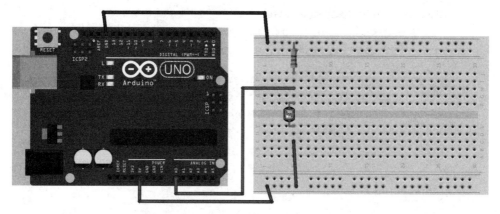

Figure 4.16 Wiring diagram for the photoresistor voltage divider circuit. The jumper wire connected to A0 needs to have its other end connected to V_{out}, between the photoresistor (R_1) and the 4.7 kΩ resistor (R_2).

Like the other resistors you've been working with, photoresistors aren't polarized, so you don't need to worry about positive-negative orientation. Connect the photocell and 4.7 kΩ resistor to the breadboard as shown in figure 4.16.

The voltage divider output, V_{out}, is available in any terminal-row hole between the photocell and the resistor (recall that the five holes in each terminal row on the breadboard are electrically connected).

Plug one end of a green jumper wire into one of those holes and the other end into pin A0 on the Uno. Hook up power to the power rail from the Uno's 5 V power and GND pins. Now you can put your breadboard aside for a moment and we'll turn to the software side.

Once the photoresistor circuit is powered (not yet! by the way), a signal of varying voltage will be present on pin A0. So *how* can we read values from that signal using our handy Johnny-Five JavaScript framework?

PROCESSING ANALOG SENSOR INPUT WITH JOHNNY-FIVE

Johnny-Five's API contains a collection of classes that can be used to interact with your development board and components. You've seen `Led`, for example. Many of the component classes, like `Led`, are for specific types of devices, such as `Accelerometer` and `Servo`. There are also a few more generic classes that have broader use, including one that can be used with analog sensors like the `Sensor` photoresistor.

> **KEEPING UP TO DATE WITH THE JOHNNY-FIVE API** Johnny-Five, like much other open source software, is constantly evolving. New features and classes get added, and the API evolves as well. You can keep up to date with the current Johnny-Five API at http://johnny-five.io/api.

USING JOHNNY-FIVE'S SENSOR CLASS

The Sensor class can be used to read and process data from analog sensors. First, create a new Sensor object in a Johnny-Five Node.js script, as shown in the next listing.

Listing 4.1   Instantiating a new `Sensor` object with Johnny-Five

```
const five = require('johnny-five');
const board = new five.Board();

board.on('ready', () => {
  const sensor = new five.Sensor({
    pin: 'A0'
  });
});
```

When instantiating a Sensor, "pin" is the only required property for the passed options object.

The internals of Sensor take care of configuring the indicated pin as an analog input pin and then automatically and continuously reading ADC data from that pin.

So what can you do with a Sensor object? You could log out its value, as the following listing shows—value is one of several parameters available on Sensor objects, and it holds the most recently read value.

Listing 4.2   Logging a sensor's value

```
board.on('ready', () => {
  const sensor = new five.Sensor({
    pin: 'A0'
  });
  console.log(sensor.value);
});
```

This will only log once (ready event fires once).

But the code in listing 4.2 will only log the value of the sensor once—that's of limited use. It's much more useful to look at sensor values over time. This is a job for event-driven JavaScript.

THE SENSOR DATA EVENT IN JOHNNY-FIVE

Different objects in Johnny-Five provide different events that your code can bind to. You can handle these events, when they occur, using a callback function.

The Sensor class, for example, has a data event that gets triggered every time the pin's value is read successfully, as shown in the next listing.

Listing 4.3   Logging values using the `data` event

```
sensor.on('data', () => {
  console.log(sensor.value);
});
```

The data event is fired every time a value is successfully read from the pin.

TRYING OUT THE PHOTORESISTOR

Let's put together our voltage-divider-enhanced photoresistor circuit with some Johnny-Five code to sense changes in surrounding light conditions. Create a new file, photoresistor.js, and populate it with the following code.

Listing 4.4 Photoresistor.js

```
const five = require('johnny-five');
const board = new five.Board();

board.on('ready', () => {
  const sensor = new five.Sensor({
    pin: 'A0'
  });
  sensor.on('data', () => {
    console.log(sensor.value);
  });
});
```

Plug in the Arduino's USB cable to your computer—now the board and breadboard circuit have power. Execute the photoresistor script:

```
node photoresistor.js
```

Once the script is running, increase and decrease the amount of light reaching the photoresistor by placing your hand over it or dimming the lights. As you do this, you should see the values in the logged output change, which will look something like the following.

Listing 4.5 Photoresistor data logging output

```
$ node photoresistor.js
1464612512404 Device(s) /dev/cu.usbmodem1421
1464612512416 Connected /dev/cu.usbmodem1421
1464612515883 Repl Initialized
>> 354
354
355
355
355
355
354
353
432
```

ADJUSTING FREQUENCY, SCALE, AND THRESHOLD

Photoresistor values are scrolling by awfully fast. By default, Sensor will read, calculate, and scale ADC data once every 25 ms. That's why your photoresistor value logging is scrolling by so briskly. It's possible to adjust the frequency of these reads with the freq parameter, as the following listing shows.

Listing 4.6   Sensor `freq` parameter

```
const sensor = new five.Sensor({
  pin: 'A0',
  freq: 1000
});
```
Values are in milliseconds: this will read once per second.

Johnny-Five event binding and `this`

Sensor object events bind `this` to the Sensor object, meaning that you could write code like the following:

```
sensor.on('data', function () {
  console.log(this.value); // `this` is bound to `sensor`
});
```

Note that because of the binding that happens with arrow functions used as anonymous callbacks, the following won't work:

```
sensor.on('data', () => {
  console.log(this.value); // --> undefined
});
```

A more elegant approach is to bind to the change event instead of the data event. The change event is fired whenever the sensor's most recent value differs by more than a threshold amount from the previously read value.

The threshold value defaults to 1, which means that—because read sensor values are integers—any change in value will trigger the change event. threshold is an attribute on the Sensor object instance and can be changed at any point to alter the threshold for triggering change events. The following listing combines this into a script that logs out any time the sensor changes value by 5 or more (remember, possible values range from 0 to 1023).

Listing 4.7   Logging changing photoresistor values

```
var const = require('johnny-five');
var const = new five.Board();


board.on('ready', () => {
  const sensor = new five.Sensor({
    pin: 'A0'
  });
  console.log(sensor.value);
```
Logs out the sensor's initial value

You can adjust the threshold attribute; default is 1

```
sensor.threshold = 5;
sensor.on('change', () => {
    console.log(sensor.value);
});
});
```

change fires when value changes by >= threshold

Because the actual voltage at V_{out} for the photoresistor circuit will vary depending on what resistor is used at R_2, the photoresistor's changing values are more relative (it's getting brighter, it's getting darker) than absolute (in foot-candles or whatever light intensity is measured in). Other kinds of sensors provide a calibrated output voltage that can be directly converted into fixed units, like degrees Celsius in the case of analog temperature sensors.

4.1.5 Using an analog temperature sensor

The TMP36 is an analog temperature sensor manufactured by Analog Devices. It's plentiful, cheap, and easy to work with. Like other analog sensors, it provides a signal of varying voltage. You don't have to build a voltage divider to use it, though: it provides a varying output voltage on a third pin. All you have to do is connect the sensor to +5 V and ground, and then read the voltage on the third, output-voltage pin (figure 4.17).

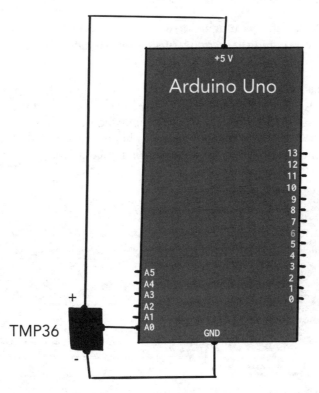

Figure 4.17   The schematic for the TMP 36 circuit

With the TMP36 and other similar analog temperature sensors, the output voltage can be used to calculate a "real" temperature value. The TMP36 sensor's voltage increases linearly with temperature—given a voltage reading from the TMP36, the Celsius temperature can be obtained by multiplying the current voltage by 100 and subtracting 50. For example, if the output voltage from the sensor is 0.7 V,

```
Temperature in Celsius = 0.7 V * 100 - 50 = 20
```

To perform this calculation, however, you'd need to convert the ADC 10-bit reading back into (approximate) voltage and also put the arithmetic into your code. To make this convenient for us, Johnny-Five offers the `Thermometer` class, which supports a number of different kinds of temperature sensors.

BUILDING THE CIRCUIT: TMP36 TEMPERATURE SENSOR

What you'll need
- 1 Arduino Uno and USB cable
- 1 TMP36 sensor
- 1 half-size breadboard
- Red (2), black (2), and green (1) jumper wires

The circuit for the TMP36 is shown in figure 4.18. Connect the TMP36 to power using red and black jumper wires, and then connect its output (middle) pin to A0 with a green jumper wire.

> **DON'T PLUG THE TMP36 IN BACKWARDS!** TMP36 sensors don't like to be plugged in backwards. Make sure you check the orientation of the flat side of the sensor when placing it into the circuit. After applying power to your circuit, touch the TMP36 sensor. If it feels unpleasantly hot to the touch—uh oh! Disconnect power immediately and check the sensor's orientation.

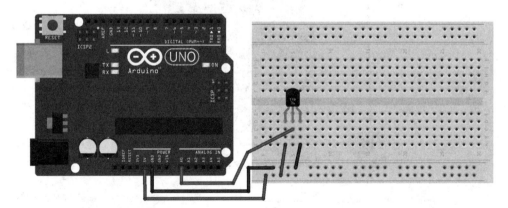

Figure 4.18   Wiring the TMP36 sensor

LOGGING AND INSPECTING TMP36 DATA

Instantiating a `Thermometer` object is similar to using the `Sensor` class, but it needs information about what kind of temperature sensor (`controller`) is being used. A simple example of logging temperature is shown in the following listing.

Listing 4.8 temperature.js

Like Sensor, Thermometer needs to know which pin it's on.

Thermometer requires a controller parameter—about 15 different temperature sensors are supported.

celsius, fahrenheit, and kelvin are all attributes on Thermometer instances.

```
var five = require('johnny-five');
var board = new five.Board();

board.on('ready', () => {
  const tmp36 = new five.Thermometer({
    controller: 'TMP36',
    pin: 'A0'
  });
  tmp36.on('data', () => {
    console.log(tmp36.celsius);
  });
});
```

INTERACTING WITH COMPONENTS USING THE JOHNNY-FIVE REPL

When a Johnny-Five script is running, you can interact with it in your terminal window. Or, you *could*, if all that `console.log` stuff wasn't scrolling by. Sometimes `console.log` is all you need, but for more convenient debugging or inspection without having to restart the script or change the code, you can take advantage of Johnny-Five's REPL (read-evaluate-print loop).

If you removed the `console.log`-ing `data` event handler from temperature.js and executed the script, you'd see something like the following.

Listing 4.9 Johnny-Five's REPL

```
$ node temperature.js
1464614001498 Device(s) /dev/cu.usbmodem1421
1464614001506 Connected /dev/cu.usbmodem1421
1464614004970 Repl Initialized
>>
```

You can type JavaScript expressions at the double-arrow prompt and press Enter on your keyboard—it's an interactive prompt. Maybe you want to see what the value of the `tmp36` temperature sensor is, in Fahrenheit, as shown in the next listing.

Listing 4.10 What if you want to get information from a Johnny-Five component...?

```
>> tmp36.fahrenheit
ReferenceError: temp36 is not defined
    at repl:1:1
    at REPLServer.defaultEval (repl.js:264:27)
    at bound (domain.js:287:14)
    at REPLServer.runBound [as eval] (domain.js:300:12)
```

```
    at REPLServer.<anonymous> (repl.js:431:12)
    at emitOne (events.js:77:13)
    at REPLServer.emit (events.js:169:7)
    at REPLServer.Interface._onLine (readline.js:211:10)
    at REPLServer.Interface._line (readline.js:550:8)
    at REPLServer.Interface._ttyWrite (readline.js:827:14)
```

This isn't game over; we just missed a step. "Injecting" something into the scope of Johnny-Five's REPL requires us to be explicit about it.

Within your Johnny-Five script, you can selectively inject things into the REPL that you'd like to have available for inspection or manipulation when the script is running, as shown in the next listing.

Listing 4.11 Injecting into the REPL

This makes the tmp36 object reference available (as tmp36).

Things are injected into the REPL as key-value pairs.

```
board.repl.inject({
  tmp36: tmp36,
  foo: 'bar'
});
```

This makes the string 'bar' available as foo.

Making the string 'bar' available as foo is kind of silly, but the point is that you can make any kind of value you like available from within the REPL. You can then use the REPL as a console for interacting with these items, as the following listing shows.

Listing 4.12 Altering temperature.js to use REPL injection

```
var five = require('johnny-five');
var board = new five.Board();

board.on('ready', () => {
  const tmp36 = new five.Thermometer({
    controller: 'TMP36',
    pin: 'A0'
  });
  board.repl.inject({
    tmp36: tmp36
  });
});
```

Now, when you run `node temperature.js`, you won't see data logging by, but you'll get a REPL prompt once the board is initialized. Then you can interact with the tmp36 object. Try typing this:

```
>> tmp36.celsius
```

Or this:

```
>> tmp36.fahrenheit
```

This can come in handy, especially when debugging or exploring more complex components.

The photoresistor is a good fit for measuring relative changes to an environmental stimulus—it's brighter, now it's dimmer, now it's brighter again. The TMP36 sensor is a good fit for measuring environmental stimulus as fixed units—degrees Celsius or Fahrenheit. Both produce voltage signals of infinite analog resolution (in theory, at least), and the range of values available for software processing is defined by the microcontroller's ADC (10-bit, in the Uno's case).

For some types of environmental sensing, though, you don't need a continuous set of values as input. For these types of applications, you can use components that generate digital signals.

4.2 Digital inputs

Pins 0 through 13 on the Uno are digital pins. Each can be configured as either an input pin or an output pin. When configured for input, a digital pin can evaluate, based on the voltage present, whether it's in a HIGH or LOW logical state.

Buttons and some switches are good examples of components that provide simple digital signals because they are binary. A button is either pressed or it isn't: it's on or it's off. This corresponds to digital input pins, whose states are also binary (LOW or HIGH).

4.2.1 Using a button as a digital input

Our challenge is to construct a circuit that correctly causes a digital pin to be in a HIGH state when a push button (a.k.a. *momentary switch*) is pressed, but in a LOW state otherwise. That way, our software can determine when a button is being pressed and do something with that information.

Push-button connection refresher

Pins that share one side of a push button are only electrically connected when the button is pressed. But pins on opposite sides of the button are always electrically connected.

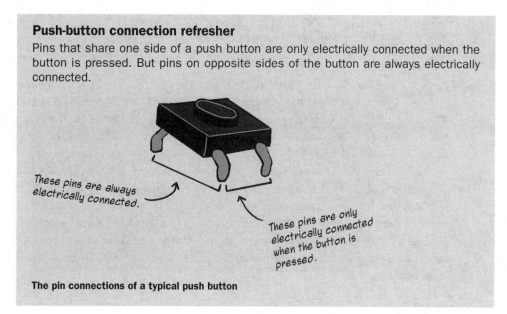

These pins are always electrically connected.

These pins are only electrically connected when the button is pressed.

The pin connections of a typical push button

UNDERSTANDING LOGIC LEVELS

The Arduino's microcontroller determines whether a given digital input pin is HIGH or LOW based on the voltage present on the pin at the time that it's read. As you might expect in the Uno's case, 5 V present on an input pin will make it logically HIGH and 0 V makes it logically LOW. There's some nuance here you need to know about, however, because it will affect the design of the button circuit.

Voltages and logic levels

A digital pin doesn't have to have exactly 5 V present to read HIGH. Similarly, low voltage of, say, 0.8 V, will result in a logical LOW. Each microcontroller has a set of voltage ranges that will result in a LOW state or a HIGH state, as well as a *noise margin* in the middle.

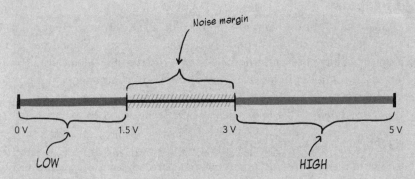

Voltage ranges for logical states on Arduino Uno pins. Any voltage below 1.5 V is LOW; anything above 3 V, **HIGH.** Voltages between 1.5 V and 3 V fall in the noise margin and should be avoided.

In the case of the Uno's ATmega 328P, input voltages from about 0–1.5 V will result in a LOW state, whereas voltages greater than 3 V will read HIGH.

Let's say you have a configured digital input pin on the Arduino but have nothing connected to it yet. What state would you expect the pin to have if you read its value? Turns out, it's impossible to predict. Could be HIGH, could be LOW. If you read it over time, you'd see LOWs and HIGHs pretty much at random. This kind of disconnected behavior is called *floating.*

This comes about because of the pin's *high impedance,* in which it takes just a teeny-tiny amount of current to move the pin between one logic level and the other. This is a useful and efficient thing—the pin can detect changes in connected components without needing to waste a lot of current to do so. Yet little blips commonly arising from electrical noise in the environment or interference from other pins on the same microcontroller are enough to make the pin swap around between LOW and HIGH basically at random.

WIRING A BUTTON WITH A PULL-DOWN RESISTOR

What you'll need

- 1 Arduino Uno and USB cable
- 1 push button
- 1 10 kΩ resistor
- 4 jumper wires
- 1 half-size breadboard

What we need to do is build a safe circuit (one that doesn't have a risk of a short circuit) that establishes a reliable "default" logic level when the button isn't pressed—LOW or HIGH, but one that won't flop around randomly. One way this can be done is by *pulling* the input pin to ground (0 V) with the aid of an additional resistor.

When a *pull-down resistor* is present in the circuit, there's always a connection between pin 2 and ground, even when the button isn't pressed (figure 4.19).

This takes care of the floating problem—if any stray current shows up uninvited when the button isn't pressed, it'll get wicked away to ground through the resistor (left side of figure 4.19). Pin 2 will continuously read LOW (0 V) when the button isn't pressed.

When the button is pressed (right side of figure 4.19), current flows at 5 V through the button, and then into both pin 2 and ground—pin 2 will read HIGH. The pull-down

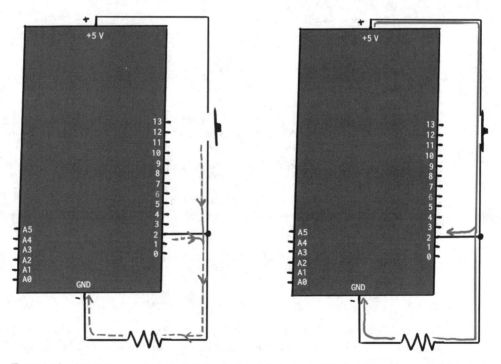

Figure 4.19 A pull-down resistor "pulls" the digital pin to logical LOW when the component (button) isn't pushed (connected).

resistor performs another role here: it prevents a short circuit when the button is pressed, limiting the current that flows.

A current divider in disguise

When using a pull-down resistor in the circuit, you'll actually be creating a current divider, even though it's not immediately obvious. Remember from chapter 3 that current division is a feature of parallel circuits (the circuit in the figure is a parallel circuit because there's more than one path an individual charge could take). When there's more than one path to choose, current will split up proportionally based on the resistance in each path.

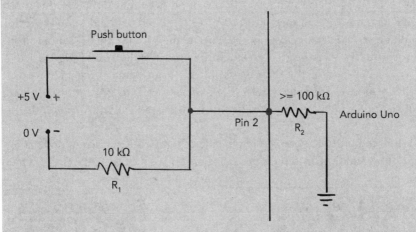

Using a pull-down resistor in combination with an input pin actually creates a current divider.

Internally, microcontroller pin circuitry includes a resistor with high resistance (on the order of 100 kΩ to several megohms) when a pin is configured for input (high impedance state). This internal resistor will play the part of R_2. For R_1, we have the 10 kΩ pull-down resistor—high resistance, but about an order of magnitude less resistant than the internal resistor (R_2).

When current flows through the circuit (the button is pressed), a whole lot more of it will go through the 10 kΩ (R_1) resistor's path than the path with the internal resistor (R_2).

In a current divider, each path gets a different current allotment, but both get the same voltage. The bit of current that does reach pin 2 is at or near 5 V, which will set the pin to HIGH.

The resulting wiring diagram (figure 4.20) isn't too complex. Go ahead and wire the button on the breadboard as shown, making sure to connect a 10 kΩ resistor between pin 2 and ground.

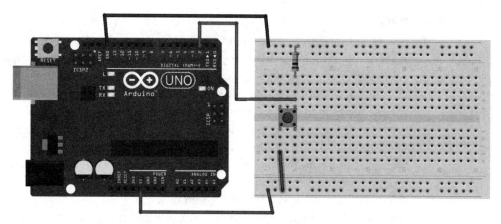

Figure 4.20   The button circuit with a 10 kΩ pull-down resistor

Johnny-Five's Button class

Johnny-Five's Button class takes care of configuring a digital output pin and provides several features that you'd want in a button, including the ability to listen for button pushes, as shown in the next listing.

Listing 4.13   button.js

```
const five = require('johnny-five');
const board = new five.Board();

board.on('ready', () => {
  const pushButton = new five.Button(2);
  pushButton.on('down', () => {
    console.log('I have been pressed!');
  });
});
```

Try out the code in listing 4.13. Connect your Arduino to USB power and run the script:

```
$ node button.js
```

Once the board is initialized, every time you press the button down, you should see this:

```
>> I have been pressed!
```

In this chapter, you've seen a few flavors of basic inputs: two kinds of analog sensors and digital input with a push button. Inputs and sensors are vital for gathering information about the physical environment, but it gets considerably more fun when you actually do something with that information—when you create output. That's what you'll be doing next.

Summary

- Analog sensors generate signals of varying voltage with (theoretically) infinite resolution, and microcontrollers convert this signal to digital value equivalents using analog-to-digital (ADC) conversion.
- The Arduino Uno has six analog input pins, which provide 10-bit ADC (1024 values). Its 14 digital pins can be configured as either input or output and have binary logic levels: LOW or HIGH.
- Each component in a series circuit receives the same amount of current, but voltage is apportioned based on the component's proportional resistance. A *voltage divider* uses this principle to convert a higher input voltage into a lower output voltage, using two resistors wired in series.
- A voltage divider circuit creates a point of reference at which you can detect changes in resistance as changes in voltage. This approach can be used to read data from resistive sensors like a photoresistor.
- Classes like `Sensor`, `Thermometer`, and `Button` in Johnny-Five or equivalent higher-level JavaScript frameworks can add convenience by abstracting away pin configuration and tedious calculations and providing relevant events to bind to.
- Each branch in a parallel circuit receives the same amount of voltage, but current is apportioned based on the branch's proportional resistance. A *current divider* uses this principle by using resistors wired in parallel.
- Using a pull-down resistor is one way to avoid a floating situation of indeterminate logic level when digital inputs are disconnected or inactive.

5

Output:
making things happen

This chapter covers

- Mastering more advanced LED-controlling techniques—animating LEDs and using full-color RGB LEDs
- Using pulse-width modulation (PWM) support to make digital output signals behave more like analog output signals
- The basics of bitshifting and binary operations in JavaScript
- Integrating a third-party weather API to create a multi-colored LED "weather ball" gadget
- Wiring up and controlling a parallel LCD module with Johnny-Five and the Uno
- Combining multiple input and output components to build an advanced timer device
- Making noises and playing tunes with piezo components and Johnny-Five

Now it's time to do something noisy. Or something bright. Or something blinky or expressive. You've tried out a few basic LED tricks, but now we're going to take a more comprehensive look at some of the ways you can integrate *outputs* into projects.

For this chapter, you'll need the following:

- Arduino Uno and USB cable
- 2 standard LEDs, any color
- 1 photoresistor
- 1 common-cathode RGB LED
- 3 push buttons
- 1 16x2 parallel LCD module
- 1 rotary potentiometer
- 1 piezo
- 3 10 kΩ resistors
- 2 220 Ω resistors
- 23 jumper wires in various colors
- 1 half-size breadboard

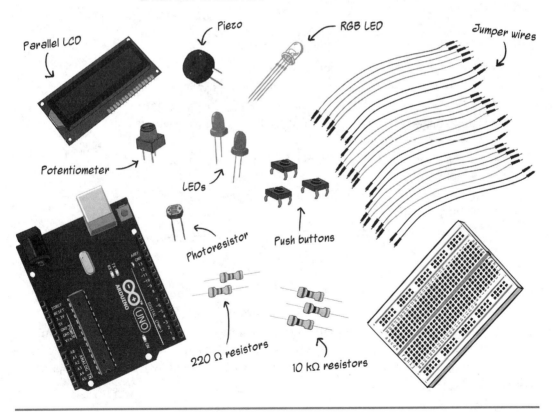

Parallel LCD

Piezo

RGB LED

Jumper wires

Potentiometer

LEDs

Push buttons

Photoresistor

220 Ω resistors

10 kΩ resistors

5.1 Lighting things up

LEDs seem to do a lot more tricks than just turn on or off. If you look around at the electronics embedded in your own electronic gadgets, you'll see them pulsing or fading out. You may even see them change color.

These common LED behaviors are, technically, illusions (figure 5.1). An LED can emit only one wavelength of light—it can only be one color. And yet, LEDs around us certainly *appear* to dim or take on different hues.

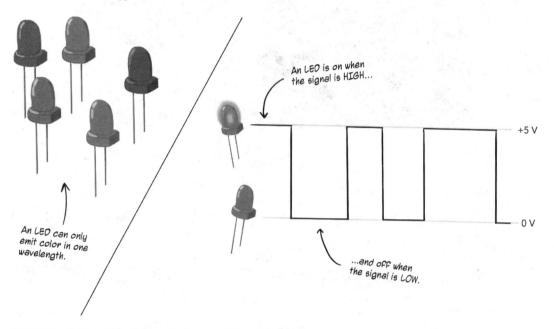

Figure 5.1 LEDs emit a single color and are either on or off.

Time to become an LED magician—there's an electronic technique we can harness to make LEDs take on depth and intrigue.

5.1.1 Fading LEDs with pulse-width modulation (PWM)

OK, so an LED can only be on or off at any point in time. You've made one blink, which is really just a cycle of periodic ons and offs. We're going to get fancier with the blinking, with the aim of tricking human eyes.

What you'll need
- 1 Arduino Uno and USB cable
- 1 breadboard
- 2 standard LEDs, any color you like
- 2 220 Ω resistors
- Yellow (2) and black (1) jumper wires

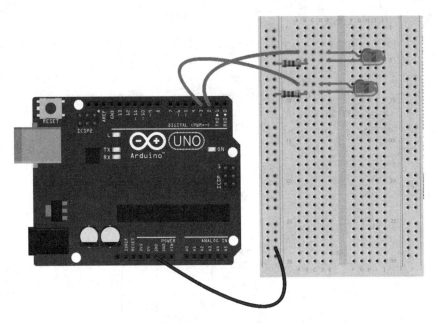

Figure 5.2   Wiring diagram for LED experimentation

First, construct the circuit shown in figure 5.2. Next, create a file and add the code shown in the following listing.

Listing 5.1   experiment-led.js

```
const five = require('johnny-five');
const board = new five.Board();

board.on('ready', () => {
  const led1 = new five.Led(2);
  const led2 = new five.Led(3);

  board.repl.inject({
    led1: led1,
    led2: led2
  });
});
```

Instantiates an Led object on pin 3

Instantiates an Led object on pin 2

Injects the Led object instances into the REPL

This code doesn't really do much. It instantiates two Led objects and makes them available in Johnny-Five's REPL as led1 and led2. Run the script:

```
$ node experiment-LED.js
```

Once it's up and running, you'll be able to type commands at the REPL prompt. First—and I know this is territory we've been through before—make one of the LEDs blink. Type the following at the REPL prompt and press Enter:

```
>> led1.blink()
```

The first LED should be blinking now, in 100 ms periods (on for 100 ms, off for 100 ms)—this is the default phase length (speed of blink periods) for the `blink` method if you don't tell it otherwise.

Now I want you to carefully gather up the Arduino and the breadboard with the LEDs in one hand and wave it in front of your face. You'll know you're waving frantically enough when the LED appears not to blink anymore but is just a smeared line.

You're fooling your own eyes. When things move too quickly, your eyes and brain can't quite keep up. Your brain, in effect, connects the dots for you and decides you're seeing a continuous line of light. If you're a photographer, you can think of it as sort of analogous to shutter speed—your own "shutter speed" isn't fast enough, and you end up with motion blur. This is why films and movies can appear fluid at 24 individual frames per second or so.

The same goes for the detection of individual blinks. If a light blinks fast enough, humans won't be able to see the blinking at all (figure 5.3). Different humans have different thresholds of perception—this explains why I get maniacally grumpy around old fluorescents or CRTs with slow refresh frequencies while some of my colleagues aren't bothered at all. But everyone reliably loses the ability to discern individual blinks at around 100 Hz (a hundred cycles per second).

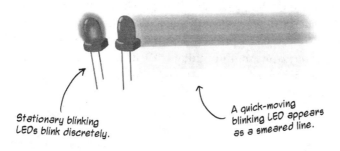

Stationary blinking LEDs blink discretely.

A quick-moving blinking LED appears as a smeared line.

Figure 5.3 We lose the ability to discern individual blinks when an LED is moving quickly.

Make it stop!

If the blinking LED is driving you nuts, you can always stop the blinking with the `Led.stop` instance method:

```
> led1.stop()
```

Depending on when the command is issued, the result may be an LED that's off or an LED that's steadily on. If the LED is on and you want it off, use this:

```
> led1.off()
```

You'll need to use both methods—you can't just skip to the `off` method. The `stop` will clear the interval that causes the blinking to happen—`off` won't.

So, great, what's the point of making an LED blink so fast that the blinks are invisible and it seems like it's always on? Can't we just *turn an LED on* steadily to get the same effect?

It turns out that interesting things come to pass if you mess around with the proportion of time that the LED is on (versus off). If you're blinking the LED really fast, humans won't be able to perceive the blink—that we've covered. But if the LED is only on one-quarter of the time (off the other three-quarters), it will also appear considerably dimmer.

Let's make this happen. Try (again in the REPL):

```
>> led1.on()
>> led2.brightness(64)
```

`brightness` is an instance method on Johnny-Five `Led` objects that takes an 8-bit value (0–255). A value of 64 is, then, one-quarter of the brightest possible value. The result of the call to `led2.brightness(64)` is that the LED spends 75% of its time off and is lit 25% of the time. All of this turning on and off is happening at frequencies too fast for the eye to pick out. You'll note that `led2` now appears less bright than `led1`—it's dimmer.

The Uno's microcontroller helps out here. It provides hardware support for a technique called *pulse-width modulation* (PWM), which does the juggling of ons and offs more quickly than software can easily provide. The percentage of time a PWM signal is HIGH (on) is called the *duty cycle*. An output that is HIGH a quarter of the time is said to have a 25% duty cycle (figure 5.4).

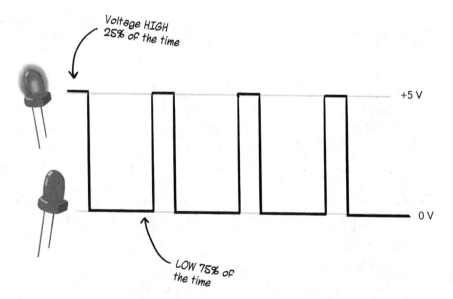

Figure 5.4   A 25% duty cycle

Digital pins that support PWM are marked with ~.

Figure 5.5   Only some of the Arduino Uno's digital pins support PWM. They're marked with ~.

PWM hardware support is common because it's quite useful, but its support varies from board to board and it's typically only available on certain pins. This is the case with the Arduino Uno. PWM is only available on pins 3, 5, 6, 9, 10, and 11.

Don't worry, you don't have to memorize that. If you look at your Arduino, you'll see that those pin numbers are silkscreened with a tilde (~) next to them (figure 5.5). That indicates that PWM is supported on that pin.

Now, back in the REPL, try this:

```
>> led1.brightness(64)
```

This won't work. You'll get an exception that starts with something like

```
Error: Pin Error: 2 is not a valid PWM pin (Led)
```

That's Johnny-Five and firmata—the software includes mappings of which pins do what on which boards.

All right, we've looked at several things in our exploration here. People can't discern blinks if they're really fast. Changing the duty cycle of the signal into an LED makes its brightness appear to change. One last thing, and then we'll do something with this knowledge.

> **BE SURE TO USE PINS WITH PWM SUPPORT FOR FEATURES THAT REQUIRE IT** Methods like brightness and several others you'll need on Led instances require the component to be connected to a pin that supports PWM. Johnny-Five will throw an error if you try to invoke a PWM-requiring method on a pin that doesn't support it. When designing your circuits, it's good to keep in mind which pins support PWM to save time and headaches later.

Try this in the REPL:

```
>> led1.on()
>> led2.brightness(128)
```

128 is exactly in the middle of the brightness range, so you may expect that these two JavaScript expressions would result in the second LED shining at half brightness compared to the first, which is on full blast. But unless you squint really hard, both LEDs look about the same. You might be able to see a slight difference, but not much.

That's because brightness wins. `brightness(128)` does result in a duty cycle of 50%—the LED is only on half of the time—but the brain skews that toward brightness. Put another way, Johnny-Five's 8-bit brightness scale 0–255 appears non-linear, entirely due to human perception.

5.1.2 Animating LEDs with PWM

Now you know how to turn an LED on or off, blink it, and, assuming it's connected to a pin that supports PWM, set its brightness. To complement this small stable of tricks, you can also *animate* the brightness of an LED, making it appear to pulse or bounce or breathe or slowly fall asleep—your imagination is the limit here.

Johnny-Five includes an `Animation` class, which offers fine-grained control over animations of—at the time of writing—the brightness of LEDs and the motions of servos (we'll meet servos in chapter 6).

Working with animations in Johnny-Five involves a few steps, shown in the next listing.

> **Listing 5.2   Steps for animating components in Johnny-Five**

Creates an options object containing animation details—more on this shortly

Instantiates an Animation object and passes it a target component—the target will be animated

```
const pulsingLED = new five.Led(3);
const options     = { /* animation details */ };
const animation   = new five.Animation(pulsingLED);
animation.enqueue(options);
```

Starts the animation with enqueue

Let's take this for a spin by making an LED appear to *pulse.* Johnny-Five needs us first to define how we want the animation to behave.

The pulsing LED should fade in and then fade out again in loops that use attractive easing. *Easing functions* are functions that vary the rate of an animation during its duration. For example, an animation that *eases out* starts out moving quickly but gets slower as it goes.

Easing functions are typically non-linear, integrating sine, cubic, exponential, and other curves into the equation. An in-out-sine easing creates an animation with a rhythm like that shown in figure 5.6. Easing functions can make an animation more lifelike or give it different qualities of motion. Of course, LEDs don't move, but changes in their brightness can definitely be animated.

The `inOutSine` easing is what we'll use for pulsing, as the changes to brightness start out slow and then accelerate midway through the brightening of the LED. A pulse is a *metronomic* animation, meaning that once the animation runs forward, it should then run backward, moving between its start and end points in a back-and-forth *loop.*

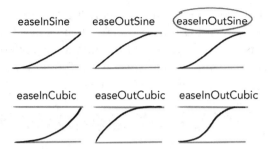

Figure 5.6 **inOutSine is one of a couple of dozen easing function options available in Johnny-Five via its dependency on the ease-component npm package.**

We also need to tell the animation what it's easing between by defining *keyframes* (figure 5.7). Keyframes define the specific states (like still frames) between which the animation should fill in intermediate frames using the easing function. The process of creating these intermediate frames or states between keyframes is known as *tweening*. For this simple pulse, the keyframes are simple: totally off (brightness 0) and totally on (brightness 255).

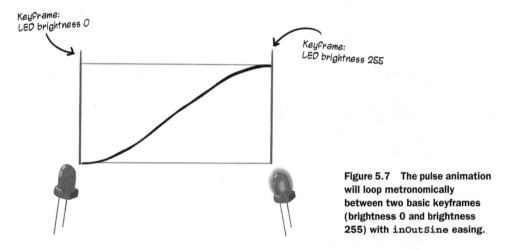

Figure 5.7 **The pulse animation will loop metronomically between two basic keyframes (brightness 0 and brightness 255) with inOutSine easing.**

Finally, we need to give the animation a *duration*, in milliseconds. Each segment of the animation—going from dark to bright or bright to dark—should take one second. Put together, the animation options look like the following code.

Listing 5.3 Animation options for pulsing

```
const options = {
  easing     : 'inOutSine',
  metronomic: true,
  loop       : true,
  keyFrames : [0, 255],
  duration   : 1000
};
```

Let's see what this looks like, shall we? You can use the circuit from the last set of experiments for this part (you won't be using the first LED). Create a new file called animate-LED.js. Paste the contents from experiment-LED.js into animate-LED.js as a starting point, and edit the code to create a single LED on pin 3. Add the `options` object after the instantiation of the pulsing `Led` object as follows.

Listing 5.4 animate-led.js

```
const five  = require('johnny-five');
const board = new five.Board();

board.on('ready', () => {
  const pulsingLED = new five.Led(3);
  const options = {
    easing     : 'inOutSine',
    metronomic: true,
    loop       : true,
    keyFrames : [0, 255],
    duration   : 1000
  };
  // ...
});
```

Steps 2 and 3 are next: creating an `Animation` object and making it go with `enqueue`.

Listing 5.5 Animation instantiation and enqueuing

```
const five  = require('johnny-five');
const board = new five.Board();

board.on('ready', () => {
  const pulsingLED = new five.Led(3);
  const options = {
    easing     : 'inOutSine',
    metronomic: true,
    loop       : true,
    keyFrames : [0, 255],
    duration   : 1000
  };
  const animation = new five.Animation(pulsingLED);   ◁─── Passes the target—the thing to animate. In this case, the LED (pulsingLED).
  animation.enqueue(options);   ◁─── Enqueues the animation and passes it the animation options.
});
```

Now run the script:

```
$ node animate-LED.js
```

And there you have it. Well, sort of. I made you do it the hard way, because as it happens, the code in the following listing does the same thing.

Listing 5.6 Easier way to pulse an LED

```
const five = require('johnny-five');
const board = new five.Board();

board.on('ready', () => {
  const pulsingLED = new five.Led(3);
  pulsingLED.pulse(1000);
});
```

> Led.prototype.pulse takes a duration in ms (default 1000).

Underneath, the implementation of `pulse` is similar to what we did earlier, but it's such a common use that it's been simplified into a method for Johnny-Five users.

Pulsing LEDs can be a nice way of grabbing attention without being too invasive. Using what we've covered, you can make a simple timer using just a few lines of code—it will start pulsing when the time's up, as the following listing shows.

Listing 5.7 The world's simplest timer

```
const five = require('johnny-five');
const board = new five.Board();

board.on('ready', () => {
  const pulsingLED = new five.Led(3);
  const timerLength = 10000;
  setTimeout(() => {
    pulsingLED.pulse();
  }, timerLength);
});
```

> Defines a timer length in milliseconds (here 10 seconds)

> Sets a timeout to start pulsing the LED after 10 seconds

Of course, this timer is of limited use. You can't change the timer's length or when the timer starts, or start a new timer. Don't worry; we'll make it better in a bit.

5.1.3 Combining input with LED output

Of course, output is more interesting if it's responding to some sort of meaningful input. The connections between input and output are what makes the internet of things tick.

One such coupling could be a photoresistor and an LED to create a brightness-aware nightlight. When the readings from the photoresistor are lower, the LED can be brighter—that is, the "nightlight" turns on at "night," when it's darker.

What you'll need

- 1 Arduino Uno and USB cable
- 1 standard LED, any color (you can reuse the pulsing LED from above)
- 1 photoresistor
- 1 10 kΩ resistor
- 1 220 Ω resistor
- Yellow (1), red (2), green (1), and black (1) jumper wires
- 1 half-size breadboard

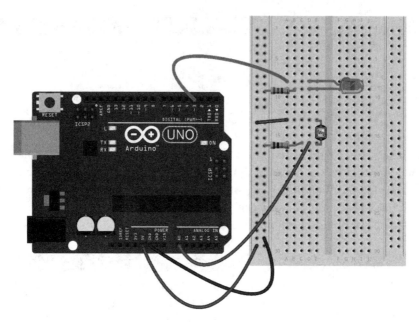

Figure 5.8   Wiring diagram for automatic nightlight

Leave the LED connected to pin 3 on the breadboard (the pulsing LED from the last example), but remove the other LED and add a photoresistor and a 10 kΩ resistor as shown in figure 5.8.

Listing 5.8 shows a first attempt at a light-sensitive nightlight using `Light`, a class in Johnny-Five that provides features for working with photoresistors (`ldr` stands for *light-dependent resistor*, another name for a photoresistor).

Listing 5.8   A naive nightlight

```
const five  = require('johnny-five');
const board = new five.Board();

board.on('ready', () => {
  const nightlight = new five.Led(3);
  const ldr        = new five.Light({ pin : 'A0', freq: 500 });
  ldr.on('change', () => {
    nightlight.brightness((ldr.value >> 2) ^ 255);
  });
});
```

> Checking light levels twice per second (every 500 ms, the value of freq) should more than suffice.

> Sets LED brightness to "the opposite" of the photoresistor's value

The following line may have made your eyes cross if you haven't spent much time in the world of bitwise operators:

```
nightlight.brightness((photoresistor.value >> 2) ^ 255);
```

Recall that the Arduino Uno's microcontroller provides ADC readings as 10-bit integers (0–1023). Meanwhile, the `brightness` method on the `Led` object expects an 8-bit number (0–255).

The expression `photoresistor.value >> 2` shifts `photoresistor.value` to the right by two bits. That means two bits pop off the right side of the number and are never heard from again (figure 5.9). In the case of `photoresistor.value >> 2`, in goes a 10-bit number, its two least significant digits are booted out, and what's returned is an 8-bit number.

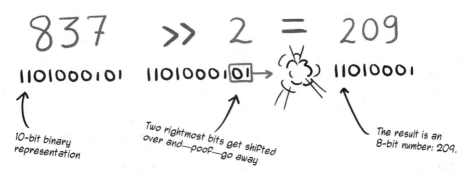

Figure 5.9 Bitshifting a 10-bit number to the right by 2 results in an 8-bit number.

You can think of the 10-bit number as being too precise for an 8-bit input; the bitshifting right by 2 "rounds" it to a lower resolution that `brightness` can use.

The `^ 255` part uses the bitwise XOR (exclusive OR) operator (`^`) to obtain what I'm going to loosely call "the opposite" 8-bit number from the left-hand argument. XOR performs a comparison on each pair of bits and returns 1 in the digit's place only when the digits evaluated are different—when one is a 1 and one is a 0 (figure 5.10).

The expression `(photoresistor.value >> 2) ^ 255` means, then, *shift* photoresistor.value *2 bits to the right (making it an 8-bit number) and subsequently* XOR *the resulting value with 255.*

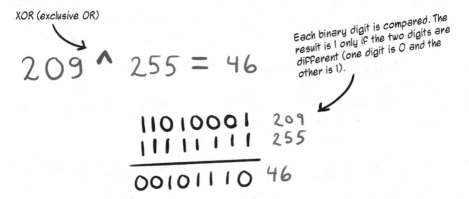

Figure 5.10 The XOR operation compares each binary digit, producing a 1 if the binary digits are different.

BITSHIFTING ALL OVER THE PLACE   Bitshifting and bitwise operations may feel foreign to software developers who usually work in higher-level code, but it comes up all over the place when working with hardware. The Mozilla Developer Network has a nice reference of JavaScript bitwise operators, which contains the key things you'll want to know (http://mng.bz/CLvy).

The first version of the nightlight has some shortcomings, which you can see in action by running it:

```
$ node nightlight.js
```

For one, the LED is always on at some brightness, even when readings for the photoresistor are near the brightest possible values. Wouldn't we want the LED to come on only when it's darker? We don't need it on during broad daylight. The second version of the nightlight code addresses that by replacing what happens inside the `change` callback function, as shown in the following listing.

Listing 5.9   Slightly improved nightlight

Light instances have a level value, which is a percentage between 0.0 and 1.0.
```
ldr.on('change', () => {
  if (ldr.level < 0.5) {                              Changes the calculation
    nightlight.brightness((ldr.value >> 1) ^ 255);   of the LED brightness
  } else {
    nightlight.off();          ⟵──── LED is off if level >= 0.5
  }
});
```

In this variant, the LED is switched off entirely if the photoresistor's `level` is greater than or equal to `0.5` (`nightlight.off()`).

If the `photoresistor.level` is less than `0.5` (50%), we know that its 10-bit `value` also must be less than 512 (because 511 is the middle of the range of possible 10-bit values, 0–1023). That means `photoresistor.value` is an integer somewhere from 0 to 511, inclusive. All of the numbers in that range are 9-bit numbers (0–511). That means we only need to shift one bit to the right to convert the `value` to an 8-bit number (0–255).

The end result is that the LED will grow increasingly bright as photoresistor values decrease from 511 to 0.

But we can still do better. As you saw in chapter 4, even when choosing the best possible resistor value for the photoresistor circuit's voltage divider, you won't be able to get the full range of voltages from 0 to 5 V. It would be better if the nightlight could calibrate itself based on the real range of conditions and readings it's encountering, as shown in the next listing.

Listing 5.10   Self-calibrating nightlight

```
const five  = require('johnny-five');
const board = new five.Board();

board.on('ready', () => {
```

```
const nightlight = new five.Led(3);
const ldr       = new five.Light({ pin : 'A0', freq: 500 });
var dimmest = 1024,
    brightest = 0;
ldr.on('change', () => {
  if (ldr.value < dimmest)   { dimmest  = ldr.value; }
  if (ldr.value > brightest) { brightest = ldr.value; }

  const relativeValue = five.Fn.scale(ldr.value, dimmest, brightest, 0, 511);
  if (relativeValue <= 255) {
    nightlight.brightness((relativeValue >> 1) ^ 255);
  } else {
    nightlight.off();
  }
});
});
```

Keeps track of the dimmest and brightest readings it sees

Updates dimmest and brightest if it encounters lower and higher values

Scales the current value to a 9-bit number between dimmest and brightest readings

The nightlight code in listing 5.10 makes two changes. One, it keeps track of the dimmest and brightest actual values seen during the nightlight's script lifetime. Then it takes advantage of the `scale` utility method available on the `Fn` object on `Board` instances.

`scale(value, fromLow, fromHigh, toLow, toHigh)` takes a `value` that currently exists in a range between `fromLow` and `fromHigh` (the `dimmest` and `brightest` values seen) and remaps it to a range between `toLow` and `toHigh` (0 and 511), proportionally.

The resulting number will be a 9-bit number (between 0 and 511). Now we can proceed, knowing that values <= 255 are in the lower half of the observed values. The nightlight will continue to adjust itself (calibrate low and high) as it runs over time.

5.1.4 *Going full-color with RGB LEDs*

All right, that's some extensive coverage of dimming an LED, but what about LEDs that seem to change color? Sure, a single LED can only ever be one color—one wavelength—but if you group red, green, and blue LEDs in a single package and control the brightness (duty cycle) of each component LED, *voilà*! All the colors of the rainbow.

RGB LEDs have four legs. There's one leg for each LED (red, green, blue). The fourth leg is either a cathode or an anode. Common-cathode RGB LEDs—where all three color LEDs share a single cathode leg—are the kind we'll be using (figure 5.11). Common-anode RGB LEDS, which have a shared *anode* leg, are also available.

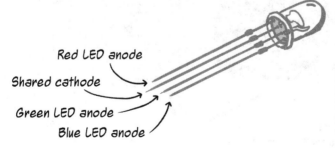

Red LED anode

Shared cathode

Green LED anode

Blue LED anode

Figure 5.11 Common-cathode RGB LEDs have three component LEDs (red, green, blue) in one package. The longest leg is the shared cathode.

Like regular LEDs, RGB LEDs allow you to control brightness with PWM, but now there are three LEDs representing the primary colors of light. For common-cathode LEDs, a higher-percentage duty cycle on a component color LED will make that color brighter, whereas a lower duty cycle makes it dimmer.

5.1.5   *Build your own "weather ball"*

I grew up in Portland, Oregon, and when I was a kid, spotting the weather ball on top of the Standard Insurance Plaza was always a little thrill. The weather ball provided a very basic encoded visual representation of the weather forecast for the next 24 hours or so. The pole-mounted weather ball was large enough to be seen throughout the city, and it was covered with lights.

It only had six possible states. Predicted temperature trend was represented by color: red if it's forecast to get warmer, white if it's getting colder, green if it's staying about the same. If precipitation was in the offing, it would blink. Simple, and yet, remarkably clear and useful. Let's make one.

What you'll need

- Arduino Uno and USB cable
- 1 common-cathode RGB LED
- 1 220 Ω resistor
- Red (1), green (1), blue (1), and black (1) jumper wires
- 1 breadboard

Wire up an RGB LED circuit as shown in figure 5.12.

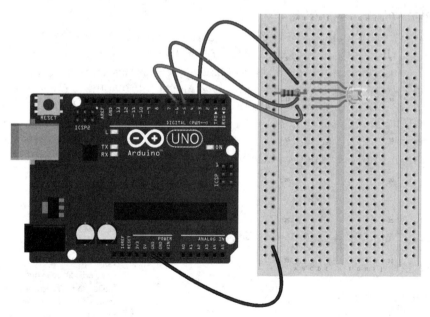

Figure 5.12   Wiring diagram for the weather ball

Now we need the weather forecast! The service Dark Sky provides a weather forecast API that, at the time of writing, provides free results for up to 1,000 queries a day. You do need to sign up for an API key, which you can do at https://darksky.net/dev/register. You may need to provide a credit card number to sign up for the service.

Once you have a developer API key, write it down and keep it somewhere reasonably safe. You'll also need your latitude and longitude, which you can find on http://mygeoposition.com/.

Create a new file called weatherBall.js. First, let's collect some settings for the weather ball, as shown in the following listing.

Listing 5.11   Settings for the weather ball

```
const API_KEY = 'YOUR API KEY HERE';
const LAT     = '43.3463760';
const LONG    = '-72.6395340';
const API_URL = 'https://api.darksky.net/forecast';
```

I'm in Vermont. Change the **LAT** and **LONG** values to your own location.

You shouldn't need to change this **URL**.

Time to take care of our dependencies:

```
$ npm install johnny-five request
```

We'll use the `request` package to make API calls to Dark Sky. Add `requires` to the top of the file, and go ahead and instantiate a board with Johnny-Five. Notice in the next listing that Johnny-Five provides a special kind of `Led` component class for RGB LEDs: `Led.RGB`.

Listing 5.12   Instantiating a board

```
const five    = require('johnny-five');
const request = require('request');
// SETTINGS AS BEFORE

var board = new five.Board();
board.on('ready', () => {
  console.log('Powered by Dark Sky: https://darksky.net/poweredby/');
  const rgb = new five.Led.RGB({ pins: [3, 5, 6] });
  // Make request to API
});
```

Next, we need to get some data about the forecast by requesting it from the Dark Sky API in the next listing.

Listing 5.13   Requesting data from the Dark Sky API

```
//...
board.on('ready', () => {
  console.log('Powered by Dark Sky: https://darksky.net/poweredby/');
  const rgb        = new five.Led.RGB({ pins: [3, 5, 6] });
  const requestURL = `${API_URL}/${API_KEY}/${LAT},${LONG}`;

  request(requestURL, function (error, response, body) {
```

Puts together the request URL

```
    if (error) {
      console.error(error);
    } else if (response.statusCode === 200) {      ◁──── If the response comes back OK...
      const forecast    = JSON.parse(body);   ◁──
      console.log(forecast);         ◁──────────────── Parses the response body as JSON
    }
  });                    Logs the forecast object to the REPL
});
```

Assuming everything went OK, you'll now have data to work with. Let's make the weather ball go, as shown in the following listing.

Listing 5.14   Make the weather ball go

```
request(requestURL, function (error, response, body) {
  if (error) {
    console.error(error);
  } else if (response.statusCode === 200) {
    const forecast    = JSON.parse(body);
    const daily       = forecast.daily.data;
    const willBeDamp  = daily[1].precipProbability > 0.2;
    const tempDelta   = daily[1].temperatureMax - daily[0].temperatureMax;
    console.log(forecast);

    if (tempDelta > 4) {
      rgb.color('#ff0000'); // warmer
    } else if (tempDelta < -4) {
      rgb.color('#ffffff'); // colder
    } else {
      rgb.color('#00ff00'); // about the same
    }
    if (willBeDamp) { rgb.strobe(1000); }
  }
});
```

daily[1] is tomorrow. Is it likely to rain?

daily.data is an Array with seven day-forecast elements.

daily[0] is today. How much is the temperature changing?

Sets the color of the RGB LED based on how much the temperature is changing

strobe is the same as blink— blink is an alias to strobe.

Troubleshooting the circuit

For maximum flexibility, methods related to colors on Johnny-Five component object instances—most relevantly, `Led.prototype.color` in this case—accept several different color formats, such as these:

- *Hex (string)*—Familiar to web developers, RGB hex values like `"#00ff00"` (bright green) can be used. It works with or without the leading #.
- *CSS color name (string)*—"red" or "darksalmon" or "lemonchiffon" or any other valid CSS color name works.
- *Array of R, G, B values (array)*—Each element of the array should be an 8-bit value, such as `[0x00, 0xff, 0x00]` or `[0, 255, 0]`.
- *Object of RGB values (object)*—Again, 8-bit values should be used, such as `{ red: 0x00, green: 0xff, blue: 0x00}`

Keep up to date with the latest at http://johnny-five.io/api/led.rgb/.

Now run your weather ball:

```
$ node weatherBall.js
```

The sensors and outputs we've used in examples so far have only required a few wires and have had simple hookups. In the next section, you'll meet a component that has a bunch of wires, but it isn't hard to work with as long as you're paying attention.

5.2 Working with parallel LCD displays

LCDs (liquid crystal displays) can display characters and shapes, making them useful outputs for tons of projects. Their resolution is often defined in terms of how many *characters* they can display. The 16x2 LCD module we'll use in the following experiments can display up to 32 characters total: 16 each on 2 lines. Each "character" slot is actually its own matrix of 5x7 dots; non-character shapes can also be represented.

LCD modules are available with different interfaces, including several serial options (you'll learn about serial communication in chapter 7). The module shown in figure 5.13 has a *parallel* interface.

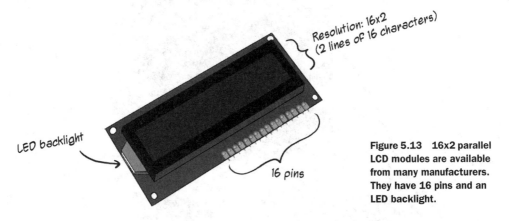

Figure 5.13 16x2 parallel LCD modules are available from many manufacturers. They have 16 pins and an LED backlight.

Don't panic when you see the wiring diagrams in this section. Wiring up parallel LCDs requires a fistful of jumper wires, but working with them isn't complicated. Make sure you pay attention to which wires go where when you're plugging things in and you'll be fine. Improving the timer project from earlier in the chapter admittedly requires more jumper wires than you've yet seen in one place, but it's a good exercise for piecing together more-complex circuits.

5.2.1 Making a full-featured timer with LCD

What you'll need

- 1 16x2 5 V parallel LCD module, such as any of SparkFun's basic 16x2 5 V parallel LCD modules
- 1 standard LED, any color
- 3 push buttons (momentary switches)

- 1 rotary potentiometer
- 1 220 Ω resistor
- 3 10 kΩ resistors
- 1 piezo (optional)
- 23 jumper wires
- 1 half-size breadboard

This smarter timer will allow you to adjust the timer's duration using buttons (even when the timer is running!) and will count down the remaining time on the LCD. You can pause and restart the timer, as well. When the time's up, an LED will pulse to (gently) grab your attention.

BUILDING THE CIRCUIT

The fully constructed circuit will look like figure 5.14. We'll break it down into a few steps to make it less intimidating.

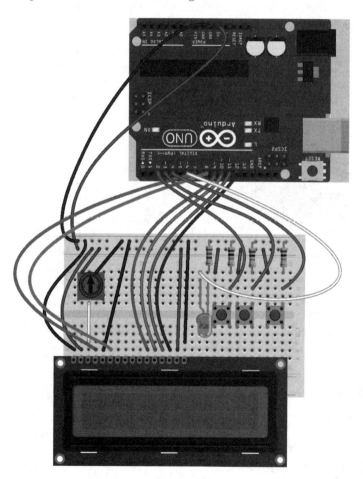

Figure 5.14   The fully built LCD timer

CONNECTING AND TESTING BUTTONS

Let's start with some buttons that will allow a user to control the timer. From left to right, the buttons in figure 5.15 are

1 A Down button (represented by `downButton` in the following code), which will subtract one second from the current timer
2 An Up button (`upButton`), which will add one second to the current timer
3 A toggling Go button (`goButton`), which will start and pause the timer

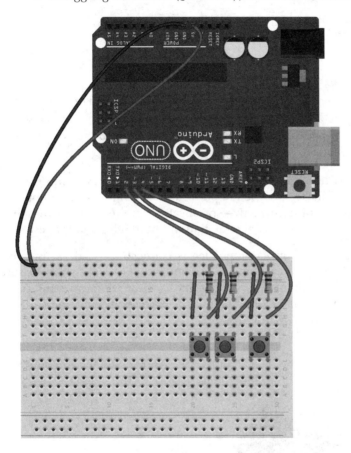

Figure 5.15 Wiring diagram showing only the buttons: Down, Up, and Go

Make sure the buttons straddle the center notch and are oriented as shown in figure 5.15. Each button is connected to ground through a 10 kΩ pull-down resistor, and to the +5 V power rail with a jumper wire.

Create a new file called timer-advanced.js and start by adding the following code to handle button presses.

Listing 5.15 Test the Buttons in timer-advanced.js

```
const five = require('johnny-five');
const board = new five.Board();
```

```
board.on('ready', () => {
  const downButton = new five.Button(2);
  const upButton   = new five.Button(3);
  const goButton   = new five.Button(4);
  downButton.on('press', () => {
    console.log('down');
  });
  upButton.on('press', () => {
    console.log('up');
  });
  goButton.on('press', () => {
    console.log('go');
  });
});
```

By beginning with some simple button handlers, you can validate that your buttons are wired correctly before moving on to other parts of the device. Run the script (`node timer-advanced.js`) and verify that pressing the different buttons logs the correct message to the console.

> **TROUBLESHOOTING THE BUTTONS** If pressing the buttons isn't giving you the results you expect, make sure the jumper wires from the button's output are connected to the Arduino correctly—specifically, that the breadboard side of the connection is in a hole between the button's output leg and the resistor.
>
> Double-check that the button's input leg is connected to power and that the 10 kΩ pull-down resistors connect each button to ground. Also make sure your push button's orientation is correct—most buttons fit more comfortably across the center notch in one orientation (the correct one) but there are lots of different kinds of buttons out there.

CONNECTING THE LCD

With the buttons squared away, we can move on to connecting the LCD module to the breadboard, connecting to most of its 16 pins (figure 5.16).

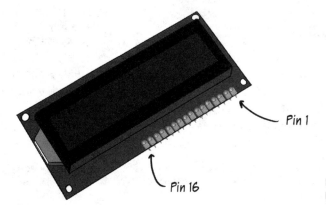

Pin 1

Pin 16

Figure 5.16   A 16x2 parallel LCD module

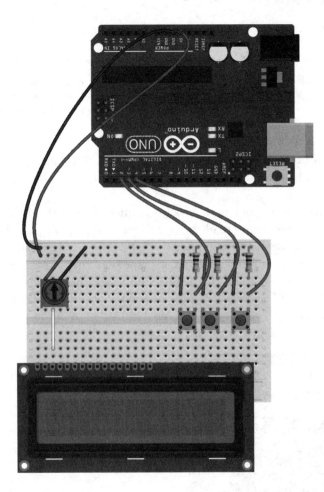

Figure 5.17 Wiring diagram of timer including potentiometer and LCD placement

Go ahead and connect the LCD to the breadboard as shown in the LCD positioning diagram (figure 5.17), making sure the leftmost pin of the LCD module is connected to the leftmost row of the breadboard, as in the wiring diagram. The LCD's pins are numbered 1–16, starting from the left in this orientation.

LCD MODULE PIN OUTS Most common 16x2 parallel modules have the same pin orientation, with pin 1 at the left and 16 at the right, when in the orientation shown in the LCD positioning diagram (figure 5.17). Double-check that your LCD module has the same pin orientation—you may need to flip your LCD around if not.

Next, connect the potentiometer to the breadboard.

WIRING A CONTRAST-CONTROL POTENTIOMETER

Like photoresistors, potentiometers are a kind of variable resistor (figure 5.18). Potentiometers have three pins: two power pins and a third, middle pin. As the knob is turned on a rotary potentiometer (or slid on other kinds of potentiometers), the

Figure 5.18   **Potentiometers are variable resistors. They come in several shapes and sizes.**

voltage on its middle pin changes. Potentiometers have internal voltage dividers, so their output voltages can be read directly—we don't have to build a voltage divider like we do with photoresistors.

In this circuit, the potentiometer's middle pin is connected directly to the LCD's pin 3. The LCD's onboard electronics read the voltage on that pin to determine the contrast of the display. Rotating the potentiometer will, therefore, adjust the contrast.

Your potentiometer might be a different size or shape than the one shown in the LCD positioning diagram (figure 5.17): that's fine. Connect its outer pins to power and ground—you can't get it backwards, as potentiometers aren't polarized. Either orientation works. Next, connect the potentiometer's middle leg to pin 3 of the LCD (remember, connections don't continue across the center notch).

COMPLETING THE LCD'S CONNECTIONS

Onward! The LCD has several power connections (figure 5.19). Connect LCD pins 1, 5, and 16 to the ground power rail and pins 2 and 15 to the source power rail.

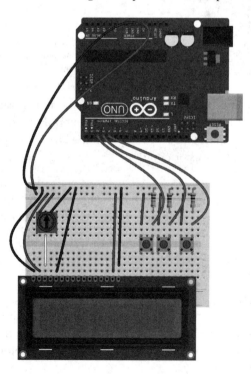

Figure 5.19   **Wiring diagram showing the breadboard power connections to the LCD**

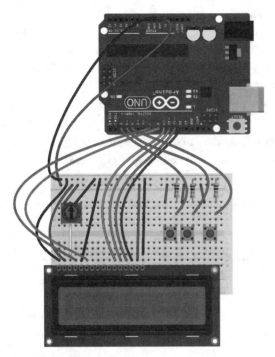

Figure 5.20   Wiring diagram showing all of the LCD connections

The connections to LCD pins 1 and 2 power the LCD itself, and LCD pins 15 and 16 power the display's LED backlight.

Pin 5 is a read/write (R/W) pin. When it's pulled to ground, it puts the LCD in write mode, which is what one often wants when using an LCD—to write to it.

The rest of the pins we'll use on the LCD will connect directly to the Arduino's pins (figure 5.20).

LCD pin 4 is the register select (RS) pin. At certain times, Johnny-Five's underlying software needs to send instructions to the LCD to tell it how to behave. At other times, it needs to send the specific data for display. This pin allows it to switch between the two different memory *registers* for instructions and data. It should be connected to pin 7 on the Arduino.

Pin 6 on the LCD is the enable (EN) pin. It should be connected to pin 8 on the Arduino. Writing a voltage to this pin prompts the LCD to read incoming data waiting for it on the data pins.

Data pins, eh? Those are the last remaining LCD connections. Pins 7 through 14 on the LCD are parallel data pins (D0–D7), which represent the bit values of data written to the registers of the device. You only need to connect four of the eight—D4 through D7 (LCD pins 11, 12, 13, and 14, connected to pins 9, 10, 11, and 12 on the Arduino respectively). Whew. There are a lot of wires!

CONTROLLING THE LCD WITH JOHNNY-FIVE

You can take your LCD for a spin by using the Johnny-Five LCD class. By default, Johnny-Five's LCD object constructor will treat the LCD as a parallel LCD. It expects an array of six pin numbers for wires attached to different pins on the LCD: register select (RS), enable (EN), and four data connections (D4, D5, D6, and D7).

The details of interacting with parallel LCDs are fairly low-level, but Johnny-Five abstracts much of that away for you. Useful LCD methods in Johnny-Five include these:

- cursor(row, column)—Positions the cursor before displaying text
- print(str)—Displays text starting at the current cursor position
- clear()—Clears the LCD's contents

Try it out by adding more code to your timer-advanced.js script, as shown in the following listing.

Listing 5.16   Test the LCD

```
const five = require('johnny-five');
const board = new five.Board();

board.on('ready', () => {
  const downButton = new five.Button(2);
  const upButton   = new five.Button(3);
  const goButton   = new five.Button(4);
  const lcd = new five.LCD([7, 8, 9, 10, 11, 12]);   ◁──┐ Instantiates a Johnny-
  /** button handler functions... **/                      Five LCD object
  lcd.cursor(0, 0).print('hello, world');   ◁──┐
  lcd.cursor(1, 0).print('hello, again');   ◁─┐│
});
```

Positions the cursor on the
0th line, 0th position (top left)
and prints "hello, world"

Writes "hello, again" to the
LCD's second line, 0th position

Run the script (node timer-advanced.js) and, once it's running, turn the potentiometer's dial to adjust the contrast on the LCD.

The LCD should display "hello, world" on the first line and "hello, again" on the second line.

> **TROUBLESHOOTING THE LCD** If your LCD doesn't seem to work right, or at all, the first thing to do is double-check all of the wire connections and make sure they're connected to the correct pins on the Arduino.
>
> If your LCD doesn't light up, check the power connections on pins 15 and 16 (backlight power).
>
> Make sure the LCD module is seated correctly and that the pins are aligned accurately.

PROGRAMMING THE TIMER'S LOGIC

Our LCD circuitry is ready. It's time to program the timer. We'll break this down into chunks, but an overview of the timer's eventual structure is shown here.

Listing 5.17 Overview of timer application structure

```
const five = require('johnny-five');
const board = new five.Board();

// constants

board.on('ready', () => {
  // Initialize J5 components for buttons and LCD
  // Initialize some variables

  function init () {
    // initialize timer
  }

  function showRemaining () {
    // format remaining timer duration and
    // update LCD display
  }

  function adjustTime (delta) {
    // add or remove delta milliseconds
    // to/from timer duration
  }

  function start () {
    // start the timer
    // use setInterval to invoke tick()
  }

  function pause () {
    // pause the timer
  }

  function tick () {
    // update timer values internally
    // if timer is over, chime() and reset timer
    // otherwise, showRemaining()
  }

  function chime () {
    // pulse the indicator LED
  }

  // add button-press handlers

  // initialize the timer
});
```

Jumping in from the top, a section of variable initialization sets up some of the values we'll need for operating the timer, as shown in the following listing. Add these to timer-advanced.js.

Listing 5.18   Setting up some values

```
const five = require('johnny-five');
const board = new five.Board();

const DEFAULT_TIMER = 60000;
const UPPER_LIMIT   = 99 * 60000;
const LOWER_LIMIT   = 1000;

board.on('ready', () => {
  const downButton = new five.Button(2);
  const upButton   = new five.Button(3);
  const goButton   = new five.Button(4);
  const lcd        = new five.LCD([7, 8, 9, 10, 11, 12]);
  const alertLED   = new five.Led(6);
  var remaining, timer, timeString, lastTimeString, timestamp, lastTimestamp;

  // ...
});
```

> 60 seconds is the default timer length, in ms. You can change this if you like.

> The upper limit of the timer is 99 minutes.

> You can't make the timer shorter than one second.

The 99-minute upper limit is based on the way the remaining time is formatted on the LCD (mm:ss). Longer durations wouldn't fit.

Speaking of display formatting, let's get that going. It's time to add a function to initialize a timer and to show the time remaining in the current timer on the LCD. The next bit of code to add defines the init() and showRemaining() functions.

Listing 5.19   Initializing and displaying timer remaining time

```
// ...
board.on('ready', () => {
  // ... components and variable initialization
  function init () {
    remaining     = DEFAULT_TIMER;
    lastTimeString = '00:00';
    timeString    = '';
    showRemaining();
  }

  function showRemaining () {
    var minutes, seconds, minPad, secPad;
    minutes   = Math.floor(remaining / 60000);
    seconds   = Math.floor((remaining % 60000) / 1000);
    minPad    = (minutes < 10) ? '0' : '';
    secPad    = (seconds < 10) ? '0' : '';
    timeString = `${minPad}${minutes}:${secPad}${seconds}`;
    if (timeString != lastTimeString) {
      lcd.cursor(0, 0).print(timeString);
    }
  }
  // ...
});
```

> Initializes a new timer and some variables

> Formats and displays the remaining time in this timer

> Only updates the LCD if the formatted string has changed

The showRemaining function will get invoked frequently when the timer is actually running. The check to make sure the time string has changed before updating the LCD (timeString != lastTimeString) will improve performance. The time remaining in the current timer will display at the top left (cursor position 0, 0) of the LCD.

Onward! upButton and downButton should adjust the timer's duration when pressed, adding or removing a second, respectively. The adjustTime() function (in listing 5.20) takes a delta in milliseconds and adjusts the timer's duration by that amount, making sure to keep the total duration within bounds.

Button handlers need to be registered to invoke adjustTime(), and this is also a good spot to initialize the timer (init()).

Add adjustTime() and the button handlers as follows.

Listing 5.20 Add time-adjustment handler functions

```
// ...
board.on('ready', () => {
  // ... variable and component initialization
  function init () { /* ... */ }
  function showRemaining () { /* ... */ }

  function adjustTime (delta) {
    remaining += delta;
    if (remaining < LOWER_LIMIT) {
      remaining = LOWER_LIMIT;
    } else if (remaining > UPPER_LIMIT) {
      remaining = UPPER_LIMIT;
    }
    showRemaining();              ◁——  The timer's duration has
  }                                     changed, so the LCD's
                                        display needs updating.
  downButton.on('press', () => { // remove a second
    adjustTime(-1000);
  });
  upButton.on('press', () => { // add a second
    adjustTime(1000);
  });
                      Don't forget to
  init();        ◁——  initialize the timer.
});
```

Now, let's hook up the Go button. That button should toggle the timer (play/pause). That means we'll also need logic for activating the timer—invoking the tick() function every 250 ms—and pausing it, as shown in the next listing.

Listing 5.21 Making the timer tick

```
    // ...
    board.on('ready', () => {
      // ... variable and component initialization
```

```
function init () { /* ... */ }
function showRemaining () { /* ... */ }
function adjustTime (delta) { /* ... */ }

function start () {
  lcd.clear();
  timestamp = Date.now();
  timer     = setInterval(tick, 250);
  tick();
}

function pause () {
  timer = clearInterval(timer);
  lcd.cursor(0, 9).print('PAUSED');
}

function tick () {
  lastTimestamp = timestamp;
  timestamp     = Date.now();
  remaining -= (timestamp - lastTimestamp);
  if (remaining <= 0) {
    timer = clearInterval(timer);
    init();
  }
  showRemaining();
}

downButton.on('press', () => { /* ... */ });
upButton.on('press', () => { /* ... */ });
goButton.on('press', () => {
  if (!timer) {
    start();
  } else {
    pause();
  }
});
init();
});
```

Clears anything currently displayed on the LCD → `lcd.clear();`

Sets an interval to invoke tick four times per second or so ← `timer = setInterval(tick, 250);`

Kicks off the timer with a tick → `tick();`

Clears the timer interval so the timer stops ticking → `timer = clearInterval(timer);`

PAUSED will get erased when the timer is started again by lcd.clear(). ← `lcd.cursor(0, 9).print('PAUSED');`

Makes sure there isn't already a timer running before starting → `if (!timer) {`

Now you can start and pause the timer, but what happens when the time runs out? We need something to alert the user that their time is up.

5.2.2   *Adding a visual LED "chime"*

As the final part of this circuit construction, you can add an LED as shown in figure 5.21. It should be connected through a 220 Ω resistor to ground, and its anode should be connected to the Arduino's pin 7.

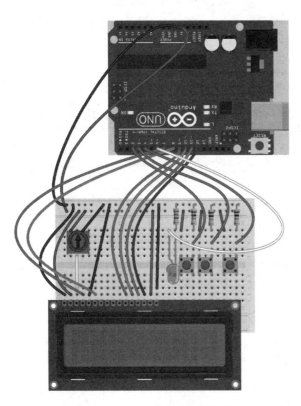

Figure 5.21 The completed wiring diagram, with LED

We'll need to make a few adjustments to the start and tick functions, and we'll add a new chime function, shown in the next listing.

Listing 5.22 Add a visual chime

```
// ...
board.on('ready', () => {
  const downButton = new five.Button(2);
  const upButton   = new five.Button(3);
  const goButton   = new five.Button(4);
  const lcd        = new five.LCD([7, 8, 9, 10, 11, 12]);
  const alertLED   = new five.Led(6);
  var remaining, timer, timeString, lastTimeString, timestamp, lastTimestamp;

  function init () { /* ... */ }
  function showRemaining () { /* ... */ }
  function adjustTime (delta) { /* ... */ }

  function start () {
    alertLED.stop().off();
    lcd.clear();
    timestamp = Date.now();
    timer     = setInterval(tick, 250);
    tick();
  }
```

Instantiates an Led object on pin 6

Any time the timer is counting down, the chime-LED should be off.

```
function pause () { /* ... */  }

function tick () {
  lastTimestamp = timestamp;
  timestamp    = Date.now();
  remaining -= (timestamp - lastTimestamp);
  if (remaining <= 0) {                        ◄────────┐ Some logic to determine if
    timer = clearInterval(timer);                       │ time's up and if so to clear
    chime();      ◄────┐                                │ the interval, and so on
    init();            │ chime()...
  }
  showRemaining();
}

function chime () {
  alertLED.pulse();                   ◄──── Pulses the LED! Time's up!
  lcd.cursor(0, 9).print('DONE!');    ◄────┐
}                                          │ Displays "DONE!" as well

downButton.on('press', () => { /* ... */ });
upButton.on('press', () => { /* ... */ });
goButton.on('press', () => { /* ... */  });
init();
});
```

Because init() is called again when time runs out, the timer can be used over and over again without restarting the program (figure 5.22). Try it!

```
$ node timer-advanced.js
```

CODE ARCHITECTURE FOR THE TIMER The logic for the timer all happens within the ready callback for the Johnny-Five board object, and it's starting to feel unwieldy. It would likely be more elegant to encapsulate the logic in an external module. You'll see examples of that in later chapters.

Figure 5.22   The timer, timing away!

5.3   *Making noise with a piezo*

First off, I'm not going to try to convince you that piezos (figure 5.23) make lovely, dulcet noises. They can produce tones, based on simple frequencies, but they sound tinny and grating. Still, you *can* make one play a song, and they're fun to noodle around with. If you'd like to add a piezo to your timer, you can swap out the LED for a piezo (as you'll see in figure 5.24). Then you'll be ready to have fun and annoy friends with your piezo!

Figure 5.23   Some piezos have wire leads, and others have legs. Piezos have two pins: + and -.

When voltage is applied to a piezo, it causes physical changes to the shape of a surface inside the piezo. Piezos *transduce* the electrical energy into mechanical energy, and we, as humans, detect that mechanical energy as sound waves. Applying voltages at specific frequencies creates vibrations that correspond to different musical notes. This phenomenon is known as the *reverse piezoelectric effect*—electricity is converted to mechanical movement.

Piezos can also be used as sensors. Used as an input, piezos can detect knocks or other kinds of vibrations. This demonstrates the reverse of the reverse piezoelectric effect, that is, the *piezoelectric effect.*

Piezos: timing and frequencies

To get a piezo to squawk out a note requires a combination of PWM and timing. To make a piezo make noise, you give it voltage at a 50% duty cycle—this creates square waves (on off on off). To make a piezo play a particular note, you adjust the frequency of these PWM cycles.

For example, the note A4, or A440 is a common reference tuning note. It's called A440 because it vibrates at 440 Hz. Every 1/440th of a second, there's a full wave period. In real life, these are smooth analog waves. With a piezo, they are square digital waves. By applying a 50% duty cycle voltage to a piezo 440 times a second, you can approximate A4.

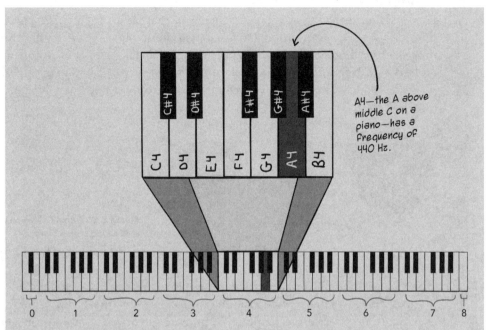

The octaves contained on a standard 88-key piano keyboard. A4 (a.k.a. A440) is the A above middle C (the A in the fourth octave).

Musical frequencies double every octave, so that by the time you get to A7, you're looking at 3520 Hz.

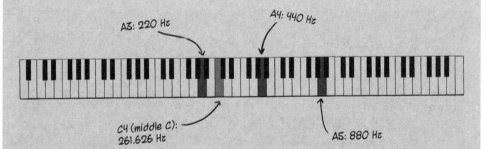

Frequency doubles every octave. A3 (220 Hz) is half the frequency of A4 (440 Hz), whereas A5 (880 Hz) is double the frequency of A4. A's have nice round frequencies. The notes between also have predictable frequencies that double every octave, such as middle C (C4) at 261.626 Hz and C5 at 523.521 Hz.

In Johnny-Five, A4 (A440) is created by alternately writing HIGH and LOW to the piezo's pin in equal intervals 880 times per second. Yep, 880—that's twice the frequency, because one full "wave" (on-off) should happen 440 times per second.

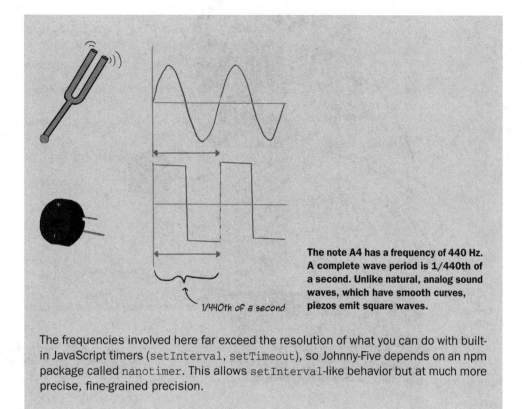

The note A4 has a frequency of 440 Hz. A complete wave period is 1/440th of a second. Unlike natural, analog sound waves, which have smooth curves, piezos emit square waves.

1/440th of a second

The frequencies involved here far exceed the resolution of what you can do with built-in JavaScript timers (`setInterval`, `setTimeout`), so Johnny-Five depends on an npm package called `nanotimer`. This allows `setInterval`-like behavior but at much more precise, fine-grained precision.

5.3.1 Adding an audible piezo chime to the timer

Depending on which kind of piezo you have, either plug it directly into the breadboard or plug its wires into the breadboard (figure 5.24). Don't forget to remove the 220 Ω resistor, as well.

PLAYING TUNES ON THE PIEZO

The code changes for the timer are minor. Inside of timer-advanced.js, instantiate a `Piezo` instead of an `Led` and remove the reference to `alertLED` from the `start()` function, as shown in the following listing.

> **Listing 5.23 Instantiating a piezo**

```
var alertChime = new five.Piezo(6);
```

Johnny-Five's `Piezo` class gives you some handy tools to make piezos play tunes, handling the complex timing and frequency conversions. Notes are exposed by their names (such as `'e5'`) so you don't have to memorize frequencies. You can pass an object representing a "tune" to the `play` method, with properties such as `tempo` (BPM) and a `song` (array of notes and their durations).

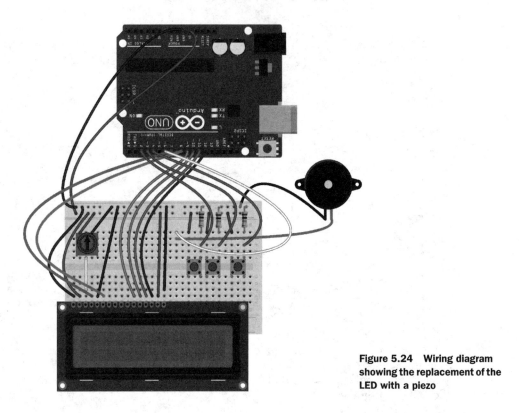

Figure 5.24 Wiring diagram showing the replacement of the LED with a piezo

Update the chime() function to play a song, as shown in the next listing.

Listing 5.24 The new chime() function

```
function chime () {
  alertChime.play({
    tempo: 120,          ⟵── tempo is an optional property.
    song: [
      ['e5', 1],         ⟵── This will play the note e5 for I "beat".
      ['g#5', 1],
      ['f#5', 1],
      ['b4', 2],
      ['e5', 1],
      ['f#5', 1],
      ['g#5', 1],
      ['e5', 2],
      ['g#5', 1],
      ['e5', 1],
      ['f#5', 1],
      ['b4', 2],
      ['b4', 1],
      ['f#5', 1],
      ['g#5', 1],
      ['e5', 2]
```

```
    ]
  });
  lcd.cursor(0, 9).print('DONE!');
}
```

You'll have to try this out to find out what the time's-up tune is!

Summary

- An LED can only emit one wavelength (color) and can only be off or on at any given time, but pulse-width modulation (PWM) can be used to fool the eye into thinking an LED is shining at different brightnesses.

- PWM support is a hardware feature, and only some pins on development boards support PWM.

- The brightness of LEDs can be "animated" to create effects and communicate information. Using different easing functions and providing different animation options can generate different outcomes with Johnny-Five.

- RGB LEDs combine three LEDs (red, green, blue) at different brightnesses—via PWM—to create different colors. Common cathode RBG LEDs have three component LEDs that share a single cathode leg.

- Parallel LCDs have a lot of connections. Johnny-Five provides a simplified interface to LCDs via its LCD class.

- Potentiometers are another kind of variable resistor, like photoresistors. Unlike photoresistors, they have their own internal voltage dividers, so changing voltage can be read on the third pin.

- Piezos take advantage of the reverse piezoelectric effect to transduce voltages at different frequencies into mechanical motion, and, as a result, sound waves.

Output:
making things move

This chapter covers

- How motors work and what makes them spin
- The inductive characteristics of motors and how to safely construct motor circuits
- Using diodes, capacitors, and transistors in circuits to control motors and protect components
- How to position things, precisely, with servos
- How to control motors using an H-bridge circuit and motor drivers
- How to build your first basic, roving robot

By now you're likely tapping your feet impatiently and wondering, "When do we get to make *robots*?" Well, your ship has come in. It's time to learn how to make things move.

The motors and servos you're about to get to know provide the fundamental control of robots' movements. There's lots to learn, but by the end of this chapter you'll have built a basic roving bot.

Making robots move involves choreographing electronically controlled movement. Motors spin, making wheels roll. Servos allow precise positioning of components: cameras, robotic arms, and so on. Let's get moving.

For this chapter, you'll need the following:

- Arduino Uno and USB cable
- 1 9 V DC motor
- 1 9 V battery and snaps
- 1 1N4001 diode
- 1 N-channel MOSFET, such as FQP30N06L
- 1 100 µF capacitor
- 1 4.8 V micro servo
- 1 Texas Instruments SN754410 Quadruple Half-H Driver
- Actobotics Peewee Runt Rover kit (or 2 gearmotors, 2 wheels, chassis)
- Breakaway male header pins
- Jumper wires
- 1 half-size breadboard

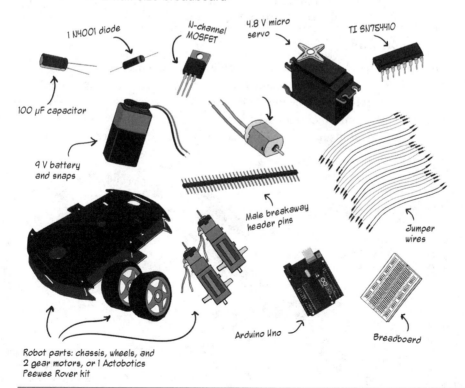

1 N4001 diode

N-channel MOSFET

4.8 V micro servo

TI SN754410

100 µF capacitor

9 V battery and snaps

Male breakaway header pins

Jumper wires

Arduino Uno

Breadboard

Robot parts: chassis, wheels, and 2 gear motors, or 1 Actobotics Peewee Rover kit

6.1   *Making motors spin*

Motors convert electrical energy into mechanical energy (figure 6.1). Current goes in and motion comes out, typically in a rotary form, such as a spinning axle.

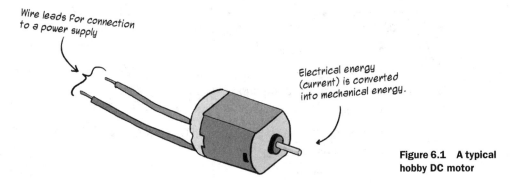

Wire leads for connection to a power supply

Electrical energy (current) is converted into mechanical energy.

Figure 6.1   A typical hobby DC motor

At the heart of a motor's electricity-to-motion alchemy? Magnets!

ACTUAL CURRENT FLOW Recall how conventional current representations show electrical current as flowing from positive to negative, but in reality the opposite is closer to the truth? The actual direction of current flow is relevant to some of the topics covered in this chapter, and, as such, the conceptual diagrams show current flowing from negative toward positive.

6.1.1   *How motors work*

When an electrical current runs through a wire, a magnetic field is also created. The magnetic field is oriented at a right angle to the current's direction (figure 6.2).

The current-induced magnetic field near a single, straight wire is weak, relatively speaking. But it's possible to concentrate the magnetic effect by winding a length of wire around (and around and around) a piece of metal. When current is applied to the *coil*

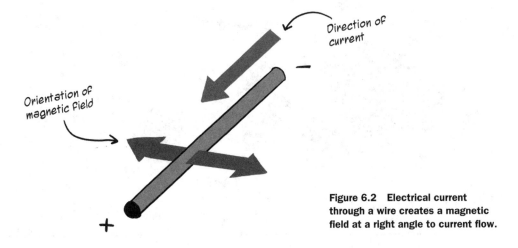

Direction of current

Orientation of magnetic field

Figure 6.2   Electrical current through a wire creates a magnetic field at a right angle to current flow.

of wire, the collective right-angle magnetic field has enough oomph to yank some of the previously disorganized atoms in the metal core into a north-south alignment. And, voila! You've created a magnet by using electricity: an *electromagnet* (figure 6.3).

If you reverse the direction of the current that's running through the coiled wire, the electromagnet's polarity will flip too—the north and south magnetic poles will swap places (figure 6.4). Cut off current from the wire, and the magnetic field will dissipate—you can turn your magnet off!

Let's envision our imaginary electromagnet being put to theoretical use. In the left side of figure 6.5, an unpowered electromagnet is mounted on an axle and suspended between two stationary magnets. As soon as current is applied to the electromagnet (the middle of figure 6.5), the electromagnet will want to align itself as magnetic forces dictate—its north pole toward the stationary magnet with the inward-facing south pole. What it will want to do is rotate half a turn to make this happen, like on the right in figure 6.5. Of course, this hypothetical motor isn't going to work: the battery is in the way and things are getting all tangled up.

Without further intervention, things would stop here—the magnets are aligned in a happy way. But if we were able to swap the current direction through the electromagnet again

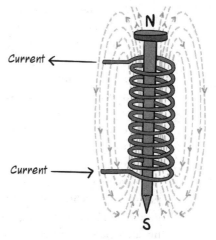

Figure 6.3   The current through the coil creates a magnetic field that magnetizes the iron core of the electromagnet.

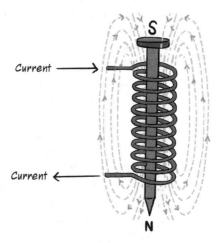

Figure 6.4   Reversing current flow reverses the polarity of the electromagnet.

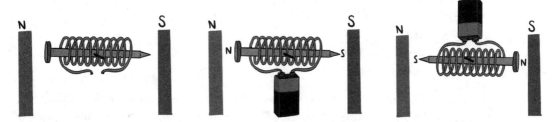

Figure 6.5   An electromagnet on an axle between two fixed magnets is going to want to orient itself—by rotating—as magnetic forces dictate.

at exactly this spot, the motion could be forced to continue, as the magnet seeks to align itself correctly once more. Reversing current polarity every half-turn could keep things going forever. Indeed, this concept is how motors work. A motor wired like the thing shown in figure 6.5 would quickly become a tangle of batteries and wires, so a real motor involves some design enhancements.

Figure 6.6 shows a—still oversimplified—*brushed DC motor*. The wall of the motor contains fixed magnets. Positive and negative power connections from the power source are connected to two stationary *brushes*, which "brush on" power in a given polarity as the motor's shaft turns and they come into contact with different parts of a split ring called a *commutator*. The current—and, thus, the magnetic field—changes polarity as the motor turns, keeping everything in motion. Brushed motors are very common, but non-brushed motors use the same general concepts—electricity and magnets—to accomplish the same thing.

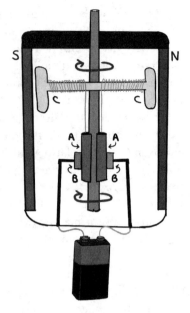

Figure 6.6   A brushed motor's electromagnets are connected to a split ring called a *commutator* (A). The commutator and electromagnets rotate as the motor spins. Fixed-position *brushes* (B) are attached to the power supply and "brush" alternating polarities onto the commutator as it rotates beneath them, changing the polarity of the electromagnets on the motor's *armature* (C).

6.1.2   *Controlling a motor with a push-button switch*

Let's ease into motor control gently by building a basic circuit that powers a motor, controlled by a push button. In a bit, we'll add the ability to control the motor with the Arduino Uno and Johnny-Five.

What you'll need
- 1 9 V battery
- 1 9 V battery snap with leads
- 1 small DC motor, rated up to 9 V
- 1 1N4001 diode
- 1 jumper wire (black)
- 1 half-size breadboard

Motors take electricity in, and put mechanical rotation out. But the inverse is also true: if the shaft of a motor is turned (mechanical energy is applied), the motor will *generate* electrical energy—it acts as a *generator*. This is how water can generate (hydroelectric) power, for example. Flowing water physically turns the shaft of a motor (generator), and

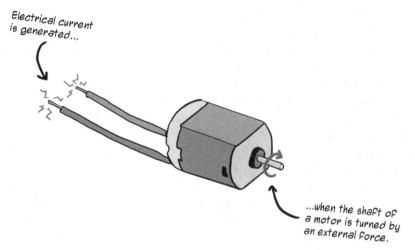

Electrical current
is generated...

...when the shaft of
a motor is turned by
an external force.

Figure 6.7 When a motor is turned by an external force, electrical current is generated.

electricity comes out. So motors also take mechanical energy in, and put electricity out (figure 6.7). This set of phenomena—the creation of voltage or motion via interactions with magnetic fields—is called *inductance*. A motor is an *inductive* component.

The characteristics of inductive components have relevance to your circuitry. Say you apply current to a motor, and it's spinning merrily along. Remove the current— shut off the power—and the motor will continue to spin on its own for a little while. During this brief time, it will be generating power, and an important thing to note is that a motor (or any inductor) will generate voltage in the *opposite direction* of the input voltage (figure 6.8).

Motor connected to power

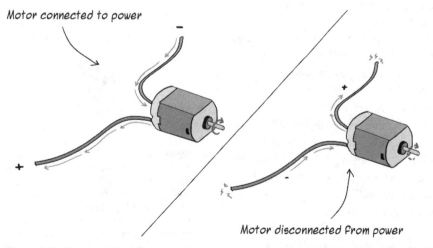

Motor disconnected from power

Figure 6.8 When a motor is connected to a power supply, current flows from negative (low potential) toward positive (higher potential). The current flow causes the motor to spin. When current flow is removed from the motor, inertia causes the motor to continue spinning briefly. During this time, the motor acts as a generator, generating electricity with voltage opposite to the previous input voltage.

This means that the electricity flow can "move around backwards" in your circuit, and the negative voltage spike can be huge (albeit for a very short amount of time). Without intervention, this *back voltage* (also called *back electromotive force* or *back-EMF*) can do nasty things, like damage components or cause actual sparks to leap around!

A circuit without protection from this back voltage works fine when the circuit is closed and current is flowing through the motor (figure 6.9), but it can be problematic when the current through the motor changes (figure 6.10), which changes when the button is released (the switch is opened, breaking the circuit).

The large negative voltage briefly generated in figure 6.10 wants so very much to make a path to the +9 V voltage that it might do crazy things, like leap through the air or through other non-conductive materials to get there. We've got to protect our circuit against this kind of inductive voltage spike.

MANAGING BACK VOLTAGE WITH FLYBACK DIODES

We've got to manage this back voltage situation for the health and safety of our circuit. We need to make sure negative voltage isn't allowed to go wandering around the circuit willy-nilly, hurting innocent components.

There's a standard method for accomplishing this, using a diode (figure 6.11). You briefly met diodes in chapter 2—LEDs are a kind of diode. A diode is a semiconductor component that only allows current to flow through it in one direction.

The diode placement in the circuit wiring diagram for the push-button-controlled motor we're about to

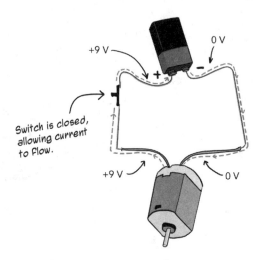

Figure 6.9   In the unprotected circuit pictured here, current flow is controlled with a push button (switch). When the switch is pressed and held, the current flows as expected, powering the motor. The motor consumes the voltage provided.

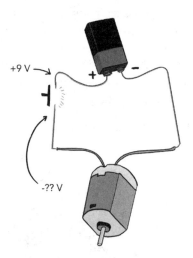

Figure 6.10   When the button is released (switch opened), the motor continues to spin for a little while. During this time it's generating negative voltage. The lead formerly connected to the positive terminal of the battery (through the switch) can build up a very large negative potential—hundreds of volts, say—which is much, much lower than the +9 V of the battery.

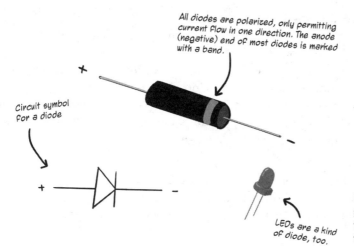

All diodes are polarized, only permitting current flow in one direction. The anode (negative) end of most diodes is marked with a band.

Circuit symbol for a diode

+ ⟶ —

LEDs are a kind of diode, too.

Figure 6.11 Diodes are semiconductor components that only permit current to flow in one direction.

construct—with the diode's cathode connected to the positive power rail—looks backwards, and it *is* (figure 6.12).

The way the diode is oriented ("backwards," or, more technically, *reverse-biased*) in the circuit means that current will be blocked from flowing through it—usually. But when the back-voltage situation arises, and the flow through the circuit is topsy-turvy, the diode becomes temporarily *forward-biased*—it's momentarily oriented so that current can flow across it. At these times, it can create a path to "wick away" dangerous negative voltage current and reroute it through the motor over and over again until the negative voltage dissipates naturally on its own (don't worry, it will, and quickly).

A diode used this way is called a *flyback diode*, or a *snubber diode* (figure 6.13).

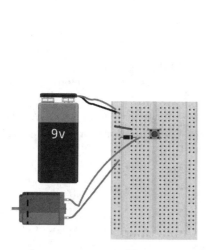

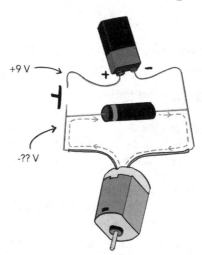

+9 V ⟶

-?? V

Figure 6.12 Circuit diagram of a basic, push-button-controlled motor, including a protective diode

Figure 6.13 If a flyback diode is used in a circuit with an inductor like a motor, it can provide a path for pent-up negative voltage that's trying to go the wrong way. It can route it back through the motor in a loop until it dissipates.

POWERING MOTORS IN CIRCUITS

Inductive elements like motors are current-hungry, especially when they're being turned on or off (by now you've probably recognized that inductors have some interesting characteristics when they're starting up or shutting down). The maximum current draw possible from a single Arduino Uno pin is only 20 mA—this isn't enough! Plus, many hobby motors are rated at 6 V or even 9 V—more than the Uno can provide, voltage-wise. We'll use a stable, separate power source for our motor—a 9 V battery—to make sure our motor gets the juice it needs.

BUILDING THE CIRCUIT

For the motor shown in figure 6.12 to spin, you'll need to create a closed path from the power source (positive battery terminal) to ground (negative battery terminal). Pressing the push button will connect this path—the motor will operate when the button is pressed.

Build the circuit as shown in figure 6.12, taking care to orient the flyback diode correctly. If you get it backwards, it's going to get really hot (at a minimum) or possibly even blow up or damage the battery.

Once you've constructed the circuit, you should be able to start the motor by holding down the push button. Those little hobby motors spin fast!

> **SPINNING MOTORS BACKWARDS**   Your motor may have red and black wire leads, implying that there's a "correct" or "polarized" way to plug the motor into a circuit. That's a little misleading: motors are happy plugged in in either orientation—swapping the connections will simply reverse the direction that the motor spins. You're welcome to try reorienting your motor's leads in the circuit and see if you can get it to run "backwards." Changing the direction of current through a motor to change the motor's direction is a key part of robotic control, as you'll see in a bit.

6.1.3   *Controlling a motor with Johnny-Five*

Our first motor experiment has a few shortcomings: there's no logic controlling the motor—just our own fingers—and the motor is either on (full speed!) or off—there's nothing in between.

Johnny-Five has a `Motor` component class that can give you more control over the motor's speed. It gives you even more control if you use more sophisticated integrated circuits or motor controllers—but let's start basic.

What you'll need
- 1 Arduino Uno and USB cable
- 1 9 V battery
- 1 9 V battery snap with leads
- 1 small 9 V DC motor
- 1 1N4001 diode
- 1 N-channel MOSFET, such as the FQP30N06L

- 4 jumper wires
- 1 half-size breadboard

In this experiment, we want to replace the human-powered push-button switch with a switching mechanism that can be controlled by the output from one of the Uno's pins. You already know that the motor needs more than the Arduino's on-board power can provide—both in terms of voltage and current—but any output signal from an Uno pin is going to be at 5 V. We're going to end up with circuitry that combines two separate power sources: 9 V (battery) and 5 V (Arduino logic).

USING TRANSISTORS AS SWITCHES

MOSFETs are *metal-oxide-semiconductor field-effect transistors* (whew, no wonder people just say *MOSFET*). Transistors are semiconductor components that play one of two roles: amplifying or switching signals. There's more to know about transistors, but in our immediate case, we're going to use a MOSFET as a very fast, reliable switch.

When a small voltage is applied to the MOSFET's *gate* pin (figure 6.14), the other two pins (*source* and *drain*) are connected, and current can flow between them—the MOSFET is turned on. The Uno can reach out with a weaker, 5 V "finger" and "push" the gate

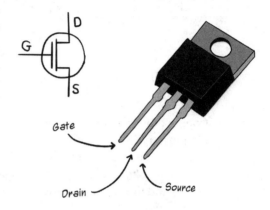

Figure 6.14   A MOSFET and its circuit symbol. A small voltage applied to the gate (G) pin will make a connection between the drain (D) and source (S) pins.

pin, completing the 9 V circuit attached to *source* and *drain*. That is, you can use a signal with low voltage and power to control a signal with higher voltage and power. The resulting motor circuit has two input power sources: the 9 V battery and 5 V input coming from the Uno.

> **MOSFET PINOUT**   Although most field-effect transistors (FETs) of this type (N-channel) use the pinout shown in figure 6.14, make sure you double-check your component's datasheet to confirm which pins are the gate, drain, and source.

One last thing: you need to connect the two power sources to a common ground. Although the input power sources are segregated—the positive power rail is only for 9-volt power—the ground for both is connected.

BUILDING THE CIRCUIT

Make sure the MOSFET's metal tab is oriented as shown in the wiring diagram for the MOSFET-switched motor (figure 6.15)—the tab should be oriented toward the right. From the top, the first pin is the gate: this should be connected to the Uno's pin 6.

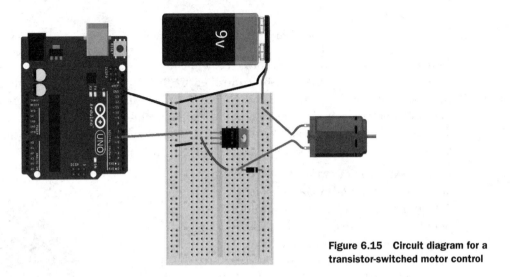

Figure 6.15   Circuit diagram for a transistor-switched motor control

Connect the bottommost pin—the source—to ground. The MOSFET's drain pin (middle pin) should be connected to one of the motor's leads and the flyback diode as shown (the diode is in parallel with the motor).

When voltage is applied to the gate pin, current will be able to flow between the source and drain pins, allowing the motor to spin.

TAKING THE MOTOR FOR A SPIN

Create a JavaScript file called motor-basic.js in your Johnny-Five working area with the following code. This script instantiates a `Motor` on pin 6 and makes it available to the REPL for your manual control.

Listing 6.1   Motor test drive

```
const five  = require('johnny-five');
const board = new five.Board();

board.on('ready', () => {
  const motor = new five.Motor({ pin: 6 });      ◁──┐ Pin 6 will control the
  board.repl.inject({                                 motor's speed with PWM.
    motor: motor       ◁──┐ You'll have access to the
  });                       motor from the REPL.
});
```

Johnny-Five's `Motor` component class has more to it, but we're starting with the most basic instantiation: identifying a single pin for controlling a motor's speed in a single direction. This is called a *non-directional motor*.

Run the script and interact with the `motor` in the REPL:

```
$ node motor-basic.js
```

Once the board and REPL are initialized, you can experiment with the available `motor` object reference by typing into the REPL. Here are some handy methods:

- `speed(0-255)`—Make your motor spin at a given speed; for example, `motor.speed(100)`.
- `stop()`—Stop the motor; for example, `motor.stop()`.
- `start()`—Start the motor using the previously set speed; for example, `motor.start()`.

Motor speed is controlled with pulse-width modulation (PWM), so it's a good thing we have a fast switch (the MOSFET) that can open and close the circuit at high frequencies.

> **Take it further: make your own temperature-controlled fan**
>
> You now have all the tools you need in your growing builder's kit to construct the temperature-controlled fan first mentioned in chapter 1.
>
> Challenge: Instead of using the REPL to control a motor, add a TMP 36 sensor to your circuit and use changes in its value to turn the fan on or off, or to change its speed. You may have more fun if you cut a fan blade out of stiff paper or cardboard and attach it to your motor's axle!

6.2 Making servos go

Servos are mechanisms for positioning things precisely, and they're indispensable in robotics and other gadgets that require things to be moved accurately (figure 6.16).

A servo's movement is powered by a DC motor, similar to the ones we've been experimenting with in this chapter. But a servo needs a few more parts to get its job done. A gear assembly translates the fast but weak rotation of the motor into a slower, but more accurate and strong (higher torque) rotation. Additional built-in circuitry monitors for input signals to tell the servo at what *angle* it should position itself, and it allows the servo to detect when it's in the correct position.

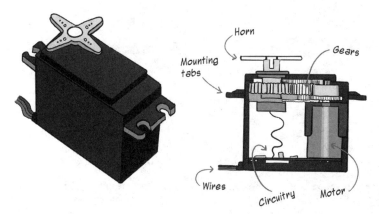

Figure 6.16 A servo and its basic parts. Horns come in different shapes and sizes: discs, stars, single arms.

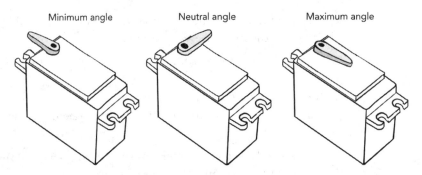

Figure 6.17 A servo (with attached horn) positioned at a minimum angle, a neutral angle, and a maximum angle. Different servos have different real-life angle ranges.

Most servos have about 180 degrees of rotation. They have a "neutral" position (90 degrees, or "up") and can rotate about 90 degrees from that neutral position in either direction (figure 6.17). The 180 degrees of rotation is best-case: inexpensive low-power servos have as little as ~150 degrees of rotation.

The circuitry within the servo package responds to coded signals on the servo's signal wire. The signal used for controlling the position of a servo is a specific kind of PWM.

Servo-flavored PWM

A servo's position, or *angle*, is controlled by sending PWM over its signal wire, but it's a special "flavor" of PWM. A servo expects to receive a pulse every 20 ms. The length of time that the pulse persists—the amount of time that the signal is HIGH—determines the position of the servo. The shorter the pulse duration, the further to the left the resulting position will be.

Typically, a pulse of 1.5 ms will cause the servo to point in its *neutral* direction (90°). A pulse of 1 ms or so will peg the servo left (0°), whereas a 2 ms pulse will position it all the way to the right (180°).

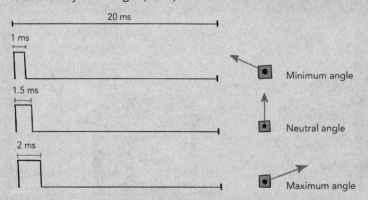

The duration of a PWM pulse determines the servo's angle. A 1.5 ms pulse positions the servo at a neutral angle. Shorter pulses equate to more acute angles, and longer pulses to obtuse angles.

6.2.1 Controlling a servo with Johnny-Five

What you'll need
- 1 Arduino Uno and USB cable
- 1 micro servo (4.8 V)
- 1 100 µF (microfarads) capacitor
- 3 male header pins, if needed
- 3 jumper wires (red, black, yellow)
- 1 breadboard

Header pins for connecting your servo

Most servos' wires terminate in a female connector with three terminals.

The easiest way to plug these into a breadboard is to obtain some *breakaway header pins*. These strips of pins come in rows of 16 to 40 pins, and you snap off the number of pins you need to connect a given component. Some are sturdier than others and may require pliers to snap apart.

Look for male header pins at a 0.1" pitch (the 0.1" pitch makes them breadboard-compatible).

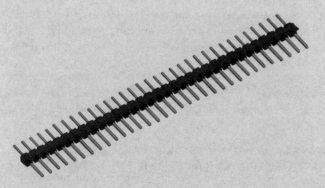

Male breakaway header pins come in strips. You "break away" (snap off) the number of pins you need for a given component.

Like motors, servos are power-hungry when they move and can cause voltage fluctuation in the circuit. However, it's possible to power low-voltage micro servos—those rated for 4.8 V or below—directly from the Uno's power supply if you take some precautions.

PROTECTING CIRCUITS WITH DECOUPLING CAPACITORS

Capacitors (figure 6.18) are passive electronic components that act kind of like batteries: they store a certain amount of charge, measured in units called *farads* (abbreviated as *F*). One farad is a lot; most capacitors for hobby electronics are measured in micro-, nano-, or even picofarads.

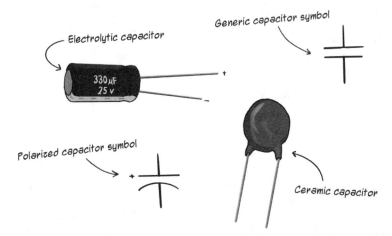

Figure 6.18 Capacitors come in a number of different packages and sizes; electrolytic capacitors and ceramic capacitors are quite common. Take care: some, but not all, capacitors are polarized.

A charged capacitor will get twitchy if there's a voltage fluctuation between source power and ground. For example, if the voltage suddenly drops to 4.5 V, the capacitor will discharge some of its stored charge to "smooth out" the voltage.

That means a capacitor can act as a tiny, boosting battery, squirting out extra charge as needed to keep the voltage steady. A capacitor used this way is called a *decoupling capacitor*, as it *decouples* the rest of the circuit from voltage noise caused by components.

Be careful with capacitors

Watch out! Capacitors are sneaky little devils and can be downright *dangerous* in certain cases. They deserve extra respect and care.

An important thing to know is that capacitors can retain their charge for long periods of time, even if current isn't running through them. They're, again, like batteries in that regard. That means that if you accidentally complete a circuit across a capacitor—and, yeah, you can cause this situation with your fingers—it could discharge immediately and violently. If you ever find yourself deconstructing old televisions or electronic camera flashes, *be very careful*. If one of those powerful capacitors discharges at you unexpectedly, you could be looking at a trip to the hospital, or worse.

A more day-to-day thing to keep in mind is that electrolytic capacitors, like the one used in this experiment, are polarized. They won't abide being plugged in backwards and they have a rather ornery habit of exploding when used in a reverse orientation. In our low-voltage, low-capacitance world, these are rather mild explosions, but they could still scare the bejeezus out of you, or melt components and boards you'd rather not melt.

BUILDING THE SERVO CIRCUIT

Connect your servo's power, ground, and control wires to the breadboard, using header pins if needed (see figure 6.19). Different servo manufacturers use different

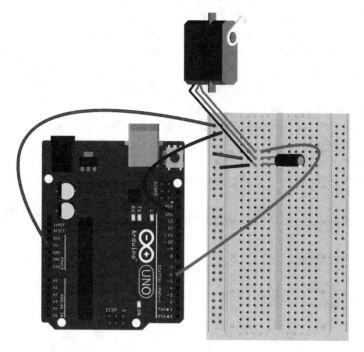

Figure 6.19   Wiring diagram for a servo with a decoupling capacitor

wire colors, but the positive power connection should be a red wire. Most servos use black for the negative lead wire, but some have a brown or maroon-ish wire. Finally, the signal wire could be white, yellow, orange, or even blue. In summary, the red wire is power, the darkest wire is ground, and what's left over is the signal wire (figure 6.20).

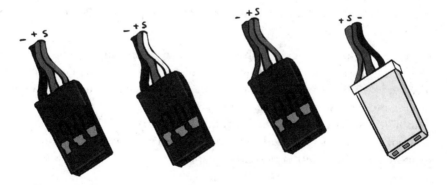

Figure 6.20   Servo wires come in various colors and have differing connectors. There should be a red wire—this connects to Vcc (source power). The darkest wire—black or brown—is ground. The remaining wire is the signal wire—abbreviated here as S—for controlling the servo's position.

Connect a 100 μF electrolytic capacitor in parallel with the servo's power connections—that is, plug the capacitor's anode into the same breadboard row as the servo's power connection and its cathode into the same row as the servo's ground connection. Connect the servo's signal wire to pin 6 on the Uno. Finally, connect the servo's power to the Uno's 5 V power and the servo's ground to the Uno's GND pin.

TAKING THE SERVO FOR A TEST DRIVE

You may by now have guessed already that Johnny-Five has a `Servo` class for controlling servos. It sure does!

Create a new file, servo-basic.js, and add the following JavaScript. This is similar to the motor test drive: it will make a reference to `servo` available to you in the REPL.

Listing 6.2 Servo test drive

```
const five  = require('johnny-five');
const board = new five.Board();

board.on('ready', () => {
  const servo = new five.Servo({ pin: 6 });
  board.repl.inject({
    servo: servo
  });
});
```

Servos require PWM control signals—make sure to use a PWM-enabled pin!

Run the script:

```
$ node servo-basic.js
```

Now you can avail yourself of the `Servo`'s methods:

- `to(deg)`—Move the servo to the `deg` value (between 0 and 180). For example, `servo.to(50)`
- `center()`—Move the servo to its center/neutral position, 90 degrees by default. For example, `servo.center()`

If you try to position your servo at the extreme ends of its range—0 or 180 or near to those values—it will likely protest, making sad grinding sounds. That's because the *effective* range of the servo is less than 180 degrees. Try experimenting to determine the lowest and highest angle values your servo can comfortably reach.

This little test drive is but a brief introduction to servos. If the next section—building a robot!—appeals to you, and robotics is an area you want to dive into, you'll have many more encounters with servos as you explore.

6.3 *Building your first robot!*

It's time to build a robot. To build a robot that can move around on wheels, you need some basic parts (figure 6.21):

- *A chassis*—Every robot needs a body. A chassis is a structure onto which you can attach motors, wheels, and other components.
- *At least two geared motors*—Motors for driving robots need to have some *gear reduction* to give them some torque. Otherwise they won't be able to climb over even the most minimal obstacles. The drive axle of a gear motor is usually (but not always) at a right angle to the spin of the motor itself.
- *Wheels or tracks*—These translate the motion of the motors. Wheels fit onto the drive axles of gearmotors.
- *A brain*—A microcontroller or processor to define the robot's logic.
- *Motor circuitry*—Your robot needs some components to translate its desired movement into motor motion.

One of the things that can be off-putting about getting into basic robotics is the combined expense of various parts. Chassis can cost up to a few hundred dollars (!), and off-the-shelf shields, boards, or other circuitry for controlling the motors can cost a bit too.

Our first roving bot will use quite inexpensive parts. You can find the suggested Acto-botics Peewee Runt Rover chassis kit for about $16 online and in electronics-supply stores.

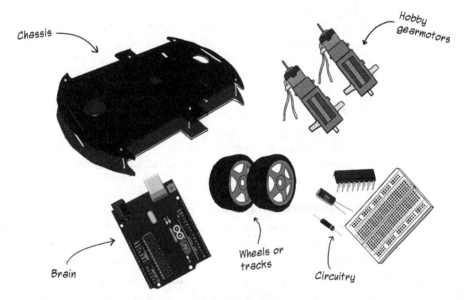

Figure 6.21 A basic robot needs a chassis (body). Two or more geared motors connect to wheels or tracks to propel the bot. Of course, you'll also need circuitry, a brain (microcontroller), and a power supply.

What you'll need

- 1 Arduino Uno and USB cable[1]
- 1 Actobotics Peewee Runt Rover robot kit or similar[2]
- 9 V battery and snaps
- 1 Texas Instruments SN754410 Quadruple Half-H Driver
- 15 jumper wires
- Double-sided tape, electrical tape, gaffer's tape, or other adhesive (optional)
- 1 half-size breadboard

OTHER OPTIONS FOR BUILDING YOUR FIRST BOT   The Actobotics Peewee Runt Rover kit is a handy option for a first robot because it's inexpensive and includes a chassis, wheels, gearmotors, and mounts—the basic pieces you'll need. But other two-wheeled chassis frames or kits are fine too. SparkFun's Shadow chassis is another cheap option (though you'll need to buy motors and wheels separately). Whatever you end up with, make sure you have a chassis, geared motors, and wheels. The instructions that follow for constructing a rover bot assume the Peewee kit, but construction shouldn't differ too much for similar kits.

6.3.1   *Robots and motors*

From our recent experiments, you've seen how a motor's speed can be controlled with PWM, and how a motor's direction can be reversed by swapping its power and ground connections. You've also seen how motor circuits are a little more complex than other circuits: you need diodes to protect your circuit's other components, and you'll likely need a more robust power supply for a motor than a development board can provide.

It gets a bit more complicated. A roving robot needs at least two motors to be steerable, and you need to be able to run those motors in a forward and a reverse direction (without physically unplugging and swapping the leads, of course). Multiple motors on a single circuit should also be isolated with decoupling capacitors so that sudden spikes caused by one motor don't affect the other motor or components. The details are starting to add up.

CONTROLLING MOTORS WITH H-BRIDGE DRIVERS

An H-bridge is a circuit with four switches and a load in the middle—the load being a motor, in our case. In concept, it's laid out roughly in the shape of the letter *H*, as shown in figure 6.22.

The arrangement of switches (that is, transistors) in an H-bridge allows the motor's direction to be controlled without you having to physically change its wiring. Closing

---

[1]   If you happen to have a longer USB A to USB B cable than the one that came with your Arduino, this would be a good time to use it.

[2]   Contains chassis, 2 gearmotors, and 2 wheels.

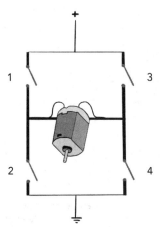

Figure 6.22 An H-bridge circuit contains four switches, with the motor in the center. Different combinations of switch states can route current through the motor in different directions.

switches 1 and 4 (figure 6.23, left) allows current to flow through the motor in one direction, whereas closing switches 2 and 3 (figure 6.23, right) allows the motor to spin in the opposite direction.

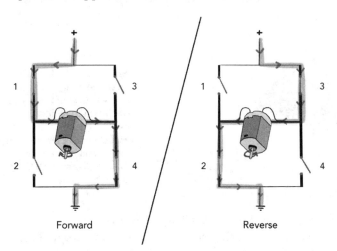

Forward

Reverse

Figure 6.23 By activating different switches in an H-bridge, a motor can be made to spin in a forward or a reverse direction.

There are 16 possible states (switch combinations) an H-bridge circuit can be in, of which the two in figure 6.23 are the most obviously useful. Several others are innocuous, allowing the motor to coast (when there's no path through the circuit) or braking the motor (both leads of the motor connected to the same voltage).

There are six switch combinations that are bad news, causing a situation called "shoot-through," more simply described as a short circuit (figure 6.24). This is not good and will fry things.

For our robot we'd need to build one H-bridge circuit per motor, not to mention adding in additional protective diodes and capacitors—that's starting to sound like a lot of connections and complications. Fortunately, H-bridges are available inexpensively as

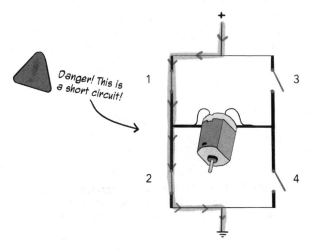

Danger! This is a short circuit!

Figure 6.24   Closing both switches on either side of the H-bridge causes "shoot-through"—a short circuit!

integrated circuit (IC) chips (figure 6.25). Even better, many inexpensive ICs package together H-bridge circuitry along with internal diodes and other gadgetry to protect your motor circuit as well as preventing shoot-through states. These chips are called *motor drivers* or just *drivers*.

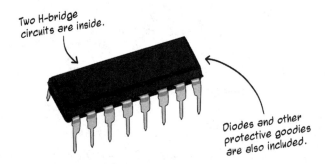

Two H-bridge circuits are inside.

Diodes and other protective goodies are also included.

Figure 6.25   Inexpensive motor drivers, like this Texas Instruments SN754410, give you logical control over internal H-bridge circuits. They also include other components, like diodes, making motor control simpler and less error-prone. The SN754410 is a dual H-bridge—it can control two motors.

The Texas Instruments SN754410 Quadruple Half-H Driver costs just a few bucks and is available from various electronics supply resellers. Yeah, its name is a mouthful (bonus hint: a quadruple half-H-bridge is equivalent to two complete H-bridge circuits), but it does everything we need to drive both motors for our first roving robot.

Before we dive into the details of the motor driver IC's pins and related circuitry, let's get started on the foundational pieces of our first robot.

6.3.2   *Building the robot's chassis base*

You'll want to attach the side supports (this may take some oomph) and your breadboard to the bottom plate of the robot chassis (figure 6.26). If you have the Peewee kit, the side supports are the pieces of plastic with the larger, rectangular holes in the middle.

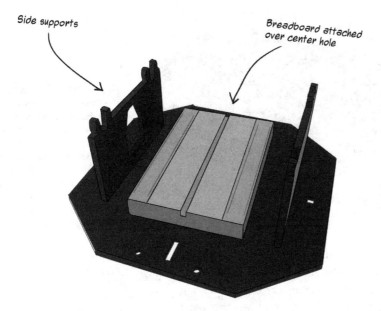

Side supports

Breadboard attached over center hole

Figure 6.26   The bottom plate of the Peewee Runt Rover chassis, with attached side supports and breadboard. If you're using a different chassis, it'll look a little different, of course.

ATTACHING THE BREADBOARD TO THE CHASSIS Most half-sized breadboards have adhesive that can be exposed by peeling off a piece of backing paper, and this can be useful for adhering the breadboard to the robot's chassis to keep it from moving around. If you can't permanently commit a breadboard to the robot—perhaps this is your only breadboard!—or if your breadboard doesn't have adhesive, you can temporarily attach the breadboard to the robot chassis using double-sided tape, electrical tape, gaffer's tape, or your choice of removable adhesive. You could also use wire ties.

Go ahead and center the breadboard and attach it to the chassis. The hole in the center of the plate will leave some of the breadboard adhesive exposed (if you're permanently attaching your breadboard). You can cut a piece of the backing paper in the shape of the hole and reattach it to cover up the exposed gummy surface, if you like. Don't attach the top plate of the chassis yet.

Gearmotors made for robots have a geared output axle for driving wheels that's (typically) at a right angle from the motor's spin. Wheels attach to the output axle, facing outward from the robot, while the motor's spinning shaft is oriented up (as in the Peewee kit, figure 6.27) or toward the back (as in the SparkFun Shadow Chassis). In all cases, you'll want to have the motors' wires on the inside.

Take the Peewee chassis' top plate and attach the gearmotors to it. The motors' leads can then be routed down through the circular hole in the middle of the top plate, for access to the breadboard below. The Peewee kit also comes with two development-board supports, in the shape of wide, shallow *U*s. These should be attached to

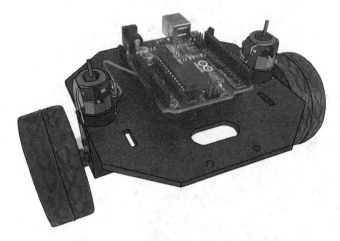

Figure 6.27   The top plate of the Peewee Runt Rover chassis, shown with attached gear motors, wheels, dev-board support, and Arduino Uno. Make sure the motors' wires are oriented toward the inside of the chassis. The motor wires can be run underneath the Uno and through the center hole of the chassis plate.

the top plate now, and you can nestle the Arduino into them, with the USB connection toward what will be the rear of the robot (the plate is symmetrical front-to-back, so you get to decide now where the rear of your bot is).

You can now slide the wheels onto the gearmotor axles. At this point, you should have a bottom plate with attached breadboard and side supports, and a top plate with attached Arduino, motors, and wheels.

6.3.3   *Controlling the robot's motors*

If you orient the SN754410 motor driver with the semicircular dimple at the top, the pins are ordered from 1 to 16, as shown in figure 6.28. Different pins have different purposes and provide connections to different things inside the chip. We'll walk through these as we build the circuit.

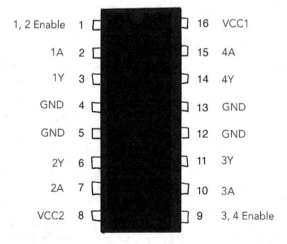

Figure 6.28   The pinout of the SN754410 motor driver

SN754410 POWER AND ENABLE CONNECTIONS

The first step for wiring up the SN754410 is connecting some of its pins to power and ground (figure 6.29).

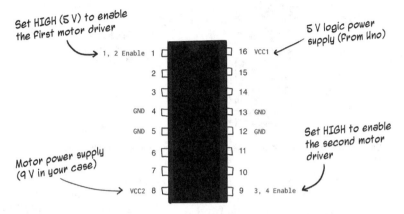

Figure 6.29 The SN754410 needs to be connected to a motor power supply on VCC2 (physical pin 8) and the logic power supply on VCC1 (physical pin 16). The two enable pins should be connected directly to 5 V to set them HIGH. There are also four GND pins that, unsurprisingly, need to connect to ground.

The driver needs to be connected to two separate power sources. The 9 V battery will power the motors themselves (the *motor power source*), whereas the logic for controlling the motors will be 5 V from the Uno (the *logic power source*).

In addition, there are two *enable* pins on the chip: one for each motor's driver. You need to "turn on" each driver by connecting each enable (EN) pin—physical pins 1 and 9—to 5 V (that is, logical HIGH).

Make connections to the power and enable pins as shown in the motor power wiring diagram (figure 6.30). Note that the ground rails are tied together (shared ground), but the power sources are isolated: the left rail for the motor power source (9 V), the right rail for the logic power source (5 V).

SN754410 LOGIC CONNECTIONS

On the SN754410, each motor is controlled via two input pins. Two corresponding output pins are connected to the motor (figure 6.31).

Different logic-level combinations on a motor's two input pins cause different things to happen with each motor, thanks to the internal H-bridge

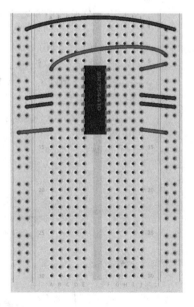

Figure 6.30 Wiring the SN754410's power connections on the robot's breadboard

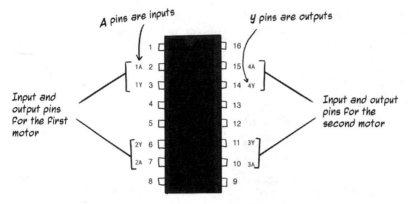

Figure 6.31   Each of the two motor drivers has two input pins and two output pins.

switches and circuitry. For each motor, one input pin can be used for controlling direction while the second input pin can be used to control the motor's speed. Let's take a look at how that can possibly be, examining how the first of the two motors is controlled (the second motor is controlled identically).

CONTROLLING MOTOR DIRECTION

We'll use pin 1A (physical pin 2 on the SN54410) to control the direction of the first motor (figure 6.32).

When pin 1A is set HIGH and pin 2A is LOW, 9 V current will be allowed to flow across the two output pins (1Y, 2Y) and the motor will spin in a forward direction (figure 6.33).

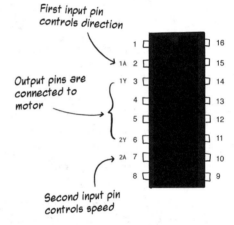

Figure 6.32   The first motor controller: two input pins and two output pins. We'll use one of the input pins to control the motor's direction and the other to control its speed.

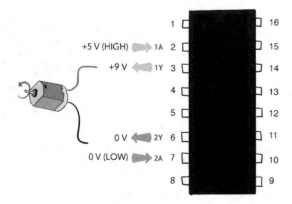

Figure 6.33   When the first input is set HIGH and the second input is set LOW, the motor will turn in a forward direction.

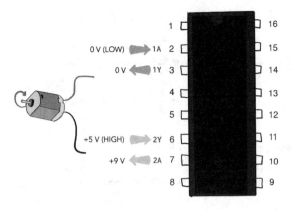

Figure 6.34 When first input is LOW and second is HIGH, the motor rotates in the opposite (reverse) direction.

Similarly, when the direction pin 1A is set LOW, the motor will spin in a reverse direction (9 V current flow is reversed) any time pin 2A is HIGH (figure 6.34).

Put another way, any time 1A and 2A have opposite logic levels, the motor will be powered to spin in the direction dictated by the logic level of pin 1A. But if both input pins have the same logic level, no current will flow through the motor (detailed in table 6.1).

Table 6.1 Motor driver direction control for motor 1

1A (direction pin) value	2A (speed pin) value	Result
HIGH	LOW	Motor spins in direction 1 (forward)
HIGH	HIGH	No current through motor
LOW	HIGH	Motor spins in direction 2 (backward)
LOW	LOW	No current through motor

CONTROLLING MOTOR SPEED

Pin 2A (SN54410 pin 7) will control the speed of the first motor, using PWM. Let's say pin 1A, the direction pin, is set LOW, indicating a reverse direction for the motor's spin, while PWM with a duty cycle of 25% is applied to pin 2A, the speed pin (figure 6.35). Seventy-five percent of the time, 1A and 2A will have the same logic levels (LOW/LOW), during which no current will flow through the motor. However, 25% of the time, the LOW/HIGH combination will allow current to flow, powering the motor. This results in what we want: the motor spinning in a reverse direction at a 25% speed setting.

The same goes for speed control in a forward direction, but there's a wrinkle. Let's say 1A (direction) is set HIGH—forward—and 2A (speed) is set to a 25% duty cycle PWM. What we intend is for the motor to spin forward at 25% speed, but what will actually end up happening is that it will spin forward at 75% speed (figure 6.36).

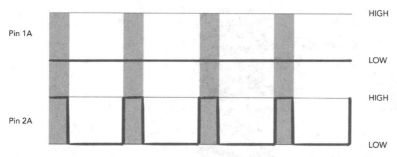

Figure 6.35   With direction set to LOW (reverse) on pin 1A and a 25% duty cycle on pin 2A (speed), the motor will be powered 25% of the time in the reverse direction.

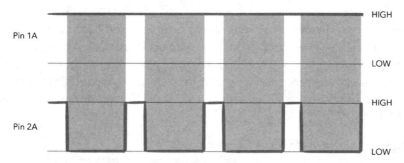

Figure 6.36   With direction set to HIGH (forward) on pin 1A and a 25% duty cycle on pin 2A (speed), the motor will be powered 75% of the time in the forward direction.

To account for this, the PWM signal needs to be *inverted* when the motor direction is forward. Some motor drivers handle this for you, automatically inverting PWM when the motor is set to spin forward. The SN54410, however, doesn't, so we'll have to account for it in our code.

COMPLETING THE MOTOR CIRCUIT

The rest of the circuit involves connections to the Arduino, 9 V motor power supply, and the two motors (figure 6.37). Connections to the Arduino and the motors should be routed through the center hole of the top chassis plate. As you finish making these connections, you can rest the top chassis plate on the bottom chassis plate and tuck the 9 V battery inside, but don't snap the pieces together yet—you need to test the motors first.

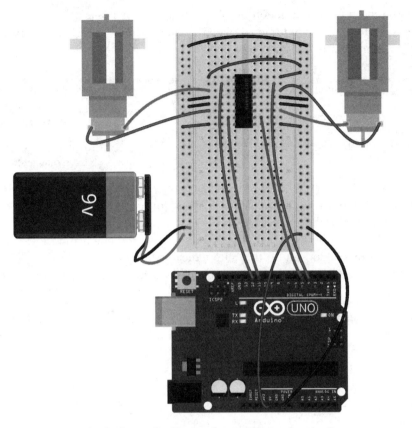

Figure 6.37 Circuit diagram for the rover's completed motor circuit

TESTING THE MOTORS WITH JOHNNY-FIVE

Before putting the robot together, you should test that the motor circuit is working as expected. Create a file called motor-test.js in your working directory, and put the following code into it.

Listing 6.3 Motor driver test drive

```
const five = require('johnny-five');
const board = new five.Board();

board.on('ready', function () {
  const motors = new five.Motors([
    { pins: { dir: 12, pwm: 11 }, invertPWM: true },
    { pins: { dir: 4, pwm: 5}, invertPWM: true }
  ]);

  board.repl.inject({
    motors: motors
  });
});
```

Let's zoom in on the instantiation of a Johnny-Five `Motors` object in the next listing. `Motors` is a Johnny-Five component collection class, akin to `Leds`. It can control multiple `Motor` components at once.

```
const motors = new five.Motors([
  { pins: { dir: 12, pwm: 11 }, invertPWM: true },
  { pins: { dir: 4, pwm: 5}, invertPWM: true }
]);
```

Options and pins for the first motor

Options and pins for the second motor

To the `Motors` constructor, you pass along an array containing options for each `Motor`. Now that each motor is controlled by two pins, Johnny-Five needs to be told which pins do what: one for direction (`dir`) and one for speed (`pwm`).

Remember that the PWM signal needs to be inverted when the motor runs forward. The hardware doesn't do this automatically, but you can let Johnny-Five know that it needs to be done, and Johnny-Five will do it for you, by using the `invertPWM` option.

> **DON'T LET YOUR BOT RUN AWAY!**   Before running the motors in the test script, lift your partially constructed robot off the ground so that the wheels are in the air. Otherwise it might run off!

Run the script:

```
$ node motor-test.js
```

When the board and REPL are initialized, enter the following command and press Enter:

```
> motors.forward(100)
```

Now look at your motors. Are they running forward, rather slowly? There's a reasonable chance that one or both of them are spinning in the wrong direction. Not a problem. Kill the script, disconnect power, and swap the connection between the motor's leads and the output pins on the motor driver for any motor that's going the wrong way. Then try again.

FINISHING THE CHASSIS CONSTRUCTION

Attach the small plastic nubbins to the bottom of the bottom plate, at front and back. These are what the bot rests on when it's not moving. Confident your motors are spinning as expected? Good. Now you can snap together the top and bottom chassis plates (figure 6.38).

WRITING THE ROBOT SOFTWARE

The rover's software will allow you to use the arrow keys on your keyboard to steer the bot (and use the spacebar to stop it). The code is going to consist of a couple of scripts

Figure 6.38 The completed robot, viewed from the front

(modules) and an extra dependency (the npm `keypress` module). Let's be a little more organized about the project's working area:

1. Create a new directory called rover, and `cd` into that new directory.
2. Run this command: `npm init --yes`. This will initialize a `package.json` file with some sane defaults.
3. Run this command: `npm install --save johnny-five keypress`. This will install the two modules listed and save information about the dependencies to package.json.

Create a file called Rover.js (listing 6.5). This module will hold a JavaScript `class` that defines the rover's basic movements. `Rover` doesn't know about the specific pins or the configuration of the motors in the `Motors` object passed to its constructor; those details are abstracted away.

Listing 6.5 The `Rover` class

```
class Rover {            ◁─── Organizing behavior with
  constructor (motors) {  ◁─── class syntax can make code
    this.motors = motors;        more readable.
  }                              The constructor creates
                                 a reference to the
  forward () {                   motors (this.motors).
    console.log('Full speed ahead!');
    this.motors.forward(255);
  }

  backward () {
    console.log('Reverse!');
    this.motors.reverse(255);
```

```
  }

  left () {
    console.log('To the left!');
    this.motors[0].reverse(200);
    this.motors[1].forward(200);
  }

  right () {
    console.log('To the right!');
    this.motors[0].forward(200);
    this.motors[1].reverse(200);
  }

  stop () {
    this.motors.stop();
    console.log('Stopping motors...');
  }
}

module.exports = Rover;
```

> Each Motor in a Motors object can be accessed with array notation.

> Steering involves running one motor forward and one backward.

> Exports the Rover class for outside consumption

Now the robot needs an interface and a way to control it. Create another file called index.js, shown in the following listing.

Listing 6.6   Structure of index.js

```
// Require dependencies
const five     = require('johnny-five');
const board    = new five.Board();
const keypress = require('keypress');
const Rover    = require('./Rover');

board.on('ready', function () {
  // 1. Instantiate Motors
  // 2. Instantiate Rover, using Motors
  // 3. Configure `keypress` to generate events on keypresses in the REPL
  // 4. Listen for `keypress` events and invoke appropriate Rover methods
});
```

Expanding on steps 1 and 2 in the preceding listing, let's instantiate the Motors and then the Rover in the next listing.

Listing 6.7   index.js: setting up the motors and the rover

```
// ...

board.on('ready', function () {
  // 1. Instantiate motors
  const motors = new five.Motors([
    { pins: { dir: 12, pwm: 11 }, invertPWM: true },
    { pins: { dir: 4, pwm: 5}, invertPWM: true }
```

> **Left motor details**

> **Right motor details**

```
   ]);

   // 2. Instantiate Rover, with motors          Passes Motors to the
   const rover = new Rover(motors);              Rover constructor

   // 3. Configure `keypress` to generate events on keypresses in the REPL
   // 4. Listen for `keypress` events and invoke appropriate Rover methods
});
```

To control the robot, you need to listen for relevant keystrokes for steering input. The third task in index.js is to configure keypress.

> **Listing 6.8   index.js: setting up `keypress`**

**Tell keypress to generate events for process.stdin
(standard input, via your keyboard)**

```
//...
board.on('ready', function () {
   // 1. Instantiate motors (as before)
   // 2. Instantiate Rover, with motors (as before)
   // 3. Configure `keypress` to generate events on keypresses in the REPL
   keypress(process.stdin);
   process.stdin.setEncoding('utf8');
   // 4. Listen for `keypress` events and invoke appropriate Rover methods
});
```

Be explicit about character encoding.

Finally, you need to listen for and handle keypresses.

> **Listing 6.9   index.js: handling keypresses**

```
//...
board.on('ready', function () {
   // 1. Instantiate motors (as before)
   // 2. Instantiate Rover, with motors (as before)
   // 3. Configure `keypress` to generate events on keypresses in the REPL
   // 4. Listen for `keypress` events and invoke appropriate Rover methods
   process.stdin.on('keypress', function (ch, key) {     Listen for keypress
                                                          events. You care about
      if (!key) { return; }          If there's nothing useful in    the key argument here.
                                     key, return (do nothing).
      switch (key.name) {
        case 'q':                        Pressing the q key will
          rover.stop();                  quit the robot. First, the
          console.log('Bye-bye!');       motors are stopped.
          process.exit();
          break;
        case 'up':                   'up' refers to the keyboard's
          rover.forward();           up arrow (and so on with
          break;                     'down', 'left', and so on).
        case 'down':
          rover.backward();
```

**process.exit()
will terminate
the robot's
process.**

```
      break;
    case 'left':
      rover.left();
      break;
    case 'right':
      rover.right();                    The robot can be
      break;                            stopped with the
    case 'space':                       spacebar.
      rover.stop();
      break;
    default:                   ◁─┐      The default case for the
      return;                    │      key switch statement is
  }                                     to do nothing.
  });
});
```

DRIVING YOUR ROBOT

Place your robot where it has a bit of space to move around, and then run the script:

```
$ node index.js
```

Once the board and REPL are initialized, you can use your arrow keys (up, down, left, right) to steer the robot around and the spacebar to make it stop.

You may feel mingled feelings both of triumph (hooray! first robot!) and restriction (adventures are limited by the length of your USB cable). There's good news: as we proceed, you'll be able to untether your robots and make them more interesting.

Before we do that, however, you'll round out the major topics of input and output by learning how to work with *serial* data.

6.4   *Summary*

- Electromagnets make motors spin. A motor provided with current will convert that electrical energy into mechanical energy—it will spin. Turning a motor's shaft causes it to act as a generator, converting mechanical energy into electrical energy.
- Building circuits with motors involves additional care. Motor circuits often combine multiple voltages, and motor power supplies tend to be isolated from lower-voltage logic circuitry.
- Motor direction can be reversed by reversing the direction of current flow through the motor, and motor speed can be controlled with PWM.
- Transistors like MOSFETs can be used as high-speed switches, using low-voltage logic to switch higher-voltage circuitry.
- Diodes and capacitors are two components that can help build safer motor circuits.
- Diodes only allow current to flow through them in one direction. A diode, oriented to be reverse-biased in parallel with a motor, can protect the circuit, acting as a flyback diode.

- Capacitors store electric charge and can be placed in parallel with components to isolate them from the circuit and smooth out voltage changes they cause. When used this way, they are called decoupling capacitors.
- Servos allow for precise positioning, converting PWM signals into angle position. Most servos' ranges are, ostensibly, 180 degrees, but the usable range is narrower on inexpensive servos.
- H-bridge circuits provide the ability to direct current through a load (motor) in multiple directions, allowing you to reverse motor direction. H-bridges, combined with other features, are packaged in motor driver ICs.
- Basic roving robots combine a microcontroller with a motor driver, gearmotors, wheels, a source of power, and a chassis.

Part 3

More sophisticated projects

This part of the book ups the ante and opens new possibilities through serial communication and the snazzy, Node.js-capable Tessel 2 development board.

To use more sophisticated sensors and exchange more complex data, you'll need to get a handle on how serial communication works, which is the topic of chapter 7. You'll get a chance to experiment with some nifty sensors, including an accelerometer, a GPS, and a compass. Along the way, you'll learn the difference between asynchronous and synchronous serial, and you'll meet the I^2C and SPI protocols. You'll also learn to solder.

In chapter 8, you'll untether your projects, going wires-free with the Tessel 2 development board. You'll get to know the Tessel, which can run your Johnny-Five scripts natively, and you'll build more complex experiments that make increasing use of third-party npm packages.

As you continue your adventure, you'll likely be starting to think of your own things to build. Chapter 9 walks through the steps of adapting existing hardware and writing your own software support for components. You'll hack a remote-controlled outlet switch and the APDS-9960 gesture sensor breakout board.

This part of the book is a step toward more independence and sophistication for your projects. You'll achieve independence from wires via the Tessel's native Node.js and onboard WiFi, and you'll try out more sophisticated components using serial communication.

Serial communication

7

This chapter covers

- What serial communication is, what it can do, and where it gets used
- How to work with asynchronous serial components like GPS modules
- An introduction to the core skills of soldering
- The basics of synchronous serial communication and the most popular protocols for hobby electronics: SPI and I^2C
- Building more complex projects by combining multiple serial device components

For this chapter, you'll need the following:

- 1 Arduino Uno and USB cable
- 1 Adafruit Ultimate GPS breakout board
- 1 Adafruit HMC5883L magnetometer (compass) breakout board

- 1 Adafruit BMP180 multisensor breakout board
- 1 Adafruit ADXL345 Triple-Axis accelerometer breakout board
- 1 16x2 parallel LCD module, or, optionally, I^2C-enabled Grove RGB LCD module
- 1 rotary potentiometer (for parallel LCD)
- Breakaway male header pins
- Soldering iron and soldering supplies
- Jumper wires
- 2 half-size breadboards

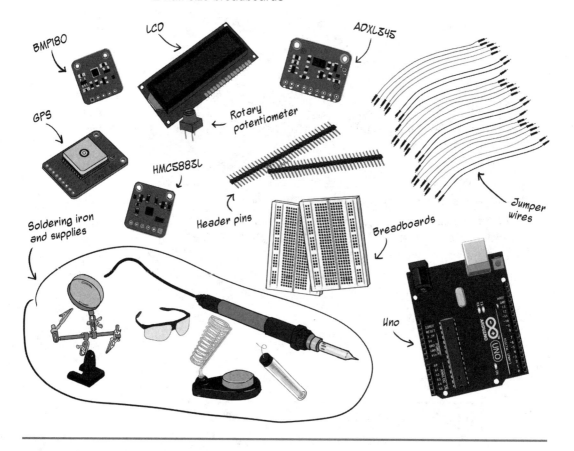

In our experiments so far, we've been able to glean some fun but straightforward data about the world around us, such as temperature (figure 7.1) or ambient light intensity. And by listening for variance in a basic digital signal (HIGH vs. LOW), we could tell if a button had been pressed.

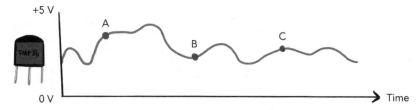

Figure 7.1   With a simple analog sensor like the TMP36, you can obtain a value for a single data point (temperature) by sampling the voltage of the signal at different points in time (A, B, C).

But there's a lot more information out there than can be (plausibly) relayed with a single analog signal. In fact, much of the interesting data is considerably more complicated and needs more refined coordination (figure 7.2). What if you want to detect physical motion in three directions simultaneously—like from an accelerometer? What about reading information from GPS chips? Precise compass coordinates and headings? More sophisticated data calls for more structured, sophisticated methods of digital communication between components.

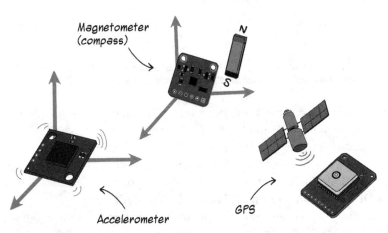

Figure 7.2   The complex digital data from sensors like accelerometers, compasses, and GPS modules requires a more sophisticated method of data exchange.

7.1   *Communicating digital data in parallel and in serial*

Serial communication: it's a single concept with myriad manifestations. The single concept at its core is dead simple: *serial* simply means that information—data—is sent one bit at time, one bit following the next. This is in contrast with *parallel* communication, in which multiple bits get sent at the same time (figure 7.3).

The benefits of communicating in parallel can be rather evident: why throw bits around one at a time if you can open the floodgates and chuck out a whole slew of bits simultaneously? It's true, parallel communication can be very fast. But there are some gotchas.

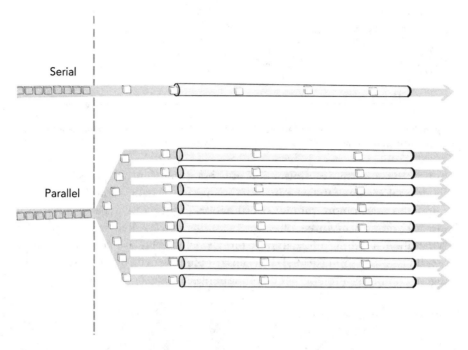

Figure 7.3   In serial communication (top), one bit is sent at a time sequentially. In contrast, parallel communication (bottom) transmits multiple bits at the same time.

In fact, you've already seen one of the downsides of parallel communication. Remember the LCD timer experiment in chapter 5? That circuit used a parallel LCD component. Think back for a moment to the circuit. One of its hallmarks was that it required an entire herd of wires. Four of those wires were responsible for sending data, in parallel, to the LCD, and that circuit only used four of a possible eight parallel data pins on the LCD. Drawback number one for parallel: tons of wires.

Parallel hardware also requires more physical bits and pieces than serial hardware. More wires leads to more expensive, complex circuits—and lots of pieces means that there are more things that might break.

It's also tricky to wrangle all of those parallel bits and make sure they get to the same place at the same time. In the end, parallel's complexity can be more trouble than it's worth. And serial, despite its simplicity, is more than fast enough. Serial is all around us: HDMI, USB, Ethernet. Serial is the data exchange method for a vast array of electronic components. So let's talk about serial.

7.2   *The basics of serial communication*

Although the core concept of serial communication isn't hard to grasp—one bit at a time down the wire—there are an intimidating number of ways that it can actually happen. How fast should those bits move around? How many bits make up each discrete grouping (*frame*) of delivered data? How are errors detected and corrected? If

Figure 7.4   For devices to exchange data using serial communication, they need to know how to talk to each other.

there are more than two components communicating, how does data get sent (*addressed*) to the correct component? Is one component in charge (the *master*) of several connected components?

All of the components conversing on the same serial communication channel, or *bus*, need to be in agreement about how that conversation is going to work (figure 7.4)—they need to use the same *protocol*. There are a lot of serial protocols, and it can feel overwhelming. The good news is that only a handful are commonly used in hobby electronics components. Get a conceptual grip on basic asynchronous serial, I²C, and perhaps SPI, and you'll be in good shape. And if you're feeling especially wary, note that nearly all of the low-level complexity can be abstracted out for you by libraries such as Johnny-Five.

7.3   *Asynchronous serial communication*

When people refer to *serial* without any further qualification, they often mean *asynchronous serial communication*—two devices transmitting (TX) and receiving (RX) data between themselves (figure 7.5). Yet even a setup as simple as this needs to have some rules.

Asynchronous serial is so called because there's no managed clock signal shared by the components. Each device has to be its own timekeeper. That's fine, but there has to be a common agreement between components about how many bits are sent per unit of time. Put another way, each component needs to know how long one bit of data will take—for example, how long will a signal remain HIGH to indicate a single 1-bit value? (Without knowing this, how would a receiver be able to tell the difference between two sequential 1 bits and a single, long 1 bit?). The speed of bits is usually expressed in bits per second (*bps*), or *baud rate*.

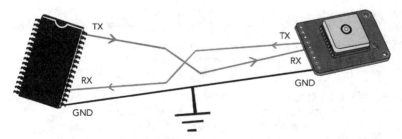

Figure 7.5   The exchange of asynchronous serial data: each of two connected devices can transmit (TX) data to and receive (RX) data from the other component. Note that one device's TX connects to the other's RX and vice versa. A GPS breakout board like Adafruit's is an example of a component that communicates its data using asynchronous serial.

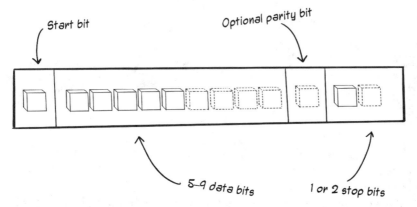

Figure 7.6   **A frame of asynchronous serial data. A single start bit is followed by 5–9 bits of data. A parity bit may be used for error detection. Then one or two stop bits indicate the end of the frame.**

But wait, there's more! Data isn't sent in endless streams of 1s and 0s. Instead, data is packaged in brief segments called *frames*. Each frame of data sent is composed of several parts: the data itself (5–9 bits of it), but also a start bit, a stop bit (or two), and, maybe (though not all that often) a *parity bit* to aid in error detection (figure 7.6).

Each asynchronous protocol configuration defines the specifics of how its data frames will be structured, as well as the baud rate. For example, 9600/8N1, a common protocol configuration, indicates a data rate of 9600 baud, 8-bit data chunks, no parity bit, and one stop bit (figure 7.7).

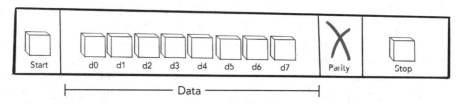

Figure 7.7   **The data frame structure of 9600/8N1: start bit, 8 data bits, no parity bit, one stop bit**

Firmata, serial, and a bit more about how Johnny-Five works

The architecture of Johnny-Five makes a clear distinction between the exposed, high-level JS API for components and the actual I/O implementation under the covers that writes data to and reads it from those connected components.

Johnny-Five assumes that compatible dev boards have the ability to perform a set of I/O operations. For example, the logic inside of the Led class assumes it's possible to enact a digital write to a pin (to set it HIGH or LOW), but it doesn't specifically care *how* that digital write is implemented. Instead, it's the responsibility of compatible *I/O plugins* to define how those operations actually take place.

When you instantiate a `Board` object, you can optionally declare which I/O plugin to use. For example, if you wanted to use Johnny-Five with the Tessel 2 board (and we will, in the next chapter), you can set an `io` option property.

Listing 7.1 Using a different I/O plugin with Johnny-Five

```
const five = require('johnny-five');
const Tessel = require('tessel-io'); // A third-party I/O plugin module
    for J5
const board = new five.Board({
  io: new Tessel() // tell Johnny-Five to use this I/O plugin
});
```

You've probably noted that, so far, we haven't been providing an `io` option in our `Board` instantiations. If the option isn't set, Johnny-Five, by default, uses *Firmata* for I/O. That default Firmata I/O layer is compatible with a slew of Arduino boards, including your Uno.

When running a Johnny-Five Node.js script on your host computer, it's Firmata that's translating your application's logic into I/O commands to send to the board. It's also running on the board as firmware and does the translation in the other direction: sending data from the board back to the host computer.

Firmata's execution is an example of asynchronous serial in action. Firmata data is transmitted in 8-bit chunks (8N1) between the host computer and the Arduino board at a fast baud rate. When you execute a Uno-compatible Johnny-Five Node.js program on your host computer ("compatible" meaning it uses the default Firmata I/O), Firmata data is sent and received through the connected USB cable. (USB does stand for Universal *Serial* Bus, after all!) On the Arduino's end, receiving and transmitting serial Firmata data is handled by the Uno's single on-board Universal Asynchronous Receiver/Transmitter (UART) (figure 7.8).

For the curious: although the Firmata protocol defines the structure of messages, and the Firmata implementation handles the packaging and processing of these messages, the actual nuts-and-bolts mechanics of serial data exchange via your computer's USB port is supported by an npm package called node-serialport.

7.3.1 UARTs

A *universal asynchronous receiver/transmitter* (UART) is a piece of hardware for handling asynchronous serial communication (figure 7.8). A UART can take a bunch of parallel data—say, data coming from several I/O pins or other sources—digest it, and spit it out in a desired serial protocol. It goes the other way, too: a UART can also decode incoming serial data and make it available as parallel data. Parallel in, serial out—and vice versa. UARTs can be configured to speak different flavors of asynchronous serial: different baud rates, and so on. That makes UARTs highly flexible and useful bits of hardware.

The term *transistor-transistor logic* (TTL) in this case refers to the use of asynchronous serial communication via UARTs. With TTL, logical HIGH is represented as the microcontroller's

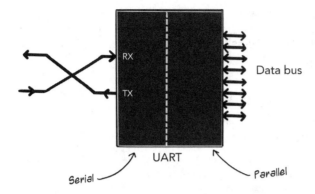

Figure 7.8   **A UART is specialized hardware for asynchronous serial communication and parallel-to-serial conversion.**

Vcc (+5 V in the case of the Uno), and LOW is represented as 0 V—that is, the voltage range is always limited to the voltages appropriate for the microcontroller at hand.

The multiple meanings of TTL

The term *transistor-transistor logic* (TTL) usually refers to a method for constructing digital circuits using transistors for logic—for example, AND gates, logical inverters, XOR gates, and so on. Standard voltages used in TTL components will look familiar: +5 V to indicate a logical HIGH and 0 V for LOW. TTL ICs, especially those compatible with the wildly popular Texas Instruments 7400 family, were widely used into the 1990s. They're still very much available and are useful for hobby projects or simpler embedded systems, though they've been superseded by other technologies for most sophisticated mass-produced electronics (for example, *complimentary metal-oxide-semiconductor*, which is abbreviated to something you may recognize: *CMOS*).

Perhaps confusingly, the term *TTL* is also applied to a device or circuit that can be connected to another device or circuit without any extra translation or interfacing. In this context, it indicates that the signal between the two will communicate logically using HIGH (+5 V) and LOW (0 V) logic levels. It's this usage that leads to the convention of alternately referring to asynchronous serial as *TTL serial*.

Your trusty Arduino Uno has one UART (more accurately, its ATmega 328P microcontroller has one UART). While a Johnny-Five script is executing on your host computer, the Uno's UART is busy receiving and transmitting messages in Firmata format.

There's a potential conflict here. Say you've got a device component you want to use in your project that communicates data using async serial. But your Uno's UART is already occupied, monopolized by the Firmata communication it needs to carry on in order to make Johnny-Five programs work.

Fortunately, there's a way! The work a UART performs is certainly more efficient and speedy when implemented in hardware, but it can be emulated in software. So-called *software serial* allows you to communicate in async serial via microcontroller pins that wouldn't normally support it at the hardware level. Software serial can be processor-intensive and it isn't as fast as a UART, but it can be *fast enough* and gets the job done.

7.3.2 *Trying out software serial with a GPS breakout board*

What you'll need

- 1 breadboard
- 1 Adafruit Ultimate GPS breakout board
- Red, black, yellow, and white jumper wires
- Arduino Uno and USB cable

Here's where it gets fun—the first time you connect up a GPS and see incoming data, it feels pretty awesome. Reading GPS data with an Arduino Uno used to feel a little arcane—lots of copying and pasting of Arduino code and relying on low-level libraries cooked up by community members. It worked, but it wasn't terribly intuitive for the non-C expert.

Interacting with GPS using Johnny-Five these days, however, is so streamlined it feels almost magical. Your little GPS chip is listening to *satellites*! It's hard to believe that something so sophisticated can be controlled and sampled with only a few, clear lines of JavaScript. Technology is cool.

GPS data and NMEA sentences

Many GPS chips output data conforming to a standard called NMEA 0183. The National Marine Electronics Association (NMEA) maintains this standard, which defines the structure of data from the kinds of hardware you might expect to find aboard a seagoing vessel: sonar, gyroscopes, marine radar—and GPS.

NMEA data is communicated over asynchronous serial as ASCII characters—ASCII characters are 7 bits, which fit nicely inside of a byte of data—and those characters are assembled into comma-delimited *NMEA sentences*. Although the standard does make mention of a particular configuration (4800 8N1), NMEA data can be sent over various configurations. The GPS breakout from Adafruit defaults to 9600 baud, but some GPS modules can transmit even faster.

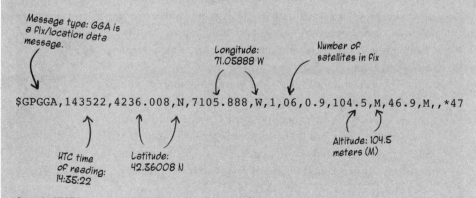

Sample NMEA sentence and some of its fields explained. Data transmitted from the GPS is sent in comma-delimited ASCII conforming to the NMEA standard.

> *(continued)*
> Johnny-Five's GPS class parses NMEA sentences from the GPS hardware using software serial and organizes them into handy properties like `latitude` and `longitude`.

The good news is that building a circuit with a GPS breakout board requires minimal connections. You'll find that the supporting electronic components are often built into breakout boards—capacitors, resistors, and so on—leaving you with just power and data connections to hook up.

On the flip side, you'll need to learn to solder now. The Adafruit GPS breakout board needs to be soldered onto headers so that you can plug it into a breadboard (figure 7.9). Soldering isn't hard, but like any new core life skill, it can take a few tries before you'll have your soldering sea legs.

The GPS module will need to be soldered onto some header pins so that it can be connected to a breadboard.

Figure 7.9   Before you can use it on a breadboard, the GPS needs to have some header pins soldered to it.

7.3.3 *Learn to solder!*

Solder is a metal alloy intended for making—*fusing*—permanent bonds between bits of metal (figure 7.10). Solder melts at a lower temperature than the legs and connections of your components, allowing it to flow, liquid, around those connections without damaging them. Once it hardens—this happens nearly instantly—you've got a permanent connection. It's sort of like conductive metal glue. Solder comes in long, thin lengths on a spool, like wire.

To provide the heat needed to melt solder and make those connections, you'll need a *soldering iron* (figure 7.11). Soldering irons range from ten bucks (U.S.) to several hundred. Unsurprisingly, you get what you pay for. Cheap soldering irons behave in, well, cheap ways and aren't adjustable. But an inexpensive soldering iron will get the job done just fine if you're not ready to invest in a quality model.

Figure 7.10   Solder comes on a wound spool, like thread.

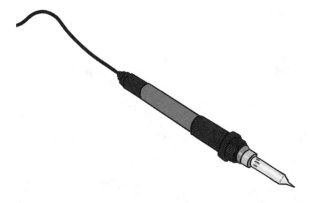

Figure 7.11   A run-of-the-mill inexpensive soldering iron. Cheap ones don't typically have temperature-control settings—they just get one flavor of hot.

Make sure your soldering iron has a *stand* to put it in when it's not in your hand (figure 7.12). You'll also need sponge for cleaning the tip of your soldering iron between solders and for tinning the tip (more on that shortly). Good soldering sponges are brass, but regular household sponges work, too. If you use a cellulose household sponge, make sure to dampen it before using it with your iron.

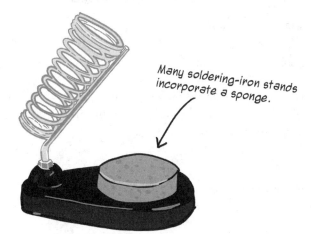

Many soldering-iron stands incorporate a sponge.

Figure 7.12   Your soldering iron needs a stand to hold it when not in use, and to protect things around it from burning.

PUTTING TOGETHER YOUR SOLDERING KIT

If the list of necessary soldering supplies seems onerous (figure 7.13), you might consider a "learn-to-solder" kit, sold by online electronics retailers, which comes with most of the items you'll need and a practice project to boot.

Solder, traditionally, is made of an alloy containing a high percentage of lead. As you likely know, lead is bad for humans. Since 2006, the use of lead in electronics has been restricted in the EU via the Restriction of Hazardous Substances Directive (RoHS), which has all but eliminated the use of lead in manufacturing solder. Lead-free solder is definitely good for people and the earth, but it's also a little more challenging to work with—it doesn't flow as smoothly as leaded solder. Both lead-free and

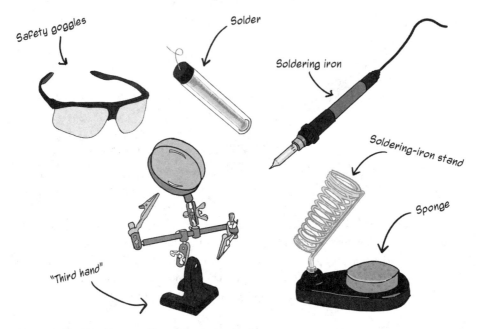

Figure 7.13   Key things you'll need to start soldering

leaded solder are available; some feel that learning to solder with leaded solder is easier than with lead-free.

You may also wish to pick up a spool of solder wick (a.k.a. *desoldering braid*). This braided copper wire acts as a chemical vacuum cleaner to undo bad solders: reheat the soldered joint and use the solder braid to wick up the misplaced solder.

HOW TO SOLDER, STEP BY STEP

Read these instructions completely before setting out to solder, so you're prepared and ready to rock:

1   Before you begin, set up your workspace using a third hand (figure 7.14) or some other method for securing your work and leaving your hands free—slotting header pins into a breadboard and positioning the board in place on top is also an option. Have the tools and parts you anticipate needing at the ready so you're not flailing around with a hot soldering iron later.

2   Plug your soldering iron in and let it heat up for several minutes. Now, especially if

Figure 7.14   Secure your components before soldering. A third hand is a convenient tool for this.

you have an inexpensive model, wait a few more minutes—that is, be patient. Working with a soldering iron that's not hot enough is a recipe for frustration and singed boards.

3 Prepare (*tin*) your soldering iron's tip. Melt a little bit of solder onto the tip of the iron and then wipe off the excess on your sponge. This should result in a shiny, bright tip on your soldering iron. If the solder doesn't melt readily when you touch it to the iron's tip, the iron isn't hot enough. Wait a few more minutes and try again.

Figure 7.15 Place the soldering iron's tip on the metal connection pad and the pin to heat them up.

4 Hold the soldering iron in your dominant hand and the solder in your other hand. Press the tip of your hot iron to the header pin and the connection pad for about one second (figure 7.15).

5 Keep the iron in place and apply the end of the solder to the opposite side of the joint (figure 7.16). You won't be melting the solder directly with the iron—solder instead comes into contact with the heated pin and board connection. Keep your soldering iron at the bottom of the pin; ignore the temptation to move it up toward the solder.

Figure 7.16 The heated pin will cause the solder to melt and flow around the joint.

6 The solder will melt and flow around the joint. Once you have a nice-looking mountain-shaped mound of solder (figure 7.17), remove the soldering iron and voila! You'll find with time that the solder kind of naturally "wants" to flow into that volcano shape.

Figure 7.17 A well-soldered connection resembles a little volcano of solder.

Soldering isn't complicated, but it can take a few rounds to get it quite right. YouTube and the web are your friend: there are tons of videos and tutorials for learning to solder. It's one of those skills that may be easier to understand if you watch it in motion. SparkFun's "Through-Hole Soldering" tutorial is clear and straightforward (http://mng.bz/cv1Z).

Common challenges for soldering newbies

Like any new physical skill, soldering takes a while to master. Here are some of the common things that can slow you down:

- *A soldering gun you know to be hot doesn't seem to "want" to melt solder, or, "it just doesn't seem to work"*—Make sure you keep the tip of your soldering iron *tinned*, that is, coated with just a bit of solder. You can tell a tip is tinned because it will be shiny. If your soldering iron's tip is black or matte-textured, it's oxidized and you need to *re-tin* it. This process can be tedious: you need to get solder melted so that it will coat the tip, but non-tinned parts of the tip don't cause the chemical reaction that causes solder to flow correctly. Take your time, be patient, and get this right, using your sponge to help direct the solder and wipe off excess.

  The best way to fix this is to keep it from happening in the first place: check your iron after every few soldered joints, and touch up the tip with some additional solder if it starts to look oxidized in any spot. Note that lead-free solder will cause your soldering iron to oxidize considerably faster than leaded solder.

- *Blackened, warped, or singed boards*—Soldering doesn't damage components if you don't apply too much heat, but it's pretty easy to mess this up by touching your soldering iron to the board (instead of the metal connections), using too high a temperature setting, holding the iron too long against a component, and so on. You'll get better at this with practice. Often singed-looking boards or components will still function okay, but sometimes you may find that you've truly fried something. Go slow, aim carefully, and try out your first few soldering tasks on inexpensive components, just in case.

- *Soldered joints don't work right*—A joint without enough solder (a "cold joint") won't conduct—plug your soldering iron back in and try again. Another common problem is accidentally using too much solder and soldering the connection to a neighboring connection as well, causing any number of woes with the circuit. An overabundance of solder can be cleaned up with *soldering wick*.

- *Solder just won't stick to the thing you're trying to stick it to*—Soldering is a chemical process. You can't solder to non-metal surfaces like plastics, and even some metals are non-solderable.

7.3.4   *Building the GPS circuit*

Once the header pins are soldered onto the GPS breakout board, building the circuit is a snap. Plug the GPS into the breadboard. Connect power and GND to the Uno's 5 V and GND pins, respectively. Connect the board's TX pin to pin 11 on the Uno, and the RX to pin 10 (figure 7.18).

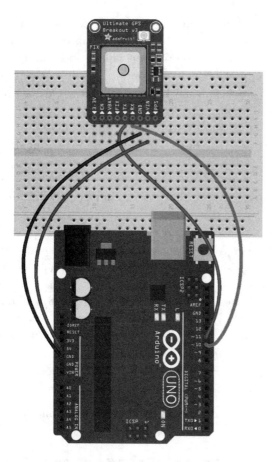

Figure 7.18   GPS circuit wiring diagram

READING GPS DATA WITH JOHNNY-FIVE

The code required is breathtakingly simple. In your Johnny-Five working directory, create a new file called gps.js and add the following code.

Listing 7.2   Johnny-Five GPS

```
const five = require('johnny-five');
const board = new five.Board();

board.on('ready', function () {
  const gps = new five.GPS([11, 10]);

  board.repl.inject({
    gps: gps
  });
});
```

> Software serial is supported on these pins—and only these pins—on the Uno.

> Makes the GPS object (gps) available in the REPL

As soon as the GPS board is connected to power, it will start trying to get a satellite fix. Until it has a fix, you'll see an onboard LED blink about once per second.

The GPS has a built-in antenna, but it won't be able to get a satellite fix without exposure to a wide slice of sky. Most likely, you'll need to go outside. With luck, this requirement won't be too cumbersome—scoop up your laptop and Uno and breadboard, and head to the great outdoors for a few minutes. Then again, it was 24 degrees (F) out and spitting snow pellets when I tested this code. Or maybe you're working on a desktop computer, which isn't going to be outdoor-friendly.

You might have luck next to a large window with a clear view of the sky, or you may be able to use a longer USB cord so that your Uno and breadboard can sit outside while your computer is inside.

It takes about 30–60 seconds to get a solid ("cold-start") satellite fix.

"But wait," you say, "my phone can get my GPS position in just a few seconds…and it works inside. What gives?"

Your smartphone uses some extra tricks to derive your location: where it is relative to local cell phone towers and nearby WiFi networks. In fact, for your phone to get a real GPS lock—the satellite kind—it can take just as long or longer than these stand-alone chips—up to several minutes.

Once your GPS chip has a satellite fix, the onboard LED will stop blinking so quickly, slowing down to one blink every 15 seconds. It doesn't matter when you start the gps.js script—before the chip has a fix or after—but, obviously, location data won't be available until the fix is solid:

```
$ node gps.js
```

Assuming you have a fix, you can now start interacting with your GPS and logging out data, as shown in the next listing.

Listing 7.3   Photoresistor data logging output

```
1479058386733 Device(s) /dev/cu.usbmodem1411
1479058386761 Connected /dev/cu.usbmodem1411
1479058388413 Repl Initialized
>> gps.latitude
42.38
>>
```

All right, cool—almost too easy! You can try inspecting other properties on your gps object, like longitude. See the Johnny-Five GPS documentation for the latest about what you can do (http://johnny-five.io/api/gps/).

Nice. You've mastered basic asynchronous serial connectivity using software serial. Let's see what else serial can do.

7.4   *Synchronous serial communication*

Async serial is straightforward and useful, but it isn't the right fit for everything. To account for small potential differences in the clocks of each of the components, each data chunk has to be surrounded by start and stop bits, and maybe a parity bit is thrown in there, too. That's a sizable overhead: best case (one start bit, one stop bit, no parity), it takes 10 bits to transmit 8 bits of information. UART hardware is complex, and software implementations are slower and processor-intensive. Getting the baud rate and other details sorted out between components can be finicky. Finally, async serial is really only cut out for letting two devices talk to each other.

Synchronous serial protocols add a shared clock line in addition to data connections for synchronizing components. Because the clock signal dictates the speed of the data transmission, the data rate of components doesn't have to be configured beforehand. Certain synchronous serial protocols also make it possible and convenient to communicate among many devices on the same communication bus. There are also drawbacks; for example, both the SPI and I²C protocols you're about to meet require connecting wires to be short—for example, you can't reasonably communicate using I²C over a 20-foot cable.

7.4.1 Serial Peripheral Interface (SPI)

Serial Peripheral Interface (SPI) is a synchronous serial protocol originally developed by Motorola in the 1980s. It allows for a "master" device to control and coordinate data exchange between itself and one or more "slave" devices. For a one-to-one master-slave connection, as few as three wires can be used (figure 7.19), but four or more are required if there are multiple slave devices (figure 7.20).

SPI's biggest advantage is that it allows for really fast data transmission rates. The receive hardware is also significantly simpler than a UART. SDCard memory cards are a popular example of real-world use of the SPI protocol.

SPI components are widely available to hobby tinkerers. Johnny-Five has support for a certain SPI barometer, for example. Also, we'll work with an LCD module (Nokia 5110)

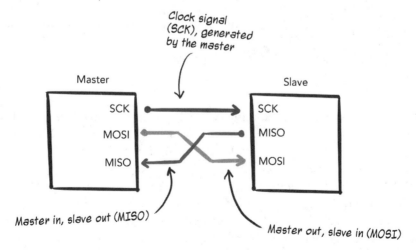

Figure 7.19 In a simple SPI configuration—one master, one slave—as few as three wires can be used for data exchange: a shared clock line (SCK) managed by the master, master-out-slave-in (MOSI), and master-in-slave-out (MISO).

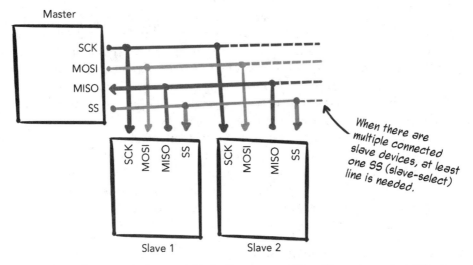

Figure 7.20 When more devices are added, at least one additional line—slave-select (SS)—is needed, though some SPI configurations require one SS line per slave device.

in chapter 10 that has an SPI interface. But SPI components aren't nearly as common as the big-hitter protocol: I²C. That's where we'll put our attention.

An aside on terminology

I'm no fan of the archaic *master-slave* terminology to describe certain metaphors in electronics and computer science. But it's entirely pervasive in serial protocols—for example, it's hard-baked into acronyms like *MOSI* and *MISO*. Thus, I am using *master-slave* language here, reluctantly, as to do otherwise could lead to confusion.

Note also that in these discussions about different serial configurations, the dev board's serial hardware is playing the part of "master," and the connected devices are the "slaves."

7.4.2 *I²C*

Inter-Integrated Circuit (more commonly written as *I²C*, pronounced "I-squared-C") is a synchronous serial protocol created by Philips Semiconductor (which is now NXP). Although it's not quite as fast as SPI, I²C makes up for it with flexibility and simplicity—only two wires (figure 7.21)!

With I²C, you can have up to, oh, about a thousand devices on a single bus (1008 if you use 10-bit addressing; the more common 7-bit addressing allows up to 127). That means that you're back to the connection simplicity of async serial—minimal wires—but you get the benefits of sync serial—multiple devices and no advance configuration.

All of the data for all connected components is carried on a single SDA (serial data) line. The second wire is SCL (serial clock), which, like SDA, is shared by all of the

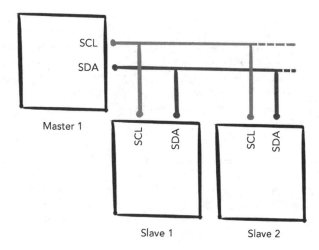

Figure 7.21 No matter how many devices are connected together, with I²C there are always just two lines: SCL (clock) and SDA (data).

connected components. Connect each device to the SDA and SCL lines (and give 'em some power!), and you're ready to go.

How I²C devices talk to each other

Because there are often many I²C components on the same bus, I²C messages have to be more structured, and something needs to take control of directing traffic. One or more *master* device on the bus has this authority. The active master (there can be more than one master device on a bus, but only one can be *actively* in charge at any given time) generates the clock signal and tells other devices when to transmit or receive data.

To start the ball rolling, the active master first transmits an *address* frame (first frame on left in the following figure) to determine which connected slave device needs to perform the subsequent action.

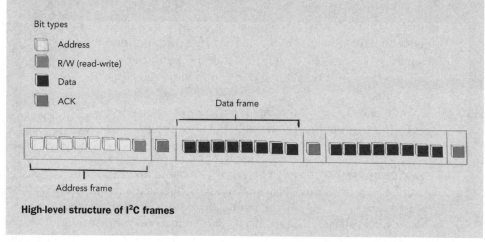

High-level structure of I²C frames

(continued)

Each connected device on the bus has its own, unique address. Commonly, this is a 7-bit address, and the full (8-bit) address frame consists of 7 address bits followed by a R/W (read/write) bit. The R/W bit designates whether the indicated device should read or write data. The addressed device is then expected to transmit a single ACK bit to indicate that all systems are go. Then data frames can be transmitted, each frame followed by an ACK bit. All this is choreographed by the shared clock signal.

The ins and outs of the protocol's details are a bit more involved—for example, you'd need to use 10-bit addresses to exercise the 1008-device bus maximum (7-bit numbers don't go higher than 127, and every device needs to have a unique address) and the exact mechanics of a read-from-slave process require identifying things like which memory register to read from. If you want to learn more, I recommend Sparkfun's "I²C" tutorial (https://learn.sparkfun.com/tutorials/i2c).

Many I²C devices ship with hardware-defined addresses. That means you can't change the device's address: if you have another device with the same (hard-wired) address, you won't be able to put them on the same bus. But some devices have configurable addresses.

7.4.3   *Making a digital compass with an I²C magnetometer*

What you'll need

- 1 Arduino Uno and USB cable
- 1 HMC5883L magnetometer (compass) 5 V-friendly breakout board, such as Adafruit's
- 1 half-size breadboard
- Red, black, yellow, and white jumper wires

The Honeywell HMC5883L is a popular I²C triple-axis *magnetometer* chip—that is, a compass—available on a 5 V-friendly breakout board from Adafruit. Determining your orientation is moments away, combining Johnny-Five's Compass class with a breakout board centered on the Honeywell chip.

You'll have to exercise your soldering skills again—the breakout board will need to be soldered onto header pins (figure 7.22) before it can slot into a breadboard.

Figure 7.22   The compass breakout board, like the GPS breakout, will need to be soldered onto header pins.

WATCH OUT FOR OPERATING VOLTAGES! Breakout boards for the HMC5883L are available from various electronics resellers, but make sure the board you choose can tolerate 5 V. Many, including Sparkfun's variant, are made for 3.3 V logic-level voltages. Connecting a 3.3 V compass to your Arduino's 5 V power and pin outputs can fry the chip. Adafruit's HMC5883L breakout board has an on-board *power regulator*, which makes it safe to provide anywhere from 3–5 V DC—it's a so-called "5 V-safe" component. Although there are ways to make 3.3 V components work safely with a 5 V board like the Uno, it requires some extra steps and hardware, so for now, make sure you have a 5 V-friendly breakout board.

As with the GPS breakout board, once the headers are soldered, the wiring is simple for this circuit: connect the breakout board's SDA pin to the Uno's A4 pin and the SCL to Uno pin A5. Connect VIN to the Arduino's 5 V power and connect the ground pin to GND (figure 7.23).

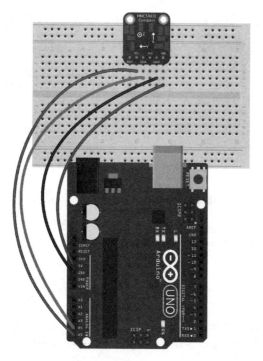

Figure 7.23   Wiring diagram for compass

I²C HARDWARE SUPPORT ON ARDUINO UNO   Note that the pin numbers for this circuit aren't arbitrary: Uno pins A4 and A5 have hardware support for I²C; other pins don't. The Uno's A4 pin provides SDA; A5 is SCL.

Johnny-Five's Compass class supports a number of different chips, so you'll need to let it know, during instantiation, which specific controller to use; see listing 7.4. The Johnny-Five Compass documentation identifies the supported components (http://johnny-five.io/api/compass/). You don't have to define which pins the compass is connected to, as there's only one way to connect I²C devices to the Uno board (pins A4 and A5).

Listing 7.4   Instantiating a Compass with a specific controller

```
const compass = new five.Compass({ controller: 'HMC5883L' });
```

Using a `controller` option to differentiate between different supported hardware is a common pattern in many of Johnny-Five's component classes. You first saw it in chapter 4, with the TMP36 analog temperature sensor.

Inside of your Johnny-Five working directory, create a file called compass.js, as shown in the following listing.

Listing 7.5 compass.js: reading HMC5883L data with Johnny-Five

```
const five = require('johnny-five');
const board = new five.Board();

board.on('ready', () => {
  const compass = new five.Compass({ controller: 'HMC5883L' });  ◁── Instantiates a Compass for the HMC588L chip
  compass.on('change', () => {  ◁── Compass object instances, like most other J5 component objects, have a change event.
    console.log(compass.bearing);  ◁── The bearing property is an object with information about the compass's orientation.
  });
});
```

Now run the script:

```
$ node compass.js
```

Once the board and REPL initialize, you'll see output in your terminal like this:

```
$ node compass.js
1479310483561 Device(s) /dev/cu.usbmodem1411
1479310483570 Connected /dev/cu.usbmodem1411
1479310485230 Repl Initialized
>> { name: 'East', abbr: 'E', low: 84.38, high: 95.62, heading: 94 }
{ name: 'East', abbr: 'E', low: 84.38, high: 95.62, heading: 91 }
```

Each `bearing` object being logged contains several properties (`abbr`, `heading`, and so on). This digital compass would be slicker if it had an output—we'll make one now.

7.5 *Pulling it together: shake-to-change multisensor widget*

This next experiment combines several I²C sensors together and displays output on an LCD. There are enough sensors here that it's tough to display all the output at once on the LCD, so we'll use an accelerometer to create a shake-to-swap-display feature. By shaking the device, you can toggle which data is displayed on the LCD: a screen with temperature and pressure data, or a screen with the current compass heading.

Pins A4 and A5 are the only I²C-compatible pins on the Arduino Uno, but that's just fine—the I²C protocol allows a whole bunch of devices on a single bus. That is, you can control multiple I²C devices using just those two pins.

What you'll need

- 1 Arduino Uno and USB cable
- 1 HMC5883L (compass) 5 V-friendly breakout board, such as Adafruit's

- 1 16x2 LCD: parallel or Johnny-Five-compatible I^{2}C LCD, such as the Grove-compatible JHD1313M1
- Adafruit 5 V-ready BMP180 breakout board (I^{2}C temperature, atmospheric pressure sensor)
- Adafruit ADXL345 triple-axis accelerometer
- Jumper wires
- 2 half-size breadboards or 1 full-size breadboard

Mixing and matching sensors

The specifics of this experiment's code and wiring are based on the items mentioned in the list of supplies, but you can mix and match other Johnny-Five-supported I^{2}C sensors:

- Other "multi" sensors (combining temperature, pressure, altimeters, and sometimes humidity): BME 280, BMP 280, HTU21D, and so on. See the Johnny-Five "Multi" API page for more supported I^{2}C devices: http://johnny-five.io/api/multi/.
- Other accelerometers. See the Johnny-Five "Accelerometer" API page for more supported I^{2}C accelerometers: http://johnny-five.io/api/accelerometer/.

Of course, you'll need to adapt the code examples to use the correct controllers for the hardware you choose.

Note that most of these sensors come on breakout boards that require you to solder header pins.

If you have a Johnny-Five-supported I^{2}C LCD like the Grove RGB LCD module on hand, you're in luck: it's a breeze to connect I^{2}C LCDs. A parallel LCD will work fine in this circuit, too, but, as you now know, it requires a slew more wires.

7.5.1 Step 1: combining a compass with LCD output

The wiring diagram in figure 7.24 shows how to orient the compass and LCD on two breadboards. (As you add sensors to this project, there won't be enough room on a single breadboard.)

WHY NOT USE THE GPS IN THIS EXPERIMENT? Using the GPS breakout in this combined-sensor project seems like it would be a nifty idea. However, Johnny-Five support for software serial is relatively fresh, and some of the complications of implementing software serial mean that it can be hard to predict how much data a sensor is going to communicate (the data exchange isn't structured like I^{2}C in that regard). Because of this, at the time of writing, combining a GPS with other sensors or output can cause garbage-y issues with the LCD's display and other unpredictable behavior.

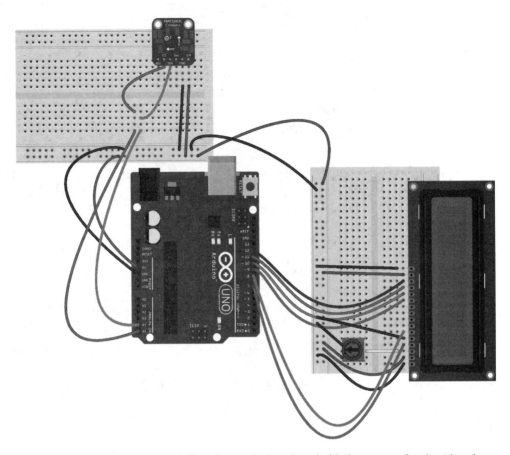

Figure 7.24   Wiring diagram, step 1. The wires on the breadboard with the compass breakout board are arranged to make room for sensors that will be added later.

CONFIGURING MAGNETIC DECLINATION FOR BETTER ACCURACY

One thing I like to do with my compass headings is correct them for my local *magnetic declination*. A compass will always give readings relative to *magnetic north*, which is in different places relative to true (geographic) north depending on where you are on the surface of the earth. In my locale, true north is about 14 degrees *west* of magnetic north—that is, there's a magnetic declination here of –14.28 degrees. You can find your magnetic declination by visiting www.magnetic-declination.com—we'll make use of it in the code for the device.

BUILDING THE MULTISENSOR CODE

Create a script called multi-sensor.js and start with this configuration code.

Listing 7.6 multi-sensor.js: configuration

Your local magnetic declination: this should be the value from www.magnetic-declination.com.

```
const five              = require('johnny-five');

const DECLINATION       = -14.28;
const UPDATE_FREQ_MS = 1000;
var lastDisplay      = null;

const board             = new five.Board();
```

How frequently to update the LCD's display

Keeps track of the last thing displayed on the LCD

Next, add a helper function to correct compass readings for local declination. The arithmetic in the following declination-correcting function will ensure that the returned value is a valid degree measurement between 0 and 360.

Listing 7.7 multi-sensor.js: correcting for declination

This function corrects a (Number) heading for local declination.

```
function correctForDeclination (heading, declination) {
  var corrected = heading + declination; // Recall: declination may be negative
  corrected += 360;
  while (corrected >= 360) {
    corrected -= 360;
  }
  return corrected;
}
```

Ensures corrected value is positive

Subtracts units of 360 (degrees) from corrected value until it's less than 360

And now, a formatting helper function to format the display of readings taken from the project's sensors. In this first round, shown in the following listing, it'll format a heading property—we'll populate it shortly with data from the compass.

Listing 7.8 multi-sensor.js: display formatting for compass heading

```
function formatDisplay (readings) {
  var displayLine1, displayLine2;
  displayLine1 = 'HEADING: ';
  displayLine2 = Math.round(readings.heading) + ':circle:';
  return [displayLine1, displayLine2];
}
```

Takes a readings object and returns what to display on each of the LCD's two lines

:circle: is a special character that can be displayed on the LCD.

Now, let's finish up this round of code.

Listing 7.9   multi-sensor.js: displaying compass heading

Tells the LCD to use the special circle character (for a degree marker)

```
/* ... */
function correctForDeclination (heading, declination) { /** ... **/ }
function formatDisplay (readings) { /** ... **/ }
```

Instantiates a parallel LCD

```
board.on('ready', () => {
  const compass      = new five.Compass({ controller: 'HMC5883L' });
  const lcd          = new five.LCD({ pins: [7, 8, 9, 5, 6, 12] });     ◁

  lcd.useChar('circle');
```

Corrects the compass reading for declination and populates readings.heading with the result

```
  function update () {
    var display = formatDisplay({
      heading: correctForDeclination(compass.heading, DECLINATION),    ◁
    });
    if (!lastDisplay || (lastDisplay.join('') != display.join(''))) {  ◁
      lcd.clear();
      lcd.cursor(0, 0).print(display[0]);
      lcd.cursor(1, 0).print(display[1]);
      lastDisplay = display;   ◁
    }
  }
```

Has the display value changed? If so, updates the LCD.

Keeps track of the last thing displayed

```
  board.loop(UPDATE_FREQ_MS, update);   ◁
});
```

Sets up a loop to invoke update every UPDATE_FREQ_MS milliseconds (1000 ms, in this example)

By only checking data every second (`board.loop` frequency) and only reprinting to the LCD if data has changed, performance is improved and excessive LCD flicker is avoided.

Try it out:

```
$ node multi-sensor.js
```

You should see a compass heading on your LCD—adjusted for magnetic declination and rounded to the nearest full degree. It should update every second as the compass is reoriented.

7.5.2   *Step 2: adding a multisensor to the device*

Johnny-Five's `Multi` component class is meant for devices like the BMP180, which combine *multiple sensors* into one package. Figure 7.25 shows Adafruit's BMP180 breakout board, which contains both temperature and atmospheric pressure sensors. Like the GPS and compass, the BMP180 board needs to be soldered onto header pins before use in a breadboard.

Figure 7.25   Adafruit's BMP180 breakout board

A `Multi` object behaves as a container for various sensor components and lets you interact with them in a coordinated manner. Each contained sensor is mapped to its own appropriate J5 component class. For example, the object instantiated as

```
const multi          = new five.Multi({ controller: 'BMP180' });
```

will contain the following instance properties:

- `thermometer`—A reference to a Johnny-Five `Thermometer` instance for the temperature sensor
- `barometer`—A reference to a Johnny-Five `Barometer` instance for the pressure sensor

The BMP180 uses I²C for communication, meaning you can connect it to the shared SDA and SCL line already in use by the compass (figure 7.26).

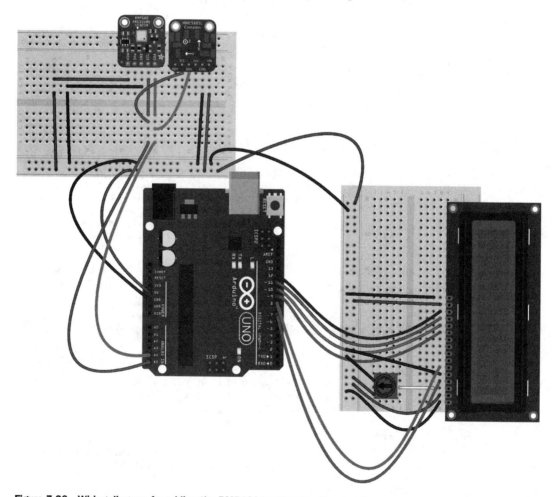

Figure 7.26 Wiring diagram for adding the BMP180 breakout to the circuit

7.5.3 *Step 3: updating the display to show temperature and pressure*

Displaying temperature, atmospheric pressure, and compass heading at the same time overcrowds the limited 16x2 character space on the LCD. It would be better if we split the display into two screenfuls: one to display temperature and pressure, and the other to show compass heading. In our first version, there won't be a way to swap between the two screens—it'll just show temperature and pressure—but we'll come back to that in a few moments.

First, add one more additional variable near the top of the file:

```
var altDisplay     = false;
```

This is simplistic way to help the program determine which screen—temperature and pressure, or compass heading—to display.

Now, update the display-formatting function, shown in the next listing.

> **Listing 7.10 multi-sensor.js: updating the display formatting**

This branch will never execute in this version of the code (it's always false).

Update to take an altDisplay parameter (Boolean).

```
function formatDisplay (readings, altDisplay) {     ◁
  var displayLine1, displayLine2;
  if (altDisplay) {
    displayLine1 = 'HEADING: ';
    displayLine2 = Math.round(readings.heading) + ':circle:';
  } else {
    displayLine1 = 'TEMP/PRESSURE:';
    displayLine2 = readings.temperature.toFixed(1) + ':circle:F';
    displayLine2 += ' / ' + Math.round(10 * readings.pressure) + 'mb';     ◁
  }
  return [displayLine1, displayLine2];
}
```

Pressure is in kPa; multiply by 10 and round to get more familiar millibars

Next, update the board's `ready` callback: instantiate a `Multi` sensor and pass more properties to the display-formatting function, as shown in the following listing.

> **Listing 7.11 multi-sensor.js: updating the board's ready callback**

Instantiates a Multi object for the BMP180

```
board.on('ready', () => {
  const compass       = new five.Compass({ controller: 'HMC5883L' });
  const lcd           = new five.LCD({ controller: 'JHD1313M1' });
  const multi         = new five.Multi({ controller: 'BMP180' });     ◁

  lcd.useChar('circle');

  function update () {
    var display = formatDisplay({
      temperature: multi.thermometer.F,     ◁
      heading    : correctForDeclination(compass.heading, DECLINATION),
```

Adds a temperature property from the BMP180's temperature value, in Fahrenheit

```
                                                        Adds a pressure property from
Passes the (currently always                            the BMP180's pressure sensor
false) altDisplay value
        pressure    : multi.barometer.pressure    ←
      },
  └─▷  altDisplay);
      if (!lastDisplay || (lastDisplay.join('') != display.join(''))) {
        lcd.clear();
        lcd.cursor(0, 0).print(display[0]);
        lcd.cursor(1, 0).print(display[1]);
        lastDisplay = display;
      }
    }

  board.loop(UPDATE_FREQ_MS, update);
});
```

Now try things out:

```
$ node multi-sensor.js
```

You should see the current temperature and pressure on the LCD's screen (but not the compass heading).

7.5.4 Step 4: adding a shake-to-swap display feature with an accelerometer

Accelerometers measure acceleration and orientation changes. By monitoring an accelerometer for acceleration—forces that exceed 1 G—you can create a shake-to-change display feature.

The ADXL345 triple-axis accelerometer breakout board from Adafruit (figure 7.27) is a 5 V-friendly accelerometer component that provides both I²C and SPI interfaces. Although the board's connections support both serial protocols, Johnny-Five's support for it uses the I²C interface (only).

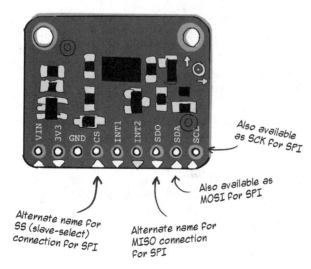

Figure 7.27   The ADXL345 triple-axis accelerometer breakout board from Adafruit. It can be connected to an I²C bus (via SDA and SCL pins) or, with some pins doing double duty as noted in the image, a four-wire SPI setup (via CS, SDO, SDA, and SCL pins).

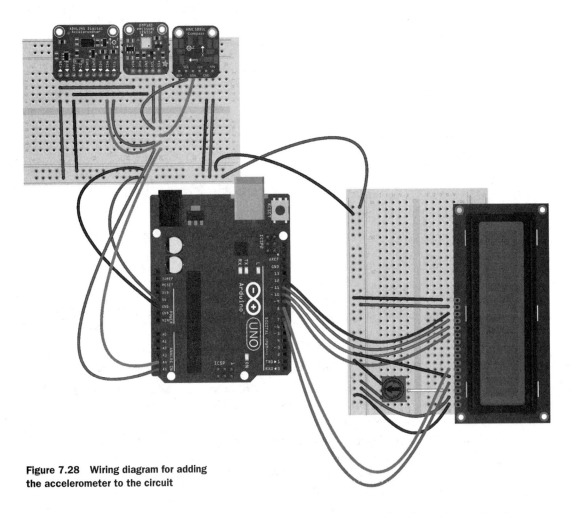

Figure 7.28   Wiring diagram for adding the accelerometer to the circuit

Add the accelerometer to the circuit (figure 7.28) once it's soldered onto header pins, connecting to the shared SDA and SCL rows on the breadboard.

The Johnny-Five `Accelerometer` class provides support for, you guessed it, accelerometers (J5 component classes are probably starting to feel old hat).

To implement the shake-to-swap display feature, we'll bind to the `Accelerometer` instance's `acceleration` event, which is fired when the device's acceleration reading has changed, and see if it exceeds a rough threshold that suggests a brisk, shaking-like movement.

Edit the following code.

First, add additional variables near the top of the file to set a shake threshold (in Gs) and to keep track of last shake detected, for debounce purposes:

```
const SHAKE_THRESHOLD = 1.15;
var lastJiggleTime = null;
```

Detecting and debouncing "shakes"

An `Accelerometer` object's `acceleration` event fires whenever the acceleration reading changes. In rough, unscientific experimentation, I found that a reasonable threshold for what should register as a shake is around 1.15 G. If you find that this is too sensitive or requires too energetic a shake, you can adjust the threshold in the code.

A real-life movement like a shake generates fluctuating acceleration values over the period of several device reads. That is, several sequential `acceleration` events are fired in a short amount of time, multiple times, with readings that exceed the threshold. If we implemented the swapping to switch displays each time the accelerometer reported acceleration above the threshold, the display would flicker wildly back and forth.

Instead, we need to *debounce* the swap, preventing it from occurring too frequently. We can do this by keeping track of the last time the display was swapped, and making sure we don't swap it more often than, say, once per second.

Inside the `ready` callback, instantiate the accelerometer:

```
const accel            = new five.Accelerometer({ controller: 'ADXL345' });
```

Also inside the `ready` callback function, add a handler for the `acceleration` event, shown in the following listing.

Listing 7.12 multi-sensor.js: acceleration handler

```
accel.on('acceleration', () => {
  if (accel.acceleration > SHAKE_THRESHOLD) {
    var jiggleTime = Date.now();
    if (!lastJiggleTime || jiggleTime > (lastJiggleTime + 1000)) {
      altDisplay     = !altDisplay;
      lastJiggleTime = Date.now();
      update();
    }
  }
});
```

If the current value of the acceleration property exceeds the G threshold...

If the display wasn't swapped within the past 1000 ms...

Update the display.

Flip the value of altDisplay.

Keep track of the time the swap happened.

It's done! Run.

```
$ node multi-sensor.js
```

Initially, you should see the temperature and pressure information displayed on the LCD. Pick up the breadboard with the sensors, and give it a brisk shake: you should see the LCD swap over to the compass-heading display.

By now, it's likely you've started noticing an elephant in the room. You've just built an orienteering-like device...that is chained by a cable to your laptop or computer.

Swapping in an I²C LCD: a case study

The wiring for the combined-sensor circuit is crowded, requiring two breadboards.

On the off chance you have an I²C-enabled LCD display hanging around (I did), you can use that instead of the parallel one. I used a Grove-compatible I²C LCD (part number, JHD1313M1). Grove is a system of components made by Seeed Studio that all share common connectors—but, alas, those connectors aren't compatible with headers or breadboards. You can purchase connector adapters, but in my case, I did some homebrew surgery: I cut the connector off the end and soldered the four stranded wires (VCC, GND, SCL, and SDA, just like any other I²C device) to solid-core hookup wire that slotted more easily into a breadboard.

The resulting circuit frees up a bunch of Uno pins and is much simpler overall. I²C is an ideal protocol for cutting down on the number of physical dev board I/O pins you'll need to support your project's components.

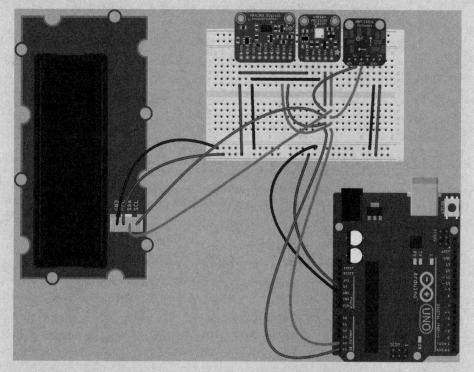

Wiring diagram using the Grove I²C LCD component. It can share the same SDA and SCL lines as the other connected sensors.

The only change to the orienteering code is in the LCD's instantiation. Instead of this,

```
const lcd = new five.LCD({ pins: [7, 8, 9, 5, 6, 12] });
```

use this:

```
const lcd = new five.LCD({controller: 'JHD1313M1'});
```

The Arduino and its attached components are helpless without the compute power on the host machine—that's where the Node.js process executes. This is, of course, a pretty ridiculous setup for hiking through the woods. Similarly, the robot you built in chapter 6 can only rove as far as its USB cable allows.

It's time to break free. In the next chapter, we'll start untethering our projects and setting them free.

Summary

- Although simple analog signals suffice for basic sensor data, reading data from more advanced components calls for a more structured way of exchanging information.
- Parallel communication is fast by its nature, but it can be cumbersome. Serial communication—one bit at a time—is the method of choice for exchanging data in hobby electronics.
- Asynchronous serial is commonplace, but it requires both devices to be configured for protocol specifics beforehand and is limited to two devices.
- TTL (transistor-transistor logic) is the type of async serial used on dev boards. UART hardware makes fast TTL serial possible on boards, but this type of serial communication can also be emulated in software (software serial).
- Synchronous serial protocols add a shared clock line to the communication bus. SPI is a protocol that requires three or four (data and clock) wires; the even more popular I^2C protocol only requires two wires.
- Serial components can be combined to make fun and more powerful projects. Although only two devices can exchange data over an async (TTL) serial connection, many devices can be added to the same SPI or I^2C buses, allowing more efficient use of development board I/O pins.
- I^2C can support up to 1008 devices on a single bus (with 10-bit addresses). Each device on the bus needs to have a unique address.
- Support for serial data exchange is usually provided at the hardware level (software serial emulation being the evident exception). On development boards, this is often dependent on the serial support provided by the microcontroller or processor.
- Serial connections are available only on certain pins. For the Arduino Uno, I^2C is supported on pins A4 (SDA) and A5 (SCL), SPI on pins 10 (SS), 11 (MOSI), 12 (MISO), and 13 (SCK).

Projects without wires

8

This chapter covers

- Why hobby electronics projects need wires, and how to get rid of them

- Using Johnny-Five with different I/O plugins on different platforms

- Configuring and working with the Tessel 2 development platform

- Adapting to 3.3 V logic levels and different pin configurations

- Deploying code wirelessly to the Tessel 2

- Taking advantage of the Node.js and npm ecosystem to create more complex software for the Tessel 2

- Using batteries to go fully wires-free with the Tessel 2

For this chapter, you'll need the following:

- 1 Tessel 2 development board

- 1 USB A to USB micro cable

- 1 standard LED, any color

- 1 100 Ω resistor
- 1 Adafruit BMP180 multisensor breakout board
- Any one of the following:
  - 3 female header pins
  - 2 lengths of 22-gauge, solid-core wire
  - 9 V battery and snaps
- Soldering iron and supplies
- 1 USB 5 V wall charger or similar, to power the Tessel 2
- 1 USB battery (sometimes called a *power bank*)
- Jumper wires
- 1 half-size breadboard
- Roving robot (motor-driving circuit and chassis) from chapter 6

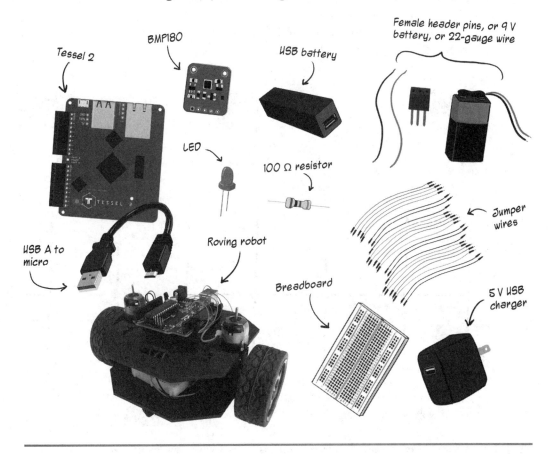

The things we're building are becoming more intricate and powerful, but there's a limiting factor: they're physically connected to a computer. These Arduino Uno-based Johnny-Five projects lack physical independence—they're wholly dependent on a host computer for logical instructions and power. For some kinds of projects, this tethered host-client setup isn't a problem. But to move further on your journey, to create JavaScript-controlled, autonomous, self-contained projects—to free yourself of wires—you'll need to expand your hardware horizons.

The ATmega328P microcontroller used on the Arduino Uno is too constrained to run a full operating system or execute JavaScript natively. If you want to control the Uno with JavaScript, you have to use something external and more powerful—a *host*—to execute the JavaScript on the board's behalf.

On the host, the logic in the JavaScript program needs to be translated into instructions the constrained microcontroller can understand. Those instructions then need to be communicated to the Uno, which acts as a thin *client*. Likewise, data coming from the Uno—sensor readings, and so on—are communicated back to the host for processing (figure 8.1).

With Johnny-Five, formatting and exchanging those instructions and data between host and client is the job of the *I/O layer*.

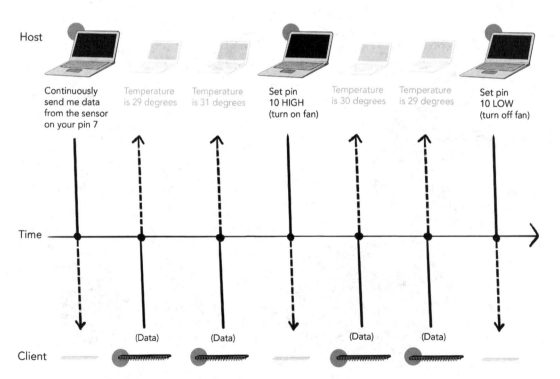

Figure 8.1 This sketch from chapter 1 outlines theoretical host-client communications for an automatic fan widget. In your experiments so far, the Arduino Uno has acted as a thin client, and your computer as the host.

Arduinos, including the Uno, are a special case with Johnny-Five: Firmata provides the I/O layer and is available by default in Johnny-Five. That is, when you instantiate a Board object, unless you tell it otherwise (with an option), Firmata (over USB) will be used for I/O. You've been using this default I/O in the previous chapters.

8.1 Why you've been tethered so far

You've used physical USB tethering for your projects thus far because the USB connection has provided both a means of I/O exchange and a supply of power. To unplug, you need to satisfy those requirements—I/O and power—in different ways, so let's dig deeper to see what's going on under the hood.

8.1.1 Data exchange, the I/O layer, and I/O plugins

Although Johnny-Five defines APIs and the logical behavior of components, exactly how data and instructions are exchanged between a Johnny-Five application and the hardware is left up to the *I/O layer*. This is how Johnny-Five keeps itself platform-agnostic: it leaves those details up to compatible *I/O plugins*.

You haven't been using any Johnny-Five I/O plugins up to this point because common Arduinos, including the Uno, are special cases with Johnny-Five. When you instantiate Board objects without specifying what I/O to use, Johnny-Five uses Firmata over USB by default—that's why it "just works." Unlike I/O plugins for other platforms, which have to be installed individually, Firmata comes with Johnny-Five (technically: it's a dependency). That can make it seem like Firmata and nitty-gritty I/O details are part of Johnny-Five's code, which isn't actually the case. As you try out Johnny-Five on other platforms, you'll see that you have to install appropriate I/O plugins. More on that in a bit.

In your host-client Johnny-Five setup with an Arduino Uno thus far, the USB cable serves as an umbilical cord for the exchange of serial Firmata-formatted messages. That's one reason you've been physically tethered.

8.1.2 USB as a power source

Something has to power the circuits in a project. The USB connection you've been using is a source of steady 5 V power. With the exception of a few inductive circuits—motors and servos, which require more current or voltage than the development board can provide—you've relied on the USB cable for power as well as for data exchange.

> **DC power for development boards**
>
> The Arduino Uno has a built-in DC barrel jack that you can use to connect it to a wall-powered DC adapter. Such "wall warts" are ubiquitous, converting wall-based AC power to the DC power that so many electronics hunger for.
>
> The wall warts of yore have barrel-jack connectors that can socket into anything from answering machines to your own development boards, like the Uno.

(continued)

DC-in barrel jack

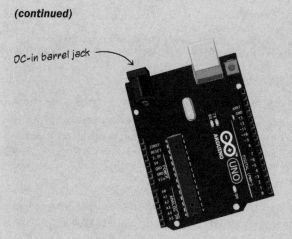

**The Uno has a DC-in
barrel jack for power**

Most dev boards (including the Uno) have onboard *voltage regulators* for their power inputs, which means it's OK to provide anywhere from 9 V to over 20 V to the Uno via DC, and it takes care of regulating that down to its needed 5 V.

Voltage regulators need to be provided with a higher voltage than their target output voltage. Like with LEDs, there's a forward voltage drop across the regulator itself—the power-adjusting circuitry on the board eats up some of the input voltage. In the Uno's case, to get a steady 5 V, at least 7 V input is needed.

Any 9 V–12 V DC adapter with center-positive polarity and a 5.5 mm x 2.5 mm plug (the most common size) is ideal for powering the Uno.

**This symbol indicates that the power adapter has center-positive polarity. That is, the tip of
the connector has positive polarity, and the sleeve is negative. A majority of DC wall warts
are center-positive polarity—that's the kind you want for powering the Uno and, typically,
other dev boards.**

Not all adapters have a polarity symbol printed on them. That's a pity, because you can't assume a given adapter is center-positive polarity—there's no default, although center-positive polarity is more common.

I keep a collection of DC wall warts, as well as 5 V USB chargers, at hand for use in projects. Long-since orphaned from their original consumer electronics, they're handy in their second life of providing power for various prototypes and projects.

8.1.3 Options for wires-free project communication

As you've seen, there are two main reasons projects have wires: data exchange and power. We'll tackle power momentarily, but let's first look at different ways to create projects that don't require physically tethered data connections.

WIRELESS HOST-CLIENT SETUPS

Certain development boards with constrained microcontrollers provide wireless communication capabilities, like WiFi or Bluetooth.

A host is still needed to execute JavaScript logic, but data and instructions can be exchanged between the host and client wirelessly—obviating the need for a physical USB data tether (figure 8.2).

The Blend Micro board can communicate using Bluetooth Low Energy (BLE).

The Particle Photon board can communicate over WiFi.

Figure 8.2 Like the Uno, these boards have constrained microcontrollers, but both can communicate wirelessly.

The Blend Micro board, for example, can be used wirelessly with Johnny-Five by making use of the blend-micro-io I/O plugin and using BLEFirmata firmware on the board. You'll meet another BLE-capable small board, Espruino's Puck.js, in chapter 12.

EMBEDDED JAVASCRIPT

Another class of development boards has microcontrollers that range from constrained to moderately sophisticated and are optimized to run JavaScript, some subset of JavaScript, or JavaScript-like code natively. The microcontrollers on these boards aren't cut out to run full-fledged OSs, but tend to be power-efficient, inexpensive, and small—all ideal characteristics for embedded systems.

Workflow varies from platform to platform. In some cases, the JavaScript you write might get compiled to something else (code that's more low-level and efficient) before being flashed to the device. In other cases, the board's microcontroller might be able to execute some subset of JavaScript directly—meaning you write in JavaScript, but you might not have access to every language feature (figure 8.3). We'll revisit constrained, embedded JavaScript platforms in chapter 10.

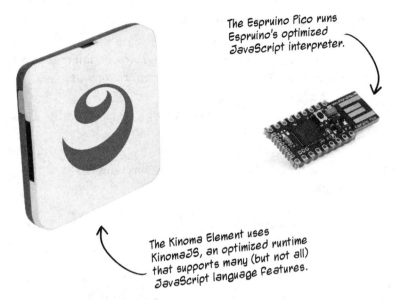

The Espruino Pico runs Espruino's optimized JavaScript interpreter.

The Kinoma Element uses KinomaJS, an optimized runtime that supports many (but not all) JavaScript language features.

Figure 8.3   This class of devices combines constrained microcontrollers with optimized variants of JavaScript and JavaScript-like runtimes. We'll explore both the Pico and the Element in chapter 10.

CONTROLLING A CLIENT WITH TINY COMPUTERS (SBCS)

Single-board computers (SBCs) are capable of running a real, multitasking operating system and provide a range of options in terms of processing power and onboard peripheral support. They can do a lot, including running Node.js, but they're correspondingly more power-hungry, more costly, and physically larger than other development boards for embedded projects.

With SBCs, the lines can be blurry between computer and dev board: some, like the popular Raspberry Pi series, combine generalized computing functionality with dev-board-like I/O on one board. Does that count as embedded logic execution, or is it a miniaturized variant of the host-client setup (with the Pi's processor serving as a host to control the I/O)? Things get even more convoluted because you can, for example, use a Raspberry Pi to control an Arduino attached to one of the Pi's own USB ports—a mini host-client setup. We'll look at more SBCs in chapter 11.

8.2   *Toward wires-free projects using the Tessel 2*

The Tessel 2 (https://tessel.io/) is an open source development platform (both the hardware and the software are open source) centered around Node.js and the npm package manager (figure 8.4). In addition to the kinds of basic I/O you've come to rely on—digital, analog, PWM, I²C, and so on—the Tessel 2 also has a few higher-level peripheral goodies, like USB ports, Ethernet, and—hooray!—WiFi. (The Tessel 2 is the only Tessel model currently available, so I'll generally just refer to it as the Tessel.)

The Tessel is an interesting and useful piece of hardware. Based on the "can run a real OS" criterion, it'd fall in the SBC category of devices—it ships with *OpenWrt*, a

Linux distribution commonly found on routers, preinstalled.

But the development workflow is more reminiscent of host-client setups and embedded-
JavaScript devices: you write code on your computer and deploy *to* the Tessel, as opposed to
writing code *on* it. And although the Tessel runs
OpenWrt and comes with some nifty software
goodies that we'll check out in a bit, it's more
constrained than SBC platforms like Raspberry
Pis. It only has 64 MB of RAM and 32 MB of Flash
space for programs. That's leagues beyond
what's available on ATmega328P-based boards
like the Uno, but it's not in the same ballpark as
a typical desktop computer.

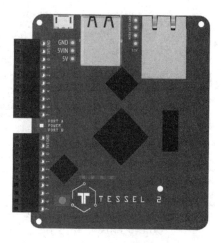

Figure 8.4   The Tessel 2 open source development board

After developing projects with Johnny-Five
for the Uno, you'll find many of the ergonomics with the Tessel familiar. Indeed, the
mechanics of working with the Tessel will feel old hat if you're used to developing with
or for Node.js in general.

There's one difference between the Tessel and the Arduino Uno that's essential to
note: the Tessel operates at 3.3 V versus the Uno's 5 V.

TESSEL 2 IS 3.3 V   The Tessel 2 operates at 3.3 V. You need to design circuits with
this in mind, and make sure to use 3.3 V-friendly components. Plugging 5 V
components or power into your Tessel 2's pins could do damage to the board.
Don't worry: we'll walk through the details as we go.

8.3   *Getting your Tessel set up*

What you'll need

- 1 Tessel 2
- 1 USB cable: USB A to USB micro

To get the Tessel ready for adventure, you need to connect it to your laptop with a USB
cable, just like with the Uno. But there are some big differences. For one, the JavaScript
code you'll write will get uploaded to and run on the Tessel itself—the Tessel doesn't
need a host to do its thinking for it. Also, the Tessel has WiFi, so you don't have to keep
it plugged into USB once it's set up—you can deploy to it wirelessly.

> **Tessel and Node.js LTS**
>
> The Tessel supports the Long Term Support (LTS) version of Node.js, which at the
> time of writing is at 6.11 (and by the time you read this, it'll likely be considerably
> further along). The code examples in this book will assume at least version 6.11, and
> the example scripts will make use of available language features in that version.
> Node.js versions newer than current LTS may not be compatible with the Tessel.

> **(continued)**
> Note that the version of Node.js running on the Tessel itself is likely different (and older) than your system Node.js version. Once your Tessel is configured, you can see what version of Node.js it's running onboard, as well as its firmware version, by using the `t2 version` command (more on the `t2` tool shortly).

8.3.1   Configuring the Tessel

The following explanations may make the setup steps feel lengthy, but the process takes just a few minutes in most cases.

STEP 1: INSTALL THE CLI

Install the command-line interface (CLI) for controlling your Tessel from your computer. This should be installed as a global npm package by entering the following command in your terminal:

```
$ npm install -g t2-cli
```

Once the module is installed, you'll be able to use the `t2` command in a terminal to control your Tessel.

> **t2 VS. t2-cli** The npm module is named `t2-cli`, but the command it makes available is `t2`.

STEP 2: CONNECT, FIND, AND RENAME YOUR TESSEL

Connect a USB cable from the USB micro port on your Tessel to a USB port on your computer. This will provide power to the Tessel, and you should see an LED blink as it boots (this can take about 30 seconds).

Find the Tessel by using this command in your terminal:

```
$ t2 list
```

You should see something like this.

Listing 8.1 `t2 list`

```
$ t2 list
INFO Searching for nearby Tessels...
    USB     Tessel-02A397D5D8A4
```

Yay! But `Tessel-02A397D5D8A4` isn't very catchy. Luckily, it's easy as pie to rename your Tessel with this command:

```
t2 rename <name>
```

I decided to call my Tessel `sweetbirch`. You can choose your own name.

Listing 8.2 `t2 rename`

```
$ t2 rename sweetbirch
INFO Looking for your Tessel...
INFO Connected to Tessel-02A397D5D8A4.
INFO Renaming Tessel-02A397D5D8A4 to sweetbirch
INFO Changed name of device Tessel-02A397D5D8A4 to sweetbirch
```

STEP 3: GET TESSEL ON WIFI AND PROVISION

Get your Tessel on your WiFi network with the following command:

```
$ t2 wifi -n <network-name> -p <password>
```

> **TESSEL'S WIFI COMPATIBILITY** It's usually easy to get a Tessel on a typical 2.4 GHz home WiFi network with a single command. But be aware, Tessels aren't, at this time, compatible with 5 GHz networks. If you run into trouble, head over to Tessel's WiFi connection setup page (http://tessel.github.io/t2-start/wifi.html) for more connection info.

Finally, provision the Tessel so that you can send code to it from your computer over WiFi:

```
$ t2 provision
```

The output of the `t2 list` command after provisioning should show the Tessel as available both on a USB connection and over WiFi (LAN), as shown in the next listing.

Listing 8.3 `t2 list` after provisioning

```
$ t2 list
INFO Searching for nearby Tessels...
    USB     sweetbirch
    LAN     sweetbirch
```

STEP 4: UPDATE YOUR TESSEL

Updates are released now and again for the Tessel's firmware. Make sure you have the latest version by running this command:

```
$ t2 update
```

If there are available updates, this process may take a few minutes.

Make sure your Tessel is still connected to USB and booted up. To get the LED-blinking code going on your Tessel, first initialize the project as shown in the following listing.

Listing 8.4 Initialize the Blinking-LED Tessel project

```
$ t2 init
INFO Initializing new Tessel project for JavaScript...
INFO Created ".npmrc".
INFO Created ".tesselinclude".
INFO Created "package.json".
```

The `t2 init` command

Newer releases of the `t2-cli` npm package require you to run the command `t2 init` within a project directory before that project's code can be deployed to your Tessel. You only need to do this once (per project). If you forget to run `t2 init`, you'll get a helpful message:

```
$ t2 run index.js
INFO Looking for your Tessel…
INFO Connected to sweetbirch.
WARN This project is missing an ".npmrc" file!
WARN To prepare your project for deployment, use the command:
WARN
WARN t2 init
WARN
WARN Once complete, retry:
WARN
WARN t2 run index.js
```

8.3.2 *"Hello World" LED blinking on the Tessel*

You can control the Tessel with JavaScript right out of the proverbial box—that's what the Tessel is made for. Create a file called hello-tessel.js and add the LED-blinking code in the following listing to it. This script will make one of the Tessel's built-in, onboard LEDs blink.

Listing 8.5   hello-tessel.js

```
const tessel = require('tessel');          ◁─┐ Imports the tessel
                                               hardware interface
tessel.led[2].on();          ◁──────┐
                               Starts by turning one of
         setInterval(function () {   the onboard LEDs on
Toggles      tessel.led[2].toggle();
LEDs         tessel.led[3].toggle();
every     }, 100);
100 ms  ▷

console.log("I'm blinking! (Press CTRL + C to stop)");
```

Now you can run the LED-blinking code on the Tessel by using the `t2 run <file>` command, as in the following listing. After the code deploys and starts running, you should see two of the Tessel's onboard LEDs blinking rapidly.

Listing 8.6   `t2 run`

```
$ t2 run hello-tessel.js --lan
INFO Looking for your Tessel...
INFO Connected to sweetbirch.
INFO Building project.
INFO Writing project to RAM on sweetbirch (89.088 kB)...
```

```
INFO Deployed.
INFO Running hello-tessel.js...
I'm blinking! (Press CTRL + C to stop)
```

THE `--lan` FLAG Johnny-Five scripts that log to the REPL (with `console`
`.log()`) do better if the script is deployed over a LAN (WiFi) connection. The
`--lan` flag for the `t2 run` command specifies that the WiFi connection should
be used (versus the wired `usb` connection).

UNDERSTANDING THE "HELLO TESSEL" EXAMPLE

There are some familiar-looking things in the hello-tessel.js code, but some details are
unique to the Tessel (as compared to controlling the Uno with Johnny-Five).

The first thing in the code is the requirement of a library called `tessel`:

```
var tessel = require('tessel');
```

Sharp-eyed observers may note that this is curious: you never `npm install`-ed any such
library or otherwise made it available to the code on your computer. The Tessel 2 Hardware API documentation (http://mng.bz/Ror5) explains this `require` statement:

> *When you* `require('tessel')` *within a script which is executed on Tessel 2, this
> loads a library which interfaces with the Tessel 2 hardware, including pins, ports, and
> LEDs...*

An important piece of the puzzle here is the phrase "executed on Tessel 2." It's true: if
you tried to run the hello-tessel.js script with Node.js on your own computer, you
wouldn't get far—you'd encounter an error about the missing module. You won't find
the `tessel` package on npm, either. Instead, `tessel` is a JavaScript API library preinstalled on the Tessel itself, and therefore available to scripts that run on Tessel 2.

Turning on and toggling the Tessel's onboard LEDs via the `tessel` object looks sort
of like working with Johnny-Five `Led` objects, but not quite:

```
tessel.led[2].on();
tessel.led[2].toggle();
tessel.led[3].toggle();
```

The `tessel` object gives you access to the ports and pins on the Tessel board, exposing
a hardware API to work with them. It's a lower-level API than Johnny-Five: you can read
and write digital, analog, and serial data, but there are no higher-level objects that
wrap, say, a temperature sensor. The Tessel 2 Hardware API documentation provides
lots more information (http://mng.bz/Ror5).

8.3.3 *Blinking an external LED with the Tessel*

What you'll need

- 1 Tessel 2
- 1 USB to USB-micro cable
- 1 standard LED

- 1 100 Ω resistor
- Jumper wires
- 1 full-size breadboard

Honoring the age-old tradition of the blinking-LED "Hello World," let's sink our teeth further into the Tessel with this classic first circuit. Instead of blinking an onboard LED, this example uses an externally connected LED. Although this experiment is pedestrian in scope, it will introduce you to the workflow and structure of Tessel projects.

> ### Tessel project structure
> Instead of writing one-off, standalone scripts as you did with the Uno, you'll structure each Tessel experiment as a proper Node.js project:
>
> - Each experiment will have its own working directory.
> - You'll use a package.json file to manage dependencies.
> - The main (entry point) script for experiments will be named index.js.
>
> If you're experienced with writing software with Node.js, this structure will look familiar.

SETTING UP A JOHNNY-FIVE TESSEL PROJECT

Before writing any code, set up the working area for the project. You'll need to create a directory and set up a package.json file using the `npm init` command. Open up a terminal and execute the following commands:

```
mkdir t2-blink
cd t2-blink
npm init -y
```

Running `npm init` will typically walk you through an interactive set of questions to set up your project. Adding the `-y` flag will skip those steps and create a package.json file with default settings. It's a faster way to get started if you're not concerned with your project's specific configuration details. Once you've run `npm init`, you'll have a package.json file.

WIRING THE 3.3 V LED CIRCUIT

Though you've build a basic LED-blink circuit before, a little arithmetic is in order to adjust for Tessel's 3.3 V supply voltage. The circuit is similar to the basic LED circuit for the Uno you built in chapter 3 (figure 8.5), but you'll need a different current-limiting resistor to account for the Tessel's 3.3 V logic.

Back in chapter 3, you made a calculation for the needed current-limiting resistor for a single LED in a series circuit by taking into account both the Uno's operating voltage (5 V) and an approximation of an LED's forward voltage (~1.8 V). You came up with this:

```
5.0 V (supply voltage)
- 1.8 V (red LED forward voltage)
-------------------------------
= 3.2 V ("remaining" voltage in the circuit)
```

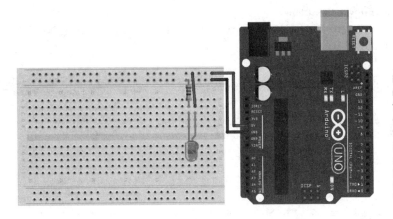

Figure 8.5 The original basic LED circuit for the Uno. The Uno operates at 5.5 V, whereas the Tessel is a 3.3 V device. The circuit needs to be adjusted for the different voltage of the Tessel.

Targeting 20 mA of current for the LED, you then used Ohm's law:

```
Resistance (R) = Voltage (V) / Current (I)
         R  = 3.2 V      / 0.02 A
----------------------------------------
             = 160 Ω
```

160 Ω isn't a common resistance value, so you rounded up to 220 Ω (which is a common value).

Adjust the values for the 3.3 V supply on the Tessel:

```
3.3 V (supply voltage)
- 1.8 V (red LED forward voltage)
--------------------------------
= 1.5 V ("remaining" voltage in the circuit)

Resistance (R) = Voltage (V) / Current (I)
         R  = 1.5 V      / 0.02 A
----------------------------------------
             = 75 Ω
```

75 Ω isn't a common resistance value, but 100 Ω is—a 100 Ω resistor will do just fine here! It makes sense that a lower resistance value is called for than in the 5 V circuit: there's less voltage left over after the LED voltage drop to account for.

Wire the circuit as shown in the Tessel LED wiring diagram (figure 8.6).

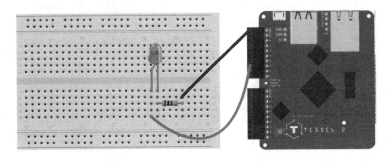

Figure 8.6 Connect the LED's anode to Tessel's port A, pin 5, and its cathode to the GND connection on port A.

WRITING THE LED-BLINKING CODE

In chapter 2, the blinking-LED experiment for the Arduino Uno using Johnny-Five used the following code.

Listing 8.7   led.js

```
const five = require('johnny-five');
const board = new five.Board();

board.on('ready', () => {
  const led = new five.Led('13');
  led.blink(500);
});
```

When the board is ready... → `board.on('ready', () => {`

Blinks the LED → `led.blink(500);`

Instantiates a Board object with no non-default options → `const board = new five.Board();`

Instantiates an Led, connected to pin 13 → `const led = new five.Led('13');`

There isn't much that needs changing to make this work with the Tessel. You need to account for two things:

- The Tessel needs different I/O-layer support to work with Johnny-Five. You'll need to make your Board object use tessel-io for its I/O (instead of the default firmata).
- The pin number that the LED is attached to needs to be updated.

Start by running the following command in your t2-blink working directory:

```
$ npm install --save johnny-five tessel-io
```

This will install the johnny-five and tessel-io packages locally and save the dependencies into the package.json file. You know the johnny-five package well already. tessel-io is the Johnny-Five I/O plugin for the Tessel.

Create a file called index.js in the same directory, and add the following code.

Listing 8.8   index.js

```
const five = require('johnny-five');
const Tessel = require('tessel-io');
const board = new five.Board({
  io: new Tessel()
});

board.on('ready', () => {
  const led = new five.Led('A5');
  led.blink(500);
});
```

Tells the Board to use tessel-io for I/O → `io: new Tessel()`

Requires the tessel-io package → `const Tessel = require('tessel-io');`

The LED is connected to port A, pin 5 on the Tessel. → `const led = new five.Led('A5');`

This code is remarkably similar to the Uno-compatible code. The only differences are the I/O plugin and the pin number. Go ahead and try it out by using the t2 run command:

```
$ t2 run index.js
```

You should see output similar to the next listing, and the LED should start blinking.

Listing 8.9   Running the LED-blink code on the Tessel

```
$ t2 run index.js
INFO Looking for your Tessel...
INFO Connected to sweetbirch.
INFO Building project.
INFO Writing project to RAM on sweetbirch (746.496 kB)...
INFO Deployed.
INFO Running index.js...
1484926245789 Device(s) Tessel 2 (Tessel-02A397D5D8A4)
1484926245946 Connected Tessel 2 (Tessel-02A397D5D8A4)
1484926246003 Repl Initialized
>>
```

8.3.4   *Exploring the Tessel's pins and capabilities*

Like the Arduino Uno, different pins on the Tessel do different things. There are 16 I/O pins on the Tessel, split between two ports (figure 8.7).

Pins are numbered A0–A7 (on port A) and B0–B7 (on port B). The top two pins in each physical port provide power connections (GND and 3.3 V). Other features, like I²C, SPI, and UART (asynchronous/TTL serial) are supported on specific pins (figure 8.8).

Although all pins can be used as digital I/O pins, analog input (ADC) is available on

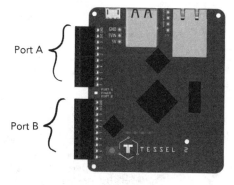

Figure 8.7   The Tessel's pins are divided into two "ports," each with 8 I/O pins.

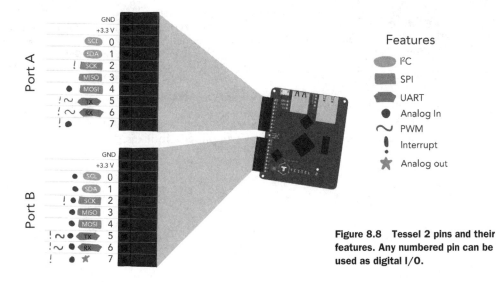

Figure 8.8   Tessel 2 pins and their features. Any numbered pin can be used as digital I/O.

pins A4 and A7 and on all port B pins. You can also see that some pins support interrupts (meaning they would be viable for "listening" for button presses or for other applications that need to accurately detect a change from LOW to HIGH or vice versa). Some, but not all, pins support PWM.

Pin B7 has a capability we haven't run into yet: analog *out.* That pin can provide digital-to-analog conversion (DAC). We won't explore that capability directly, but it is available on the Tessel.

8.4　*Projects without wires on the Tessel*

Hey, wait! The LED example still has you tethered. Next you'll start removing some wires.

First, you'll untether the Tessel from your computer but use a wall outlet to provide power.

What you'll need

- 1 Tessel 2
- 5 V–12 V USB charger
- 1 LED
- 1 100 Ω resistor
- 1 half-size breadboard

Wall power for the Tessel

If your Tessel didn't come with a USB DC adapter, you can use a 5 V USB charger, like a tablet or phone charger, to power the Tessel.

Like the Arduino Uno's DC input jack, the Tessel's USB micro connection has a power regulator to regulate input voltage down to the needed 3.3 V. The standard 5 V (USB voltage) is just right for input voltage.

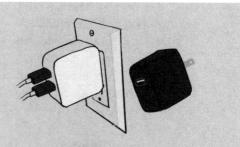

USB wall adapters that provide 5 V DC power are widespread. They're especially popular as chargers for phones and tablets.

Just to prove you can, you'll adapt the LED blink code a bit to make the LED pulse. You can do this because the LED is connected to a PWM-capable pin on the Tessel.

To make that change, find the following line in index.js:

```
led.blink(500);
```

Replace it with this:

```
led.pulse(500);
```

Now, plug your Tessel into wall power anywhere you like, as long as it's within range of the same WiFi network that your computer's on. Allow it time to boot before trying to deploy code to it.

Now, back at your computer, you can try deploying in a slightly different fashion. In your working directory, execute this command:

```
t2 push index.js
```

The t2 push command differs from the t2 run command. With t2 run, the Node.js process will execute on the Tessel only until the host computer kills the process (typically via Ctrl-C). With t2 push, the program will be flashed to the Tessel and will run as long as the Tessel has power. If you unplug the Tessel and plug it back in again, it will resume executing the program.

Now you have an LED pulsing somewhere yonder, but that's not terrifically exciting. It's time to build something a little more functional that can also hook into the Node.js ecosystem available on the Tessel. You can use the Tessel as an independent weather station: reading data from one or more sensors and serving that data by running a local web server (figure 8.9).

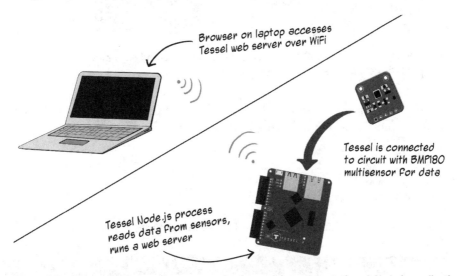

Browser on laptop accesses Tessel web server over WiFi

Tessel is connected to circuit with BMP180 multisensor for data

Tessel Node.js process reads data from sensors, runs a web server

Figure 8.9 A Tessel serves as the nerve center for a mini weather station. A Node.js application running on the Tessel will read data from the BMP180 multisensor and run a web server so that other computers on the same WiFi network can view weather information in a web browser.

8.4.1 *Wires-free data: a remote weather station*

What you'll need

- 1 Tessel 2
- 1 USB-micro to USB-A cable
- 1 5 V–12 V USB charger

- 1 Adafruit BMP180 I²C multisensor
- Jumper wires
- 1 half-size breadboard

There's a nifty feature of the Adafruit I²C sensors used in chapter 7: they're happy at both 5 V and 3.3 V. Their breakout boards each contain voltage regulator hardware and can handle level shifting—that is, they can account for the different logic-level voltages of 3.3 V and 5 V microcontrollers. You can use these sensors as easily with the Tessel as with the Arduino Uno.

The circuit is straightforward: wire the BMP180 I²C sensor to the Tessel as shown in figure 8.10.

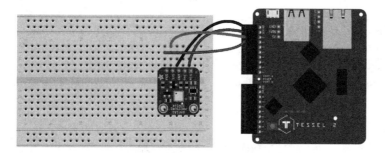

Figure 8.10   Connect the BMP180 I²C sensor to power (GND and 3.3 V pins of port A), SCL (A0), and SDA (A1).

In your terminal application, set up a new working project directory and install dependencies in the same way as for the LED example:

```
mkdir t2-weather
cd t2-weather
npm init -y
npm install --save johnny-five tessel-io
```

Create a file called index.js and add the following code.

Listing 8.10   index.js

```
const five = require('johnny-five');
const Tessel = require('tessel-io');

const board = new five.Board({
  io: new Tessel()              ⟵─┐ Don't forget to specify
});                                │ tessel-io as the I/O layer.

board.on('ready', () => {
  const weatherSensor = new five.Multi({
    controller: 'BMP180'
  });
```

```
weatherSensor.thermometer.on('change', function () {
  console.log(this.F);
});
});
```

When the change event fires on the sensor's thermometer instance...

...logs out the current reading in Fahrenheit

As with the previous LED-blinking code, the abstraction of I/O out of Johnny-Five core components makes this code look nearly identical to how you'd use an I²C sensor on the Arduino Uno. In fact, the only difference here is that you're passing a different I/O plugin option when creating the `Board` object. You don't have to mess with pin numbers because the `board` already knows which pins support I²C on the Tessel (and it will default to port A).

The preceding code accesses the `thermometer` instance via `weatherSensor`. A `Multi` object instance for controller `BMP180` contains `thermometer` and `barometer` properties, which are references to component class instances representing the BMP180's temperature and pressure sensors. Each multisensor component generates events independently, and events are also aggregated up to the `Multi` instance collectively:

```
weatherSensor.on('change', () => {
  // This will get invoked any time ANY of the multi component's sensors
  // have a change
});

weatherSensor.barometer.on('change', () => {
  // This gets invoked only when the barometer's reading changes
});
```

Other *collection* component classes in Johnny-Five (such as `Buttons` and `Leds`) behave in a similar fashion.

With your Tessel connected via USB for now, use `t2 run` to try the script out on the Tessel:

```
$ t2 run index.js --lan
```

You should see something like this:

```
$ t2 run index.js --lan
INFO Looking for your Tessel...
INFO Connected to sweetbirch.
INFO Building project.
INFO Writing project to RAM on sweetbirch (440.832 kB)...
INFO Deployed.
INFO Running index.js...
1487876926840 Device(s) Tessel 2 (sweetbirch)
1487876926995 Connected Tessel 2 (sweetbirch)
1487876927051 Repl Initialized
>> 72.14
72.32
72.14
72.32
```

To do something useful with the sensor's readings—something more intuitive and visual—you'll take advantage of the Tessel's ability to support npm packages and execute more sophisticated Node.js code—let's see how to build a web app.

BUILDING MORE SOPHISTICATED APPS ON THE TESSEL

To serve web content from the Tessel, you'll need to create a few additional files. At the very least, you'll need to start with a basic HTML document.

Create a directory called "app" inside the t2-weather directory. Create an index.html file inside of that directory, as shown in the following directory structure.

Listing 8.11   Project directory and file structure, so far

```
t2-weather/
├── app
│   └── index.html
├── index.js
├── node_modules
└── package.json
```

Open up index.html and add the following content.

Listing 8.12   index.html

```html
<!DOCTYPE html>
<html lang="en">
 <head>
  <title>Current Conditions</title>
 </head>
 <body>
  <h1>Current Conditions</h1>
  <p>Data coming soon!</p>
 </body>
</html>
```

When you execute code on the Tessel, the Tessel knows to copy over and use the script you're running as well as the Node.js modules installed for the project. But you need to tell it explicitly if it needs to use assets outside of those items. You can do this by placing a .tesselinclude file in the root level of your project.

Create a .tesselinclude file and add the following to it:

```
app/
```

Each line in a .tesselinclude is a *glob*, a pattern for matching files. For example, app/ matches all the files in the app directory. This will ensure that the Tessel copies over all of the files in the app directory when it deploys.

After adding .tesselinclude, your file structure should look like this.

Listing 8.13 Project directory and file structure with .tesselinclude

```
t2-weather/
├── .tesselinclude
├── app
|   └── index.html
├── index.js
├── node_modules
└── package.json
```

Next, you'll tackle building a web app to show weather station data in two steps:

1 You'll set up a basic, static web server by combining the Express (http://expressjs.com/) web application framework with built-in Node.js modules. This will serve a basic web page that will be the container for the weather station data.

2 You'll set up a socket.IO server on the Tessel (the web server) and connect to it from the client (from the JavaScript that runs in the browser). You'll also spiff up the HTML with some CSS and structured markup.

SETTING UP A STATIC WEB SERVER

You'll start simple by spinning up a basic, static web server in your app's code. *Static* here means that the web server will deliver assets (like HTML, images, JavaScript, and the like) without performing any dynamic, server-side processing on them—it'll just deliver the files it's asked for from a designated directory.

Begin by installing the express web framework. Make sure you're in the t2-weather directory, and execute the following command in a terminal:

```
$ npm install --save express
```

Returning now to the index.js script, add the following code to the top of the file.

Listing 8.14 index.js

```
const five = require('johnny-five');
const Tessel = require('tessel-io');          Requires
const express = require('express');           Express

const path = require('path');                 Requires some built-in
const http = require('http');                 Node.js modules
const os = require('os');
                                              Instantiates a
var app = express();                          new Express app
app.use(express.static(path.join(__dirname, '/app')));    Tells the app to serve
var server = new http.Server(app);                        static assets out of the
                                                          app/ directory
const board = new five.Board({
  io: new Tessel()              Creates an HTTP server
});                            and passes it the app

board.on('ready', () => {
  const weatherSensor = new five.Multi({
```

```
     controller: 'BMP180'
   });
   server.listen(3000, () => {
     console.log(`http://${os.networkInterfaces().wlan0[0].address}:3000`);
   });
 });
```

Makes the server listen for requests on port 3000

Omit or comment out the console.log lines from the previous version.

It's not necessary to npm install the modules os, path, or http because they're built into Node.js.

Try it out!

```
$ t2 run index.js --lan
```

You should see results like the following.

Listing 8.15   Running index.js

```
$ t2 run index.js
INFO Looking for your Tessel...
INFO Connected to sweetbirch.
INFO Building project.
INFO Writing project to RAM on sweetbirch (933.376 kB)...
INFO Deployed.
INFO Running index.js...
1487884455497 Device(s) Tessel 2 (sweetbirch)
1487884455635 Connected Tessel 2 (sweetbirch)
1487884455691 Repl Initialized
>> http://192.168.1.16:3000
```

The app is getting larger as you add more dependencies.

This is the Tessel's internal address and actively listening HTTP port.

You can now open up a web browser and view the URL logged in the console (make sure you use the URL that displays in your output—not the one shown in the preceding example output).

The Tessel's IP address

Your Tessel needs to be connected to the same network as your computer for this experiment to work. This will likely be a WiFi network, as discussed in the setup section, though the Tessel does also have an Ethernet port.

Being connected to the network results in the Tessel being assigned its own IP address, which you'll need to know to access the web server running on it. The following line in the index.js code conveniently displays this for you:

```
console.log(`http://${os.networkInterfaces().wlan0[0].address}:3000`);
```

You can copy and paste the output of this from your terminal app into a browser's URL bar. Visiting the output URL in a browser will render the current index.html file (figure 8.11).

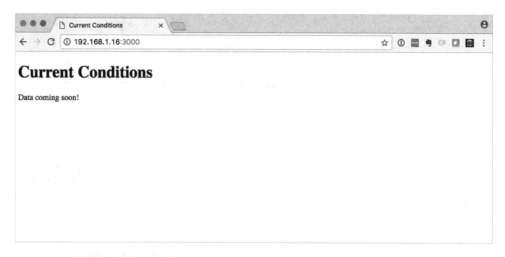

Figure 8.11   Nothing fancy! Navigating to the Tessel's IP address and port in a browser displays the index.html file, which doesn't do anything much yet.

USING SOCKET.IO TO DISPLAY LIVE DATA

One option for a simple web app would be to include the current sensor values within the markup of the HTML document that's served. This is a perfectly valid approach, and it follows a traditional HTTP model: the browser is in charge of asking the server for more data, in the form of a full document (web page) request. The side effect is that a user would have to reload the page in the browser to see new readings.

There's a better way!

The WebSocket API is a web standard that lets a client (a browser) and a server exchange asynchronous messages over a single TCP *socket*. Each can push messages to the other, allowing for the exchange of near-real-time data.

WebSocket is supported by many, but not all, browsers. To help plug the gaps, you'll use Socket.IO, an API that uses WebSocket when it can (when the browser supports it), but that has a long list of other fallback transports to emulate WebSocket behavior. In short, it makes using WebSocket features easy and worry-free.

With Socket.IO, when sensor readings change, the socket server can "push" the new data to the client (assuming the client is listening for it and does something useful with the updated data). The net effect is that you can make the sensor readings update in the browser frequently, without page reloads.

The first step is to install the `socket.io` npm package:

```
npm install --save socket.io
```

Next, update the contents of index.js with the following code.

Listing 8.16   index.js

```
const five    = require('johnny-five');
const Tessel  = require('tessel-io');
const express = require('express');
const SocketIO = require('socket.io');                  Requires the
                                                        socket.io library

const path = require('path');
const http = require('http');
const os   = require('os');

const app    = new express();
const server = new http.Server(app);                    Creates the
const socket = new SocketIO(server);                    socket.io server
app.use(express.static(path.join(__dirname, '/app')));

const board = new five.Board({ io: new Tessel() });

board.on('ready', () => {
  const weatherSensor = new five.Multi({
    controller: 'BMP180',                               Has Johnny-Five reduce the
    freq: 5000                                          frequency of sensor reads
  });                                                   down to five seconds

  socket.on('connection', client => {                   Registers a callback for when a
    weatherSensor.on('change', () => {                  client requests a connection
      client.emit('weather', {
        temperature: weatherSensor.thermometer.F,
        pressure: (weatherSensor.barometer.pressure * 10)
      });
    });
  });

  server.listen(3000, () => {
    console.log(`http://${os.networkInterfaces().wlan0[0].address}:3000`);
  });
});
```

Dialing down the sensor-read frequency to every five seconds keeps performance within bounds and establishes a reasonable threshold for how often the client will receive new data over the socket. Every five seconds is the maximum frequency that the socket server will trigger updates, because the weather event will only get fired if the sensor readings change.

Let's examine the Socket.IO connection handling more closely in the following listing.

Listing 8.17   index.js

```
// Register a callback for when a client (browser) tries to connect.
// The callback is passed a reference to the `client`
socket.on('connection', client => {
  // Listen for change events on the J5 Multi (representing the BMP180)
  weatherSensor.on('change', () => {
```

```
    // Emit a `weather` event on the client
    // And pass an object representing current sensor values
    // The client can listen for this event and handle it accordingly
    client.emit('weather', {
      // This is the temperature in Fahrenheit;
      // change to `C` if you'd prefer Celsius
      temperature: weatherSensor.thermometer.F,
      // Multiplying by 10 converts the sensor's readings in kilopascals
      // to more commonly used millibar units
      pressure: (weatherSensor.barometer.pressure * 10)
    });
  });
});
```

CODE NOT PRODUCTION-WORTHY   The code in these examples is pared down to a minimum for clarity and brevity. That's fine for at-home prototyping, but the code in index.js isn't production-ready. In a "real" codebase, you'd want to be sure that the socket server doesn't willy-nilly accept every incoming connection, that a maximum number of connections is enforced, and so on. In addition, although the index.html markup contains valid HTML, it lacks a few accessibility and polish niceties, and greater care could be taken in the CSS for supporting older browsers and diverse browsing environments (such as mobile devices).

The socket server won't be too useful if there isn't also a client that takes advantage of it. First, you need to prepare the HTML to display sensor values by adding some structured markup, as shown in the next listing.

Listing 8.18   index.html

```
<!DOCTYPE html>
<html lang="en">
<head>
  <script src="/socket.io/socket.io.js"></script>        ⟵ Includes the client socket.io JavaScript
  <link rel="stylesheet" href="style.css" type="text/css" />   ⟵ You'll create this CSS file shortly.
  <title>Current Conditions</title>
</head>
<body>
                                    ⟵ Marks the content up in some container elements that will render as a row
  <main role="main">
    <h1>Current Conditions</h1>
    <div class="row">
      <div class="col">
        <div class="data">
          <h2>Temperature</h2>
          <span class="data--value" id="temperature">--.--</span>   ⟵
          <small class="data--unit">F</small>
        </div>
      </div>
      <div class="col">                              The .data—value spans will be populated with sensor data.
        <div class="data">
          <h2>Pressure</h2>
```

```
            <span class="data--value" id="pressure">---.--</span>
            <small class="data--unit">mBar</small>
          </div>
        </div>
      </div>
    </main>

  </body>
</html>
```

This line may be causing you to scratch your head:

```
<script src="/socket.io/socket.io.js"></script>
```

Where'd that JavaScript file "magically" come from?

In index.js, you started up socket.io by giving it a `server` instance—it makes client-side code available automatically, via the server, at /socket.io/socket.io.js.

As for this line:

```
<link rel="stylesheet" href="style.css" type="text/css" />
```

You'll make that stylesheet now. Within the t2-weather directory, navigate into the app subdirectory and create a file called style.css. Add the following code to it.

Listing 8.19   style.css

```
html {
    font-family    : "Helvetica Neue", "Helvetica", "Arial", san-serif;
}
.row {
  display          : flex;
  justify-content  : center;
  max-width        : 48rem;
  margin           : auto;
}
.row .col {
  margin           : auto;
  padding          : 2rem;
}
h1, h2 {
  margin           : 0;
  text-align       : center;
}
h2 {
  font-size        : 1.5rem;
}
small {
  color            : #999;
  font-size        : 0.65em;
}
.data {
  padding          : 1.5rem;
```

```
  background-color: #eee;
  border-radius    : 10px;
  font-size        : 3rem;
}
.data--value {
  font-weight      : bold;
}
.connected { /* Make font color green to show that websockets updating works
      */
  color            : #093;
}
```

CSS flexbox

The CSS here makes use of the "flexible box" layout mode, a.k.a. *flexbox*. Flexbox allows you to arrange and position elements without the confusion of floats and collapsing margins. Flexbox is increasingly well supported, but if you're using Internet Explorer, things may lay out a bit funky (Edge browsers do, however, support flexbox). If all this is gibberish, not to worry. The CSS here just styles the web page and isn't critical to understanding the functionality of the project.

Listing 8.20   Complete file and directory structure of project

```
t2-weather/
├── .tesselinclude
├── app
│   ├── index.html
│   └── style.css
├── index.js
├── node_modules
└── package.json
```

Now, finally, the linchpin. The client needs to connect to the socket server, listen for relevant events (weather, in this case), and respond to them in some useful manner. Return to index.html and add the following code to the file, just before the body closing tag (</body>).

Listing 8.21   index.html

When the page's DOM is all loaded...

Create a Socket.IO client.

Handler function for the weather event: parses updated data and updates page display

```
<script>
  window.addEventListener('DOMContentLoaded', function () {
    var socket = io();
    socket.on('weather', updateData);
  });
  function updateData (data) {
    ['temperature', 'pressure'].forEach(function (dataPoint) {
      document.getElementById(dataPoint).innerHTML =
        data[dataPoint].toFixed(2);
```

Register a callback for weather events.

```
    });
    document.querySelectorAll('.data--value').forEach(function (el) {
      el.classList.add('connected');
    });
  }
</script>
```

Let's look more closely at the preceding code.

When the DOM has loaded, you need to create a Socket.IO client and tell it to invoke a callback (updateData) whenever a weather event happens:

```
window.addEventListener('DOMContentLoaded', function () {
  var socket = io();
  socket.on('weather', updateData);
});
```

WHERE'D IO() COME FROM?   The io function, for initializing a Socket.IO client, is made available globally via the inclusion of the /socket.io/socket.io.js script.

The updateData function takes the updated data object and updates the page's DOM to include the new values, as the following listing shows.

Listing 8.22 updateData() detail

```
// `data` is an object containing a `temperature` and `pressure` properties
function updateData (data) {
  ['temperature', 'pressure'].forEach(function (dataPoint) {
    document.getElementById(dataPoint).innerHTML = data[dataPoint].toFixed(2);
  });
  document.querySelectorAll('.data--value').forEach(function (el) {
    el.classList.add('connected');
  });
}
```

First, the HTML elements with IDs temperature and pressure are updated—their HTML content is set to the value of the temperature and pressure sensors, respectively:

```
['temperature', 'pressure'].forEach(function (dataPoint) {
  document.getElementById(dataPoint).innerHTML = data[dataPoint].toFixed(2);
});
```

The sensor values are formatted such that two digits display after the decimal.

Then, as a visual cue, an additional class—connected—is added to the #temperature and #pressure elements (the CSS styles this as green text) to show that data is being received over the socket:

```
document.querySelectorAll('.data--value').forEach(function (el) {
  el.classList.add('connected');
});
```

DOM-manipulation code, jQuery style

To avoid excessive client dependencies, the JavaScript in index.html uses the browser DOM API directly; for example, `document.querySelectorAll()`. But lots of people are more familiar with jQuery-style syntax, which makes DOM traversal and manipulation more readable and intuitive.

You can use jQuery if you like. To do this, you'd need to add a `<script>` tag to include it. Using their CDN-hosted code (https://code.jquery.com/) is recommended so you don't have to add another file to the app directory.

The updated index.html script would then look something like this:

```
$(function () {
  var socket = io();
  socket.on('weather', updateData);
});
function updateData (data) {
  $('#temperature').html(data.temperature.toFixed(2));
  $('#pressure').html(data.pressure.toFixed(2));
  $('.data--value').addClass('connected');
}
```

It's ready! You can position the Tessel, plugged into wall power, anywhere within your wireless network's range. Then, once again, from your computer, enter this command:

```
t2 run index.js --lan
```

Open a browser to the URL indicated in the console (figure 8.12).

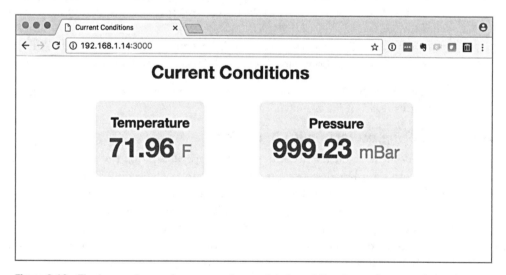

Figure 8.12   The temperature and pressure values update in real time in your browser, via websockets.

T2 PUSH DEPLOYMENT FOR FULL INDEPENDENCE

Remember, when deploying a project with t2 run, the Tessel still has some dependence on your computer: the process only runs on the Tessel as long as it isn't terminated from your computer. With t2 push, the Tessel can reach full autonomy.

Take note of your Tessel's current IP address and web server port. If you need to be reminded, run t2 run index.js again and copy the logged IP address and port combination somewhere you can access. When deploying via t2 push, you won't be able to see output from console.log anymore.

Now, run this command:

```
$ t2 push index.js
```

You should see output like the following.

Listing 8.23 t2 push output

```
$ t2 push index.js
INFO Looking for your Tessel...
INFO Connected to sweetbirch.
INFO Building project.
INFO Writing project to Flash on sweetbirch (1400.832 kB)...
INFO Deployed.
INFO Your Tessel may now be untethered.
INFO The application will run whenever Tessel boots up.
INFO     To remove this application, use "t2 erase".
INFO Running index.js...
```

Give the Tessel several seconds to finish spinning up the web server and get started, and then view the weather station web page (at the Tessel's IP address, port 3000) in your browser.

Even if your Tessel loses power, it will start running the weather station script once it regains power and boots up. The Tessel doesn't need your computer anymore.

> **MAKE IT STOP** You can use t2 erase to make the Tessel stop running the weather station program.

8.5 *Powering projects with batteries*

There's one wire left: a wall connection that provides power for the Tessel and its circuit.

There are myriad options for powering projects, such as wall power, alkaline or rechargeable household batteries, many forms of lithium-ion batteries, or solar panels. The options can feel overwhelming. Let's break it down a bit.

First, what exactly needs to be powered? For a project like the weather station, the Tessel itself (dev board, microcontroller, processor) needs to be powered, and the Tessel subsequently provides power at 3.3 V to the BMP180 breakout board. In that case, it's natural to think of providing power to the dev board and assume the dev board will serve as a power source for the rest of the circuit and its components.

That's a fine concept when the project circuitry requires little in the way of power, but it's different when projects contain motors or other current-hungry components. Back in chapter 6, the circuitry for the rover robot contained two DC motors and required more current than the Arduino Uno pins could provide directly. That project included a secondary power source to drive the motors: a 9 V alkaline battery (figure 8.13).

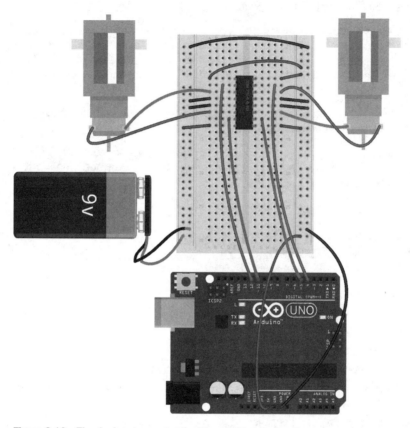

Figure 8.13   The dual-motors setup for the robot in chapter 6 used a power source external to the Uno for powering the DC motors: a 9 V battery.

In any case, whatever you select to provide power for your project needs to power the whole project—sometimes all of the power will flow through the dev board, sometimes not, depending on what's in the circuit.

For your first foray into completely battery-powered freedom, we'll use a *USB power bank*. Perhaps you already have one on hand: these little power packs are often used to provide extra juice for mobile phones and tablets on the go. They provide a steady 5 V current over USB and are easy to charge with USB wall chargers. They're great as an extra battery for your mobile device, but they're also great for powering projects that can run on 5 V power.

Battery capacity

The amount of "juice" in a given battery is measured in terms of current over time. A battery's capacity is measured in *Amp hours* at its rated voltage, or, in the context of household batteries, *milliamp hours* (mAh). A 1.5 V battery with a capacity of 500 mAh should be able to provide, at 1.5 V, a steady current of 100 mA for 5 hours. Or a steady current of 10 mAh for 50 hours.

Of course, it's not quite that simple. A battery's actual capacity varies based on a lot of variables: discharge rate (higher discharge rates result in lower total capacity), ambient temperature (batteries don't like the cold), time elapsed since the battery was charged (batteries naturally and normally slowly discharge), the battery's chemistry, and more.

Consumer 1.5 AA batteries can range in capacity from 400 to over 3000 mAh depending on their chemistry and other factors. That's a big range!

The beefiest of my current collection of USB power banks provides 8000 mAh (8 Amp hours). On the opposite end, some of my smaller lithium polymer (LiPo) batteries are only a few hundred mAh.

The power needs of the Tessel (not a particularly low-power board) and motors call for a higher-capacity battery like that USB brick, whereas a project combining an Arduino Nano (a small and efficient Arduino board) and a low-power temperature sensor would do fine on a lower-capacity LiPo.

8.5.1 *A battery-powered robot with the Tessel*

What you'll need

- 1 Tessel 2
- 1 constructed roving robot and chassis from chapter 6
- 1 USB "power bank" battery with a USB micro connection
- 3 female header pins *or* a length of solid-core wire (22-gauge solid-core is ideal) (optional)
- Soldering gun and supplies

By making some minor alterations, the robot you built with the Arduino Uno in chapter 6 can be set free (of wires). Won't that feel more like a real robot?

To liberate the bot, you'll need to do the following:

1 Solder some connections to the Tessel to make a 5 V power source available to the motors (optional)
2 Replace the Uno in the circuit with a Tessel
3 Initialize a project working directory, copy the rover code into the new project, and adjust pin numbers for the motor-driver pins

POWERING THE MOTORS

In chapter 6, the roving robot's motors were powered with a 9 V battery. The Tessel's 3.3 V operating voltage is too low to power the motors—and besides, the current restrictions on the pins would be problematic. But Tessel boards provide access to 5 V power with enough current to get the job done (figure 8.14). The trick is accessing it—you'll need to do a bit of soldering.

The most flexible option is to solder *female headers* to the three power pins on the Tessel, resulting in reusable "sockets" you can plug jumper cables into (8.15).

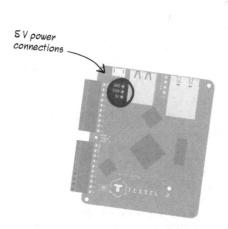

Figure 8.14 The Tessel can provide 5 V power from the power pins highlighted here.

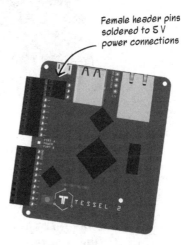

Figure 8.15 Soldering female header pins to the 5 V power pins provides handy reusable slots for jumper wires.

Soldering female header pins (figure 8.16) is a little different than soldering on male breakaway headers: you turn the board upside down and solder the pins on the bottom. Use a piece of tape to keep the pins in place on the top so they don't fall off the board when you invert it.

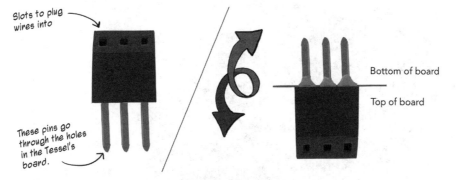

Figure 8.16 To solder female headers to the board, flip the board over and solder on the bottom. You'll need a piece of tape to hold the pins in place from the top while you solder.

Figure 8.17   Soldering solid-core wires to the power pins is also an option.

Alternatively, you could solder lengths of wire to the +5 V and GND pins (figure 8.17). However, this results in permanently attached wires.

   If this seems like too much hassle, you could opt to use two power supplies for this project: the existing 9 V battery for the motor power rail, and the USB battery to power the Tessel—a wiring diagram for each is provided in the next section.

   DON'T POWER THE MOTORS FROM 3.3 V   The Tessel's 3.3 V power pins provide neither the voltage nor the current the motors require. Don't attempt to power the motors directly from the Tessel's 3.3 V pins.

(RE-)BUILDING THE ROBOT CIRCUIT

Take the top off of the Uno-powered robot chassis (figure 8.18) so that you can access the inside, and alter the circuit to use the Tessel instead of the Uno. If you soldered connections to the Tessel's 5 V power, build the circuit as shown in figure 8.19. If you opted to continue using the 9 V battery, wire the circuit as shown in figure 8.20.

Figure 8.18   By replacing the Uno in chapter 6's roving bot with a Tessel, making a couple of wiring adjustments, and plugging in a USB battery to the Tessel, you can create a wires-free roving bot.

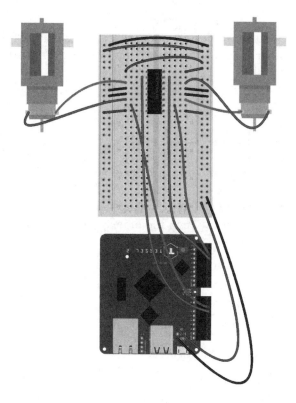

Figure 8.19   The rover robot circuit using the Tessel and the Tessel's 5 V power. The Tessel's 5 V power needs to power both power rails—make sure you connect the positive columns of the power rails together using an additional (red) jumper wire (near the top).

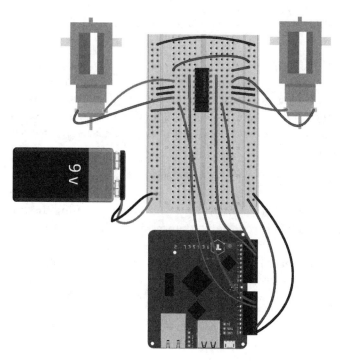

Figure 8.20   The rover circuit using two power sources: the Tessel's 3.3 V and a 9 V battery for the motors.

UPDATING THE ROVER CODE

Create a working directory and install some dependencies. In a terminal (making sure you're not inside the t2-weather or any other preexisting project directory), enter these commands:

```
mkdir t2-rover
cd t2-rover
npm init -y
npm install --save johnny-five tessel-io keypress
```

The keypress package is used to capture keyboard input, so the bot can be steered with the arrow keys.

Copy the two robot scripts into the t2-rover directory—index.js and Rover.js (or flip back to chapter 6 to find the source). Open the index.js file in a text editor and make the following changes:

1   Add a require for tessel-io near the top of the file:

```
const Tessel = require('tessel-io');
```

2   Update the board instantiation to specify the I/O plugin:

```
const board = new five.Board({ io: new Tessel() });
```

3   Update the motor pins:

```
const motors = new five.Motors([
  { pins: { dir: 'A4', pwm: 'A5' }, invertPWM: true },
  { pins: { dir: 'B4', pwm: 'B5' }, invertPWM: true }
]);
```

That's it! Your bot is ready to go, wires-free. Nestle the Tessel board into place on the roving bot where the Uno was previously. Plug in the USB power supply (and 9 V battery, if you're using one) and use tape or Velcro to secure it to the robot chassis. Make sure the Tessel is fully booted and visible over the LAN (use t2 list to make sure). Then run this command:

```
$ t2 run index.js --lan
```

You should be able to control your robot from your computer using the arrow keys, and the rover should be able to roam much more widely than when it was tethered with a USB cable.

Through the experiments in this chapter, you've seen how you can start setting your projects free from physical tethers. You're past the basics now. It's time to give you more tools to invent your own experiments and create things that haven't been created before.

Voltages and the motor driver

The Arduino Uno-based rover used 5 V logic levels, and the motors were provided with 9 V of power from a battery. Remember, there are two power sources here—one for the motor driver's logic and one to power the motors themselves.

In the Tessel-based setup, the motor driver is connected to 3.3 V logic levels and the motors only get 5 V (unless you're using a 9 V battery). The motor driver works on 3.3 V logic because 3.3 V HIGH is enough to register as a logical HIGH for the 5 V motor driver device—oftentimes you can use 5 V logic with 3.3 V because the range of valid HIGH voltages for a 5 V device usually includes 3.3 V.

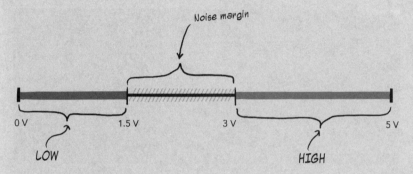

3.3 V logic is sometimes compatible with components that have 5 V logic levels. The voltage range that's interpreted as HIGH for 5 V logic-level devices often encompasses 3.3 V. That is, a +3.3 V signal (HIGH from the 3.3 V device) will be interpreted as HIGH on the 5 V device because it falls within its HIGH voltage range.

You'll notice that the motors aren't as zippy with 5 V as on 9 V. That's to be expected. But they're still good enough to rove.

Summary

- There are two main reasons that projects require wired connections: data and communication exchange, and power.
- Using Johnny-Five with Arduino Uno is an example of a host-client setup. A tether must exist between a host computer and the Uno at all times. Some constrained hardware like the Photon Particle can communicate wirelessly with Johnny-Five, but a host computer is still required to do the thinking.
- Tessel 2 is an open source platform that runs embedded Linux and Node.js directly on the board itself. The Tessel can execute code independently of a host computer.
- The Tessel 2 operates at 3.3 V. It has two ports of 8 pins each and supports different features on different pins.

- For the most part, the only adaptations required to write Johnny-Five scripts for the Tessel versus the Uno (or to port between the platforms) is to use the `tessel-io` I/O plugin for Johnny-Five and change the pin numbering for components.
- Because the Tessel can run Node.js natively and supports npm packages, it's possible to create sophisticated, high-level applications and execute them directly on the Tessel.
- There are many options for powering projects. So far you've used wall power, alkaline batteries, and a USB power bank. USB batteries are handy because they have multiple applications, including charging up mobile devices, and they're easy to use.

Building your own thing

 For this chapter, you'll need the following:

- 1 Tessel 2
- 1 set of remote-controlled wall outlets
- 1 SparkFun 3.3 V APDS-9960 breakout board

- Soldering iron and supplies

- Push buttons and/or LEDs for debugging circuits (optional)

- 6 photocouplers (opto-isolators), such as the 4N25

- 6 100 Ω resistors

- 1 full-size breadboard

- Jumper wires

- 1 multimeter

- 0.1" male breakaway headers

- 22AWG solid-core wire (optional, for soldering to remote control circuitry)

Hardware toolkit for chapter 9 (optional 22AWG solid-core wire not shown)

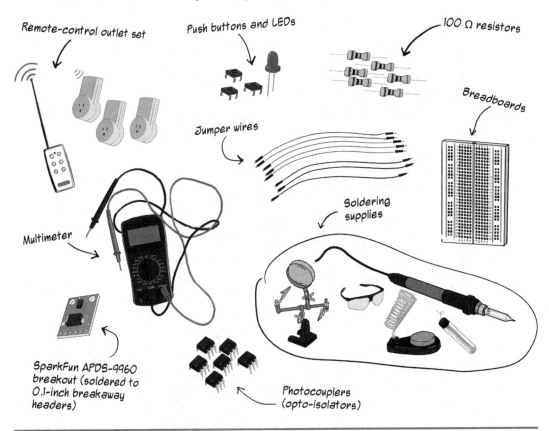

Already you've moved well beyond the light-up-an-LED world, and you might be chafing to start building things with electronics that haven't been built before, to chart your own course. Let's take a tour through the arc of an entire example project—

remixing a remote-controlled set of outlet switches—from inception, through proto-typing, troubleshooting, iteration, and improvement. Instead of relying upon preex-isting schematics, instructions, and software, you'll forge your own way through some parts of the project.

The projects in this chapter will expose you to more software complexity than ear-lier experiments. Depending on your level of JavaScript expertise, this might hit a sweet spot, or it might feel like more than you want to bite off right now. If it's too much, that's just fine: it's always valid to put together projects from preexisting com-ponent support.

Real-world projects have ups and downs. It takes a touch of bravery to jump into more elaborate projects with unknowns. Making it work in the end is sweetly reward-ing, and I hope you'll learn to relish the plunge.

9.1 Hacking consumer electronics

One of the most electrifying moments (if you'll pardon the wretched pun) during the growth of my electronics expertise was when I realized that I had enough basic know-how to mess around with existing consumer electronics: to make them better, or to invent creative mash-ups—scratching whatever inventor's itch might arise. Why design, buy parts for, and laboriously build a circuit if you've got an unused electronic trinket lying around the house that already performs the same function?

9.1.1 Modifying RF-controlled outlet switches

Wandering around a room to turn on (or off) several individual lamps can be tire-some, especially if their switches are inconveniently located. Wirelessly controlled plug-in switches for electrical outlets can be handy. For about $20 you can buy a set of three with a remote control (figure 9.1).

With the battery-operated remote in hand, you can turn each of the plugged-in switches (and, by turn, the lamps plugged into them) on or off, individually. This is a

Figure 9.1 Sets of remote-controlled outlets are inexpensive and widely available at hardware stores and home centers. The remote control unit is powered by a low-voltage battery.

step up from having to make a physical lap around the room. But there are some things which could be improved upon.

It's not possible—at least with the model I have—to turn all of the switches (and thus their lights) on or off at the same time. Each has to be switched individually.

More interestingly, wouldn't it be nice to be able to trigger the lights in other, possibly automated, ways? Maybe you want the lights to turn on when it gets dark, or from another room in your home, or using some other form of input that you've dreamed up.

Good news! The circuitry inside these little remote controls is both low in complexity and in oomph—low voltage, low current. They're easy to understand and probably won't zap you terribly if you mess something up. Let's get hacking. Using the guts of the remote control, you'll cobble together your own personalized device.

Always be careful!

Although the circuitry in many low-voltage, battery-powered consumer electronics is benign, every device is different, and you need to exercise common sense.

Unless you're a qualified electrician, *don't* open up or alter the outlet components of the remote-control system—keep your hackery confined to the remote-control unit. The outlets plug into the wall, and I make it a policy never to get near mains power in my electronics explorations—this keeps me out of the hospital.

Remove batteries from electronics when you're working with them. And always, always give capacitors a wide berth. They can hold a charge for a long time, even when not connected to power.

DISASSEMBLING THE REMOTE CONTROL UNIT

You'll need to dismantle the remote control assembly. Your remote control unit may be slightly different, but to disassemble the remote control that I have, I removed two small screws. Inside of the case, I found just a few things (figure 9.2):

- A 3 V coin-cell battery (lithium CR2032 in this remote)
- The physical, pressable buttons, which are all attached together on one flexible bed of plastic
- A small circuit board containing the contact pads for the buttons, battery contacts, and a status LED (among other things, like the radio transmitter)
- A telescoping antenna, attached to the circuit board

Each button has a corresponding pad beneath it on the circuit board, which looks like a zig-zag pattern. When the overlying button is pressed, it makes a connection between the two different sides of the zig-zag, completing the circuit. You can connect the circuit yourself, acting like a single pressed button, by using a jumper wire and touching one end to each side of the zig-zag (figure 9.3).

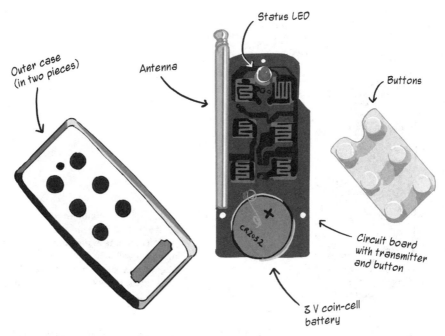

Figure 9.2   The deconstructed remote control

Figure 9.3   When a button is pressed, it makes contact with both sides of the zig-zag contacts underneath it. You can reproduce this effect by connecting the two sides with a jumper wire.

ADDING ONTO THE REMOTE'S CIRCUITRY

One side of the zig-zag is connected to ground. You need to determine which side that is so that you can wire up your own "buttons" correctly (that is, not backwards). The best way to do this is with a multimeter, but if you don't want to purchase a multimeter right now, you can try touching the LED's leads to each side of the button contacts and

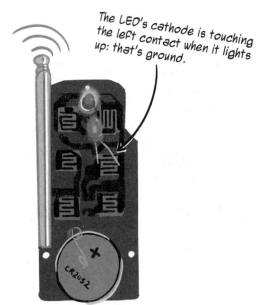

The LED's cathode is touching the left contact when it lights up: that's ground.

Figure 9.4   No multimeter? You may be able to use an LED to figure out which side of the button contacts is the ground side. An LED is a diode—it will only allow current to flow if it's aligned correctly in the circuit. When it lights up, that means its cathode is on the ground side of the button.

see when it lights up—whichever side the cathode of the LED is touching at that point is the ground side (figure 9.4). Keep in mind that you run the risk of sacrificing the LED if it ends up getting too much current or balks at being connected backward.

Mastering multimeters

A multimeter, which can measure voltage, current, and resistance, is an essential tool for an electronic-tinkerer's toolbox. They're inexpensive—tolerable hobby-quality ones can be had for less than $20.

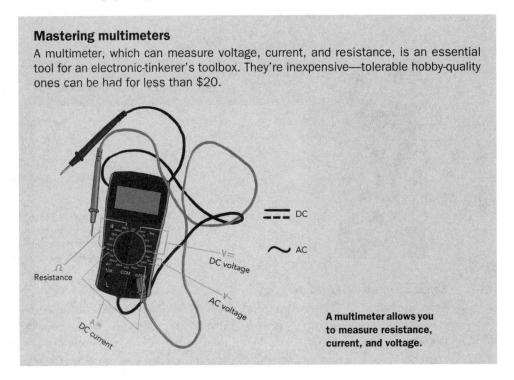

A multimeter allows you to measure resistance, current, and voltage.

In our current experiment, you can determine which side of the button contact pads are connected to ground by looking at the difference in voltage potential between the two sides of the zig-zag. To do this, set the multimeter to a DC voltage setting. I chose 20 V—the device should operate around 3 V based on its battery. The 20 V setting can display voltage readings up to 20 V; the device's voltage is just a tad too high to use my 2 V setting.

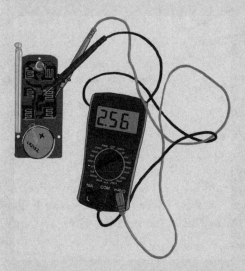

With the multimeter set to an appropriate DC voltage setting, the reading will be positive when the ground probe is on the ground side of the button contacts.

When you touch the multimeter's probes to each side of the button contacts, you should see a voltage reading on the device. If the number is negative, swap the probes. Once you see a positive reading—mine was about 2.5 V—you've found the positive side (red probe connection) and the negative side (black probe connection). Take note of these for each button connection.

The controls can look intimidating at first, but multimeters are a great friend to have for sanity checking and debugging circuits. SparkFun's "How to Use a Multimeter" tutorial is a good one: http://mng.bz/9f03.

The next step may require some ingenuity depending on the specifics of your device's circuit board: you need to attach wires to each side of the button zig-zags (two wires per button). Subsequently you'll be able to turn remote switches on and off by controlling—making and breaking—connections between these wires.

If you're lucky, you can solder wires directly to the button contact pads (figure 9.5). In my case, the remote control's *printed circuit board* (PCB)—a board manufactured specifically for this product with connections *silkscreened* onto it and *traces* connecting different elements—made this challenging. Although the button contacts were electrically

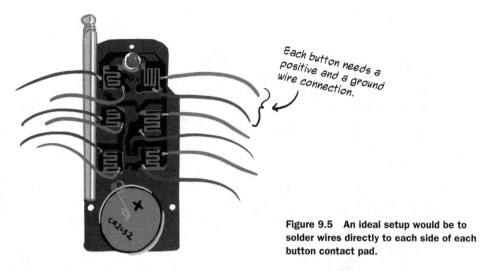

Each button needs a positive and a ground wire connection.

Figure 9.5   An ideal setup would be to solder wires directly to each side of each button contact pad.

conductive, solder would not adhere to them. Try as I might, all I achieved was globbing solder onto my wires and making a mess. Securing the wires to the pads using electrical tape was frustrating and finicky and kept falling apart on me.

Finally, poking around using my multimeter, I was able to find holes on the circuit board that corresponded to button contacts. Those holes still didn't hold solder, but they served as anchor points through which I could stick wires into an underlying breadboard (figure 9.6).

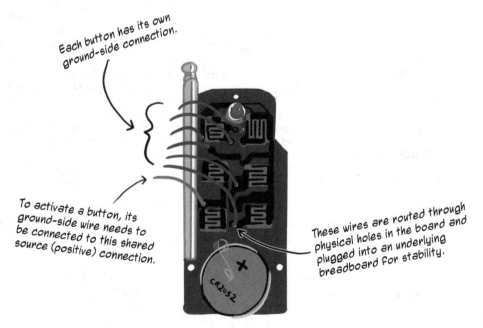

Each button has its own ground-side connection.

To activate a button, its ground-side wire needs to be connected to this shared source (positive) connection.

These wires are routed through physical holes in the board and plugged into an underlying breadboard for stability.

Figure 9.6   My home-brew wiring solution, taking advantage of the structure of the particular circuit board

It turned out that each button on the circuit board had its own separate connection to ground (blue wires—top six in figure 9.6). But all of the buttons were connected via traces to a single shared positive power source (yellow wire—bottom in figure 9.6). To activate any one button, it was necessary to complete the circuit by connecting the button's specific ground connection to the shared positive source.

Learning to have patience when inventing

When you're blazing new trails and inventing your own things, chances are you'll have at least one point in each project where things don't go as expected (probably more, to be honest). It can be a letdown. Whether it's a problem soldering a wire to a connection or a component that doesn't fit into a breadboard, you'll need to be resourceful and thoughtful to get through it.

Try not to rush or get flustered—easier advised than done, of course! It's all part of the experience. Try to use the right tool for the job, even if that means putting your project aside for a few days while you wait for the right online-ordered tool or part to arrive in the mail. Even if you do have the necessary materials on hand, sometimes it's a good idea to take a breather.

It does get better! As you go on, you'll learn to foresee certain gotchas. You'll also be building your toolset, so you'll have more options to fall back on when you need to fix a glitch or troubleshoot. And you'll learn how long it really takes to build a project from scratch: it can take longer than you'd think!

If you'd like to experiment, you can wire up a few momentary switches (push buttons) to your button wires and use those to make connections, thus turning on or off the remote switches (figure 9.7).

So far, this has been an interesting exercise in understanding how things work, but you may have realized that it doesn't accomplish anything useful. It still requires pokes from human fingers to operate the controls. Instead, let's design it so you can control the device based on whatever input or logic you desire.

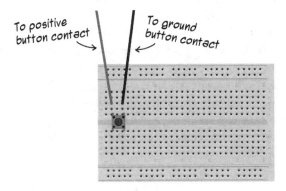

To positive button contact →

To ground button contact ←

Figure 9.7   If you like, you can connect up one or more of your wired buttons to a push button to test it out.

USING PHOTOCOUPLERS TO KEEP CIRCUITS ISOLATED

When interfacing with circuits in other electronics, it's best to keep the power sources and circuit components of the target device isolated from your development board and circuit. You wouldn't want vagaries of current or voltage in the remote to damage the electronics in the dev-board circuit or vice versa. You want your development board and the devices connected to it to be able to *control* the flow of current through the remote (making and breaking connections for different buttons), but you don't want to actually *connect* to the remote's circuitry (figure 9.8).

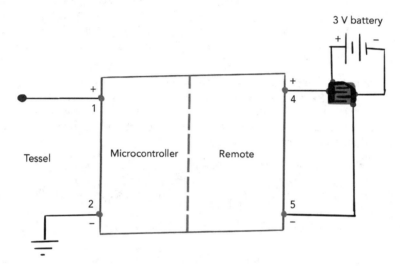

Figure 9.8   For each button on the remote, you want to be able to press and release the button using the Tessel as a switch-like controller. You want it so that applying current across points 1 and 2 (the input side) causes current to flow between points 3 and 4 (the output, remote side), but you don't want the two circuits to be physically connected.

This is where *photocoupler* components shine (literally). When current is flowing between two pins on the input side of a photocoupler component, current is allowed to flow between two pins on the *output* side. That is, the output-side switch is closed (figure 9.9). If this notion strikes you as somewhat reminiscent of how transistors work—a small input current that allows current to flow between two other pins—you're right. But in this case, the input current activates the output transistor without "touching" it with its current. Instead, an internal LED is powered by the current flowing across the input pins. The output-side transistor is photosensitive and activates (closes the switch) when light hits it.

As you've seen with some other components, a photocoupler goes by many alternative names: you may see them referred to as *optocouplers* or *opto-isolators*.

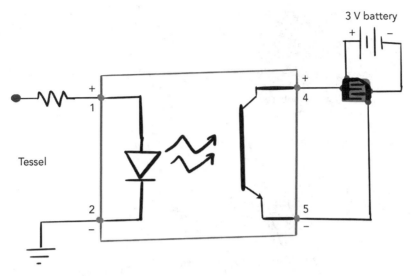

Figure 9.9   Current applied to the input side of a photocoupler activates an internal infrared LED. The LED shines onto a photosensitive transistor, activating it and allowing current to flow on the output side.

9.2   Controlling the remote switches with a Johnny-Five component plugin

Your first experiment with remotely controlling the remote control (oh, it's getting meta!) will involve using existing Johnny-Five features, but cobbling them together in new ways.

In this first iteration, you'll make it so you can control each on and off switch—virtually pressing buttons—using application logic running on the Tessel.

9.2.1   Prototyping the switch project

Instead of going all-in and wiring up all of the photocouplers and switches at once—six photocouplers and related components in my case—it can be helpful to start with one chunk of the circuit and make sure it works. Then you can whip up some less-than-polished code to check that things are behaving as expected before doing any fine tuning.

This process of *prototyping* can help you validate your approach and troubleshoot issues on a smaller scale before diving in too deep.

PROTOTYPING THE HARDWARE

Wire up the first set of on and off buttons as shown in figure 9.10. Yellow wires should connect to positive button connections, black to negative (in my case, all yellow wires connect to the same, shared positive source). Make sure the dot indicating pin 1 on the photocouplers is oriented correctly. Connect pin 2 of both photocouplers to ground.

Connect pin 1 of the first photocoupler to pin A0 on the Tessel through a 100 Ω resistor, and pin 2 to GND. The current-limiting resistor is needed here because there's an

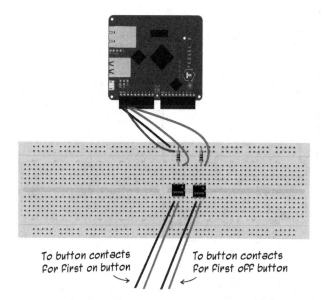

To button contacts
for first on button

To button contacts
for first off button

Figure 9.10   Wiring diagram for the first set of on/off buttons

LED inside of the photocoupler. Connect pin 5 of the photocoupler to the positive wire of the first switch's *on* button, and pin 4 to the ground wire for that button.

Connect the second photocoupler in a similar fashion, but connect it to pin A1 on the Tessel (source) side and to the positive and ground wires of the first switch's *off* button.

PROTOTYPING THE SOFTWARE

Here's something to consider. What does it mean to "press a button" on the remote? The connection that the button-press makes doesn't stay connected forever, nor is it an instantaneous blip—think of a human finger pressing and then releasing the button. On my remote, in fact, I'd noticed in the past that if I pressed a button too fast—releasing it too quickly—the switch didn't always respond. There's a bit of press-and-hold involved.

You can imitate this with software by enabling a button's connection via the photocoupler and keeping it on for a period of time, say half a second, before turning it off again. This is probably easier to conceptualize by looking at actual code. Let's go.

First, set up the project:

```
mkdir remote-switches
cd remote-switches
npm init -y
```

Next, install the standard dependencies and create an index.js file:

```
npm install --save johnny-five tessel-io
touch index.js
```

Instead of using a higher-level Johnny-Five component class like `Led`, you'll write digital values—HIGH (1) or LOW (0)—to pins A0 and A1 directly. A pin can be configured as a digital output pin, like this:

```
board.pinMode('A0', five.Pin.OUTPUT);
```

Once configured, it can be written to like this:

```
board.digitalWrite('A0', 1); // set HIGH (3.3V on Tessel)
board.digitalWrite('A0', 0); // set LOW (0V)
```

To "press" the button that turns the first switch on, you'll want to set pin A0 HIGH—"turning on" the photocoupler and allowing current to flow across the first button. After 500 milliseconds, you'll set A0 LOW again, breaking the circuit connection and "releasing" the button.

Add the following prototype switching code to index.js.

Listing 9.1 Prototype button-pressing code

```
const five = require('johnny-five');
const Tessel = require('tessel-io');

const board = new five.Board({ io: new Tessel() });

const switchPins = {                     ◁——┐ These two pins are
  on: 'A0',                                  │ connected to the source side
  off: 'A1'                                  │ of the two photocouplers.
};
const pressDuration = 500;          ◁——┐ "Presses and holds" buttons
                                        │ for 500 milliseconds to
board.on('ready', () => {               │ ensure switch activation

  board.pinMode(switchPins.on, five.Pin.OUTPUT);   ◁——┐ Configures A0 and A1
  board.pinMode(switchPins.off, five.Pin.OUTPUT);      │ as digital output pins

  const pressButton = function (pin) {
    board.digitalWrite(pin, 1);      ◁——┐ To press a button, first set the
    setTimeout(() => {                   │ associated photocoupler pin HIGH.
      board.digitalWrite(pin, 0);
    }, pressDuration);          ◁——┐ Then set a timeout for
  };                               │ pressDuration (500 ms) before
  const turnOn = function () {     │ setting the pin LOW again.
    pressButton(switchPins.on);
  };
  const turnOff = function () {
    pressButton(switchPins.off);
  };

  board.repl.inject({         ◁——┐ For the prototyping phase,
    turnOn: turnOn,               │ make turnOn and turnOff
    turnOff: turnOff             │ available to the REPL.
  });
});
```

Try it out. Deploy the code to the Tessel over LAN (you need to deploy over LAN for the REPL to function):

```
$ t2 run index.js --lan
```

Try invoking the `turnOn()` and `turnOff()` functions from the REPL. Note that both functions return `undefined`—this is fine and not an error.

```
1492612088185 Available Tessel 2 (sweetbirch)
1492612088341 Connected Tessel 2 (sweetbirch)
1492612088415 Repl Initialized
>> turnOn()
undefined
>> turnOff()
undefined
```

Doing this should "press" the on and off buttons on the remote and turn the associated wall outlet on and off.

BUILDING OUT THE REST OF THE CIRCUIT

Once you're feeling more confident that your first circuit is doing what you expect, expand on it as shown in figure 9.11. Make sure to pay attention to each photocoupler's orientation.

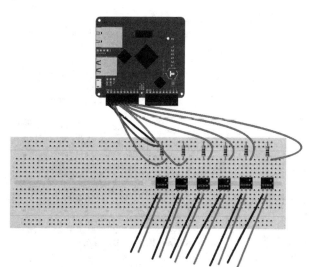

Figure 9.11   The completed switch/photocoupler wiring. The outputs from the photocouplers should connect to the button contact wires.

9.2.2   *Writing the RemoteSwitch plugin*

Now that you've polished the circuit, it's time to polish the code. Instead of having a motley collection of code in the application's main module (index.js), you can encapsulate the behavior of each of the three on/off switch combinations in a custom component called `RemoteSwitch`. Whisking away the component-specific code will allow you, back in index.js, simply to instantiate a `RemoteSwitch` object for each of the three on/off pairs (or however many switch pairs your remote has) and turn them on or off at will.

Let's walk through the steps of creating a reusable Johnny-Five component plugin.

> **JOHNNY-FIVE COMPONENT PLUGINS VS. COMPONENT CLASSES** Built-in *component classes* like `Led` and `Motor` are part of Johnny-Five's core. Creating a new component class requires changes to the Johnny-Five codebase itself. On the other hand, *component plugins* can be created without making any modifications to Johnny-Five—ergo the terminology *plugin*. The structure of a component plugin bears many similarities to the structure of component class code, but the two things—component class versus component plugin—are different animals, so don't get confused (you are making a *plugin*)!

COMPONENT PLUGIN STRUCTURE BASICS

Create a new file in the remote-switches directory called RemoteSwitch.js to contain the plugin module. The structure of the module will start out as shown in the following listing. This skeleton structure follows some Johnny-Five component plugin conventions to make it modular and flexible.

Listing 9.2   RemoteSwitch.js: starting point

Consuming module provides a reference to Johnny-Five (five).

This will initialize a new RemoteSwitch object (this is its constructor).

You'll add three prototype methods to control the switch component.

```
module.exports = function (five) {
  return (function () {
    function RemoteSwitch (opts) { /* ... */ }
    RemoteSwitch.prototype.toggle = function (turnOn) {};
    RemoteSwitch.prototype.on = function () {};
    RemoteSwitch.prototype.off = function () {};
    return RemoteSwitch;
  }());
};
```

The `RemoteSwitch` module doesn't have a direct dependency on Johnny-Five. Instead, it takes a Johnny-Five object reference as an argument to its exported function. That way the plugin can work on top of whichever Johnny-Five object is in play when it's included. The passed Johnny-Five object might contain a `board` configured with the Tessel I/O plugin, or it might have an Arduino with a Firmata I/O layer, or perhaps something else—this way the plugin doesn't have to care about logistics or valid pin numbers or anything. The passed-in Johnny-Five object will take care of that, leaving you free to deal with the logic at hand.

The plugin needs to have a constructor that can take some options, perform any setup it needs to do, and register itself with Johnny-Five. The instantiation of a `RemoteSwitch` will look like this when you're done:

```
const switch1 = new RemoteSwitch({ pins: { on: 'A0', off: 'A1' } });
```

You'll work on that constructor next.

CODING THE PLUGIN

Add the following code to `RemoteSwitch.js`.

Listing 9.3   RemoteSwitch.js: constructor

```
module.exports = function (five) {
  return (function () {
    function RemoteSwitch (opts) {
      if (!(this instanceof RemoteSwitch)) {
        return new RemoteSwitch(opts);
      }
      five.Board.Component.call(this, opts = five.Board.Options(opts));

      // opts.pins should contain two properties, `on` and `off`,
      // defining their pin numbers, respectively
      this.pins     = opts.pins;
      this.duration = 500;
      this.isOn     = undefined;
      this.isActive = false;

      this.io.pinMode(this.pins.on, this.io.MODES.OUTPUT);
      this.io.pinMode(this.pins.off, this.io.MODES.OUTPUT);
    }
    // ...
  }());
};
```

This (boilerplate) pattern ensures the function is called with the "new" keyword.

Registers the component

You don't know, technically, whether the switch is on or off at the outset.

isActive is true when one of the switch's buttons is activated (being pressed).

Configures the switch's on and off pins to be digital output pins.

Now it's time to add the methods that turn the switch on and off.

Listing 9.4   RemoteSwitch.js: prototype methods

```
module.exports = function (five) {
  return (function () {
    function RemoteSwitch (opts) { /* we already wrote this */ };

    RemoteSwitch.prototype.toggle = function (turnOn) {
      if (this.isActive) { return false; }
      this.isActive = true;
      if (typeof turnOn === 'undefined') {
        turnOn = !this.isOn;
      }
      const pin = (turnOn) ? this.pins.on : this.pins.off;
      this.io.digitalWrite(pin, 1);
      setTimeout(() => {
        this.io.digitalWrite(pin, 0);
        this.isActive = false;
        this.isOn = !!turnOn;
      }, this.duration);
    };
    RemoteSwitch.prototype.on = function () {
      this.toggle(true);
    };
    RemoteSwitch.prototype.off = function () {
```

Doesn't activate the switch if it's already active (busy)

Determines toggle behavior if turnOn is missing

Switch is no longer active; isActive should be false again

Denotes that the switch is currently active

Determines which of the switch's pins (on or off) to activate

Keeps track of the switch's current state

```
            this.toggle(false);
        };
    }());
};
```

You'll notice that everything centers around the `toggle` method. The single `toggle` argument, `turnOn`, defines what happens. If it's truthy, the switch will turn on. If it's falsy, the switch will turn off. If it's *missing* (`undefined`), the switch will toggle from whatever state it's currently in. To support that functionality, the switch's current state is stored in the `isOn` property.

To prevent the remote from trying to send two signals at once, the `isActive` property is used as a flag. `toggle` won't write to any pins if `isActive` is true.

REFACTORING INDEX.JS TO USE REMOTESWITCH

You can now update index.js to contain the following code.

Listing 9.5   Refactored index.js

```
const five = require('johnny-five');
const Tessel = require('tessel-io');
const RemoteSwitch = require('./RemoteSwitch')(five);          ⟵  Imports the
                                                                   RemoteSwitch
const board = new five.Board({ io: new Tessel() });                module and passes
                                                                   it the five reference
board.on('ready', () => {
  const switch1 = new RemoteSwitch({
    pins : { on: 'A0', off: 'A1' }
  });
  const switch2 = new RemoteSwitch({
    pins: { on: 'A2', off: 'A3' }
  });
  const switch3 = new RemoteSwitch({
    pins: { on: 'A4', off: 'A5' }
  });
  board.repl.inject({
    switch1: switch1,
    switch2: switch2,
    switch3: switch3
  });
});
```

Try it out:

```
t2 run index.js --lan
```

Once it's running, you can interact with the switch objects in the REPL:

```
1492618175517 Available Tessel 2 (sweetbirch)
1492618175671 Connected Tessel 2 (sweetbirch)
1492618175746 Repl Initialized
>> switch1.on()
```

```
undefined
>> switch1.off()
undefined
>> switch2.on()
undefined
```

ITERATION: QUEUING AND CALLBACKS

Right now, the `toggle` method on `RemoteSwitch` instances won't do anything if `isActive` is true—that is, it won't allow multiple simultaneous switch activations. The downside is that, as it's currently written, commands to `toggle` will be effectively thrown away and ignored if they happen while the switch is already active. Say for some reason you wanted to blink the switch on and off again several times, and you had the following code in index.js to try to accomplish that:

```
for (var i = 0; i < 10; i++) {
  switch1.toggle();
}
```

The switch would toggle once as expected, sure. But the subsequent nine calls to `toggle` would happen immediately afterward—while the switch is still activated from the first invocation (and, thus, while `isActive` is true). They'd be ignored. As a result, the switch would only toggle once, not 10 times.

You can fix that by throwing in simple FIFO queueing (first in, first out—analogous to "calls are answered in the order they're received") for toggle commands that come in while the switch is active. This requires just a few lines of code.

While you're in there, you can also add some *callback* support to `RemoteSwitch`'s methods, as shown in the next listing. This is consistent with other J5 components and makes it possible to register a function to be called when the switch command (on/off/toggle) is complete. Right now this is gravy, but it'll be useful later.

Listing 9.6 The complete `RemoteSwitch` plugin

```
module.exports = function (five) {
  return (function () {
    function RemoteSwitch (opts) {
      if (!(this instanceof RemoteSwitch)) {
        return new RemoteSwitch(opts);
      }
      five.Board.Component.call(this, opts = five.Board.Options(opts));

      this.pins     = opts.pins;
      this.duration = opts.duration || 500;
      this.isOn     = undefined;
      this.isActive = false;
      this.queue    = [];                      ⟵  Instantiates an empty array
                                                   to hold queued "commands"

      this.io.pinMode(this.pins.on, this.io.MODES.OUTPUT);
      this.io.pinMode(this.pins.off, this.io.MODES.OUTPUT);
    }
```

```
RemoteSwitch.prototype.toggle = function (turnOn, callback) {
  if (this.isActive) {
    this.queue.push([turnOn, callback]);
    return;
  }
  this.isActive = true;
  if (typeof turnOn === 'undefined') {
    turnOn = !this.isOn;
  }
  const pin = (turnOn) ? this.pins.on : this.pins.off;
  this.io.digitalWrite(pin, 1);
  setTimeout(() => {
    this.io.digitalWrite(pin, 0);
    this.isActive = false;
    this.isOn = !!turnOn;
    if (typeof callback === 'function') {
      callback();
    }
    if (this.queue.length) {
      this.toggle.apply(this, this.queue.shift());
    }
  }, this.duration);
};

RemoteSwitch.prototype.on = function (callback) {
  this.toggle(true, callback);
};
RemoteSwitch.prototype.off = function (callback) {
  this.toggle(false, callback);
};
return RemoteSwitch;
}());
};
```

Now accepts a callback

Pushes things onto the queue if the switch is busy

The toggle action is complete: invokes the callback, if there is one

Calls toggle on the next item in the queue, if there is one

on and off handler functions take a callback argument and pass it on to toggle.

Now if you add the following code to index.js, it should work as expected:

```
for (var i = 0; i < 10; i++) {
  switch1.toggle(); // This will cause the switch to toggle 10 times
}
```

YOUR HARDWARE MAY VARY The switch should toggle 10 times, based on the software we've written. It's worth noting, however, that there may be hardware limitations that prevent this from actually being the case. For example, your remote's electronics may not allow a switch to be toggled that frequently.

So far, you've hacked into consumer electronics, built a small prototype, and then expanded that into a more polished circuit with a custom Johnny-Five component plugin for output (switches).

You could trigger your RemoteSwitch components with some of the input devices you've seen before. You could use a photoresistor and trigger the switches when it gets dark in the room. You could use a motion or proximity sensor to turn them on when your cat walks by (and turn them off automatically after a certain amount of elapsed time). But what happens when you have your heart set on controlling the switches with a kind of input that isn't supported by Johnny-Five? What then?

9.3 *Writing software for sophisticated hardware*

There's this nifty I²C device that caught my eye. The Avago APDS-9960 device (figure 9.12) contains multiple sensors: an RGB ambient light sensor, a proximity sensor, and a sophisticated gesture sensor. SparkFun sells an inexpensive (about $15) breakout board based on the chip. Neat! A gesture sensor! What a fun way to control your remotely switched lamps. Why poke buttons when you can swipe through the air like a magician?

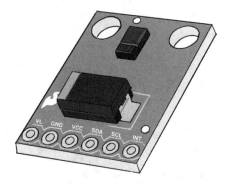

The problem is, at the time I stumbled upon the APDS-9960, there was no preexisting Johnny-Five support for it. There's no component class for gesture sensors. That means you need to create that support! When preexisting

Figure 9.12 The APDS-9960 crams three sensors into one package, including a gesture sensor. SparkFun offers a breakout board that makes working with the chip easier.

software doesn't exist for something you want to use, you've got two options: substitute another piece of hardware that does have support, or create that support yourself.

9.3.1 *Project: Johnny-Five support for APDS-9660 gesture sensor*

The APDS-9960 is going to test your mettle (it's a sophisticated device), but the high-level structure of the plugin you'll create for it will mirror that of `RemoteSwitch`. The following project process is based on a real experience and highlights some common phases, setbacks, and results encountered while creating new support for a piece of hardware.

To build the support, you'll do the following:

1 Define the goals and scope
2 Gather information and do research on the APDS-9960
3 Build a quick, proof-of-concept prototype
4 Define the API surface and plugin lifecycle
5 Write the code for the plugin
6 Test that the plugin works
7 Finish the project, integrating the APDS-9960 plugin with your `RemoteSwitch` from earlier in the chapter

GOALS FOR THE GESTURE SENSOR PLUGIN

Before plugging in wires, soldering, or slinging code, the first thing to do is ask yourself what you're trying to accomplish.

You want to make a Johnny-Five component plugin for the gesture sensor on the APDS-9960. A reasonable API consistent with other Johnny-Five components would include exposing gesture events that could be listened for and responded to by application code.

What's not in scope? Given the complexity of the APDS-9960's gesture sensor alone, don't try to tackle support for its other sensors. Likewise, to save on development time and headaches, you'll go ahead and hard-code many of the default settings and feature support that could later be managed in another way, such as through options passed to the plugin.

Designing the code to be usable on multiple hardware platforms is a good goal, as is keeping flexibility for the future in mind as you go. Writing a module that conforms to Johnny-Five component plugin conventions—like `RemoteSwitch`—will aid with the cross-platform objective. Being mindful about how constants are managed, paying attention to the consistency of the API surface, and keeping methods modular will help make the software easier to modify and to expand upon later.

You'll be writing this gesture-sensor support based on the Tessel. There's no reason to think it wouldn't work on other (3.3 V) Johnny-Five-compatible platforms, but you won't be taking the time in this project to do testing beyond the Tessel.

GATHERING INFORMATION ABOUT THE APDS-9960

With your goals and scope defined, it's time to gather information. There are many questions to answer:

- *Physical hardware and protocols*—What is the operating voltage of the device? What are the pins and connections? What communications protocol does it use?
- *Communicating*—What are the particulars for reading data from and writing it to the device?
- *Configuration and setup*—What steps need to be taken to initialize the device, set defaults, and enable needed features?
- *Data*—What kind of data is produced by the device? How do you interpret and process the data?

Your first stop on the discovery journey is to read SparkFun's APDS-9960 hookup guide and documentation (http://mng.bz/MapU). SparkFun's breakout board for the APDS-9960 takes care of some of the hardware-level busywork for you—jumpers and power connections. The resulting board can be wired up like other I²C components you've encountered. But there's one addition: a connection to an interrupt-capable pin. We'll come back to that. Another really important detail is that this device operates at 3.3 V—that's totally fine for the Tessel, but don't try to connect it to a 5 V Arduino.

Next, get your hands on the datasheet for the APDS-9960 and give it a scan (http://mng.bz/by50). The great news is that the APDS-9960's datasheet is excellent, as datasheets go. But it's still a datasheet for a nontrivial device: don't panic if an initial peek makes your eyes cross a bit. Read page 1 in its entirety—it's a good summary.

From the datasheet you can obtain vital details like the device's hard-coded I²C address (it's `0x39`; see p. 8).

By reviewing existing software and firmware support for the APDS-9960, you can get a big leg up. Shawn Hymel at SparkFun authored a complete and excellent open source Arduino library (for 3.3 V Arduinos only!) that supports every feature of the device (http://mng.bz/8gE7). It's outstanding: readable and exhaustively commented. Cross-referencing between the Arduino library and the datasheet fleshes out some other details about working with the device.

HOW TO WORK WITH THE APDS-9960

Before gesture data can be generated, the APDS-9960 hardware needs to be initialized and have its gesture mode enabled. This is, conceptually, a two-step process.

First, there's a *setup* phase in which defaults and settings are written to a number of different individual registers on the APDS-9960. Subsequently, there's an *enable* phase in which the gesture mode is activated (as opposed to a mode for one of the device's other sensors) and some gesture-specific settings are written to some more registers (figure 9.13).

To use a very sloppy, inaccurate metaphor: *setup* is like turning the chip on and booting it up, whereas *enable* is like launching a gesture-specific app on the device. Although your implementation will only support gesture sensing—which means enable will always happen right after setup without user intervention—keeping these two phases distinct will make it easier to add additional sensor support later.

Which registers and what values need to be written during setup and enable? All of that info is in the datasheet; it requires time and patience and attention to detail to organize it all.

With setup and enable completed, the APDS-9960 will be actively sensing for gesture movement. When the device senses motion and begins to produce data, it will

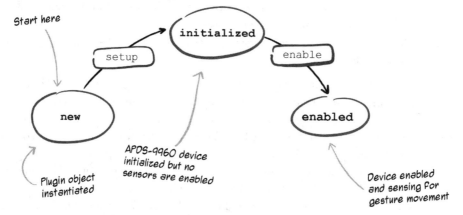

Figure 9.13 In this simplified partial state machine representation of your plugin, a plugin object instance starts out in a `new` state. Via a `setup` method it moves into an `initialized` state, at which point the APDS-9960 device is initialized but not actively sensing gestures. An `enable` method enables the gesture mode on the device.

pull the interrupt pin LOW, signaling that a gesture has been detected. That is, the voltage on the Tessel pin connected to the breakout board's interrupt pin will change from 3.3 V to 0 V. That so-called *falling edge* from HIGH to LOW is the sign that your software should read gesture data from the device.

The data representing a gesture is composed of a collection of 4-byte datasets, each containing 1 byte (a value from 0 to 255) for each direction (up, down, left, right). By analyzing the way these values change for each direction over the set of dataset samples, it's possible to derive an overall gesture direction.

When the device detects gesture movements, it pulls the interrupt LOW and then starts stashing datasets into memory registers. There are 128 bytes of space on the device for this—up to 32 readings of 4 bytes each—and the data is put into these registers in a FIFO (first-in, first-out) manner (figure 9.14).

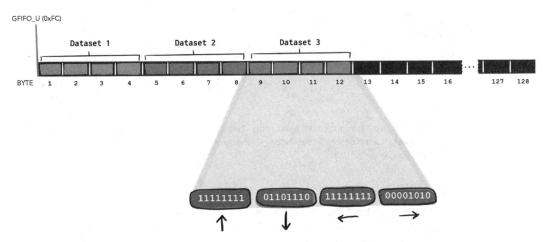

Figure 9.14 There are 128 bytes of FIFO RAM, starting at memory address 0xFC, available to hold gesture data. In this example, there are three datasets available in the FIFO queue. A dataset is composed of four bytes, each representing data for a different direction—up, down, left, and right.

When the controlling device—your Tessel—reads data bytes out of those registers, it frees up space, and more data can be pushed into the FIFO RAM. This cycle continues—the controller reads, the device puts more data in the FIFO—until no more gesture data is coming in and the FIFO is emptied. Then the data can be processed by the controlling device (figure 9.15).

TECHNICALLY SPEAKING: INTERRUPTS Technically, the device will trigger an interrupt on detecting gesture data because you'll configure it to do so as part of the enable step. The APDS-9960 is highly configurable, and gesture interrupt is an optional feature. Even more technically, it will trigger an interrupt after four datasets (samples) have been put into the FIFO RAM. Precisely when that interrupt triggers is, yep, also configurable.

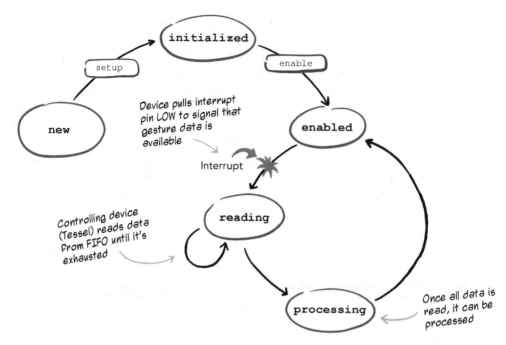

Figure 9.15   The plugin's state machine gains more detail as research continues. When an interrupt is detected, the plugin instance enters a reading cycle phase and then a processing phase before returning to the active-listening enabled state.

PROTOTYPING A PROOF-OF-CONCEPT

Before tackling the plugin implementation, a sanity check is in order. You're going to establish a working area, wire up the chip, and make sure you can establish I²C communication with it. That will make you feel more confident as you get into the more detail-oriented development phases.

Wiring up the APDS-9960 breakout board is easy, though you'll need to solder header pins onto it first. Connect it as shown in figure 9.16. The interrupt pin is connected to pin A2 on the Tessel, which is an interrupt-capable pin.

Create a new project working area and install these dependencies:

```
mkdir gesture
cd gesture
npm init -y
npm install johnny-five tessel-io
```

Copy the RemoteSwitch.js file into the gesture directory, as well. You'll be using it again later.

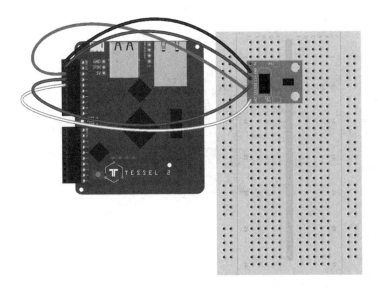

Figure 9.16 Wiring diagram for APDS-9960 breakout board

Creating and sharing circuit and wiring diagrams

To create the wiring diagrams used in this book, I used the open source Fritzing software (http://fritzing.org/home/), which is available on Mac, Windows, and Linux platforms. It comes with a variety of parts, including boards and components that you can build diagrams with. In addition, parts manufacturers like SparkFun and AdaFruit often provide Fritzing parts for their products. I was able to find a part for the APDS-9960 in SparkFun's Fritzing_Parts repository, for example (http://mng.bz/Hsa2).

It's possible to create schematics as well as diagrams with Fritzing, though I find it finicky. Considerably more heavy-hitting in the schematic and PCB-design software world is EAGLE by Autodesk. It has, unsurprisingly, a learning curve, but it's widely used and there is a cross-platform free version if you want to take it for a spin (www.autodesk.com/products/eagle/free-download).

KiCad EDA is another option for cross-platform, open source schematic and PCB design software (http://kicad-pcb.org/).

If you're keen on experimenting with simulating electronics circuitry—not high-level breakout boards and microcontrollers, but fundamentals like capacitors, logic gates, transistors, and transformers—you might try the iCircuit App ($9.99), available for iOS, Android, and Windows (desktop and phone). This isn't a static drawing or drafting app. Instead, it's a live-simulation engine that allows you to see what really happens as you make changes to circuits.

One of the many registers on the APDS-9960 is a read-only DEVICE_ID register, with address 0x92 (p. 25 of the datasheet). When reading a byte from that address, you should always get the value 0xAB (figure 9.17). This isn't useful for your further operation of the chip, but it is a convenient way to make sure that I²C communication is working and that you are, indeed, connected to an APDS-9960.

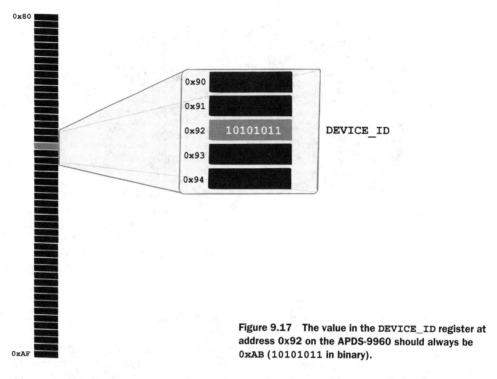

Figure 9.17   The value in the DEVICE_ID register at address 0x92 on the APDS-9960 should always be 0xAB (10101011 in binary).

Create a file called i2c-test.js and add the following code to it.

Listing 9.7   Testing the connection to the APDS-9960

Starts I²C communications with slave address 0x39.
This is the APDS-9960's hard-coded I²C address.

```
const five = require('johnny-five');
const Tessel = require('tessel-io');
const board = new five.Board({ io: new Tessel() });

board.on('ready', () => {
  board.i2cConfig({ address: 0x39 });
  board.i2cReadOnce(0x39, 0x92, 1, data => {
    if (data[0] !== 0xAB) { // DEVICE_ID register should return 0xAB
      throw new Error('Unable to establish connection with APDS9960');
    } else {
      console.log('Connected to APDS-9960!');
    }
  });
});
```

Reads I byte from the 0x92 register of the device at address 0x39

If that register doesn't contain the data 0xAB, something went wrong.

DEFAUL I²C INTERFACE   Tessel has two I²C interfaces. Johnny-Five, via tessel-io, will automatically use the one on port A if not told otherwise in options passed to board.i2cConfig().

I²C capabilities in Johnny-Five

The `i2cReadOnce(address, register, bytesToRead, handler(arrayOfBytes))` method reads the given number of `bytesToRead` starting from the `register` indicated. The callback is called and passed an array of bytes when the read is complete.

`i2cReadOnce` is distinct from a related method, `i2cRead`. Like the name implies, `i2cReadOnce` *reads once*, whereas `i2cRead` will *continuously* read from the indicated address/register combination. `i2cRead` is handy if you want to read from the same register(s) over and over again to watch for changes. In your case, you'll be using the interrupt capability of the APDS-9960 to let you know when there's new gesture data, not polling using `i2cRead`.

The actual underlying implementation of these I²C utility methods—which also, unsurprisingly, include the ability to *write* to an I²C device—is up to the active I/O plugin. In the Tessel's case, this is handled by `tessel-io`; for Arduino, it would be Firmata doing the heavy lifting here.

Try this test code out on your connected Tessel and APDS-9960 circuit:

```
$ t2 run i2c-test.js --lan
```

Once you successfully see the logged message "Connected to APDS-9960!" it's time to move on and build the component plugin itself.

WRITING THE APDS9960 PLUGIN

Create a file called APDS9960.js and start with the code shown in the following listing. To complete the plugin's code, you'll fill these sections in.

> **Listing 9.8 APDS9960.js starting point**

```
// Dependencies
const Emitter = require('events').EventEmitter;
const util    = require('util');

/** CONSTANTS HERE **/

module.exports = function (five) {
  return (function () {
    /**
     * @param {Object} opts Options: pin, address
     * pin denotes interrupt pin connection
     *
     * Sample initialization:
     * var gesture = new APDS9960('A2');
     * var gesture = new APDS9960({ pin: 'A2'});
     * gesture.on('up', () => { ...do something ...});
     */
    function APDS9960 (opts) {
      // Constructor: Set up instance properties and kick off initialization
    }

    // Extend Node.js' EventEmitter class so that our object can emit events
    util.inherits(APDS9960, Emitter);
```

```
    /* Reset this instance's current gesture data */
    APDS9960.prototype.resetGesture = function () { };

    /* `setup` and `enable` are invoked from the constructor */
    APDS9960.prototype.setup = function (callback) { };
    APDS9960.prototype.enable = function () { };

    /* When interrupt is pulled LOW, `readGesture` reads data out of the
     * FIFO until the data are exhausted, then invokes `processGesture`
     * and `decodeGesture` to process the resulting data
     */
    APDS9960.prototype.readGesture = function () { };

    /* `processGesture` performs some computations over read data and
     * determines some ratios and deltas in the directional samples.
     */
    APDS9960.prototype.processGesture = function () { };

    /* Using `deltas` computed by `processGesture`, "decodes" the
     * information into a gesture (up, down, left, right) when possible
     * and emits events.
     */
    APDS9960.prototype.decodeGesture = function () { };

    return APDS9960;
  }());
};
```

Methods in the high-level API surface represent the complete state machine (figure 9.18).
Now you need to implement those methods.

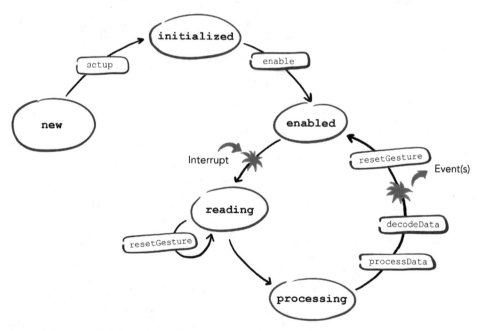

Figure 9.18   The plugin's state machine is now complete. The next step is to implement it.

CONSTANTS AND CONFIGURATION SETTINGS

You'll get some constants defined first, as there are a lot of them. But don't panic. The constants in APDS9960.js define register addresses, bitmasks, default values, and some other configuration bits and bobs.

Figuring out which registers need to be written to set up and enable the device is a detail-oriented exercise of datasheet reference (and peeking at other software implementations when available).

Figure 9.19 shows some of the registers to which configuration settings are written during setup and enable. Some registers' values are set to a simple sensible default value, such as GPENTH, which is set to the binary representation of 40. Others are disabled—GOFFSET_U is set to 0x00. And some are bitmasks, setting several flags—configuration values—at once (GCONF1, GCONF2).

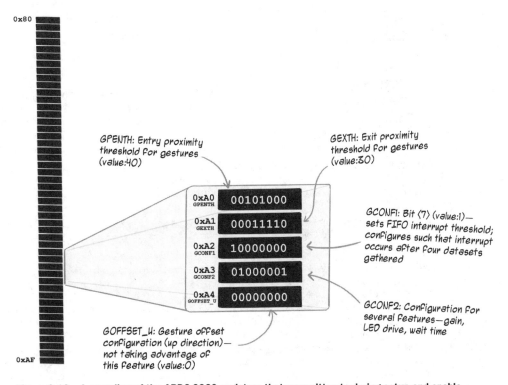

Figure 9.19   A sampling of the APDS-9960 registers that are written to during setup and enable

USING BITMASKING TO MANAGE FEATURE CONFIGURATION   The APDS-9960 plugin makes use of *bitmasking* to manage configuration settings on the APDS-9960—several configuration values are often contained within a single byte, with different bit positions corresponding to the values for different features. Several mask flags are bitwise-OR'ed together to compose the multifeature byte.

For example, the register at address 0xA3 (GCONF2), contains configuration for three features (figure 9.20).

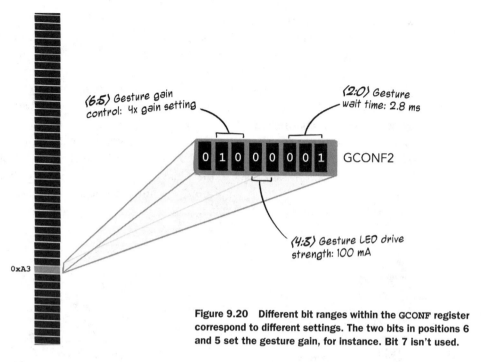

Figure 9.20   **Different bit ranges within the GCONF register correspond to different settings. The two bits in positions 6 and 5 set the gesture gain, for instance. Bit 7 isn't used.**

Once again, I point you to MDN's excellent article on bitwise operators and bitmasking (http://mng.bz/CLvy).

Fill in the constants as shown in the following listing.

Listing 9.9   **APDS9960 constants**

```
const REGISTERS = {
  ENABLE    : 0x80, // Enable different sensors/features (p.20)
  WTIME     : 0x83, // Wait time config value (p.21)
  PPULSE    : 0x8E, // Proximity pulse count and length (p.23)
  CONFIG2   : 0x90, // Second configuration register (p.24), for LED boost
  DEVICE_ID : 0x92, // Contains device ID (0xAB) (p.25)
  GPENTH    : 0xA0, // Entry proximity threshold for gestures (p.27)
  GEXTH     : 0xA1, // Exit proximity threshold for gestures (p.28)
  GCONF1    : 0xA2, // Gesture config 1: gesture detection masking (p.28)
  GCONF2    : 0xA3, // G config 2: gain, LED drive, gesture wait time (p.29)
  GOFFSET_U : 0xA4, // Gesture offset (up) (p.30)
  GOFFSET_D : 0xA5, // Gesture offset (down) (p.30)
  GPULSE    : 0xA6, // Gesture Pulse count and length (p.31)
  GOFFSET_L : 0xA7, // Gesture offset (left) (p.30)
  GOFFSET_R : 0xA9, // Gesture offset (right) (p.31)
  GCONF4    : 0xAB, // Gesture config 4: interrupts, mode enable (p.32)
  GFLVL     : 0xAE, // Gesture FIFO level: # of datasets in FIFO (p.32)
  GSTATUS   : 0xAF, // Gesture status; bit 0 indicates available data (p.33)
  GFIFO_U   : 0xFC, // 1st FIFO register in (RAM)—read data from here (p.33)
};
```

```
const FLAGS = {
  GFIFOTH   : 0b10000000, /* FIFO threshold: trigger interrupt after
                              4 datasets in FIFO (GCONF1 <7:6> p.28) */
  GGAIN     : 0b01000000, /* Gesture gain control:
                              4x (GCONF2 <6:5> p.29) */
  GLDRIVE   : 0b00000000, /* Gesture LED drive strength:
                            * 100mA (GCONF2 <4:3> p.29) */
  GWTIME    : 0b00000001, /* Gesture wait time:
                              2.8ms (GCONF2 <2:0> p.29) */
  GPLEN     : 0b11000000, /* Gesture pulse length:
                              32µs (GPULSE <7 :6> p.31) */
  GPULSE    : 0b00001001, /* Gesture pulse count:
                              10 (9 + 1) (GPULSE <5:0> p.31) */
  GVALID    : 0b00000001, /* GSTATUS register value
                              indicates valid data if 0th bit is 1 */
  PPLEN     : 0b10000000, /* Proximity pulse length:
                              16µs (PPULSE <7 :6> p.23) */
  PPULSE    : 0b10001001, /* Proximity pulse count:
                              10 (9 + 1) (PPULSE <5:0> p.23) */
  LED_BOOST: 0b00110000, /* LED drive boost:
                              300% (CONFIG2 <5:4> p.24) */
  GIEN      : 0b00000010, /* Gesture interrupt enable:
                              yes (GCONF4 <1> p.32) */
  GMODE     : 0b00000001, /* Gesture mode:
                              yes! (GCONF4 <0> p.32) */
  ENABLE    : 0b01001101, /* Enable features:
                              Gesture, Wait, Proximity, Power on
                              (ENABLE, p.20) */
};

// During setup, (value) is written to each register (key)
const SETUP_DEFAULTS = {
  ENABLE    : 0x00,             /* Disable all things,
                                   effectively turning the chip off (p. 20) */
  GPENTH    : 40,               // Entry proximity threshold
  GEXTH     : 30,               // Exit proximity threshold
  GCONF1    : FLAGS.GFIFOTH, // FIFO interrupt threshold
  GCONF2    : FLAGS.GGAIN | FLAGS.GLDRIVE | FLAGS.GWTIME, // Gesture gain,
  ↳ LED drive, wait time
  GOFFSET_U: 0x00,             // no offset
  GOFFSET_D: 0x00,             // no offset
  GOFFSET_L: 0x00,             // no offset
  GOFFSET_R: 0x00,             // no offset
  GPULSE    : FLAGS.GPLEN | FLAGS.GPULSE // pulse count and length,
};

// During enable, each (value) is written to register (key)
const ENABLE_VALUES = {
  WTIME  : 0xFF,                      /* Wait time between cycles in
                                         low-power mode: 2.78ms (p. 21) */
  PPULSE : FLAGS.PPLEN | FLAGS.PPULSE, // Proximity pulse length and count
  CONFIG2: FLAGS.LED_BOOST,
  GCONF4 : FLAGS.GIEN | FLAGS.GMODE,
```

```
        ENABLE : FLAGS.ENABLE
    };

    // For processing read data
    const GESTURE_THRESHOLD_OUT = 30;
    const GESTURE_SENSITIVITY = 10;
```

TECHNICALLY SPEAKING: HOW IT ACTUALLY WORKS   The APDS-9960 senses "gestures" by detecting changes in the amount of energy reflected back to it by a built-in, infrared LED. Details of this LED's configuration—how much power is used to drive it, how many times it pulses, and how long each pulse lasts per detection cycle—pop up frequently in the defined configuration values.

9.3.2   *Implementing constructor and initialization methods*

Next, you'll flesh out the constructor as well as the methods for initializing and enabling the device into gesture mode.

The basic structure of the constructor is the same as the RemoteSwitch constructor. The constructor also kicks off setup and enable, as shown in the next listing.

Listing 9.10   APDS9960: constructor and gesture data reset

Registers the component with the active board

Interrupt will pull from HIGH to LOW to activate; starts with a HIGH value (I)

```
function APDS9960 (opts) {
    if (!(this instanceof APDS9960)) {
        return new APDS9960(opts);
    }
    five.Board.Component.call(this, opts = five.Board.Options(opts));
    this.interruptState = 1; // Interrupt is active LOW
    opts.address       = opts.address || I2C_ADDR;
    this.address       = opts.address;
    this.io.i2cConfig(opts); // Get I2C comms started for the device

    this.io.i2cReadOnce(this.address, REGISTERS.DEVICE_ID, 1, data => {
        if (data[0] !== DEVICE_ID) { // DEVICE_ID register should return 0xAB
            throw new Error('Unable to establish connection with APDS9960');
        }
    });
    this.resetGesture();
    this.setup(this.enable);
}

util.inherits(APDS9960, Emitter);

APDS9960.prototype.resetGesture = function () {
    this.gestureData = {
        raw: [],
        deltas: {},
        movements: { // A gesture can have movements along more than one axis
            vertical  : false,
            horizontal: false,
```

Readies the I²C address to pass to i2cConfig

Retains the I²C address on the component object, too

this.io is a reference to the active board instance.

Resets (initializes) gesture-holding data object

Kicks off setup (followed by enable)

```
    up        : false,
    down      : false,
    left      : false,
    right     : false
  },
  valid: false, // Was gesture decoding successful?
  direction: undefined
};
};
```

Next, the initialization methods: setup and enable.

```
APDS9960.prototype.setup = function (callback) {
  for (var rKey in SETUP_DEFAULTS) {                    ◄──   Writes default values
    this.io.i2cWrite(this.address,                            (SETUP_DEFAULTS) for
      REGISTERS[rKey], [SETUP_DEFAULTS[rKey]]);               device setup to various
  }                                                           registers
  if (typeof callback === 'function') {
    callback.call(this);                      ◄──   Invokes callback
  }                                                 (enable, in this case)
};


                                                              Configures the
                                                              connected interrupt
                                                              as a digital input pin
APDS9960.prototype.enable = function () {
  // Set up interrupt handling
  this.io.pinMode(this.pin, this.io.MODES.INPUT);    ◄──
  // Interrupts from device are active LOW—when pin goes LOW we should act
  this.io.digitalRead(this.pin, data => {             ◄──
    if (data !== this.interruptState && data === 0) { ◄──   Reads values
      this.readGesture();                                   continuously from
    }                              When interrupt goes       the interrupt pin
    this.interruptState = data;    from HIGH to LOW,
  });                              invokes readGesture
  for (var rKey in ENABLE_VALUES) {          ◄──   Like setup, writes
    this.io.i2cWrite(this.address,                  configuration for gesture-
      REGISTERS[rKey], [ENABLE_VALUES[rKey]]);      mode-specific features
  }
};
```

READING SENSOR DATA

With that code for initialization and setup squared away, let's attack the real meat of the plugin: reading and processing gesture data. When the interrupt pin goes LOW, readGesture is invoked, reading data from the APDS-9960.

```
APDS9960.prototype.readGesture = function () {
  // GSTATUS value determines whether valid data is available (p.33)
  this.io.i2cReadOnce(this.address, REGISTERS.GSTATUS, 1, status => {
```

```
        if (status & FLAGS.GVALID === FLAGS.GVALID) {
          // There should be valid data in the FIFO
          // GFLVL will report how many datasets are in the FIFO (p.32)
          this.io.i2cReadOnce(this.address, REGISTERS.GFLVL, 1, fifoLevel => {
            // Read the number of 4-byte samples indicated by sampleCount
            // And split them out into their directional components
            this.io.i2cReadOnce(this.address,
              REGISTERS.GFIFO_U, (fifoLevel * 4), rawData => {
                for (var i = 0; i < rawData.length; i += 4) {
                  this.gestureData.raw.push({
                    up   : rawData[i],
                    down : rawData[i + 1],
                    left : rawData[i + 2],
                    right: rawData[i + 3]
                  });
                }
                return this.readGesture(); // Keep reading data...
              });
          });
        } else { // No (more) data to gather about this gesture
          this.processGesture();
          this.decodeGesture();
          this.resetGesture();
        }
      });
    };
```

First, readGesture reads a byte from the GSTATUS register. If the value in that register has its least significant (0th) bit set to 1, you're in business: there's valid data to be read out of FIFO. But how much data? The value of the GFLVL (gesture FIFO level) register will tell you how many dataset samples are available in the FIFO at the moment. Then it goes ahead and reads that many samples out of the FIFO registers, which start at GFIFO_U (address 0xFC).

Recall that each dataset is four bytes (one byte for each direction), so the total number of bytes to read out of the FIFO is fifoLevel * 4. readGestures makes use of the i2cReadOnce method once more, this time reading fifoLevel * 4 bytes instead of a single byte. Then it iterates over each full dataset and stuffs individual bytes corresponding to each direction into the raw data structure for later processing. Then it calls itself (recursively) again to see if there's more data available to read (figure 9.21).

This cycle repeats until the GSTATUS register value indicates that no valid data is left to read—the first conditional fails and execution continues in the else clause. When the data-read cycle is complete, the processing of that data begins.

PROCESSING AND DECODING GESTURE DATA

The methods in your APDS9960 plugin distinguish between *processing* and *decoding* gesture data (figure 9.22).

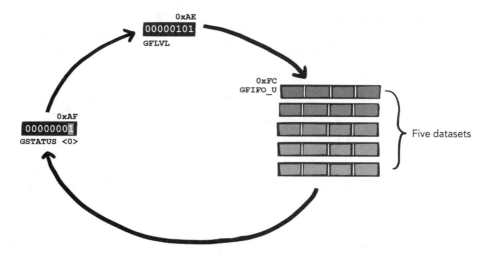

Figure 9.21 The read cycle begins by checking that the 0th bit in the GSTATUS register is 1. If so, GFLVL is read to see how many samples are available (0101, that is, 5), and then the indicated number are read from the FIFO. The cycle continues until GSTATUS<0> is 0.

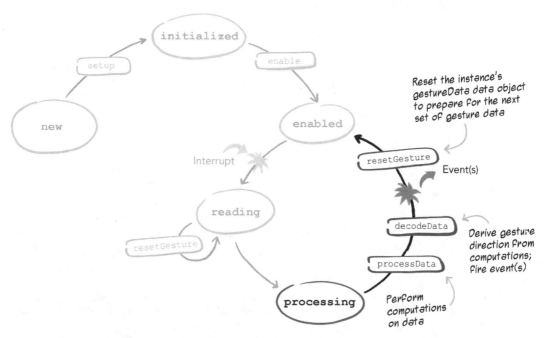

Figure 9.22 processData performs arithmetic on data; decodeData derives gesture direction from the computed results and fires events. Finally, the gesture data object is reset on the instance so it's ready to collect data from the next gesture.

In the processing step, math happens. The complete raw collection of samples is filtered to include only readings in which every direction's value exceeds a defined threshold constant. Then the change (delta) in the ratios of readings over time is computed on each axis (up/down and left/right).

Listing 9.13   Processing gesture data

```
APDS9960.prototype.processGesture = function () {
  const raw = this.gestureData.raw;
  const directionDelta = function (el1, el2, dir1, dir2) {          ◁
    var el2r = ((el2[dir1] - el2[dir2]) * 100) / (el2[dir1] + el2[dir2]);
    var el1r = ((el1[dir1] - el1[dir2]) * 100) / (el1[dir1] + el1[dir2]);
    return el2r - el1r;
  };
  const exceedsThreshold = raw.filter(sample => {                    ◁
    return (sample.up > GESTURE_THRESHOLD_OUT &&
            sample.down > GESTURE_THRESHOLD_OUT &&
            sample.left > GESTURE_THRESHOLD_OUT &&
            sample.right > GESTURE_THRESHOLD_OUT);
  });
  if (!exceedsThreshold.length || raw.length < 4) {                  ◁
    // If not enough data or none exceed threshold, nothing to do
    // This will result in gesture data being ignored and discarded
    return false;
  }

  const first = exceedsThreshold[0];
  const last = exceedsThreshold[exceedsThreshold.length - 1];
  const deltas = {
    upDown: directionDelta(first, last, 'up', 'down'),
    leftRight: directionDelta(first, last, 'left', 'right')
  };
  this.gestureData.deltas = deltas;                                 ◁
};
```

Computes deltas by comparing ratios of different directions' readings

Filters samples to include only those with readings exceeding the threshold

Makes sure there is valid data to process

Ultimately, cooks up some deltas

Finally, the decoding step in the following listing translates the deltas computed by the processGesture method into derived directions for the overall gesture. It then fires a corresponding event—up, down, left, or right—or, if it can't determine a clear, single gesture direction, it will fire a generic gesture event, as shown in the next listing.

Listing 9.14   Decoding gesture data

```
APDS9960.prototype.decodeGesture = function () {
  const deltas = this.gestureData.deltas;
  const verticalMotion = Math.abs(deltas.upDown);
  const horizontalMotion = Math.abs(deltas.leftRight);
  if (verticalMotion > GESTURE_SENSITIVITY) { // Determine meaningful
➥ movement on vertical axis
    this.gestureData.valid = true;
```

```
      this.gestureData.movements.vertical = true;
      this.gestureData.movements.up = (deltas.upDown >= 0);
      this.gestureData.movements.down = (deltas.upDown < 0);
    }
    if (horizontalMotion > GESTURE_SENSITIVITY) { // Determine meaningful
 ➥ movement on horizontal axis
      this.gestureData.valid = true;
      this.gestureData.movements.horizontal = true;
      this.gestureData.movements.left = (deltas.leftRight >= 0);
      this.gestureData.movements.right = (deltas.leftRight < 0);
    }
    if (this.gestureData.valid) {
      if (verticalMotion > horizontalMotion) {
        this.gestureData.direction = (this.gestureData.movements.up) ?
          'up' : 'down';
      } else {
        this.gestureData.direction = (this.gestureData.movements.left) ?
        'left' : 'right';
      }
    }
    // Emit a directional event if there is a direction
    if (this.gestureData.direction) {
      this.emit(this.gestureData.direction, this.gestureData);
    }
    // Always emit a generic gesture event, even if decoding failed
    this.emit('gesture', this.gestureData);
};
```

With that, the code for the plugin is complete!

9.3.3 *Integrating the gesture sensor and remote switches*

You can now edit index.js to add some quick testing code, as shown in the following listing. Before you get to the big combination step—hooking up the remote switches—you can test for different direction swipe events and log them to the console.

> **Listing 9.15 APDS9960 test drive**

```
const five = require('johnny-five');
const Tessel = require('tessel-io');
const Gesture = require('./APDS9960')(five);

const board = new five.Board({ io: new Tessel() });

board.on('ready', () => {
  const gesture = new Gesture({ pin: 'A2'});
  gesture.on('right', () => console.log('right'));
  gesture.on('left', () => console.log('left'));
  gesture.on('up', () => console.log('up'));
  gesture.on('down', () => console.log('down'));
});
```

Run index.js on the Tessel (`t2 run index.js --lan`) and try moving your hand over the top of the gesture sensor—the best distance is around eight inches (20 cm).

COMBINING APDS9960 AND REMOTESWITCH

You've already got the ingredients to control individual on/off switch combinations using the gesture sensor and RemoteSwitch. For example, you could do something like what's shown in the following listing.

Listing 9.16   APDS9960 controlling a single switch with the gesture sensor

```
const five = require('johnny-five');
const Tessel = require('tessel-io');
const Gesture = require('./APDS9960')(five);
const RemoteSwitch = require('./RemoteSwitch')(five);

const board = new five.Board({ io: new Tessel() });

board.on('ready', () => {
  const gesture = new Gesture({ pin: 'A2'});
  const switch1 = new RemoteSwitch({ pins : { on: 'A3', off: 'A4' } });
  gesture.on('right', () => switch1.on());
  gesture.on('left', () => switch2.on());
});
```

So far, so good. But wasn't one of the stated goals way back at the beginning the ability to turn all of the switches on or off at once? The good news is that you're about to make that happen. The other news is that you need to take another step to make it so.

THE CHALLENGES OF ORCHESTRATING SEVERAL SWITCHES

The design of RemoteSwitch takes into account the need to stagger switch activations: it queues "commands" that come in when one of the buttons is already active, sticks them in a FIFO queue, and executes the next queued command when it's no longer active. In addition, it will invoke a provided callback when it's done with a command. So you could execute the code in the following listing without fear of the switch stepping on itself.

Listing 9.17   A pair of buttons managed by a RemoteSwitch instance has a queue

```
switch1.on();   // Happens right away
switch1.off();  // Gets queued
switch1.on();   // Gets queued
switch1.off(() => console.log('hi!')); // Gets queued; logs 'hi!' to the
➥ console when it's done
```

But, alas, there's a shortcoming: the queueing is managed individually for each switch pair. Different RemoteSwitch instances have no idea of each other; see the following listing.

Listing 9.18   Each RemoteSwitch has its own queue

```
switch1.on();   // Happens right away
switch1.off();  // Gets queued in `switch1`'s queue
switch2.on();   // `switch2`'s queue is empty...happens right away (uh oh)
switch3.on();   // `switch3`'s queue is empty...happens right away (oh dear)
```

It's quite probable that `switch2` and `switch3` will try to activate while `switch1` is still busy—the equivalent of mashing several buttons on the remote at the same time. That's probably not good. `RemoteSwitch` was designed in such a way that each switch pair is unaware of each other. That's a nice nod toward hardware abstraction, but our reality is that multiple switch pairs are sharing the same transmitter on a single remote device.

CONTROLLING MULTIPLE SWITCHES WITH COLLECTION

Hooboy, another inflection point in the project. You could tear `RemoteSwitch` apart and rewrite it to handle multiple sets of switches and their co-mingled queues. Or you could write some code for managing multiple switch pairs inside the application-specific logic.

Both of those options have drawbacks. It would be tedious to adapt `RemoteSwitch` without breaking its existing API or overcomplicating it (this option would seem more attractive if you were starting from scratch). Dumping related logic into your main application code would be ugly and distracting. After some mulling, I settled on a pragmatic—if slightly cobbled-together—third option that takes advantage of a Johnny-Five mixin called `Collection`.

Built-in *collection classes* like `Motors` (which you saw in chapter 6) make use of the `Collection` mixin in Johnny-Five, which provides features for managing multiple components within a single container-like object. You can use some of the features offered by this mixin to create a component that can manage multiple `RemoteSwitch` objects. Once finished, you'll be able to write code like that in the following listing from within your main application module.

Listing 9.19 Using `RemoteSwitches`

```
const switches = new RemoteSwitches([
  new RemoteSwitch({ pins : { on: 'A3', off: 'A4' } }),
  new RemoteSwitch({ pins: { on: 'A5', off: 'A6' } }),
  new RemoteSwitch({ pins: { on: 'A7', off: 'B0' } })
]);
// You can act on all switches at once...
switches.on(); // Turn all switches on
// Or a single switch...
switches.off(1); // Turn the second switch off
```

Create a file called RemoteSwitches.js in your working directory, and add the following code.

Listing 9.20 `RemoteSwitches`

```
const util    = require('util');

module.exports = function (five, RemoteSwitch) {
  return (function () {
    function RemoteSwitches (opts) {
      if (!(this instanceof RemoteSwitches)) {
```

```
      return new RemoteSwitches(opts);
    }
    // RemoteSwitch is the "type" of each individual component object
    // that will be managed by this RemoteSwitches instance
    Object.defineProperty(this, 'type', { value: RemoteSwitch });
    // Make it go: register and initialize the collection component objects
    five.Collection.call(this, opts);
    this.isActive = false; 1((CO11-1))
    this.queue = [];
  }
  // Use the Collection mixin
  util.inherits(RemoteSwitches, five.Collection);

  // The nuts-and-bolts logic for (de-)activating a given switch
  // Note that this is not on the prototype (inaccessible externally)
  const write = function (whichSwitch, turnOn) {
    if (this.isActive) {
      this.queue.push([whichSwitch, turnOn]);
      return;
    }
    this.isActive = true;
    // An individual RemoteSwitch object's "toggle" method
    // is invoked
    whichSwitch.toggle.call(whichSwitch, turnOn, () => {
      this.isActive = false;
      if (this.queue.length) {
        write.apply(this, this.queue.shift());
      }
    });
  };

  // Prototype methods take optional `idx` argument to designate which
  // switch to activate. If not provided, all switches will be affected.
  RemoteSwitches.prototype.toggle = function (idx, turnOn) {
    if (typeof idx !== 'undefined' && this[idx]) {
      write.call(this, this[idx], turnOn);
    } else {
      this.each(whichSwitch => write.call(this, whichSwitch, turnOn));
    }
  };

  RemoteSwitches.prototype.on = function (idx) { this.toggle(idx, true); };
  RemoteSwitches.prototype.off = function (idx) { this.toggle(idx, false); };
  return RemoteSwitches;
}());
};
```

9.3.4 *Pulling the whole project together*

All the pieces are ready now to make a combined project, bringing together software and circuit modules into a gesture-controlled remote control.

Combine the two circuits—remote control and gesture—as shown in figure 9.23. The output sides of the photocouplers should connect to the remote control's button

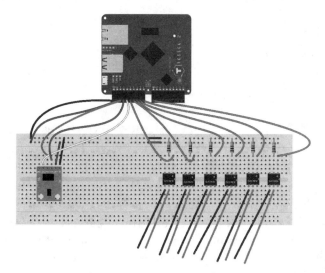

Figure 9.23   Wiring diagram showing the combination of the APDS-9960 breakout board and the button/photocoupler circuits.

contacts. Note that the photocouplers are now connected to different pins on the Tessel to make room for the APDS-9960.

> **USING FULL-SIZE BREADBOARDS**   If you use a full-size breadboard, as shown in figure 9.23, make sure you connect the power rails as shown midway along the board's length: the power rail connections have a break in the middle.

You can think of a full-size breadboard as two half-size breadboards glommed together.

FINALIZING THE SOFTWARE

Your gesture directory should now contain the following:

- *APDS9960.js_*—Gesture sensor plugin
- *RemoteSwitch.js*—(Individual) remote switch plugin
- *RemoteSwitches.js*—Remote switch collection
- *index.js*—Application logic

To make room for the APDS-9960 connections, the connections for the photocouplers have to jog down a couple of pins (see figure 9.23)—those updated pin numbers are accounted for in the final version of index.js, as shown in the next listing.

Listing 9.21   Pulling it all together in index.js

```
const five = require('johnny-five');                                    Requires the
const Tessel = require('tessel-io');                            RemoteSwitches module
const Gesture = require('./APDS9960')(five);
const RemoteSwitch = require('./RemoteSwitch')(five);
const RemoteSwitches = require('./RemoteSwitches')(five, RemoteSwitch);  ◁

const board = new five.Board({ io: new Tessel() });
```

```
board.on('ready', () => {
  const gesture = new Gesture({ pin: 'A2'});
  const switches = new RemoteSwitches([
    new RemoteSwitch({ pins : { on: 'A3', off: 'A4' } }),
    new RemoteSwitch({ pins: { on: 'A5', off: 'A6' } }),
    new RemoteSwitch({ pins: { on: 'A7', off: 'B0' } })
  ]);
  gesture.on('up', () => switches.on());
  gesture.on('down', () => switches.off());
  gesture.on('right', () => switches.on(1));
  gesture.on('left', () => switches.off(1));
});
```

You can, of course, change which gestures correspond to what switch behavior.

That was a lot of work! But there are some solid results here. You've definitely carved a few more triumphant notches on your pole of electronics-hackery experience. Of course, there are still wires going everywhere, something you'll tackle in a bit when we look into different kinds of project enclosures for different form factors.

Speaking of form factors, you've been giving tons of attention to the Arduino Uno and the Tessel, using both with Johnny-Five. But there are a lot more options for JavaScript-controlled hardware out there. It's time to meet some of the other players.

Summary

- Battery-operated, low-voltage consumer electronics can often be repurposed into parts and components for your own projects (provided you exercise care!). Photocoupler components can help isolate the circuitry in those electronics from your microcontroller circuits.

- Invention requires ingenuity but also persistence and patience. It often requires thinking creatively to solve unexpected problems.

- Datasheets can be overwhelmingly data-dense, but they're vital, and over time you'll learn the ropes and be able to find key information within them—like memory register addresses and configuration steps—more quickly.

- Even personal hobby projects can benefit from an organized development approach: identifying goals and scope, researching, prototyping, and iterating.

- Encapsulating behavior into modular, component-level chunks is a good development practice, especially for abstraction and cross-platform support. With Johnny-Five, you can create component plugins, and you also took advantage of the `Collection` mixin.

Part 4

Using JavaScript with hardware in other environments

This part of the book explores some other environments in which you can use JavaScript to control hardware, and it looks toward the future.

You'll start in chapter 10 by looking at JavaScript and JavaScript-like environments on highly constrained devices, prototyping some experiments with the Espruino Pico and Kinoma Element devices.

Both chapters 10 and 11 walk through a set of reusable steps for getting to know new platforms, quickly. In chapter 11, we'll turn our attention to beefier hardware: general-purpose single-board computers (SBCs) that have onboard I/O capabilities. You'll get up and running with the Raspberry Pi 3 and Beagle-Bone Black and adapt some Johnny-Five experiments to run on both platforms.

Chapter 12 provides a taste of some other pieces of the IoT ecosystem and examines what's possible from within a web browser. You'll use a cloud service to package and deploy a Johnny-Five application to a BeagleBone Black, and you'll explore the leading edge of Web Bluetooth and the Physical Web with the Espruino Puck.js device.

When you're finished with this part of the book, your JavaScript on Things toolkit will be well-stocked, and you'll be ready to strike out on your own into the brave, inspiring world of JavaScript and embedded systems.

JavaScript and constrained hardware

10

In the first half of this book, electronics fundamentals were demonstrated by using a tethered Arduino Uno—a *host-client* setup. In the past few chapters, though, you've met the Tessel 2, which has the oomph to run Node.js natively within its OpenWrt operating system—that's a *single-board-computer* (SBC) setup.

Now we're going to take a look at a third class of JavaScript-controlled platforms: constrained embedded hardware with native support for JavaScript (or, often, something that's JavaScript-*like*). To accomplish this feat with such limited hardware resources, these platforms tend to rely on highly optimized custom JavaScript engines.

These devices are evolving quickly, entering (and exiting) the market more rapidly than can be captured well in print. At this very moment, the Espruino platform—we'll be looking at the Espruino Pico shortly—seems to be maintaining robust momentum (figure 10.1). The Kinoma Element—also on-deck for our investigations—has been in prerelease for quite some time. Although Kinoma's embedded runtime has been held up as an early pioneer in supporting most ECMAScript 6 features, the Element product may not end up taking off. It's hard to say with things moving so quickly.

Obsolescence is pretty much guaranteed for IoT hardware and software information committed to print, which is why this chapter focuses more on tasks and puzzles common across embedded JavaScript platforms. Specific products and platforms come and go, but there are a bunch of common research steps that can help you get up to speed, quickly, on whichever product you choose.

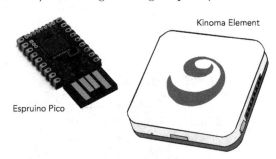

Figure 10.1   Two embedded JavaScript platforms: Espruino Pico and Kinoma Element

---

 For this chapter, you'll need the following:

- 1 Espruino Pico
- 1 Kinoma Element
- 1 USB micro cable
- 18 (two strips of 9 each) 0.1" male breakaway header pins
- 1 USB 2.0 A to USB A female (a.k.a. a USB extension cord) cable
- 1 Adafruit BMP180 I^2C multisensor breakout board
- 1 Nokia 5110 84x48 LCD display module
- 1 100 Ω resistor
- 1 Adafruit HMC5883L magnetometer (compass) breakout board

- 1 full-sized breadboard
- Jumper wires

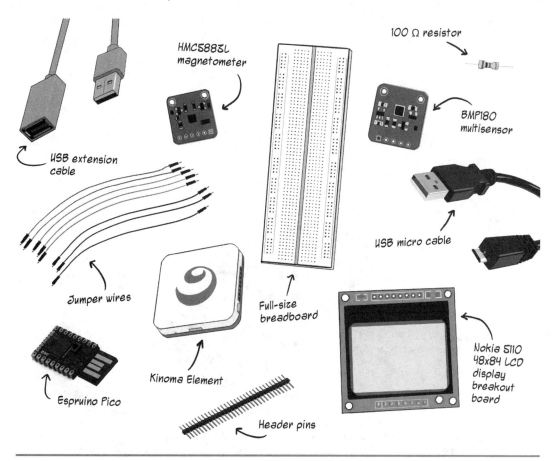

HMC5883L magnetometer

100 Ω resistor

USB extension cable

BMP180 multisensor

Jumper wires

Full-size breadboard

USB micro cable

Kinoma Element

Espruino Pico

Header pins

Nokia 5110 48x84 LCD display breakout board

10.1 *The Espruino Pico platform*

The Espruino Pico has less memory and less computational power than the Tessel 2. There's no WiFi and no USB peripheral support, so why use it? Because it shines at other things: it's cheaper, it's tiny, it's reliable, and it's power-efficient—hallmarks of low-power embedded platforms.

Espruino describes both the hardware family itself and the firmware runtime interpreter that comes preflashed on Espruino devices. Espruino-the-interpreter supports most JavaScript features, but not all of them. You can't get away with omitting semicolons, for example, and regular expressions aren't supported.

It's important to differentiate JavaScript and JavaScript-esque from Node.js: this isn't Node.js, so you can't use Johnny-Five or any npm modules.

Instead, Espruino provides its own JavaScript API for interacting with the hardware I/O (www.espruino.com/Reference#software). You've got enough experience under your belt now that aspects of the API likely ring familiar—there's an analogRead function, for example, that takes a pin number as an argument. There are also Espruino-specific modules that encapsulate the behavior of specific electronic components, as you'll see.

Before examining the Pico in more depth, you'll get it set up and take a Hello World LED-blinking script for a spin.

10.1.1 Setting up the Pico

The Pico needs to be soldered onto header strips (figure 10.2). Your Pico may have come with header strips, but if not you'll need two strips of nine pins each.

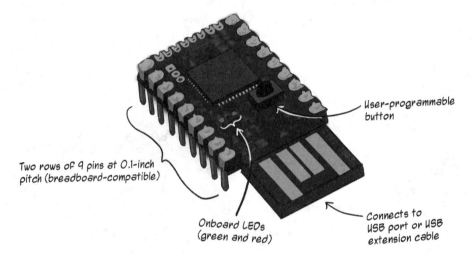

Figure 10.2 The Pico has 18 pins (two rows of 9 each) at a 0.1-inch pitch—breadboard-compatible. They'll need to be soldered onto header pins. One end of the Pico board is shaped so that it can be plugged directly into a USB port.

The Pico plugs right into a USB port. Some versions of the Pico have an additional USB micro connection, but you may well be stuck with just the USB A connection. This can be convenient, because you can plug your Pico right into your computer, but if you want to use the Pico on a breadboard—which is necessary when you want to try out any of the I/O pins—it gets a little tricky. The Pico is designed to connect to a USB A female connector. You can use the kind of cable marketed as a USB extension cable to get the USB A to USB A female connections the Pico needs (figure 10.3).

Things are evolving quickly enough in the Espruino family that including exhaustive setup instructions here would be foolish. Instead, head to https://espruino.com to get started.

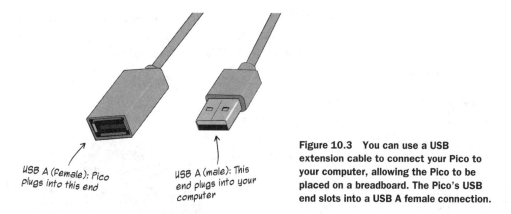

USB A (Female): Pico plugs into this end

USB A (male): This end plugs into your computer

Figure 10.3   You can use a USB extension cable to connect your Pico to your computer, allowing the Pico to be placed on a breadboard. The Pico's USB end slots into a USB A female connection.

These are the basic steps, after plugging your Pico into USB:

1   Get the Pico ready for your platform:
   a   Mac users likely don't need to do anything else.
   b   Windows users will probably need a driver.
   c   Linux users may need to adjust permissions.
2   Install the Espruino IDE Chrome app (and the Chrome browser if you don't have it installed).
3   Launch the Chrome app, and connect to and update the Pico's firmware.

For the purposes of experimenting with the Pico, you'll be using Espruino's web-based IDE (Chrome app)—that means you'll connect to, communicate with, and deploy code to the Pico from within the Chrome app.

Connect to or disconnect from Pico

Upload code to Pico

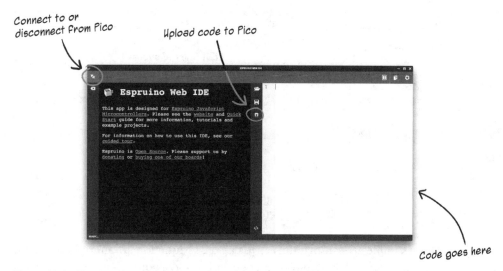

Code goes here

Figure 10.4   The Espruino Chrome app IDE

On the left side of the app's interface, you'll see a terminal-like console area. Once you're connected to a Pico, you can type expressions here directly, sort of like a Node.js interpreter or the Johnny-Five REPL. On the right side is an area where you can compose scripts.

10.1.2 *Hello World LED blink*

Let's try it out with the requisite blinking of an LED. For this experiment, you'll be using one of the Pico's onboard LEDs, so you can plug the Pico into your USB port directly or stick it on a breadboard with a USB extension cable: the choice is yours.

An assortment of variables are available at a global level in Espruino scripts, pertaining to platform features and pins. This includes the variables LED1 and LED2 for the Pico's built-in red and green LEDs, respectively (figure 10.5).

Fire up the Espruino IDE Chrome app and connect to the Pico. Enter the code shown in the following listing into the code-composition area of the screen (the right side) and click the Send to Espruino icon in the center (figure 10.6).

The Pico's built-in LEDs

Figure 10.5   This experiment will cause the Pico's onboard LEDs—one red, one green—to blink alternately. Access to the LEDs is provided via the global variables LED1 and LED2.

Listing 10.1   Blinking the Pico's LEDs

```
var ledStatus = false;
function toggleLED () {
  if (!ledStatus) {
    digitalWrite(LED1, 1);
    digitalWrite(LED2, 0);
  } else {
    digitalWrite(LED1, 0);
    digitalWrite(LED2, 1);
  }
  ledStatus = !ledStatus;
  setTimeout(toggleLED, 500);
}

toggleLED();
```

LEDl (the red onboard LED) and LED2 (green) are available in Pico scripts.

Uses setTimeout to make the function call itself every 500 ms

Kicks off the toggling

This example uses Espruino's digitalWrite function to alternately set LEDs HIGH and LOW. Once you deploy the code to the Pico, you should see the Pico's red and green LEDs blinking, one at a time. You'll also see some output on the left side of the IDE window.

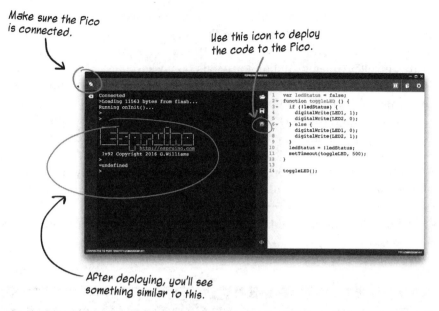

Make sure the Pico is connected.

Use this icon to deploy the code to the Pico.

After deploying, you'll see something similar to this.

Figure 10.6   Entering the LED-blink code into the Espruino IDE (font size increased for visibility)

10.2   *Learning about new platforms*

Now that you've gotten hands-on, let's back up a bit. How do you know that the Pico has two built-in LEDs (red and green), and how do you know that there are variables LED1 and LED2? By now, conventions like digitalWrite being a name for a function that writes logic levels to digital outputs probably seems sensible. But it may still seem somewhat magical or random. Where does one start?

There are a series of sleuthing steps you can apply when facing a new platform to get you scooting along in short order. You'll tackle these to learn about the Pico specifically now, but you can reuse them to evaluate different embedded platforms in the future:

1   Discover the platform's core features
2   Find a pinout or hardware diagram
3   Learn about the configuration and development workflow
4   Find examples and simple tutorials and get hands-on
5   Use the reference API documentation

Let's look at each of these.

10.2.1   *Discovering a platform's core features*

Before you even get your hands on a new dev board or platform, you'll probably want an overall sense of what it can do.

Often the key details are summarized on the manufacturer's or supplier's web site. In the Pico's case, a list of features the Pico's web page gives us the scoop: it's a 3.3 V device, petite in form factor (33 mm x 15 mm), it's powered by a STM32F401CDU6 microcontroller (no, my cat didn't just walk on my keyboard; ST—the manufacturer— has naming conventions that are unromantic, but quite precise), and it uses an ARM Cortex M4 processor (www.espruino.com/Pico).

Also in the key features list are bullet points about power consumption (figure 10.7). Even if the specific numbers cited here don't hit home, you can see that they're making noise about being power efficient.

There are 22 GPIO pins on the device, including 3 I^2C interfaces and 3 (hardware) SPI interfaces—not shabby for something so small. If you click through to the microcontroller's datasheet (http://mng.bz/i7r8), you can see that you have the STM32F401D/E family to thank for that (there's a section about communication interfaces on the front page).

Figure 10.7   The Espruino Pico's key features, listed on Espruino's website

A couple of other features jump out. One is a nice nod to the ubiquity of 5 V logic—"All GPIO is 5 volt tolerant (Arduino compatible)"—a kindness to those of us who have to swap between the two a lot. Output will always be 3.3 V, but 5 V input won't give the Pico heartburn.

Another detail worth noting: although 18 pins (two rows of 9) are at a breadboard-standard 0.1" pin pitch, 8 pins on one short end are only 0.05" apart (figure 10.8). You won't be using those pins in your explorations, as they don't slot easily into a breadboard, but there are physical shims you can get to make it possible.

Granted, this particular list of features doesn't mention that this a JavaScript-powered device, which is kind of key, but you can certainly glean that from Espruino's home page (www.espruino.com).

These pins have a 0.05-inch pitch and thus are not breadboard-compatible.

Figure 10.8 Eight of the Pico's I/O pins are at a 0.05 inch pitch: too narrow to slot into breadboards.

ARM Cortex M MCUs and embedded JavaScript

Both the Espruino Pico and the Kinoma Element are based on microcontrollers from the ARM Cortex M family. Just as ATmega MCUs are found on all sorts of Arduino-compatible, host-client-class boards (like the Arduino Uno and its brethren), ARM Cortex M MCUs are very popular for the class of embedded platforms that include the Element and the Pico. ARM's site claims that 10s of *billions* of devices have been produced using products from the Cortex M family.

The 32-bit microcontrollers in the Cortex M family outclass 8-bit ATmegas while still operating at low power (most are predictably not quite as cheap). Embedded JavaScript (or JavaScript-like) runtimes need more processing power than an 8-bit ATmega can provide.

As you continue to experiment with new platforms, chances are you'll continue to encounter Cortex M variants.

Another thing that's handy to understand is the platform's financial and licensing model. Is the hardware or software (or both) open source, or are they proprietary? This can be relevant if you're considering using a platform commercially, extending hardware or software, or otherwise making contributions to a platform. (Espruino platforms are fully open source.)

10.2.2 *Finding a pinout diagram*

Maybe it's because I have a love for maps, but finding and analyzing a board's pinout diagram is usually when things really click home. These diagrams show you which pins can do what: communication interfaces, PWM, power pins, and so on.

From the Pico's diagram (figure 10.9), we can note a few things (see it in a larger size with more detail on Espruino's Pico documentation page: www.espruino.com/Pico). For one, pin numbers aren't sequential; they jump around a bit, and you'll find both A and B pins on both of the two sides you'll be using. You can also see that there's PWM support on nearly every GPIO pin. Finally, you can see which pins have hardware support for I²C and SPI, and which can support ADC (analog-to-digital conversion).

A combination of sensible overall pin layout (hardware design) and high-quality pinout diagrams can make for a better development experience.

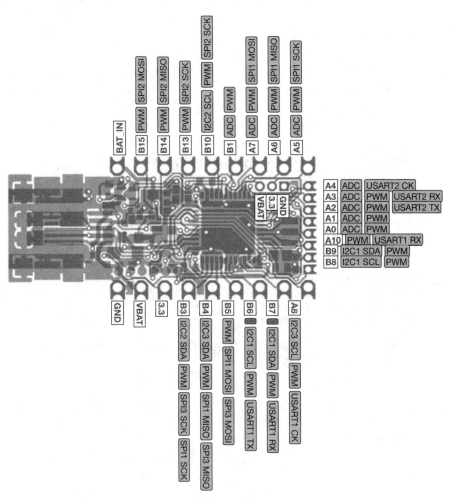

Figure 10.9   Detail of pinout diagram for the Espruino Pico

10.2.3 *Learning about configuration and workflow*

How is code written? Deployed? How is the device managed, configured, and updated? Is it supported for your operating system? Is the configuration process overwhelming and tedious? That could be a sign of an ongoing headache.

In the Pico's case, we've taken the recommended route of using the Chrome app IDE. This can be convenient—code authoring, device management, and deployment are in one place—but if you're the kind of person who has an attachment to your own editor or IDE for writing JavaScript, it might drive you nuts.

Get a sense of the high-level software constructs: are there plugins or other modularized components? Is there a general hardware-oriented API? Espruino has both of these.

10.2.4 *Finding examples and tutorials*

Stepping through some Hello World examples is next, and you've already done that with the Pico. When experimenting with a new platform, figure out how to accomplish some common tasks, such as blinking LEDs, reading data from an analog sensor, working with displays, and controlling I²C devices. Ideally, you'll get hands-on at this step, getting a sense for how it really feels to interact with the platform during development.

Once you've got your head around the big picture, and seen (and tried) a few applied examples, hitting up reference documentation can help fill in the details.

10.2.5 *Using reference API documentation*

If you glance at Espruino's API documentation (10.10), you'll see familiar JavaScript classes—`String`, `Math`, `Boolean`, `JSON`—along with Espruino-specific classes relevant to hardware stuff: `I2C`, `SPI`, `WLAN`. The `Globals` section lists hardware functions like `digitalWrite()` available to Espruino scripts, and also some standard JavaScript global goodies like `setTimeout()` and `eval()`.

There's also a page that lists available modules for Espruino and how to use them (www.espruino.com/Modules). More on that as we explore the Pico more fully.

As you learn more about a platform and gain experience with it, you'll find yourself moving from a learning phase, where you're seeking out prebaked examples, concepts, and tutorials, to a reference phase, where you're searching for details on how to accomplish specific tasks.

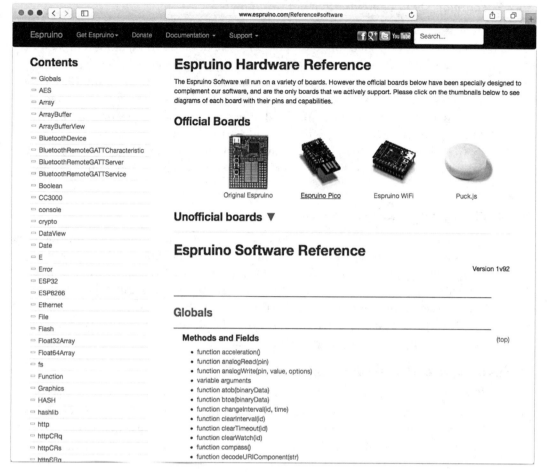

Figure 10.10   Espruino's API documentation at www.espruino.com/Reference

10.3   *Experimenting with the Pico*

Next, you'll take the Pico for a spin and try out a few experiments. First, you'll revisit the BMP180 weather multisensor, but you'll be combining it with a Nokia 5110 LCD display component to build a nice-looking, self-contained mini weather station.

10.3.1   *The Pico and the BMP180 multisensor*

What you'll need

- 1 Espruino Pico
- 1 full-size breadboard
- 1 USB extension cable
- 1 BMP180 breakout board
- Jumper wires

Because you're using the Web IDE, working with Espruino modules is as easy as using a `require()` statement in the Espruino code with the name of the module you're after. These modules provide encapsulated support for different types of components. And, huzzah, there's an existing module for your trusty BMP180 temperature and pressure multisensor. The module's called `BMP085` because it's also compatible with the similar BMP085 sensor. Once the module is imported, you can use the API it provides to interact with the BMP180 sensor. Let's see what that looks like.

THE BMP085 ESPRUINO MODULE

This experiment will log the current temperature (in Celsius) and pressure (in pascals) as obtained from the I²C BMP180 sensor.

The code required to log readings from a BMP180 isn't too dense, as you'll see in listing 10.2. It makes use of the exposed `I2C1` global to configure an I²C interface that it then passes to the `connect` method of the `BMP085` module.

As you've seen, Johnny-Five provides several constructs for performing continuous, periodic actions like sensor reads—`board.loop`, for example. But you're not using Johnny-Five here. Instead, you'll follow Espruino convention, which makes use of `setInterval` for repeated I/O.

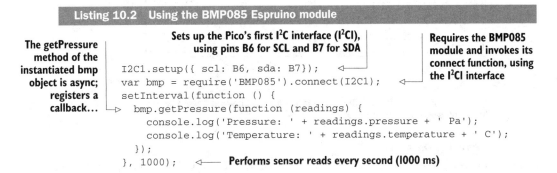

Listing 10.2　Using the BMP085 Espruino module

> The getPressure method of the instantiated bmp object is async; registers a callback...

> Sets up the Pico's first I²C interface (I²CI), using pins B6 for SCL and B7 for SDA

> Requires the BMP085 module and invokes its connect function, using the I²CI interface

```
I2C1.setup({ scl: B6, sda: B7});
var bmp = require('BMP085').connect(I2C1);
setInterval(function () {
  bmp.getPressure(function (readings) {
    console.log('Pressure: ' + readings.pressure + ' Pa');
    console.log('Temperature: ' + readings.temperature + ' C');
  });
}, 1000);
```

> Performs sensor reads every second (1000 ms)

How do you know that pins B6 and B7 support I²C SCL and SDA respectively? From the pinout (figure 10.11).

BUILDING THE BMP180 CIRCUIT

To construct this, you'll want to put the Pico on a full-size breadboard and use a USB extension cable. Construct the circuit shown in figure 10.11.

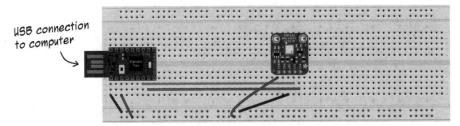

USB connection to computer

Figure 10.11　Wiring diagram for the Espruino Pico and BMP180 sensor

The setup may seem a bit cockamamie at the moment. "Why stick the BMP180 sensor so far away from the Pico?" you may reasonably be wondering. There's a method to this madness: the resulting gap will allow for the expansion of this circuit to accommodate the Nokia 5110 LCD component in upcoming experiments.

FULL-SIZE BREADBOARD CONNECTIONS   If this is your first time using a full-size breadboard, note that it really is effectively two half-size breadboards joined end-to-end, in terms of electrical connections. A gotcha with full-size breadboards is that the power rails have a break in their connections halfway down the board (figure 10.12).

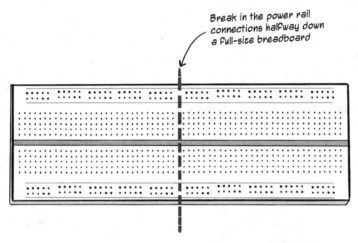

Break in the power rail connections halfway down a full-size breadboard

Figure 10.12   Don't forget! The power rails on a full-size breadboard have a break midway down the board.

DEPLOYING THE CODE

Enter the code from listing 10.2 into the right side of the IDE, and click the Send to Espruino up-arrow icon to execute the code on the Pico. The logged pressure and temperature will appear on the console/terminal (left) side of the IDE window (figure 10.13).

10.3.2 *The Pico and the Nokia 5110 LCD*

What you'll need

- 1 Espruino Pico
- 1 Nokia 5110 48x84 LCD breakout board
- 1 full-size breadboard
- 1 100 Ω resistor
- Jumper wires

The Nokia 5110 48x84 pixel display (figure 10.14) was originally used in the popular Nokia 51xx family of phones, which date from the late 1990s (great phones, by the way—they were known for their durability, excellent battery life, and ease of use).

```
1 ▾ I2C1.setup({ scl: B6, sda: B7});
2   var bmp = require('BMP085').connect(I2C1);
3 ▾ setInterval(function () {
4 ▾   bmp.getPressure(function (readings) {
5       console.log('Pressure: ' + readings.pressure + ' Pa');
6       console.log('Temperature: ' + readings.temperature + ' C');
7     });
8   }, 1000);
```

```
Temperature: 120.98125 C
Pressure: 124684 Pa
Temperature: 120.98125 C
Pressure: 124684 Pa
Temperature: 120.98125 C
Pressure: 124680 Pa
Temperature: 120.96875 C
Pressure: 124680 Pa
Temperature: 120.96875 C
Pressure: 124680 Pa
Temperature: 120.96875 C
Pressure: 124680 Pa
Temperature: 120.96875 C
Pressure: 124680 Pa
Temperature: 120.96875 C
Pressure: 67078 Pa
Temperature: -91.7125 C
Pressure: 67078 Pa
Temperature: -91.7125 C
Pressure: 124674 Pa
Temperature: 120.94375 C
Pressure: 98125 Pa
Temperature: 23.94375 C
Pressure: 98119 Pa
Temperature: 23.9375 C
Pressure: 98131 Pa
Temperature: 23.94375 C
Pressure: 98121 Pa
Temperature: 23.91875 C
>
```

Figure 10.13   Once the BMP180 script is uploaded to the Pico, you should see output logging to the left side of the screen once per second.

Nokia 5110 LCD units can be found online for as little as $6, but they're easier to find at around $10 each. They're great little components: 48x84 pixels isn't infinite real estate, but it's a lot more than the 16x2 we've seen so far. There's room to draw, animate, and do fun things.

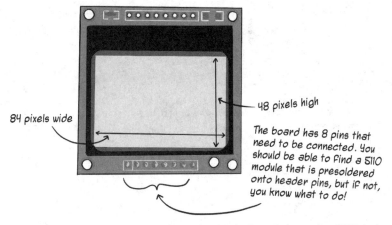

84 pixels wide

48 pixels high

The board has 8 pins that need to be connected. You should be able to find a 5110 module that is presoldered onto header pins, but if not, you know what to do!

Figure 10.14   The Nokia 5110 LCD has 48x84 pixel resolution and an SPI interface provided by its Phillips Semiconductor PCD8544 driver. The display is shown here the right side up.

The display is controlled by a Philips Semiconductor driver named, in that non-memorable way that such components often have, the PCD8544. The PCD8544 provides an SPI interface to the display, and (yay!) there's an Espruino module for this controller.

You'll start by creating a visual countdown timer using the Nokia 5110 on its own, and then you'll combine it with the BMP180 to make a little weather station.

Nokia 5110/PCD8544 pinouts

Different PCD8544/Nokia 5110 modules have different pinouts! Check your board's pin labeling before trying to follow the wiring diagram in figure 10.15. The connections should be silkscreened on the board.

The layout used in the wiring diagram is based on the 5110 variant available on SparkFun's product page (http://mng.bz/lld1), with connections as shown in the following figure. It's worth noting that the SparkFun module's pinout is different from the one assumed in the "Pico LCD Display Hello World" tutorial on Espruino's site (http://mng.bz/604s), but the layout documented by SparkFun seems to be more common.

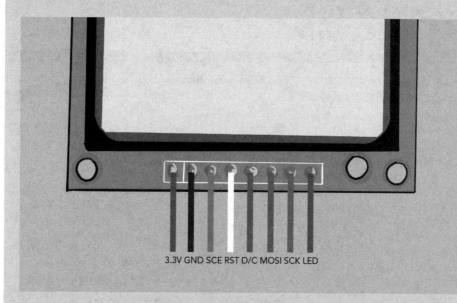

3.3V GND SCE RST D/C MOSI SCK LED

The wiring diagram in this chapter is based on the SparkFun version of the Nokia 5110 and assumes a pinout as shown here. Check your 5110's pinouts and adjust the connections in the circuit if they differ.

See table 10.1 for the specifics of which LCD modules pins connect to what on the Pico.

CONNECTING THE LCD TO THE PICO

Leave the BMP180 connected from the previous experiment—you'll use it again in a minute—and connect the Nokia 5110 to a free section of the full-sized breadboard as shown in figure 10.15 (and summarized in table 10.1).

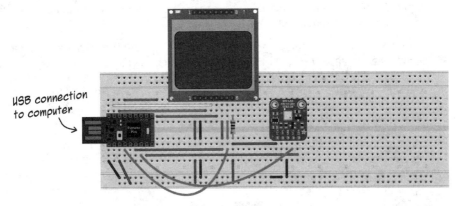

USB connection to computer

Figure 10.15 Wiring diagram for the addition of a Nokia 5110 LCD component to the circuit

Table 10.1 Nokia 5110 LCD connections

LCD module pin	LCD pin function	Connect to Pico pin	Wire color in diagram
VCC or Vin	3.3 V source power	3.3 V	Red
GND	Ground	GND	Black
CE or SCE	SPI chip select	B14	Blue
RST	Reset	B15	White
DC or D/C	Data/command	B13	Orange
MOSI or DN	SPI master out, slave in	B10	Green
SCK or SCLK	SPI clock	B1	Yellow
LED	3.3 V source for LED backlight	3.3 V, through 100 Ω resistor	Red

Wiring diagrams and aesthetics

If you study figure 10.15, you'll notice a few details that are a nod toward clarity and aesthetics, both in the diagram itself and the resulting circuit.

For example, note the power connections (red wires). The BMP180 and Nokia 5110's backlight LED are now sharing one of the positive power connections. The LCD's backlight LED power is connected through a 100 Ω resistor—it's an LED, so this resistor value of 100 Ω is a good one for a 3.3 V circuit.

(continued)

Keep in mind that the full-size breadboard's power rails have a break in their connections midway along the long side of the breadboard (a full-size breadboard really is equivalent to two half-size boards stuck together). Hence the short extra ground wire in this diagram: it connects the ground power to the other half of the board's ground rail, bridging the connectivity gap.

When you work with circuit diagrams, you'll often see affordances made to keep the circuit "tidy" in appearance, like that split ground connection. Yet another example in figure 10.15 is the orange wire for the Nokia 5110's D/C (data/command mode); the connection is split into two segments so that it doesn't have to overlap other components or wires visually. Other connections are bridged across the breadboard's central notch before using separate wires to complete the connections.

There are many ways to achieve the same resulting circuit. Each of the multiwire connections could be made with a single wire, if you're looking to save on time or wires needed.

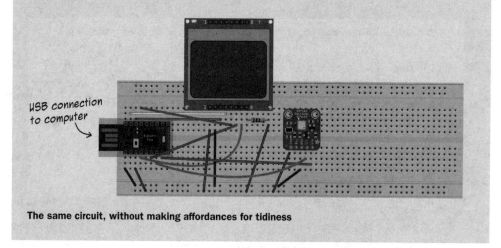

USB connection to computer

The same circuit, without making affordances for tidiness

MAKING A VISUAL COUNTDOWN TIMER WITH THE NOKIA 5110

To get acquainted with the Nokia 5110 and Espruino's Graphics capabilities, this experiment creates a 10-second timer that shows its progress using an animated progress bar on the LCD (figure 10.16). You can, of course, adjust the timer's duration in the code. The timer is started by pressing the Pico's itty-bitty built-in button.

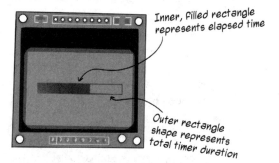

Inner, filled rectangle represents elapsed time

Outer rectangle shape represents total timer duration

Figure 10.16   The timer's display. The filled-in rectangle is "animated" and grows to the right as time elapses.

THE ESPRUINO PCD8544 MODULE

To write a program for the timer, you'll use the Espruino PCD8544 module. The code first sets up some variables and creates an initialization function to set up the timer (10.3), as shown in the next listing.

Listing 10.3   Setting up the timer

Keeps track of whether the timer is currently running ⊢▷

Determines how many "ticks" (frames) long the timer lasts

```
var lcd;
var progress      = 0; // Current timer progress
var frameDuration = 200; // ms (5fps)
var timerSeconds  = 10;
var timerLength   = timerSeconds * 1000 / frameDuration;
var timerActive   = false;
```

Invokes the onInit() function to get things going ⊢▷

Configures an SPI interface for the LCD

```
function onInit () {
  SPI1.setup({ sck: B3, mosi: B5 });
  lcd = require('PCD8544').connect(SPI1, B13, B14, B15);
}

onInit();
```

Uses the PCD8544 Espruino module to instantiate an object representing the LCD

Next, you need to find a way for a user to activate the timer. You can use the Pico's onboard push button as a trigger to start the timer by making use of some Espruino global goodies: the setWatch(function, pin, options) function and the virtual BTN pin.

The setWatch() function provides interrupt-like behavior, allowing you to register a callback that's invoked when the watched pin's value changes. In listing 10.4, set-Watch() is used to watch BTN continuously. Before starting the timer, the code makes sure there isn't another timer already running, and then it resets the timer's progress and kicks things off.

> **INTERRUPT-LIKE BEHAVIOR?** The setWatch function provides interrupt-*like* behavior. The technicality is explained in Espruino's API documentation on setWatch (http://mng.bz/EE71): "Internally, an interrupt writes the time of the pin's state change into a queue, and the function supplied to setWatch is executed only from the main message loop."

Listing 10.4   Starting the timer

The second argument to setWatch specifies the pin to watch— the Pico's onboard button.

Invokes the draw function every frameDuration (200 ms)

```
// variables
function onInit() { /* ... */ }
setWatch (function (e) {
  if (!timerActive) {
    progress = 0;
    setInterval(draw, frameDuration);
    timerActive = true;
  }
},
  BTN,
  { repeat: true });
```

The third argument is options, here specifying that the watching should continue indefinitely (repeat: true).

The timer runs by repeatedly invoking a function named `draw` at a calculated interval. But what is the `draw` function? You'll need to write it! Your `draw` function's tasks will include incrementing the timer's progress and rendering its proportional progress onto the LCD screen.

The object returned by the PCD8544 module's `connect` method—assigned in your code to the variable `lcd`—provides a few LCD-specific methods like `flip()`, which takes the current contents of a buffer and displays them on the screen, and `setContrast()`—that method does what it sounds like it would do. In addition, the object inherits from Espruino's `Graphics` library (www.espruino.com/Graphics), giving you tools to render text strings as well as draw lines and shapes.

The `draw` function in listing 10.5 uses the `drawRect(x1, y1, x2, y2)` method to draw the outline of a box representing the total timer duration. Then `fillRect(x1, y1, x2, y2)` is used to draw a filled-in progress bar at a width representative of the time elapsed so far. The only real math the `draw` function needs to do is determine how wide that filled rectangle should be—how many of the LCD's available 84 horizontal pixels represent the proportion of time that has elapsed. That's calculated and assigned to the `rightEdge` variable. To summarize: an empty rectangle—the progress bar's outline—is drawn, vertically centered on the screen, and then a filled rectangle of the calculated width is drawn inside of it.

Listing 10.5   Drawing the timer

```
// ...
function draw () {
  progress++;
  if (progress > timerLength) {        ← If the timer is done,
    clearInterval();                     turns it off and stops
    timerActive = false;
  }

  var rightEdge = Math.floor((progress / timerLength) * 84) - 1;   ← Calculates the x-axis position of the right side of the filled progress rectangle
  lcd.clear();
  lcd.drawRect(0, 19, 83, 27);        ← Uses drawRect(xl, yl, x2, y2) to draw an empty box vertically centered, eight px high
  lcd.fillRect(0, 19, rightEdge, 27);   ← Uses fillRect(xl, yl, x2, y2) to draw a filled box representing progress so far
  lcd.flip();                          ← Draws everything to the LCD screen
}
```

Paste the timer code into the right side of the Espruino IDE, connect to the Pico, and upload the code. Press the Pico's button to start the timer.

You can make adjustments to the code if you'd like. You could change the timer's duration, or you could make the LCD display a message when the timer is complete, for example.

10.3.3 *Building a power-efficient weather gadget with the Pico*

You're getting to be rather an expert at building mini weather gadgets, and here's another one to add to the arsenal. By combining your old friend the BMP180 sensor with the Nokia 5110 display, you can cobble together an independent, nicely formatted, low-power weather device (figure 10.17).

If you followed along through the previous two experiments, you already have the circuit you need: the BMP180 and the Nokia 5110 connected to the Pico on a full-sized breadboard (figure 10.18). You'll rely on some more features of the Espruino `Graphics` library to allow you to draw vector fonts and more shapes to format the display of the data, and you'll deploy the resulting code to the Pico's flash memory so that the Pico will independently run the program any time it's provided with power.

Figure 10.17 The weather gadget's output will show temperature and air pressure, nicely formatted.

As with the timer, you'll start by setting up some variables and an initialization function, shown in listing 10.6. Pressure readings on the BMP180 are considerably more accurate if you adjust them for your local altitude (in meters). The `getSeaLevel` method, available on objects returned by the `BMP085` module's `connect()` function, gives you a handy way to perform that altitude correction. Note that the `getPressure` method is used here to read both pressure and temperature at the same time. Make sure to adjust the value of the `altitude` variable in the next listing to your local altitude (in meters).

> **Listing 10.6 Setting up the weather gadget**

```
var altitude = 300; // Local altitude in meters: CHANGE ME!
var lcd;

function onInit () {
  clearInterval();
  I2C1.setup({ scl: B6, sda: B7});
  var bmp180 = require('BMP085').connect(I2C1);
  SPI1.setup({ sck: B3, mosi: B5 });
  lcd = require('PCD8544').connect(SPI1, B13, B14, B15, function () {    ◁
    setInterval(function () {
      bmp180.getPressure(function (readings) {
        draw(readings.temperature,
            bmp180.getSeaLevel(readings.pressure, altitude));    ◁
      });
    }, 1000);
  });
}

onInit();    ◁
```

Once the LCD is set up, then kick off the setInterval.

Invokes draw with the current temperature and the pressure adjusted for altitude

Don't forget to invoke the onInit function!

LINES, CIRCLES, AND TEXT WITH ESPRUINO GRAPHICS

As with the timer, you need to write the `draw` function. The code in listing 10.7 makes use of more shape-drawing methods from the `Graphics` library: `drawLine(x1, y1, x2, y2)` and `drawCircle(x, y, radius)` (figure 10.18). It also avails itself of some methods for deriving dimensions: `getWidth()` and `getHeight()`, for example, which return the display's usable area, in pixels, for the x and y axes, respectively. Finally, `stringWidth(str)` calculates the pixel width of the given string, using the current font settings.

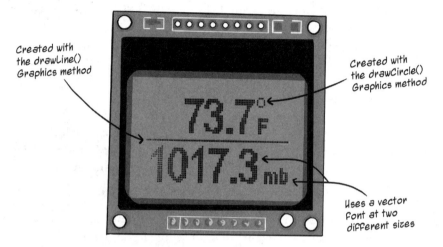

Created with the drawLine() Graphics method

Created with the drawCircle() Graphics method

Uses a vector font at two different sizes

Figure 10.18   Using Espruino's `Graphics` support to create shapes and draw text strings

Let's talk fonts. There's a tiny bitmap font available whose characters are 4 x 6 pixels in size. To use the bitmap font, you use the `setFontBitmap()` method to make that font active. In this example, however, you'll use a vector font. The vector font can be used at various sizes—it scales. The `setFontVector(size)` method will set the active font to a scaled vector font with a height of `size` pixels.

There are a lot of numbers in the following `draw` function. It's a bit finicky-looking, but everything here is unsophisticated pixel arithmetic to position elements of text and shapes. Note that the string "mb" in the drawing function (the abbreviation for *millibars*) is "hand-kerned," because I found that drawing the string in one go at that font size ran the letters together illegibly.

Listing 10.7   Rendering the weather display

```
function draw (temperature, pressure) {
  lcd.clear();
  // Convert temperature to Fahrenheit and format to one decimal place
  var tempString = (temperature * (9 / 5) + 32).toFixed(1);
  // Convert pressure from pascals to millibars and format to one decimal
⇥ place
```

```
var pressString = (pressure / 100).toFixed(1);

// Draw a vertically centered line across the display
lcd.drawLine(0, (lcd.getHeight() / 2), lcd.getWidth(),
➥ (lcd.getHeight() / 2));

// Set the active font to 18 pixels high
lcd.setFontVector(18);
// Calculate the pixel width of the temperature value at 18px font
var tempWidth  = lcd.stringWidth(tempString);
// Calculate the pixel width of the pressure value at 18px font
var pressWidth = lcd.stringWidth(pressString);
// The temperature will be horizontally centered
// Determine the x coordinate for where the value should be displayed
var xTemp      = ((lcd.getWidth() - tempWidth) / 2);

// Render the temperature at point (xTemp, 2)
lcd.drawString(tempString, xTemp, 2);
// Render a degree symbol (circle) of radius 2px
// at point (xTemp + tempWidth + 4, 5)
// The center of the circle will be 4px to the right of the
// end of the temperature value string
lcd.drawCircle(xTemp + tempWidth + 4, 5, 2);
// Render the pressure value left-aligned, 2px below vertical center
lcd.drawString(pressString, 0, (lcd.getHeight() / 2 + 2));

// Set a smaller font for the unit characters
lcd.setFontVector(8);
// Draw an "F" to denote Fahrenheit
lcd.drawString('F', xTemp + tempWidth + 2, 12);
// Draw "mb" (millibar) string.
lcd.drawString('m', pressWidth + 3, (lcd.getHeight() / 2 + 12));
lcd.drawString('b', pressWidth + 12, (lcd.getHeight() / 2 + 12));
lcd.flip();
}
```

Put all of the code for the weather gadget into the code side of the Espruino IDE, and use the Send to Espruino icon to run the code on the Pico. It'll show the temperature and pressure until it's unplugged from the USB port of your computer.

But you can do a little better! On the left side of the IDE, type the command save() and press Enter. This will flash the code to the Pico. Now, anytime the Pico has power, it will resume running this code. Try it out by plugging the Pico into a USB power source, like a phone charger.

POWER EFFICIENCY AND THE LCD'S BACKLIGHT To make the weather gadget more power-efficient, you might consider disconnecting the LCD's LED backlight connection from power. You won't be able to read the LCD in a dark room, but it'll draw less power.

10.4   Experimenting with the Kinoma Element platform

To rinse and repeat the process of platform exploration, we'll take a brief look at another embedded-JavaScript platform: the Kinoma Element.

The Element is a small, JavaScript-powered IoT platform with 16 programmable pins (figure 10.19). Like the Espruino Pico, it's inexpensive—an Element will set you back about $20 or maybe a little more. Also like the Pico, it lacks the bells and whistles of its more beefy (and costly) brethren—you won't find onboard USB, Ethernet, SDCard, or other peripheral goodies—but it has the basic bits needed for IoT products in an efficient little package. Also, it has built-in WiFi support.

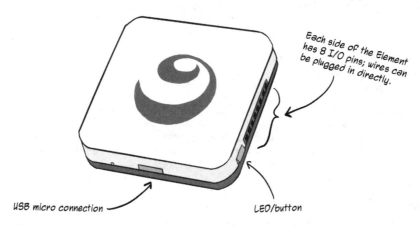

Each side of the Element has 8 I/O pins; wires can be plugged in directly.

USB micro connection

LED/button

Figure 10.19   The Kinoma Element

10.4.1   *The Element's core features*

Chipmaker Marvell produces the Element (http://mng.bz/w1lR), which features its Marvell MW302 System-on-a-Chip (SoC), which in turn uses a 200 MHz ARM Cortex M4. The board, enclosure, JavaScript runtime, and framework software are open source.

To run JavaScript natively with only 512 KB RAM, the Element uses a technology called XIP (execute in place). The Element runs FreeRTOS, a streamlined and minimal open source operating system. The board's operating voltage is 3.3 V.

The Element comes packaged in an enclosure, which makes it look less like a board and more like a finished device (the enclosure design is open source too). Instead of having dedicated power pins, you configure any of the Element's 16 pins (8 on each side of the board) as 3.3 V or ground as needed.

Kinoma uses its own (Apache-licensed) JavaScript engine, XS6, which, with minor exceptions, claims ES6 compatibility. Note that the Element's IDE software is available for Mac and Windows (beta), but it doesn't have Linux support.

10.4.2 *Pinout and hardware diagram*

The Element's pin layout is rather straightforward (figure 10.20). It's a simpler device than the Pico in terms of I/O feature support; for example, there are two I²C interfaces but no support for SPI. On the flip side, it's less complex to figure out which pins do what, and the numbering is easy to follow.

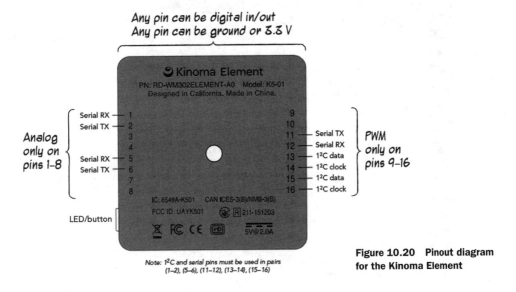

Figure 10.20   Pinout diagram for the Kinoma Element

10.4.3 *Configuration, management, workflow*

The Element is a tidy, self-contained package that won't require any soldering or prep. Jumper wires can plug right into it directly.

The configuration and workflow is similar to the Pico in that there's an IDE for configuring, authoring, and deploying. If you have an Element on hand, you can head over to the quick-start guide for details (http://mng.bz/84cS), but these are the general steps:

1 Download and install the Kinoma Code IDE.
2 Get the Element set up on your WiFi network.
3 Apply the firmware update.

Code projects for the Element, developed in the Kinoma Code IDE (figure 10.21), can be deployed over USB or WiFi b/g/n. Setup involves getting the Element on your local WiFi network. It will be assigned its own IP address.

Application projects for the Element have some structure to them. For example, each must contain a project.json file, which defines an entry point—the script that will get executed on the device. The entry point defaults to main.js.

As with Espruino, Kinoma provides some global objects to help you interact with hardware, and there is the notion of modules for the encapsulation of component

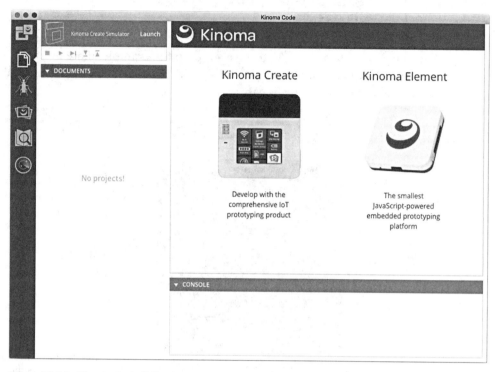

Figure 10.21   Kinoma Code IDE software

behavior. Kinoma modules for controlling hardware components are known as *Blinking-Light Libraries* (BLLs) and they involve interacting with the hardware through a (built-in) *Pins* module. You can use CommonJS style `require` statements to pull other JS files into your projects and any built-in or custom BLL modules (but remember, this isn't Node.js: you can't use npm modules).

10.4.4 *Examples and tutorials*

Kinoma's site has some code examples for the Element: http://mng.bz/1BaB. Looking at the blinking-LED example code (http://mng.bz/5t61), it's immediately evident that the structure of Kinoma projects is more formal than that of some other platforms (figure 10.22). Blinking an LED involves a project.json file to define the project, a main.js (entry point) to initialize the board and configure the pin for the LED, and an led.js BLL module that provides the logical support for blinking via a `toggle` method. (The .project file and the XML file in the project appear to be for Kinoma-site-specific build and metadata support.)

You'll also need to bring your own LED and resistor to the party, as there's no evident onboard LED you can use. The code inside of this project's main.js file assumes you're using pins 9 and 10 (ground), but there's no wiring diagram provided.

You'll learn more about what the code in a Kinoma main.js script looks like in just a bit.

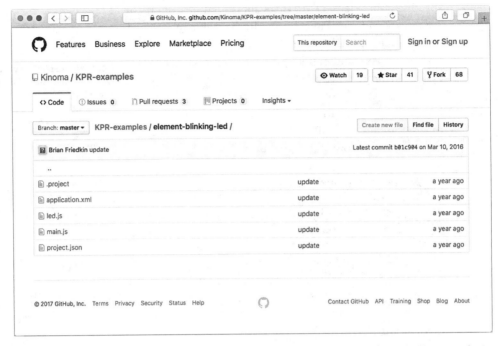

Figure 10.22   **The source for a blinking-LED Kinoma example project. The structure of a Kinoma project is more involved than that of an Espruino project.**

10.4.5   *API reference*

Kinoma modules provide the API for hardware interaction. The most immediately relevant module is `Pins`, which provides basic I/O support for the kinds of things you'd expect: digital and analog input and output; pulse-width modulation (PWM); serial (I^2C, for example). You can find a programmer's guide on the Kinoma site (http://mng.bz/w1lR).

10.4.6   *Case-study project: live-updating compass readings*

What you'll need

- 1 Kinoma Element
- 1 USB A to USB micro cable
- 1 breadboard
- 1 HMC5883L magnetometer breakout board
- Jumper wires

The Element, with its onboard WiFi and web utility libraries, lends itself to acting as a web server a little more obviously than the Pico.

In this experiment, you'll take a look at the high-level process of creating a project with the Element, crafting a custom BLL to support the HMC5883L I^2C magnetometer (compass). you'll use Kinoma's available WebSocket module to run a WebSocket server on the Element that can emit changes when the compass heading changes. Finally, you'll construct an HTML document that will connect to the Element's Web-Socket server and update as the compass heading changes (figure 10.23).

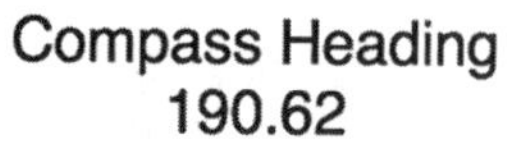

The HMC5883L module will be connected to a bread-board. By rotating the breadboard, you can change the magnetometer's orientation and see the updated heading within the browser—in real time.

Compass Heading 190.62

Figure 10.23   Detail of browser display, showing compass heading. The compass heading will update, live, without requiring a browser reload. In this case, the current heading was 190.62 degrees—a little bit west of south.

WebSocket browser support

You've met the WebSocket protocol before. In chapter 8, you used socket.IO in the Tessel 2 weather station application to show live-updating temperature and pressure. Socket.IO uses WebSockets for browsers that have WebSockets support, and it falls back to other methods for browsers that don't support WebSockets.

In this example, you'll use WebSockets proper: the application won't work in browsers that don't support WebSockets. A lack of WebSockets support is exceedingly rare in browsers these days, so it's unlikely you'll run into problems.

BUILDING THE CIRCUIT

Place the HMC5883L on a breadboard and connect it to the Element as shown in figure 10.24. The SDA and SCL pins on the breakout board connect to the Element's pins 13 and 14, which, as shown in the pinout in figure 10.20, have support for I²C. Any pin on the Element can be configured as power or ground; pins 11 and 12 are used here because of their proximity to the I²C pins.

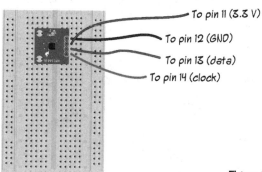

To pin 11 (3.3 V)
To pin 12 (GND)
To pin 13 (data)
To pin 14 (clock)

Figure 10.24   Kinoma Element and HMC5883L

STRUCTURING THE PROJECT

The Element live-compass project consists of four files (figure 10.25):

- A package.json file with Kinoma project metadata
- A main.js file serving as the app's main module (entry point)
- An HMC5883L.js file, which is the custom Kinoma BLL module for the compass
- An index.html file, which is the client-side code—you view it in a web browser

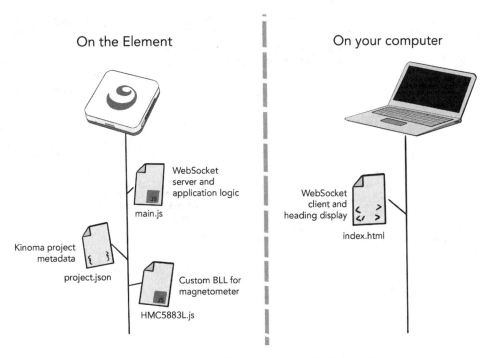

Figure 10.25 The structure for the Element live-compass project. The main.js file provides application logic and a WebSocket server, relying on support from the BLL in HMC5883L.js to interact with the magnetometer. The project.json file defines the project, using Kinoma conventions. Index.html is run in a web browser on your computer and shows live-updating compass headings.

First, create the package.json file and enter some metadata, as shown in the next listing.

Listing 10.8 project.json

```
{
  "id": "compass.websockets.lyza.com",
  "title": "hmc5883L",
  "Element": {
    "main": "main"
  }
}
```

ID strings should be in "dotted domain name style" according to the documentation.

The app's entry point will be main.js.

CREATING THE APPLICATION'S STRUCTURE

Kinoma project application modules—main.js in this case—have a general structure. They need to export a `default` function that implements some event handlers, such as `onLaunch()` and `onQuit()`. The launch handler configures the board's pins and kicks things off.

The module's basic structure is as follows.

Listing 10.9   Structure of main.js

This is the built-in Pins module, upon which much in Kinoma apps depends.

Kinoma has a built-in websocket module; you'll need to use the WebSocketServer from it.

```
import Pins from 'pins';
import { WebSocketServer } from 'websocket';

var formatMsg = heading => JSON.stringify({ heading: heading.toFixed(2) });
var main = {
  onLaunch () {
    Pins.configure({
      // Configure the HMC5883L via a custom BLL module that still needs
      to be written
    }, success => {
      if (success) {
        // Set up a WebSocket server
        // read compass headings and emit changes
      } else {
        // Handle failure with the built-in `trace` function
        trace('Failed to configure\n');
      }
    });
  }
};

export default main;
```

This is a convenience function for formatting compass headers (not used yet).

onLaunch() will be invoked automatically on launch.

Pins.configure takes a callback function, invoked when it's complete.

Once the custom HMC5883L module is ready, you'll come back and fill in the blanks in main.js.

A CUSTOM BLL FOR THE HMC5883L

A BLL, or *blinking-light library*, encapsulates Kinoma-compatible component behavior in a module. A BLL module needs to do certain things. According to the Kinoma documentation, a BLL must export at minimum a `pins` object defining the type of pins it uses, a `configure` function, and a `close` function.

The following listing shows an excerpt from the completed HMC5883L BLL module.

Listing 10.10   BLL code detail

```
// From datasheet: various register addresses for the device
var registers = {
  CRA: 0x00,
  CRB: 0x01,
  MODE: 0x02,
  READ: 0x03,
};

/* ... */

// Required export object
// Configure the pins involved as I2C at address 0x1E (from datasheet)
```

```
exports.pins = {
  compass: {type: 'I2C', address: 0x1E }
};

// Required export function
exports.configure = function () {
  this.compass.init(); // Get I2C going
  // Derived from Johnny-Five Compass class support for HMC5883Ls
  this.compass.writeByteDataSMB(registers.CRA, 0x70);
  this.compass.writeByteDataSMB(registers.CRB, 0x40);
  this.compass.writeByteDataSMB(registers.MODE, 0x00);
};

// Required export function
exports.close = function () {
  this.compass.close(); // Cleanup; boilerplate
};

// Can be invoked repeatedly to read data from sensor
exports.read = function () {
  // Derived from Johnny-Five Compass class, again
  var bytes = this.compass.readBlockDataSMB(registers.READ, 6, 'Array');
  var data = {
    x: int16(bytes[0], bytes[1]),
    y: int16(bytes[4], bytes[5]),
    z: int16(bytes[2], bytes[3])
  };
  return toHeading(data.x, data.y);
};
```

writeByteDataSMB() is provided by the Kinoma I²C API; it reads from a specific register address.

readBlockDataSMB(), again from the API, is used to get six bytes from the READ register as an array.

int16() is a utility function to make a 16-bit integer from two bytes (implementation not shown).

toHeading() uses math to derive a heading from the data (implementation not shown).

HMC5883L data consists of two bytes for each of the three axes.

Credits for the HMC5883L Kinoma BLL module

I cobbled together this BLL myself as an exploration into how BLL modules and I²C work on the Element, but the code draws heavily from pre-existing work. It's effectively a port of the Johnny-Five support logic for the sensor (http://mng.bz/TxHV), written by Johnny-Five inventor Rick Waldron. The Johnny-Five code in turn relies on an earlier implementation for Arduino (http://mng.bz/nB4V), which in turn relies on the datasheet for the device (http://mng.bz/j67k).

This kind of complex pedigree is par for the course in open source software, but as a reminder, always check your licenses and make sure you honor them. Also, give shout-outs to the inspiration for your work.

Listing 10.10 only shows a portion of the completed BLL. The complete version of the 5883L BLL can be found in the book's code repository. You'll need it if you want to build this experiment: place it in the same directory as the other project files.

FINISHING THE APPLICATION CODE

With the BLL sewn up, the bits in main.js that rely on on the BLL can be filled in. As shown in the following listing, the onLaunch handler sets up the compass sensor on the Element by passing a settings object to Pins.configure().

Listing 10.11   Configuring pins

```
/* ... */
var main = {
  onLaunch () {
    Pins.configure({
      compass: {
        require: 'HMC5883L',          ◁——  The custom BLL module, by
        pins: {                             filename, no extension
          compass: { sda: 13, clock: 14 },
          ground: { pin: 12, type: 'Ground' },
          power: { pin: 11, type: 'Power' }
        }
      },
    }, success => {    } );            ◁——  Callback function
  }
};
```

You also pass a callback function as a second argument to Pins.configure().

Within that callback, you first need to get a WebSocket server going, as shown in the next listing. This code uses the API of the built-in Kinoma WebSocketServer (WebSocketServer was required in listing 10.9).

Listing 10.12   WebSocket server setup

```
/* ... */
var main = {
  onLaunch () {
    Pins.configure({             ES6 feature
      /* ... */                  support, so Set
    }, success => {              can be used
      if (success) {                                   Starts a WebSocket
        const clients = new Set();        ◁——          server on the
        const wss = new WebSocketServer(80);  ◁——      Element's port 80
        let lastResult = 0;

        wss.onStart = client => { // When a client (browser) connects
          clients.add(client);
          // Immediately send the latest compass heading
          client.send(formatMsg(lastResult));
          // Clean up when closing later
          client.onclose = () => clients.remove(client);
        };
      }
    });
  }
};
```

Holds the last compass heading reading ⟶ (points to `const clients = new Set();` / `let lastResult = 0;`)

The code in listing 10.12 emits an initial compass reading when a client connects, but how are compass readings obtained in the first place, and how does the client receive updates when the readings change? The last bits of code for main.js, shown in the following listing, take care of those things.

Listing 10.13 Reading and updating compass headings

```
/* ... */
var main = {
  onLaunch () {
    Pins.configure({
      /* ... */
    }, success => {
      if (success) {
        /* ... */
        Pins.repeat('/compass/read', 500, result => {
          if (Math.abs(result - lastResult) >= 0.5) {
            clients.forEach(recipient => {
              recipient.send(formatMsg(result));
            });
          }
          lastResult = result;
        });
      }
    });
  }
};
```

Reads every 500 → (annotation pointing to `Pins.repeat('/compass/read', 500, result => {`)

If the new result (the heading, in degrees) differs from the last result by some threshold amount... (annotation pointing to `if (Math.abs(result - lastResult) >= 0.5) {`)

...it has meaningfully changed. Send the new value to each of the connected clients. (annotation pointing to `clients.forEach(recipient => {`)

Functions as paths in BLLs

Functions in BLLs are referenced externally by path:

```
Pins.repeat('/compass/read', 500, result => { });
```

Here, /compass/read is a "path" to the read function in the BLL module. The line of code here repeatedly invokes read every 500 ms, and a callback function receives the result of the latest read operation. See it in play in listing 10.13.

CLIENT CODE (HTML)

Finally, you'll need an HTML page to serve as a WebSocket client and to show the compass headings in real time. This page can be viewed in a browser.

Listing 10.14 Client code (HTML page) for showing compass heading

```
<!doctype html>
<html lang="en">
  <head>
    <meta charset="utf-8">
    <title>Live Compass Heading</title>
```

```
<style>
  #compass {                          ⟵── Styling for the heading display
    text-align: center;
    font-size: 2em;
    font-family: "Helvetica", sans-serif;
    margin: 2em;
  }
</style>
<script>
  window.addEventListener('load', function () {    ⟵
    var ws = new WebSocket('ws://10.0.0.17:80');   ⟵
    ws.onmessage = function (message) {
      var data = JSON.parse(message.data);
      document.getElementById('direction').innerHTML = data.heading;
    };
  });
</script>
</head>
<body>
  <div id="compass">
    <label for="direction">Compass Heading</label><div id="direction">...
    ➡ </div>
  </div>
</body>
</html>
```

On load, connects to the WebSocket server

Important! You need to change this to your own Element's IP address.

When new data comes in, updates the HTML in the #direction element to display the new heading

DEPLOYING THE COMPASS CODE

Code is deployed to the Element via the Kinoma Code IDE. Note that the index.html file isn't served from the Element in this example. Instead, you open that file in a browser once the Element is running the compass application. See the Element quickstart guide (http://mng.bz/84cS) for step-by-step instructions about how to connect to and deploy code to your Element from the Kinoma Code IDE, if you haven't done so already.

Once the code is deployed and running, you can open up the index.html file in a browser and rotate the breadboard with the attached compass to see the display update in real time.

Summary

- Embedded JavaScript platforms use optimized hardware and firmware to execute subsets of JavaScript natively. Both Kinoma and Espruino maintain their own, open source JavaScript engines (KinomaJS and Espruino JavaScript, respectively) to make this possible.

- Embedded JS platforms tend to have more sophisticated processors—often 32-bit—but still have significant constraints on memory and program space.

- Espruino's open source family of products includes the Pico, a diminutively sized development board. Espruino projects can make use of Espruino-specific modules to work with different kinds of components.

- The Kinoma Element is another open source JavaScript-powered device. Creating projects for the Element involves the use of component modules called BLLs (blinking-light libraries).
- Although there are many platform options out there, you can speed your learning process with new platforms by following certain steps: learning about core details, finding hardware and pinout information, understanding the workflow, trying out examples, and seeking out API documentation.

Building with Node.js and tiny computers

11

This chapter covers

- Getting started with Node.js hardware development on single-board computer (SBC) platforms

- Corralling components and setting up a Raspberry Pi 3 Model B system

- How GPIO works on the Raspberry Pi, and some different options for controlling it with JavaScript

- Adapting a Johnny-Five weather station app to work on several different platforms—Tessel 2, Raspberry Pi, Arduino, and BeagleBone Black

- Working with the GPIO-rich BeagleBone Black open source SBC

Single-board computers (SBCs) are tiny powerhouses that combine general-purpose computing with the characteristics of embedded systems (figure 11.1). These itty-bitty computers pack a host of peripherals and goodies into a small package: multiple USB ports, Bluetooth, WiFi, Ethernet—the features you'd expect from a desktop

Figure 11.1 Single-board computers (SBCs), left to right: Intel Edison module with Arduino breakout, Raspberry Pi 2 Model B, and BeagleBone Black

computer. But they have several features that lend themselves well to embedded applications: their cut-down size, lower price point, GPIO support, and relative power efficiency (while not as power-miserly as simpler embedded platforms, they certainly require less juice than their desktop brethren).

This isn't the first time you've seen SBCs in this book, but let's revisit what an SBC is, broadly speaking. There's no formal definition of the term, but SBC platforms tend to do the following:

- Run high-level operating systems; in most cases you can install a different OS if you choose (typically, but not always, Linux)
- Offer general-purpose desktop-like features, such as support for USB peripherals, displays, sound, and so on
- Provide GPIO options, though these sometimes play second fiddle to other features of the platform

The juggernaut in this category is the Raspberry Pi platform, a family of SBCs that are enjoying epic popularity. Accordingly, we'll spend most of this chapter diving into Node.js and the Raspberry Pi 3 Model B. But we'll also take a briefer tour of the BeagleBone Black board as a second example of a platform in this SBC class.

For this chapter, you'll need the following:

- 1 Raspberry Pi 3 Model B and 5 V power supply
- 1 microSD card and adapter
- 1 Adafruit T-Cobbler, SparkFun Pi Wedge, or similar, or an assortment of male-to-female jumper wires
- 1 standard LED, any color
- 1 100 Ω resistor
- 1 Adafruit BMP180 multisensor breakout board
- Jumper wires
- 1 BeagleBone Black
- 1 Arduino Uno
- 1 half-size breadboard

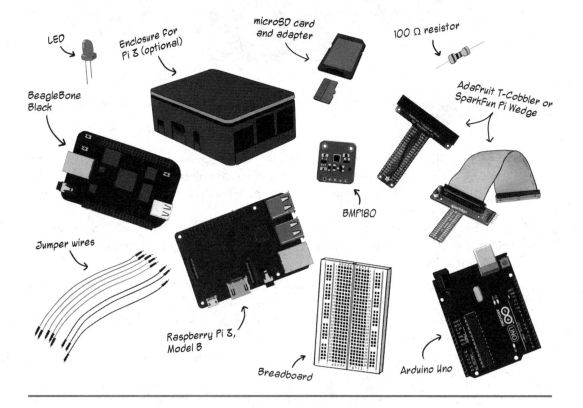

The Tessel 2 and the definition of single-board computers

The Tessel 2 is almost a device category unto itself. Its USB peripherals, networking capabilities, and high-level OS (OpenWrt Linux) seem to suggest SBC territory. Yet its limited RAM and Flash storage, as well as its lack of desktop-like peripheral support (such as a display) are signs that it's designed for embedded applications.

So is it an SBC? I'd tend to lean toward a qualified yes, but if your own definition of *SBC* emphatically involves the ability to plug in a display and use it as a desktop computer, then nope!

11.1 Working with tiny computers

SBCs are certainly more sophisticated than their simpler dev-board brethren. They can also be, correspondingly, more involved to set up and configure out of the box. In many cases, you'll be dealing with copious amounts of choice in both software and hardware realms. Don't panic, though: getting from zero to zoom on a Raspberry Pi 3 using an SD card preflashed with *NOOBS* (New Out-of-Box Software) for Raspberry Pis can be breathtakingly simple. But you'll need to roll up your Linux sleeves and spend some time in a terminal to get a comfortable, Node.js-centric workflow sorted out.

Don't be nervous. Should anything go awry when following the setup steps for either of the SBCs we'll examine—the Raspberry Pi 3 and the BeagleBone Black—you can always start again from scratch without doing irreparable harm.

SBCs, embedded systems, and (Debian) Linux

There has been a Big Bang of Linux projects and distributions targeted at embedded and mobile devices over the past several years. For example, the Tessel runs a pared-down Linux originally developed for routers: OpenWrt.

As we dig into higher-performance SBCs, you'll see that there are decisions to be made—most platforms will happily run a number of different Linux distributions.

With the Raspberry Pi, we'll stick with the default and most common choice: Raspbian, a Debian-based Linux. For consistency, the BeagleBone Black exploration at the end of the chapter reflashes the board with Debian Linux instead of using the default (Ångström) that it ships with.

Debian releases are named after *Toy Story* characters. At the time of writing, Debian stable is at version 9 (Stretch), but most embedded and SBC platforms are still using builds of version 8 (Jessie). One sometimes sees version 7 (Wheezy) builds, though they're becoming less common.

11.1.1 *The Raspberry Pi platform*

The Raspberry Pi (figure 11.2) is everywhere you look. What the Arduino platform is to simpler dev boards, the Pi platform is to SBCs: ubiquitous.

With each sequential numbered Pi generation (1, 2, and 3 so far), the platform has become more powerful, efficient, stable, and jam-packed with features. The exception is the Pi Zero family, which is even smaller and cheaper—but at the cost of some performance and features.

Despite its power and flexibility, the Raspberry Pi platform isn't always the ideal choice for electronics beginners. The sheer number of things you can do with a Pi can be distracting, as can the task of handling Linux administration and other configuration details. It's easy to get off on a Google-search tangent, wallowing for hours amidst forums and project ideas and options.

In addition, Pi pinouts are fairly complex and have multiple, confusing numbering and naming systems. Despite the large number of pins, some GPIO support is completely missing. There's no onboard analog-to-digital conversion (ADC), for instance. Other key GPIO features are limited. Of the 40 GPIO pins on a Raspberry Pi 3 Model B (figure 11.3) only two are PWM-capable.

On the other hand, you've learned enough about the basics that some of these potential pitfalls may not seem so daunting anymore. Raspbian—the Pi's default Debian-based

Figure 11.2   Raspberry Pi 2 Model B (left), Raspberry Pi Zero (center foreground), and Raspberry Pi 3 Model B (in a case, with attached SparkFun Pi Wedge)

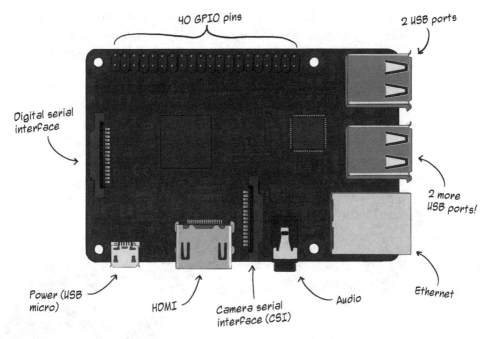

Figure 11.3   The Raspberry Pi 3 Model B

OS—is widely used, sensible, and reliable. Because so many people use Pis, there are scads of resources designed to assist even rank beginners, and there are vast troves of forums, wikis, Stack Overflow and blog posts, and so on, to aid you with every last detail.

GETTING YOUR KIT IN ORDER

The following sections provide two different options for setting up a Raspberry Pi 3 Model B-based system:

- Traditional configuration—The traditional and more beginner-friendly way to configure a Raspberry Pi is to treat it like a desktop computer—plug in a USB mouse, a USB keyboard, and an HDMI display, and work at it directly.
- Headless configuration—If you don't want to devote that many peripherals to your Pi, you can opt to treat it more like an embedded system. If that notion appeals, the headless configuration section is for you!

For a first-time setup, Pi starter kits, available from all of the major online electronics retailers—are a great, if more costly, way to go (versus buying the Pi board and supporting components separately). Here are some things to look for in a kit:

- A microSD card preflashed with NOOBs or Raspbian—Preferably also with an SD card adapter so that you can use a standard-sized card reader/writer to update the card's contents
- An enclosure (case)—This gives your Pi physical stability, protection, and, in some cases, a suave appearance.

- Power supply—The Pi's power connection is USB micro, so you could alternatively use a 5 V USB device charger. Keep in mind, however, that the Pi's current needs may not be met by all phone chargers: the Pi website recommends an adapter that can supply 2.5 A or more.
- Hardware to provide easier access to the Pi's GPIO pins—These come in the form of the Adafruit Cobbler, the SparkFun Wedge, and other similar options (figure 11.4).

Figure 11.4   Constructed Raspberry Pi 3 Model B SparkFun kit with Pi Wedge, here shown connected to a breadboard. Also shown is an Adafruit T-Cobbler (right), which provides the same kind of functionality as the Wedge.

Kits may offer other useful goodies—the SparkFun one includes a USB microSD card reader, for example—but they have the downside of often including things you probably already have: breadboards, jumper wires, LEDs, and the like.

A Raspberry Pi 3 Model B board on its own is about $40, whereas full kits are about $90. The current Pi 3 starter kits from Adafruit and SparkFun contain all the parts you need for this section.

Making GPIO connections on the Pi

The pins on Pis are male—if you connect directly to them, you'll need male-to-female jumper wires, and you may end up with a rat's nest and frustration, because there isn't silkscreened info on the Pi itself.

There are third-party hardware components aimed at making the Pi's GPIO easier to work with. SparkFun's Pi Wedge and Adafruit's T-Cobbler are two examples: these breakouts organize pins into more intuitive groupings (with silkscreened hints) and provide a breadboard-compatible form factor. Your Pi kit may come with them, or they can be purchased separately.

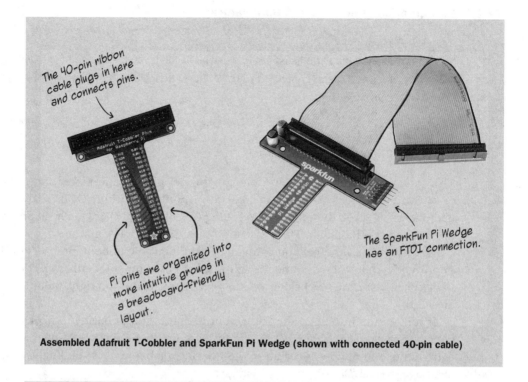

The 40-pin ribbon cable plugs in here and connects pins.

Pi pins are organized into more intuitive groups in a breadboard-friendly layout.

The SparkFun Pi Wedge has an FTDI connection.

Assembled Adafruit T-Cobbler and SparkFun Pi Wedge (shown with connected 40-pin cable)

FTDI (Future Technology Devices International)

FTDI makes chips that allow for asynchronous serial communication between embedded devices and computers. FTDI chips translate the TTL or RS-232 signals (RS-232 is another asynchronous serial protocol) coming from a device into USB signals that a computer can understand, and vice versa. FTDI connections can be used to monitor serial output from a device. In some cases, they can also be used to program or control the device.

SparkFun's Pi Wedge includes an FTDI interface. You also need a cable or a breakout board to connect to the FTDI pins (a SparkFun FTDI breakout board with mini-USB connector is visible connected to the Pi Wedge in figure 11.4).

What you'll need

Steps follow for both a traditional, desktop-style Pi setup and a headless setup. You'll want to choose only one of these options, but no matter which path you follow, you'll need the following:

- 1 Raspberry Pi 3 Model B
- 1 5 V USB micro power supply
- 1 enclosure (optional but recommended)
- 1 Adafruit T-Cobbler, SparkFun Pi Wedge, or similar; or a set of male-to-female jumper wires

11.1.2 Configuration option 1: the traditional way

What you'll need

In addition to the parts listed in the previous section, you'll also need the following:

- 1 microSD card, preflashed with NOOBS or Raspbian OS (with desktop)
- 1 USB keyboard
- 1 USB mouse
- 1 monitor
- 1 HDMI cable for the monitor

This configuration option involves plugging in peripherals and power and following on-screen instructions. Pop in a microSD card preflashed with NOOBS and power it up. NOOBS gives you the option of installing one of several OSs. Go ahead and select the first choice—Raspbian. The installation process takes a few minutes.

Once the OS is installed and configured, you'll be able to boot into the PIXEL (Pi Improved Xwindows Environment, Lightweight) environment. Setting up the WiFi is straightforward: start by clicking on the WiFi icon in the top-right menu bar (figure 11.5).

If you want to be able to shell in to your Pi later, without having to work at the Pi directly, you need to enable SSH. To do this, use the Preferences > Raspberry Pi Configuration menu option. Navigate to the Interfaces tab and click the Enabled option next to SSH. Click OK to apply the change.

That's it for the moment! If you run into any difficulty whatsoever, head on over to the Raspberry Pi Software Guide (http://mng.bz/P8Hu), which is illustrated and user-friendly.

WiFi icon here

Figure 11.5 The PIXEL desktop. Note the WiFi icon at top right.

11.1.3 *Configuration option 2: headless*

This more pared-down, straight-to-the-essentials approach obviates the need for peripherals and cables. On the flip side, it's a less common approach, and it requires more time in a terminal. Raspbian is ever-evolving, but the following steps worked reliably as of mid-2017.

If you've already set up your Pi using the desktop approach, you can skip this set of steps. You can skip forward to section 11.8.

What you'll need

In addition to the parts listed at the end of section 11.1, you'll need the following:

- 1 microSD card
- 1 SD card adapter
- 1 SD card reader/writer (or a computer that has a built-in reader)
- 1 Ethernet cable

Because you're going headless, you'll need to configure the Pi so that you can communicate with it in some way, as you'll lack a keyboard and monitor.

First you'll need to create a bootable SD card that will enable you to ssh to the Pi over a wired Ethernet connection. Then you'll shell in and configure WiFi on the command line.

CREATING A BOOTABLE RASPBIAN DISK IMAGE

You'll need to put an operating system on a microSD card so that the Pi can boot:

1 Download Raspbian (not NOOBS) from the Raspbian download page (www.raspberrypi.org/downloads/raspbian/) (figure 11.6).

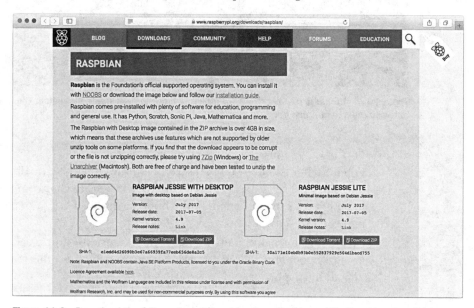

Figure 11.6   Download the full version of Raspbian from Raspberry Pi's Raspbian download page.

Once the large download is complete, unzip the resulting zip file. If things go right, you should end up with an IMG file (a bootable disk image).

BIG, HONKING RASPBIAN ZIP FILE   As noted on the Raspbian download page (figure 11.6), the resulting zip file is big, and your default unzip utility may not be up to the task of unzipping it (mine wasn't). As suggested there, try The Unarchiver for Mac or 7Zip for Windows if you run into problems.

2   Create a bootable microSD card:

   a   Install the free Etcher application (https://etcher.io/), available for Windows, Mac, or Linux. This will allow you to take the Raspbian IMG file and burn it onto the microSD card.

   b   Insert the microSD card into the SD card adapter, and then insert the whole kaboodle into your computer or SD card reader/writer.

   c   Launch Etcher and follow the steps to put the IMG file on the microSD card (figure 11.7).

Figure 11.7   Etcher is a straightforward utility: select the disk image file, select the drive (it often auto-selects for you), and go.

3   Add a file to the microSD card to enable SSH:

   a   When Etcher is done—it takes several minutes to create the disk image—the microSD card will be soft-ejected (unmounted) from your computer. Unplug it, plug it back in, and open up the boot partition (this may be the only partition you can see).

   b   Create an empty file named "ssh"—no extension—and place it at the top level of boot. This will enable SSH on the Pi, which is otherwise disabled by default in Raspbian.

4 Install the OS:

a Eject the SD card adapter from your computer, remove the microSD card from the adapter, and insert the microSD card into the Pi 3.

b Boot the Pi.

5 Establish communication with your Pi over Ethernet:

a Connect the Pi 3's Ethernet interface directly to your wireless router with an Ethernet cable.

b Find your Pi's IP address. Your Pi 3 should automatically get assigned an IP address (via DHCP), but you'll need to figure out what that IP address is.

There are many ways to skin this cat. Google "IP scanner" or "LAN scanner" and you'll find a plethora of free utilities for various platforms, or you can use a command-line tool. I use LanScan for the Mac (figure 11.8). The idea is to determine what IP was assigned to your Pi.

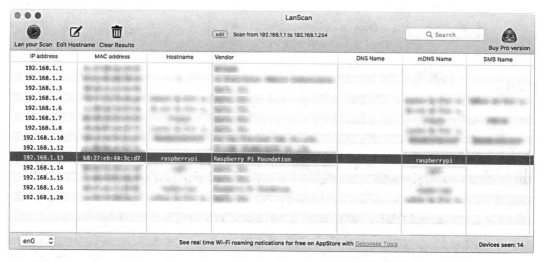

Figure 11.8   Using LanScan for Mac, I can see that the Raspberry Pi's Ethernet interface was assigned the IP address 192.168.1.13.

6 Once you've obtained the Pi's IP address, open a terminal and enter this command:

```
$ ssh pi@<your Pi's IP>
```

DEFAULT PI USERNAME AND PASSWORD   The default username on Raspberry Pi is `pi` and the password is `raspberry`. It's a good idea to change the password for the `pi` user. You can do this (when logged in as the `pi` user) by typing `passwd` at the command prompt and following the onscreen instructions. Do it. Do it now.

CONFIGURING WiFi ON THE PI

The last step is to get WiFi configured for your Pi so you don't have to use a wired Ethernet connection. This involves messing with the Pi's `wpa_supplicant` setup. Sometimes this can be finicky and frustrating if you try to edit the configuration file directly. I've found that the most failsafe way is to use the wpa_cli command-line utility:

RASPBERRY PI 3'S WIFI SUPPORT   The Pi 3, like the Tessel 2, doesn't support 5 GHz WiFi networks.

1 SSH into your Pi if you haven't already.

2 Start an interactive wpa_cli session by entering this command:

```
$ sudo wpa_cli
```

This will put you in an interactive mode. You can type subsequent commands at the > prompt.

3 Scan for available wireless networks to make sure your Pi can see the desired WiFi network. To do so, type this:

```
> scan
```

Then this, to see the results of the scan:

```
> scan_results
```

Does your network show up? If not, check your router's settings and make sure it's a compatible WiFi network (not 5 GHz). If it does, yay! Carry on.

4 Execute each of the following commands to add, configure, and enable the desired WiFi network connection in the Pi's `wpa_supplicant` config:

```
> add_network 0
> set_network 0 ssid "<your network's SSID>"
> set_network 0 pwk "<your network's password>"
> enable network 0
> save_config
```

5 Press Ctrl-C to exit the wpa_cli.

6 To verify that it worked, type this:

```
$ ifconfig wlan0
```

If it's all good, you should see an assigned IP address (figure 11.9).

You can unplug the Ethernet connection if you like. The Pi will now automatically connect to the WiFi network configured here every time it boots up. Handy!

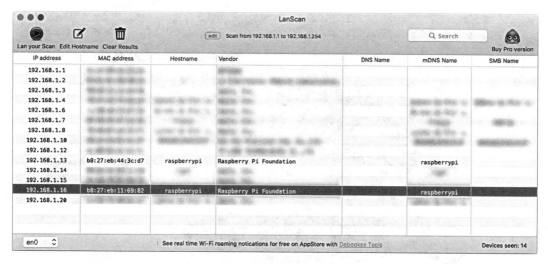

Figure 11.9   After configuring WiFi, the Pi now has two IP addresses—one for the Ethernet interface and one for its WLAN (WiFi) interface.

IF YOU NEED A DO-OVER   It's not too hard to start over if your Pi is misbehaving or you feel confused or stuck. Power the Pi down, eject the microSD, and reflash it with the desired OS: NOOBS for a user-friendly, visual setup; Raspbian; or any other compatible OS of your choice. Booting from that updated SD card will give you a clean slate.

11.2   Learning about the Raspberry Pi 3

Now that you've a configured Pi with WiFi connectivity, let's apply the platform-learning steps first outlined in chapter 10 to get a better understanding of the Raspberry Pi 3 platform overall.

11.2.1   Core features

SBCs really up the ante for processing power, commensurate with their additional bells and whistles. Microcontrollers from ARM's 32-bit Cortex M family are at the heart of a slew of platforms that can run embedded JavaScript. With full-blown SBCs, you'll be taking another step up in processor oomph. These 32- and 64-bit processors often sport multiple cores, 3D graphics acceleration, higher clock speeds, and complex subsystems.

The Pi 3 boasts a quad-core, 64-bit ARM (A8) CPU running at 1.2 GHz. That's a far cry from the Uno's 8-bit ATmega at 20 MHz (at the risk of comparing apples to oranges). Other specs noted on the product information page (figure 11.10) include 1 GB of RAM, onboard WiFi and Bluetooth, 4 USB ports, video and stereo outputs, HDMI interface, and more (www.raspberrypi.org/products/raspberry-pi-3-model-b/).

GPIO-wise, it's a mixed bag. There are multiple SPI and I²C interfaces, and lots of pins overall. As mentioned earlier, there's no ADC support, and PWM is limited. Add-on accessories and certain peripherals may require connections to some of the

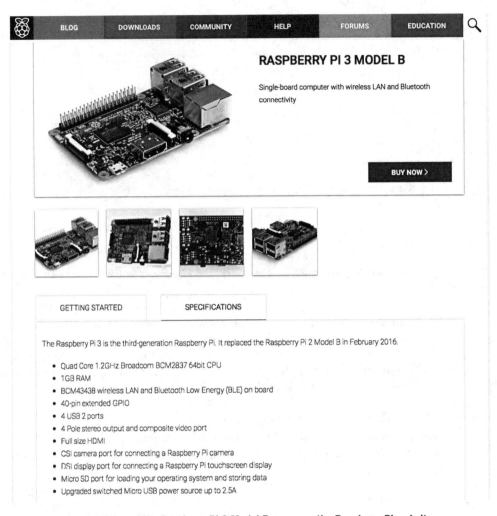

Figure 11.10 Highlights of the Raspberry Pi 3 Model B specs on the Raspberry Pi website

pins, meaning you might not have I/O access to all of the 40 pins, depending on your configuration.

Because of the Pi 3's general-purpose market, the core feature list on its product page doesn't mention that its GPIO logic level voltage is 3.3 V, but you should know that: the Raspberry Pi 3 is a 3.3 V device.

SERIOUSLY, THE PI IS A 3.3 V DEVICE   Don't apply 5 V power to any of the Pi's pins or you might find yourself with a dead Pi.

11.2.2 *GPIO features and pinouts*

Pi pinouts are complicated. For starters, there are a lot of pins (40), many different pin numbering and naming schemes, and a given pin may already be monopolized by a component, process, or peripheral. Groups of related connections, such as SPI or I²C pins, aren't necessarily physically adjacent to each other, either. The pinout.xyz website is a good resource for the nitty-gritty details on Pi pinouts.

As an example of the many faces of a single Raspberry Pi GPIO pin, physical pin 33 (figure 11.11) is alternately known as BCM 13 (Broadcom pin number), by its primary functional name of PWM1 (it's one of the PWM-capable pins), and as WiringPi pin 23. It also has several functionally named aliases, such as AVEOUT VID 9. And will it even be available for GPIO use? It won't be if you have a parallel external display connected to the Pi—it's one of the pins needed for that. And it might not be if you want to use a JTAG debugging interface or SMI (Secondary Memory Interface) device; it's one of the pins used in those kinds of connections too.

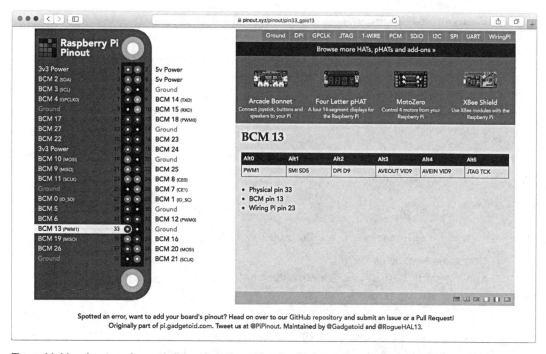

Figure 11.11　pinout.xyz is a website entirely devoted to Raspberry Pi pinout information. This detail from pinout.xyz shows the many aliases of physical pin 33.

SBCs and platform-specific hardware terminology

It seems like each SBC platform adds more jargon terms to the IoT vocabulary. Just as Arduino-compatible expansion boards are called *shields*, boards that fit on the Raspberry Pi are typically called *hats*, and those that mesh with the BeagleBone Black are called *capes*.

11.2.3 *Configuration and workflow*

The possibilities of what you can do and how you can do it are virtually unbounded on the Pi platform—it's a full-fledged computer, after all. Let's narrow that a bit by concentrating on config and workflow options for a Node.js-centric electronics-hacking setup.

At this point you should have a working Pi—whether it's set up as a standalone computer or a headless device. You have three more steps to take to get the configuration and workflow solid:

1. Make sure the Pi's software is up to date.
2. Get a tolerably recent version of Node.js installed on the Pi.
3. Figure out a way to author code and get it onto the Pi's filesystem.

UPDATING THE PI'S SOFTWARE

Make sure the Pi has the latest software updates:

1. ssh into the Pi (headless) or use a terminal (desktop). Make sure the Pi is connected to the internet.
2. Run the following command:

```
$ sudo apt update
```

   This may take a few minutes to complete.
3. Run this command:

```
$ sudo apt full-upgrade
```

   This also may take several minutes to do its job.

UPGRADING NODE.JS ON THE PI

Still logged in to the Pi or in a terminal window, try running this command:

```
$ node --version
```

This will output the current version of Node.js on the Pi. At time of writing, the preinstalled Node.js version was v0.10.29, which is archaic. Bring that up to LTS (Long-Term Support), so we don't run into compatibility or security issues in your projects:

1. If you haven't just run a full system update (as shown in the previous section), first run this command:

```
$ sudo apt update
```

2. Download and run a Node.js setup script for the target version by executing this command:

```
$ curl -sL https://deb.nodesource.com/setup_6.x | sudo -E bash -
```

At time of writing, LTS was v6.x. This will have changed by the time you read this, so you're welcome to replace the `setup_6.x` portion of the URL with the appropriate major version number. See the NodeSource Binary Distributions repository for more info (https://github.com/nodesource/distributions).

3 Install Node.js:

```
$ sudo apt install -y nodejs
```

4 Verify that it worked by running this command:

```
$ node --version
```

MANAGING FILES ON THE PI

The JavaScript files and resources for your Pi projects will be executed on the Pi and need to exist on the Pi's filesystem. There are, unsurprisingly, an awful lot of ways to get your files on the Pi. Here are some options:

- Author the files on the Pi itself. You can use a terminal-based editor, such as `vi` or `nano`. Or, if you have a desktop setup for your Pi, you can use a GUI editor like the preinstalled Leafpad application. Or you can install any number of additional text-editing applications.

- Use a utility to copy files from your computer to the Pi. You could use the Unix command-line tool scp (secure copy) to move files, or a GUI application that supports it, for example.

- Set up a file server on the Pi so you can access it as a remote share from other computers on your network. One of the many possible methods for doing this is to use a Samba (SMB) server.

Configuring a Samba (SMB) server on the Pi

One way to make your Pi's files easy to get at is to set up a file server on the Pi itself. The following steps set up a Samba (SMB) share called `projects` that can be read-write accessed by the `pi` user. Once configured, this share should show up in your system's Finder or File Explorer as a networked drive. Note that these instructions assume a general familiarity with the Linux command line:

1 `ssh` into the Pi as the `pi` user (headless) or use a terminal application (desktop).

2 Make sure you're in the `pi` user's home directory by typing this command:

```
$ pwd
```

You should see the following output:

```
/home/pi
```

3 Create a directory to keep project files in:

```
$ mkdir projects
```

(continued)

4 Install Samba:

```
$ sudo apt install samba
```

5 Set up a Samba password for the pi user by entering the following command and following the prompts:

```
$ sudo smbpasswd -a pi
```

6 Samba doesn't use system passwords; it maintains its own.
7 Edit the Samba configuration file. First make a backup to your home directory, just in case:

```
$ sudo cp /etc/samba/smb.conf ~/
```

8 Now edit the configuration:

```
$ sudo vi /etc/samba/smb.conf
```

9 (You can use a different editor, such as nano, if you prefer, in place of vi.) Scroll down to the very bottom of the file and add these lines, including the spaces around the = characters:

```
[projects]
    path = /home/pi/projects
    valid users = pi
    read only = No
```

10 Save the file and exit.
11 Restart the Samba service:

```
$ sudo service smbd restart
```

12 Check your config if you like:

```
$ testparm
```

You should now be able to connect to the SMB share from other computers on the same network (using Map Network Drive in Windows File Explorer or Connect to Server or Cmd-K on a Mac). The connection string takes this form:

```
smb://user@host/sharename
```

You should end up with something like this:

```
smb://pi@<your Pi's IP>/projects
```

Samba shares can be imperfect at times, and it's possible you may need to adjust permissions or user metadata to make it work just right. There are tons of user forums and help articles on the web if you need support.

CREATE A "PROJECTS" AREA Creating a directory called "projects" inside of the pi user's home directory is one of the steps in the sidebar on configuring a Samba server. Even if you don't set up a share on the Pi, go ahead and create a directory to corral your upcoming code experiments. The rest of the chapter will assume the existence of a `~/projects` directory (a directory called "projects" inside your home directory).

11.2.4 Examples and tutorials

There's no one way to blink an LED on a Raspberry Pi—the options are almost countless. You'll try a few ways here, emphasizing JavaScript options.

What you'll need

- 1 configured Raspberry Pi 3
- 1 SparkFun Pi Wedge, Adafruit T-Cobbler, or similar; or male-to-female jumper wires
- 1 standard LED, any color
- 1 100 Ω resistor
- 1 breadboard
- Jumper wires

The right way to `sudo`

Because of the conservative permissions for interacting with GPIO in Raspbian, you'll likely need to execute the following code examples using `sudo`. For example,

```
$ sudo ./blink.sh
```

or

```
$ sudo node index.js
```

Without `sudo`, you may get permissions errors like these:

```
./blink.sh: line 4: /sys/class/gpio/gpio4/direction: Permission denied
./blink.sh: line 5: /sys/class/gpio/gpio4/value: Permission denied
./blink.sh: line 7: echo: write error: Operation not permitted
```

Try to only use `sudo` with commands that require it, such as when executing these scripts. Don't use `sudo` to install npm modules or create files, or the like. You might end up creating things with wonky permissions if you do that. When in doubt, try to do something first without `sudo` and see if it works.

BUILDING AN LED CIRCUIT

Each of the following examples uses the same physical circuit configuration: the LED's anode should be connected to the Pi's physical pin 7 (WiringPi pin 7, BCM pin 4). The cathode should be connected to a GND pin.

Wiring diagrams are shown for direct-to-Pi connections (figure 11.12), Adafruit's T-Cobbler (figure 11.13), and SparkFun's Pi Wedge (figure 11.14).

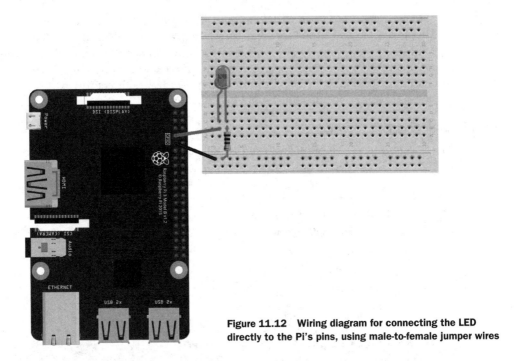

Figure 11.12   Wiring diagram for connecting the LED directly to the Pi's pins, using male-to-female jumper wires

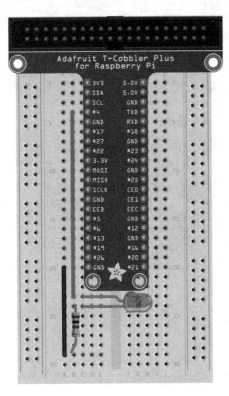

Figure 11.13   Wiring diagram, using Adafruit's T-Cobbler

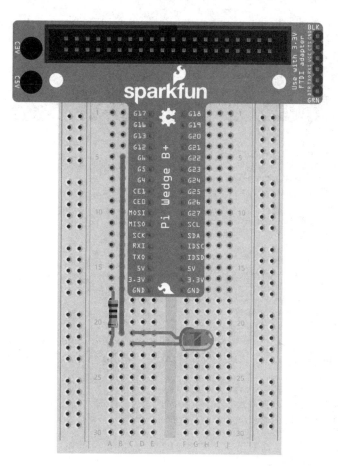

Figure 11.14 Wiring diagram, using SparkFun's Pi Wedge

BLINKING AN LED WITH SYSFS

Sysfs is a Linux pseudo-filesystem that organizes the configuration of attached devices and systems into a filesystem hierarchy. Each entity exported by sysfs into the user space is represented by a directory. Sysfs mounts at /sys, and from within /sys/class/gpio it's possible to control the Pi's GPIO pins.

For each pin you want to use, you need to do the following:

1 Export the pin. This is done by writing the pin number to the file at /sys/class/gpio/export using the BCM number scheme. This will create a directory for the pin (<pin_directory>).

2 Configure the pin, such as by writing the value 'in' or 'out' to /sys/class/gpio/<pin_directory>/direction.

3 Interact with the pin, such as by reading from the /sys/class/gpio/<pin_directory>/value file or writing a value to it.

4 Clean up. Unexport the pin by writing the pin number to the file at /sys/class/gpio/unexport.

This is likely easier to understand by example. Blinking an LED connected to physical pin 7, BCM GPIO 4, a single time—turning it on then off again—can be accomplished by using a shell script, as shown in the following listing.

To try out sysfs, create a "blink-sysfs" directory inside your ~/projects directory.

Listing 11.1   A bash script to blink an attached LED once

```bash
#! /bin/bash
# Export the pin so we can work with it
echo "4" > /sys/class/gpio/export
# Set the pin up as an output pin
echo "out" > /sys/class/gpio/gpio4/direction
# Turn on the LED by setting the pin to HIGH ("1")
echo "1" > /sys/class/gpio/gpio4/value
# Do nothing for one second
sleep 1
# Turn off the pin by setting it to LOW ("0")
echo "0" > /sys/class/gpio/gpio4/value
sleep 1
# Unexport the pin to clean up after ourselves
echo "4" > /sys/class/gpio/unexport
```

To run the blink.sh script, you need to make the file executable. You should be able to do that by running this command inside the ~/projects/blink-sysfs directory:

```
$ chmod +x ./blink.sh
```

Now try it out by typing the following:

```
$ sudo ./blink.sh
```

BLINKING AN LED WITH SYSFS AND NODE.JS

At the end of the day, these are just filesystem actions, so you can also do this with Node.js using the built-in `fs` module, as shown in the next listing.

Listing 11.2   Blinking an LED with sysfs and Node.js

```javascript
const fs = require('fs');
const sysfsPath = '/sys/class/gpio';
const ledPin = '4';                          Note that the pin number
const blinkTotal = 10;                       and all written values in
                                             this example are strings.
var blinkCount = 0;
var ledStatus = false;

// Export and configure the pin as an output
fs.writeFileSync(`${sysfsPath}/export`, ledPin);
fs.writeFileSync(`${sysfsPath}/gpio${ledPin}/direction`, 'out');

var blinker = setInterval(() => {
```

```
if (ledStatus) {
  // The LED is on. Turn it off.
  fs.writeFileSync(`${sysfsPath}/gpio${ledPin}/value`, '0');
  blinkCount++; // This completes one blink cycle
  if (blinkCount >= blinkTotal) {
    console.log('All done blinking');
    // Clean up after ourselves
    fs.writeFileSync(`${sysfsPath}/unexport`, '4');
    clearInterval(blinker);
  }
} else {
  // The LED is off. Turn it on.
  fs.writeFileSync(`${sysfsPath}/gpio${ledPin}/value`, '1');
}
ledStatus = !ledStatus; // The LED has swapped status
}, 1000);
```

Try it out by using this command:

```
$ sudo node index.js
```

Don't forget to unexport

You really do need to `unexport` objects in the gpio directory when you're done or it'll be problematic for you next time you want to use that pin. If you see an error like this when trying to run the Node.js blinking script, it's likely the pin didn't get unexported correctly:

```
Error: EBUSY: resource
busy or locked, write
```

You can execute the following command in a terminal to clean up manually:

```
$ echo "4" > /sys/class/gpio/unexport
```

You could fill an encyclopedic tome with all of the things you can do with `sysfs`, but let's move on. It's good to know about `sysfs`, but working with it directly requires patience and involves a learning curve.

WIRINGPI

WiringPi is an abstracting wrapper that attempts to make pin numbering more sane, and it exposes an API that's more familiarly Arduino-style. It's written in C, but Ruby and Python libraries for it are popular. There's an npm package that provides Node.js bindings: `wiring-pi`.

If you want to try this out, create a directory in your ~/projects area named blink-wiring-pi. Inside of that directory, run this command:

```
$ npm install wiring-pi
```

Then create an index.js file with the contents shown in the following listing. In this script, the status value toggles between 0 and 1, turning the LED off and on, respectively.

Listing 11.3   index.js

Note status is a Number (0 or 1), not Boolean as before.

Same physical pin as before, but using WiringPi numbers, which are actually JavaScript Numbers (not Strings)

pinMode() and the OUTPUT constant echo the Arduino Language API.

status here is either I (HIGH) or 0 (LOW).

Inverts the Boolean equivalent of status and makes it a Number again (+ operator)

```
const wpi = require('wiring-pi');
const ledPin = 7;
const blinkTotal = 10;
var blinkCount = 0;
var status = 1;

wpi.setup('wpi');
wpi.pinMode(ledPin, wpi.OUTPUT);

var blinker = setInterval(() => {
  wpi.digitalWrite(ledPin, status);
  if (!status) {
    blinkCount++;
    if (blinkCount >= blinkTotal) {
      console.log('All done blinking!');
      clearInterval(blinker);
    }
  }
  status = +!status;
}, 1000);
```

To run the script, use this command:

```
$ sudo node index.js`
```

JOHNNY-FIVE WITH THE RASPI-IO I/O PLUGIN

To round out the blinking extravaganza, we'll return to our old friend Johnny-Five. Just as the `tessel-io` Johnny-Five I/O plugin makes it possible to use Johnny-Five with the Tessel, the npm package `raspi-io` allows you to use J5 on the Raspberry Pi.

Go ahead and create one more directory in the ~/projects directory called blink-j5.

Inside of the blink-j5 directory, run this command to install the Johnny-Five and `raspi-io` packages:

```
$ npm install johnny-five raspi-io
```

For your next trick, you'll take one of the very first LED scripts you ever tried—from way back in chapter 2—and adapt it to work on the Pi, as shown in the following listing. The only changes required are including and using the `raspi-io` plugin to provide I/O, and changing the pin number for the LED. That's it!

Listing 11.4 Blinking the LED with Johnny-Five

```
const five = require('johnny-five');
const Raspi = require('raspi-io');          ◄─── Requires the raspi-io
                                                 I/O plugin module

const board = new five.Board({io: new Raspi()       ◄───┐
});                                                      │ Uses a Raspi
                                                         │ object for io
board.on('ready', () => {
  const led = new five.Led(7);       ◄───┐ Uses the WiringPi
  var blinkCount = 0;                    │ numbering scheme
  const blinkMax = 10;

  led.blink(500, () => {
    blinkCount++;
    console.log(`I have changed state ${blinkCount} times`);
    if (blinkCount >= blinkMax) {
      console.log('I shall stop blinking now');
      led.stop();
    }
  });
});
```

`Raspi-io` supports multiple Pi pin-numbering schemes. Pins passed as JavaScript `Number` values are automatically assumed to be WiringPi numbers. But you can also use physical pin numbers and functional names (such as `GPIO4`). See the plugin's documentation for more details (https://github.com/nebrius/raspi-io).

11.2.5 API documentation

Given that there are umpteen ways to control hardware with a Pi, there's no single source of API documentation. Instead, we'll be making use of Johnny-Five, Node.js, and the `raspi-io` I/O plugin, so you'll want to keep the documentation websites for those APIs at your fingertips as we explore.

11.3 Writing Johnny-Five applications for different platforms

As seen in listing 11.4, adapting Johnny-Five applications to work on different platforms (such as migrating from Arduino Uno to Raspberry Pi) can be quite easy. Often it's a matter of selecting the right I/O plugin and updating some pin numbers in the code.

In the next several experiments in this section, you'll adapt the live-updating BMP180-based weather application originally created for the Tessel in chapter 8 (figure 11.15). In keeping with your exploration of SBCs and the Raspberry Pi 3 specifically, you'll implement the weather station first on the Pi 3 and then subsequently make it work on an Arduino Uno.

You can find the source code for the Tessel version of the weather station application in the book's source code repository on GitHub.

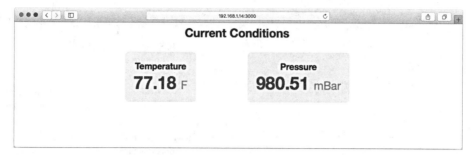

Figure 11.15   The mini weather app provides live-updating temperature and pressure data that can be viewed in a browser on any computer on the same network.

11.3.1 *Adapting the mini weather station for the Pi 3*

What you'll need

- 1 configured Raspberry Pi 3
- 1 SparkFun Pi Wedge, Adafruit T-Cobbler, or similar; *or* male-to-female jumper wires
- 1 BMP180 multisensor breakout board
- 1 breadboard
- Jumper wires

As a refresher, the weather application has two main components:

- Server code—This includes Johnny-Five code to handle I/O and reading sensor data, a static web server (using `express`), and a socket.IO server that emits events representing weather data updates (socket.IO clients can listen for those events).
- Client code—This is in the form of a single HTML page—index.html—which will be served by the `express` static web server. Once loaded in a browser, index.html connects to the socket.IO server as a client, so it can receive and display weather data without a user having to refresh the page.

This pattern—I/O handling and web server combined with a browser-based front end—can be reused to build many different kinds of IoT applications. It's a useful pattern to have in your back pocket.

BUILDING THE CIRCUIT

First, you need to build the circuit by connecting the BMP180 breakout to your Pi. As with the blinking LED, the specifics will depend on your setup. Wiring diagrams are provided for direct connections to the Pi (figure 11.16), SparkFun Pi Wedge (figure 11.17), and Adafruit's T-Cobbler (figure 11.18).

> **Raspi-io AND I²C**   The BMP180 is I²C. `Raspi-io` supports I²C just fine, but to enable it you'll need to reboot (if you haven't yet) after installing `raspi-io`. (Hint: `sudo reboot` is a handy command.)

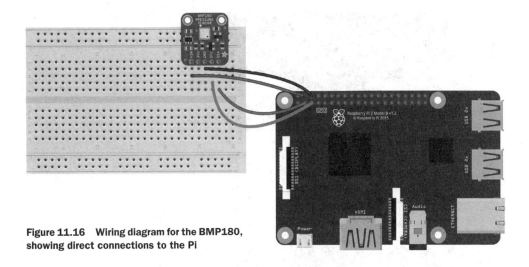

Figure 11.16 Wiring diagram for the BMP180, showing direct connections to the Pi

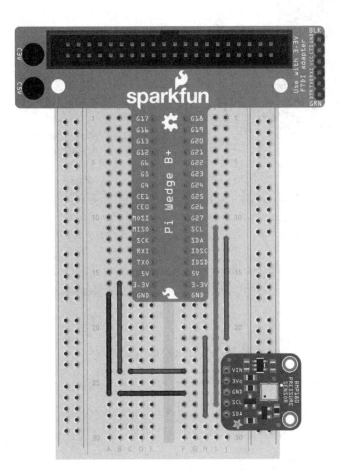

Figure 11.17 Wiring diagram for the BMP180 and the SparkFun Pi Wedge

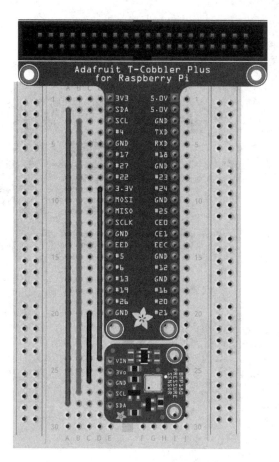

Figure 11.18   Wiring diagram for the BMP180 and the Adafruit T-Cobbler

TESTING THE BMP180

Before adapting the Tessel's weather station software, you're going to whip up a basic script to log BMP180 temperature and pressure data to the console. This will confirm that the combination of Raspbian, `raspi-io`, I²C, and the BMP180 are working together in harmony:

1 Establish a working area. Create a directory called "weather" within your Pi's projects directory:

```
$ mkdir weather
```

2 Inside of the weather directory, run this command:

```
$ npm install johnny-five raspi-io
```

3 Create an index.js file and populate it with the code shown in the next listing.

Listing 11.5 Testing the Pi, Johnny-Five, `raspi-io`, and BMP180

```
const five = require('johnny-five');
const Raspi = require('raspi-io');

const board = new five.Board({
  io: new Raspi()          ⟵┐  Once again, uses the
});                          └  raspi-io plugin for I/O

board.on('ready', () => {
  const bmp180 = new five.Multi({
    controller: 'BMP180'
  });
  bmp180.on('change', () => {
    var temperature = bmp180.thermometer.fahrenheit.toFixed(2);
    var pressure    = bmp180.barometer.pressure.toFixed(2);
    console.log(`${temperature}°F | ${pressure}kPa`);
  });
});
```

In the preceding listing, note that you don't have to designate which pins the BMP180 is connected to in the instantiation of the `Multi` sensor component (assigned to the `bmp180` variable). `Raspi-io` "knows" where the I^{2}C-capable pins are on the Raspberry Pi and takes care of configuring the interface for you! That's handy.

Try it out. Still inside of the weather directory, run this command:

```
$ sudo node index.js
```

You should see temperature and pressure data logging to the console, something like the following.

Listing 11.6 Sample output for the test BMP180 script

```
>> 77.54°F | 98.05kPa
77.54°F | 98.05kPa
77.54°F | 98.05kPa
77.54°F | 98.05kPa
77.54°F | 98.06kPa
77.54°F | 98.05kPa
77.72°F | 98.06kPa
77.72°F | 98.06kPa
77.54°F | 98.05kPa
```

MAKING PI-SPECIFIC CHANGES

Now you'll make some Pi-specific changes. Create a new working area, a directory called "pi-weather". Copy the original weather application source files from the book's GitHub repository into this directory, but omit .tesselinclude. You should end up with a structure that looks like the following.

Listing 11.7   Project directory and file structure

```
pi-weather/
├── app
│   ├── index.html
│   └── style.css
├── index.js
└── package.json
```

DON'T COPY OVER THE NODE_MODULES DIRECTORY   If you inadvertently end up with a node_modules directory inside of pi-weather (copied from earlier experiments with the Tessel), blow it away before proceeding:

```
$ rm -rf node_modules
```

There are two places in the code that need changes:

- package.json—You'll need to update dependencies.
- index.js—You'll need to use raspi-io for I/O.

UPDATING THE PACKAGE.JSON DEPENDENCIES

Start by editing package.json. It should contain, in part, a `dependencies` object, which should look similar to what's shown in the following listing, though your version numbers may be different. Remove the `tessel-io` dependency, as you won't need it for the Raspberry Pi version.

Listing 11.8   Package.json dependencies from the Tessel project

```
        "dependencies": {
          "express": "^4.14.1",
          "johnny-five": "^0.10.4",
 Delete   "socket.io": "^1.7.3",
this line. └─▷ "tessel-io": "^0.9.0"
        }
```

> Don't forget to delete the trailing comma if the tessel-io entry is the last one.

Now install the remaining dependencies:

```
$ npm install
```

Then add a new dependency—raspi-io—using the `--save` flag to write the change to the `dependencies` in package.json:

```
$ npm install --save raspi-io
```

UPDATING INDEX.JS

The changes needed in index.js are simple.

1 Replace this line,

```
    const Tessel   = require('tessel-io');
```

with this one:

```
const Raspi   = require('raspi-io');
```

2 Update the `board` instantiation to use `raspi-io` instead of `tessel-io`, changing this line,

```
const board = new five.Board({ io: new Tessel() });
```

to look like this:

```
const board = new five.Board({ io: new Raspi() });
```

The resulting index.js contents should look like the following.

Listing 11.9   A Pi-compatible version of index.js

```
const five     = require('johnny-five');
const Raspi    = require('raspi-io');
const express  = require('express');
const SocketIO = require('socket.io');

const path = require('path');
const http = require('http');
const os   = require('os');

const app    = new express();
const server = new http.Server(app);
const socket = new SocketIO(server);
app.use(express.static(path.join(__dirname, '/app')));

const board = new five.Board({ io: new Raspi() });

board.on('ready', () => {
  const weatherSensor = new five.Multi({
    controller: 'BMP180',
    freq: 5000
  });

  socket.on('connection', client => {
    weatherSensor.on('change', () => {
      client.emit('weather', {
        temperature: weatherSensor.thermometer.F,
        pressure: (weatherSensor.barometer.pressure * 10)
      });
    });
  });

  server.listen(3000, () => {
    console.log(`http://${os.networkInterfaces().wlan0[0].address}:3000`);
  });
});
```

No changes are needed in app/index.html because that's client-side code—it runs in the user's browser, and it isn't affected by platform changes.

Run the application by using this command from within the weather directory:

```
$ sudo node index.js
```

Once the server code is initialized, it will log out the URL where you can access the weather display from other computers on the same network as the Pi (as shown in the following listing). Point your computer's browser to the logged URL to see the weather station in action.

Listing 11.10   Sample output when starting the weather station application

```
pi@raspberrypi:~/projects/weather $ sudo node index.js
1499532864338 Available RaspberryPi-IO
1499532864960 Connected RaspberryPi-IO
1499532864984 Repl Initialized
>> http://192.168.1.16:3000
```

11.3.2   *Adapting the mini weather station for the Arduino Uno*

Making the weather application work on other Johnny-Five-supported platforms is similarly straightforward. It's quick work to make the weather application work on an Arduino Uno tethered to your own computer, instead of on the Pi.

What you'll need
- 1 Arduino Uno
- 1 breadboard
- 1 BMP180 multisensor breakout board
- Jumper wires

1   Copy the Pi version of the application—the weather directory and its contents, minus the node_modules directory, to your computer.
2   Edit package.json. Remove the `raspi-io` dependency; I/O support for Arduino platforms is built into Johnny-Five and doesn't require an I/O plugin.
3   Install dependencies:

```
$ npm install
```

4   Edit the index.js file:
   a   Remove the `require` statement for `raspi-io`.
   b   Change the `board` instantiation. Remove the reference to `Raspi` such that it reads as follows:

```
const board = new five.Board();
```

5   Connect the BMP180 to the Arduino Uno as shown in figure 11.19.

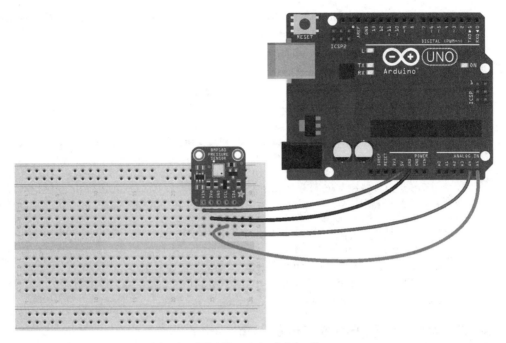

Figure 11.19 Wiring diagram for the BMP180 and the Arduino Uno

Connect the Uno to your computer and run the application. You won't need `sudo` here:

```
$ node index.js
```

11.4 *Using the Raspberry Pi as a host*

Remember, the Raspberry Pi 3 is a "real" computer, so there's no reason you can't use it as the host in a host-client setup, with its own tethered Arduino, just like you do with your own computer.

What you'll need
- 1 configured Raspberry Pi 3
- 1 Arduino Uno
- 1 breadboard
- 1 BMP180 multisensor breakout board
- Jumper wires

1   Copy the Arduino Uno version of the weather application code—again, without the node_modules directory—to the Pi.

2   Install dependencies:

```
$ npm install
```

3 Plug the Arduino Uno—connected to the BMP180 as in figure 11.23—into one
   of the Pi's four USB ports.

4 Run the application:

```
$ node index.js
```

(You don't need to use sudo here as you're not using the Pi's GPIO.)

WEATHER STATION WITH RASPBERRY PI 3 AND TESSEL 2   There's no technical
reason you can't deploy the Tessel 2 version of the weather app to the Tessel
from the Pi (instead of from your own computer). First, however, you'll need
to install t2-cli on the Pi and provision the Tessel from it as detailed in Tessel's "Install Tessel 2" page (http://tessel.github.io/t2-start/).

At the end of the day, the Raspberry Pi platform is a vast world of options and choice.
A true computer in its own right, the Pi 3 packs the punch to act as a host in a host-client
setup, which is especially nice if you don't want to bother with the Pi's somewhat convoluted GPIO. But if you do want to dive into the Pi's onboard GPIO, there are certainly
a multitude of ways to get the job done.

11.5 *Case study: BeagleBone Black*

The Pi isn't the only game in town—there are a host of other SBC platforms. To get a
sense of the commonalities and differences between them, let's take a brief tour of the
BeagleBone Black (figure 11.20), one of the BeagleBoard family of SBCs.

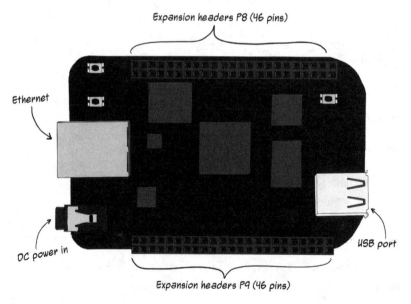

Figure 11.20   The BeagleBone Black SBC

11.5.1 *Learning about the BeagleBone Black*

Comparing any two SBCs is often an apples-to-oranges affair; different platforms are targeted at different applications. The Pi 3 wins the CPU and peripherals contest (multicore CPU, higher clock speed, more USB ports, and so on), but the BeagleBone Black outstrips the Pi in terms of GPIO features, and it's more power-efficient at idle. Rev C of the BeagleBone Black also ups the RAM ante: it has 4 GB.

Another important distinction is that, although the various Linux distributions you can run on the Raspberry Pi are open source, its hardware is not. Pis are exclusively manufactured by the Raspberry Pi Foundation and contain some closed-source components. BeagleBoards, in contrast, are open source hardware.

A rev C BeagleBone Black will set you back about $55.

CORE FEATURES

As alluded to moments ago, the BeagleBone Black's CPU is single-core and runs at 1.0 GHz, which is slower than the Pi 3's 1.2 GHz. Both are ARM v8 chips, however, so they're not too dissimilar overall. If you get the rev C, you'll score 4 GB of RAM (older versions have 512 MB). Like the Pi, the BeagleBone Black has a microSD slot, but it also has 4 GB of onboard eMMC flash storage. It has a single USB port, a mini-HDMI interface, and an Ethernet interface (figure 11.21).

Figure 11.21 The BeagleBone Black's information page on BeagleBoard's website

The BeagleBone Black and non-Ethernet connectivity options

The basic BeagleBone Black doesn't have onboard WiFi, but you can add support using a third-party adapter. You can find a list of supported WiFi adapters on the BeagleBone Black page of the Embedded Linux Wiki (http://mng.bz/Uj9d).

Another networking approach allows you to ssh to your BeagleBone Black over a USB connection. This may require you to install some drivers or tweak some other configuration; see the "Getting Started" page on BeagleBoard's site for more details (http://beagleboard.org/getting-started).

GPIO FEATURES AND PINOUTS

The BeagleBone Black boasts a smorgasbord of GPIO. There are 92 (ninety-two!) pins. There's hardware support for 4 UARTs, 65 interrupt-capable digital I/O pins, 8 PWM pins, and 7 analog inputs. Whereas the Pi is a computer that also does GPIO, the BeagleBone is more like a GPIO champ that also does computing.

The BeagleBone Black's pins are laid out in two sets of *expansion headers* with 46 pins in each. With the board's DC power connection at the top, expansion header P9 is on the left, P8 on the right (and as to what happened to P1–P7: no idea). As with the Pi, many of the BeagleBone Black's pins can play multiple roles.

You're going to use another Johnny-Five I/O plugin to control the BeagleBone Black's GPIO. Figure 11.22 shows the pins supported by the `beaglebone-io` Johnny-Five I/O plugin and their features. To reference a pin with `beaglebone-io`, you prefix the pin's physical number with the header number, such as `P9_11` for pin 11 on P9. You'll only be using the I²C interface, so you won't need to provide pin numbers at all—`beaglebone-io` will know automatically to use pins `P9_19` (SCL) and `P9_20` (SDA).

> **BEAGLEBONE BLACK VOLTAGE** The analog input pins on the BeagleBone Black only accept input voltages up to 1.8 V.

It's important to note that the pin features shown in figure 11.22 aren't indicative of all of the hardware support that the BeagleBone Black provides on those pins, but the support that the `beaglebone-io` plugin provides (for Johnny-Five scripts).

For example, there's no UART/TTL serial support shown here, but the BeagleBone Black does have several UARTs. Sometimes the search for a relevant pinout diagram can be complicated by the reality that what the pins actually do depends on how you're using them.

> **BBB GPIO BEYOND JOHNNY-FIVE** Do you plan on using your BeagleBone Black in other, non-Johnny-Five, contexts? You'll want to seek out a more complete pinout diagram. There are tons of other BeagleBone Black pinout diagrams available on the web. The BeagleBone Black has a bumper crop of 96 pins, each capable of playing upward of five or six different roles and referenced by different naming conventions. This can lead to some rather overwhelming diagrams. Take your time and be patient: it's not you—it really *is* a lot of information to take in visually.

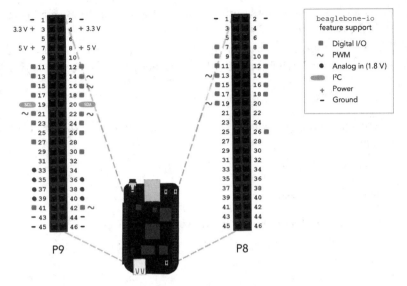

Figure 11.22 BeagleBone Black pin features available via the `beaglebone-io` Johnny-Five I/O plugin

CONFIGURATION AND WORKFLOW

One way to configure the BeagleBone Black closely mirrors the Raspberry Pi 3 setup from earlier in the chapter, minus the WiFi setup (there's no WiFi to configure).

The board ships with Ångström, an embedded Linux distribution, but this setup process replaces that with Debian. For more details about creating a bootable microSD (steps are abbreviated here), refer to the previous Raspberry Pi 3 setup in section 11.4:

1 Download the latest Debian image for BeagleBone at http://beagle-board.org/latest-images.

2 Burn the image to an SD card using the Etcher application.

3 Instead of repeatedly booting from the SD card, what you want to do is flash the OS image to the onboard eMMC flash storage. This requires an additional, slightly finicky, step here: a configuration file needs a simple edit.

After you flash the SD card with the Debian image, it may not be readable by your computer (it wasn't with mine). Instead, you can go ahead and boot the BeagleBone Black directly from the SD card, once, so that you can edit that config file:

a Insert the microSD card with the Debian image on it into the BeagleBone Black.

b Connect the BeagleBone Black directly to your router with an Ethernet cable, and then plug in power to the BeagleBone Black. It'll take a minute or two for the BeagleBone Black to boot up and get an IP address on your network.

   c Fire up your LAN- or IP-scanning utility to figure out the BeagleBone Black's IP address.

   d From your computer, in a terminal, `ssh` into the BBB with the `debian` user (`ssh` is enabled by default in the Debian image you're using here):

```
$ ssh debian@<BBB IP>
```

There's a default password for that user, which will be displayed to you on first login.

   e Edit the configuration file in question:

```
$ sudo vi /boot/uEnv.txt
```

(or use your preferred editor if you don't like `vi`).

Toward the bottom of the file, find the following line and uncomment it (remove the #):

```
#cmdline=init=/opt/scripts/tools/eMMC/init-eMMC-flasher-v3.sh
```

Save and exit the file. Uncommenting that line will allow the BeagleBone Black to run a script on startup that will copy (flash) the contents of the SD card to the built-in eMMC.

4 Now power down the BeagleBone Black. With the SD card still inserted, hold down the BOOT/USER button (figure 11.23) and reconnect the power. Keep holding the button down for a few more seconds until all of the onboard LEDs light up solid for a moment. Then you can let the button go.

5 The eMMC-flashing process takes a while—BeagleBoard's site says 30–45 minutes. You can tell when it's done because all of the BeagleBone Black's blue LEDs will turn off (frankly, a welcome respite from all of its default blinking!).

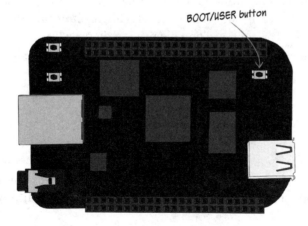

Figure 11.23 The BOOT/USER button on the BeagleBone Black

6 Power down the BeagleBone Black and eject the SD card. Power it back on again.

7 From your computer, ssh into the BeagleBone Black as the `debian` user.

8 Run this command:

```
$ lsb_release -a
```

You should see output similar to the following:

```
No LSB modules are available.
Distributor ID:   Debian
Description:      Debian GNU/Linux 8.7 (jessie)
Release:    8.7
Codename:    jessie
```

9 To see what Node.js version you have, run this command:

```
$ node --version
```

I got `v4.8.0`.

10 You're welcome to update the Node.js version if you'd like, but v4.8.x is good enough to support the rest of the code examples in this section.

EXAMPLES AND TUTORIALS

Next you'll take the BeagleBone Black for a Hello World spin, LED-style, using Johnny-Five and the `beaglebone-io` plugin. There's an onboard LED you can access, so this is a quick endeavor (no circuitry required).

Connect to your BeagleBone Black over SSH and create a working area (a projects directory or similar). Inside of this directory, install Johnny-Five and the `beaglebone-io` I/O plugin:

```
$npm install johnny-five beaglebone-io
```

Create an index.js file and add the contents from the following listing.

Listing 11.11 LED blinking on the BeagleBone Black

```
var five = require('johnny-five');
var BeagleBone = require('beaglebone-io');

var board = new five.Board({
  io: new BeagleBone()          ⟵  Using the beaglebone-io plugin
});

board.on('ready', function () {
  var led = new five.Led();     ⟵  No pin number is given here:
  led.blink(500);                  beaglebone-io will automatically
});                                use the onboard LED.
```

Now run it! As with the Pi, you'll need sudo here:

```
$ sudo node index.js
```

You should now see one of the BeagleBone Black's blue LEDs blinking on and off every 500 ms.

API DOCUMENTATION

Once again, you're taking the Johnny-Five route here. Documentation for the beaglebone-io plugin contains vital information about pin support and plugin usage details (https://github.com/julianduque/beaglebone-io).

11.5.2 *Adapting the weather station for the BeagleBone*

What you'll need

- 1 configured, networked BeagleBone Black and power supply
- 1 breadboard
- 1 BMP180 multisensor breakout board
- Jumper wires

By now, the overall adaptation pattern for the weather application is getting familiar:

1   Connect the BMP180 to the BeagleBone Black, as shown in figure 11.24.
2   Make a weather directory on the BeagleBone Black, and copy the original (Tessel variant) weather station source code into it, without node_modules.
3   Edit package.json to remove the tessel-io dependency.
4   Run $ npm install to install dependencies.
5   Run $npm install --save beaglebone-io to install the beaglebone-io plugin and save it to package.json.
6   Edit index.js:

   a   Remove the tessel-io dependency and replace it with beaglebone-io:

```
const BeagleBone = require('beaglebone-io');
```

   b   Change the board instantiation to use the beaglebone-io plugin:

```
const board = new five.Board({
  io: new BeagleBone()
});
```

The BeagleBone Black is going to require just a couple more quick tricks from you.

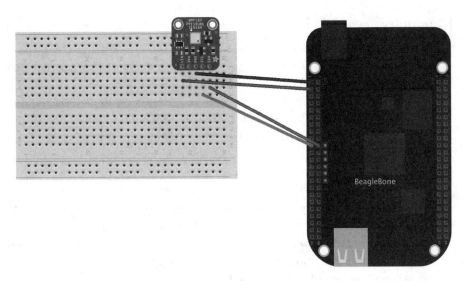

Figure 11.24   Wiring diagram for the BMP180 and the BeagleBone Black

As it turns out, the BeagleBone Black, by default, already has a server running at port 3000. And it doesn't have WiFi, so there's no wlan0 network interface. To account for this, edit the code for server.listen() as follows.

Listing 11.12   Updated `server.listen()`

> **Change the port number to something else; 4000 works fine.**

```
server.listen(4000, () => {
  console.log(`http://${os.networkInterfaces().eth0[0].address}:4000`);
});
```

> **Use eth0 instead of wlan0 here, and also update the port number.**

All done! Make it so:

```
$ sudo node index.js
```

Now open the logged URL in a browser on your computer.

Keeping the I/O details sequestered to I/O plugins makes Johnny-Five applications relatively portable between platforms. Details do pop up, like the unavailability of port 3000 on the BeagleBone Black, but overall it's usually not too bad to move things between platforms. If you'd like, you can also run the Arduino-compatible variant of the weather application, using the BeagleBone Black as a host. SBCs give you a whole constellation of options.

Summary

- Single-board computers (SBCs) add tons of features and general-purpose goodies, but they use more power and are more complicated to configure and administer than more constrained platforms.

- The Raspberry Pi 3 is the third-generation Raspberry Pi platform, and it can be used for general-purpose computing as well as for embedded applications. Raspbian is a Debian-based Linux OS specifically optimized for the Pi family.

- Common setup steps for SBCs and Node.js development include flashing (or otherwise installing or upgrading) an OS, configuring networking, updating Node.js versions, and establishing a filesystem workflow.

- Sysfs is a Linux pseudo-filesystem that allows interaction with connected components and hardware via virtual directories and files.

- There are myriad ways to hack hardware on a Raspberry Pi, with frameworks and libraries for nearly any programming language you can think of.

- WiringPi is a popular abstraction for Raspberry Pi GPIO. It's written in C, but there are libraries for it in several other languages. Other frameworks not based on WiringPi (including the `raspi-io` plugin) support WiringPi's pin-numbering scheme because its Arduino-emulating clarity can be less confusing than other numbering schemes.

- The `raspi-io` and `beaglebone-io` I/O plugins support Johnny-Five compatibility on the Raspberry Pi and BeagleBone Black platforms, respectively.

- Adapting Johnny-Five applications to work cross-platform commonly involves swapping out I/O plugins and updating pin numbers. Often those are the only changes necessary.

- The Raspberry Pi can also be used in a host-client setup, acting as the host. It can control a tethered Arduino Uno (client), for example.

- The BeagleBone Black is an open source SBC with features in the same ballpark, overall, as a Raspberry Pi 3, but it's more targeted to embedded and GPIO applications.

12

In the cloud, in the browser, and beyond

This chapter covers

- Using a cloud-based service (resin.io) to deploy and manage an application across a fleet of devices
- Bleeding-edge web platform technologies for interacting with hardware, including Web Bluetooth and the Generic Sensor API
- Building the Physical Web with the open Eddystone protocol and Bluetooth Low Energy (BLE) beacons
- Controlling hardware from a web page using Web Bluetooth and Puck.js
- Reading data from and writing commands to a BLE device

For this chapter, you'll need the following:

- 1 BeagleBone Black and 5 V power supply
- 1 Espruino Puck.js

- 1 Adafruit BMP180 multisensor breakout board
- 1 half-size breadboard
- Jumper wires

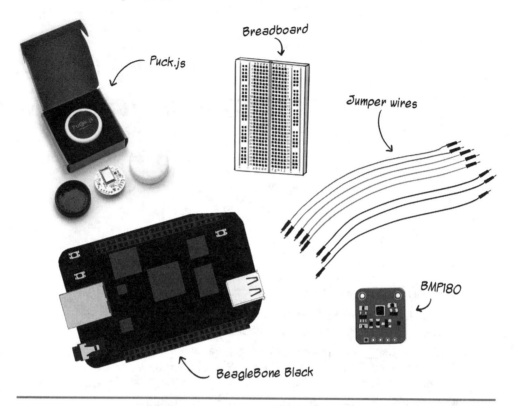

This chapter opens up some grand vistas. Yet this grandness of scale bumps up against limited space. Topics merely touched upon here are entire specialties; there's enough to learn about each to fill books, shelves, or even entire libraries: security; the web standards process; the intricacies of Bluetooth and Bluetooth LE (BLE) architecture; provisioning and managing fleets of IoT devices, at scale.

As such, this chapter doesn't mark the end of a learning journey but is instead a springboard for subsequent adventures. Its first half pulls back the curtains on the world of cloud-based IoT service offerings. The second half wears a futurist's hat, pushing at the edges of what we can do on the web and in a browser today, and at what might be coming tomorrow.

CODE IS NOT PRODUCTION-READY The code in this chapter isn't ready for a production environment. Security, performance, graceful degradation, and accessibility diligence are sacrificed here in pursuit of clarity and brevity.

12.1 IoT and the cloud

This book has been primarily concerned with illustrating core electronics principles and wrangling hardware with JavaScript. But the cloud is an indispensable part of IoT—you can't have the internet of things without the internet. Commercial IoT cloud services provide inventors and entrepreneurs with ways of bringing their IoT visions to life, offering supporting services like data stores, deployment tools, RESTful APIs, analytics, security, testing, benchmarking, debugging, monitoring, development frameworks—wow! It turns out that IoT is complex. And, boy, is there a lot of jargon involved!

The already-vague notion of IoT cloud services is muddied further by the fact that some IoT companies' products aren't limited to software. Indeed, some companies combine physical hardware platforms with their cloud services, creating a top-to-bottom package (figure 12.1).

Particle, for example, manufactures the Electron board, which has onboard 2G/3G connectivity. You deploy your code to and read data from a given Electron using cellular networks—depending on Particle's proprietary cloud services for this deployment and I/O, naturally. In this case, the company—Particle—is providing the hardware (the Electron device), the software (you program your Particle boards using their

Figure 12.1 Both Particle (https://www.particle.io) and Samsung's ARTIK services (https://www.artik.io) are so-called "end-to-end" offerings for IoT.

API), and the cloud infrastructure (you deploy to your Particle device fleet using their centralized web-based tools).

Another example of this so-called end-to-end product offering is Samsung's ARTIK platform. You could use one of the ARTIK hardware "modules" standalone—their 5-, 7-, and 10-series boards are all capable SBCs that ship with Fedora Linux—but the hardware itself is just one part of their integrated ecosystem. They're hoping you'll opt to use their cloud services too.

This is a deep ocean to dive into. It can be overwhelming if you have no familiar landmarks against which to chart your voyage, and there's a painful amount of jargon and buzzword business-speak. In an attempt to temper this novel onslaught, we won't start a project from scratch but will instead adapt our old friend, the mini weather station with the browser interface, to work on the BeagleBone Black.

We'll take the same weather-station application code—with some minor tweaks—but instead of working directly on the device to manage the OS and run the app code, we'll have resin.io do that work for us.

12.2 Containerized deployment with resin.io

What you'll need

- 1 BeagleBone Black and power supply
- 1 Ethernet cable
- 1 microSD card and adapter
- 1 breadboard
- 1 BMP180 multisensor breakout board
- Jumper wires

Resin.io (https://resin.io/) is a service that offers *containerized* deployment to and management of internet-connected, *provisioned* Linux IoT devices. That's a mouthful—there's some of that jargon I warned you about—so let's unpack it by coming at it from the angle of what problems services like resin.io are actually trying to solve.

Recall from chapter 11 that SBCs (like the BeagleBone Black) are typically capable of running various flavors of Linux, but that the tradeoff for such flexibility is that the installation and administration of Linux can add some overhead (and pain) to an SBC-based workflow. Getting code files onto a device from your preferred development environment (such as your laptop) can be a chore. Managing environment settings and configuration can be a headache. You may have an itch to work iteratively, using familiar software development methodologies and tools (such as Git for version control) and collaborating with other devs. Getting that all set up piecemeal can take time and energy, or it may even stump you entirely.

Now imagine that your IoT application needs to run not just on one BeagleBone (or Pi, or other SBC) but on an entire fleet of them, possibly scattered geographically across states, provinces, countries. Keeping tabs on the devices, keeping things in sync, sending the right version of the code to each device, monitoring devices for failures, pushing out OS or security updates—doing all of this manually isn't going to scale well. Then there are all of those requirements for software and hardware products that are used by real people: analytics (how much use has a particular device been getting?), security (let's make sure we're uploading that user's heart rate over a secure connection!), and so on.

There's a lot going on here. To accomplish much of it, resin.io (and some other similar services) employ several key strategies:

- *Containerization*—The key idea here is that you want the same application to run in the same way on each of your devices. Resin.io uses Docker containers to package applications and their dependencies cleanly and reliably. Your app's container gets deployed to each of your provisioned devices.
- *Provisioning*—A given device needs to be able to get a hold of resin.io, identify itself, and receive application updates. To accomplish this, you download a custom disk image from resin.io and boot each device from it. Once a device has been successfully provisioned, it will appear on the web dashboard for the associated resin.io app, as you'll see shortly.
- *Version control integration*—Pushing code to a particular remote of a specified Git repository automatically triggers redeployment of the application to all connected, provisioned devices. Part of setting up a resin.io project is defining which Git repository to use as the application source.

Containers, containers, containers!

You can't swing a cat on the internet these days without running into someone who's saying something (usually vague, but almost always laudatory) about containers. You'll read that containers are the greatest solution ever for app deployment, for security, for performance, for ensuring world peace, and so on, but what's harder to track down is an explanation of what the heck a container is and what it, in real terms, does.

A container serves both to encapsulate and isolate an application and the bits and bobs it requires to function correctly (dependencies, settings, and the like). A single server or computing device may run numerous separate containers at the same time without them interfering with each other. Likewise, the same container can be deployed to a whole bunch of different computers, and—because the container holds all of the things needed to define the app's environment as well as all of its dependencies—you can feel confident that the app will behave the same way on each of the different devices.

Resin.io uses Docker containers. Docker is both the name of a particular containerization technology platform and the company that created it. Docker is, by far, the most popular container technology in the industry.

Once a resin.io project and its devices are set up, you can develop your app iteratively. When you push changes to your resin.io Git remote, resin.io rebuilds your application's container with the updated code and deploys that container to all of the connected, provisioned devices for that app, wherever they may be (figure 12.2).

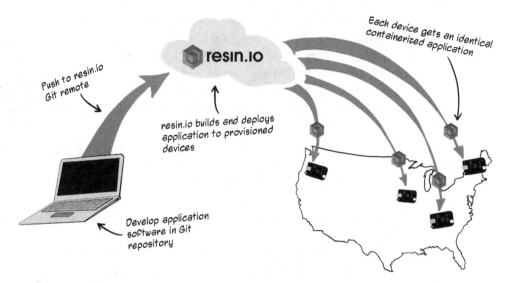

Figure 12.2   **Devices that will run the application are provisioned by installing and booting a custom-tailored resin.io OS image on each. Pushing application code to a project-specific resin.io Git remote triggers the rebuilding of the app's container and its redeployment to connected, provisioned devices.**

GIT-TING UP TO SPEED   Code for your resin.io application will be managed within a Git repository—you'll need to have Git installed on your computer. The "Installing Git" section on the git-scm website documents how to do this on several different platforms (https://git-scm.com/book/en/v2/Getting-Started-Installing-Git).

Although the instructions for building a resin.io app include all of the Git commands you'll need to get an app up and running on a BeagleBone Black, a working knowledge of Git should be part of every dev's mental toolbox. It takes minutes to learn the Git basics (though, honestly, a lifetime to master). GitHub has an interactive tutorial (https://try.github.io/levels/1/challenges/1), and there are copious other online Git-education resources—many of them free.

12.2.1   *Creating a resin.io application*

You're going to create a resin.io app for your weather station software, for deployment to your BeagleBone Black. Resin.io offers a free tier that allows deployment and management for up to five devices. Head on over to https://resin.io/ and create an account (figure 12.3).

Next, create an application. You'll be prompted for a name and a device type for your application. You can name it whatever you like—I called mine `beagleweather`. For the Device Type field, select `BeagleBone Black` from the long list of options (figure 12.4).

NO BEAGLEBONE BLACK?   No BeagleBone Black on hand? You can use a Raspberry Pi instead, if you like. You'll need to use the Pi version of the weather application code (find it in the chapter-11 folder of the book's GitHub repository)—with the `raspi-io` I/O plugin—but otherwise the steps should be the same. Oh, and, of course, make sure to select `Raspberry Pi 3` instead of `BeagleBone Black` as the Device Type for your resin.io application.

Figure 12.3 Sign up for an account at resin.io.

Figure 12.4 Detail of application-creation step showing the list of supported device types

12.2.2   *Provisioning the BeagleBone Black*

Resin.io generates a custom *OS image* for every project. The resin.io OS is a lightweight Linux. It can run your app's Docker container, and it also takes care of housekeeping jobs like provisioning the device and keeping an eye out for deployed updates.

Once you've defined your resin.io application, you can go ahead and download the generated OS image (there's a link provided, as shown in figure 12.5) and install it on your devices (or, in our case, a single *device*). See section 11.2.3 in chapter 11 for more details on the steps here:

1 Download the OS image.
2 Using the Etcher app, burn the IMG file to the microSD card.
3 Insert the microSD card into the BeagleBone Black and connect the Beagle-Bone Black's Ethernet interface to your router.
4 Hold down the USER/BOOT button (figure 12.6) and plug power into the Bea-gleBone Black. Keep holding down the button until the LEDs start blinking madly. Release the button.

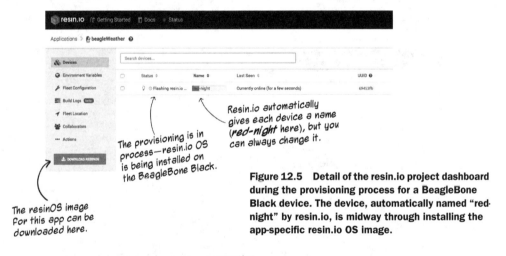

Figure 12.5   Detail of the resin.io project dashboard during the provisioning process for a BeagleBone Black device. The device, automatically named "red-night" by resin.io, is midway through installing the app-specific resin.io OS image.

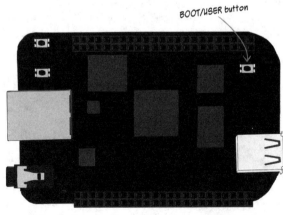

Figure 12.6   Hold down the BeagleBone Black's BOOT/USER button to boot from the SD card.

Back at your own computer, you should see the device show up on your resin.io application's dashboard after a few moments. From the dashboard, you'll be able to track the device's progress through the provisioning process.

12.2.3 *Adapting the weather application software*

To get the weather app software running on the provisioned BeagleBone Black, there are a few more steps:

1 Set up and configure a Git repository for the app.
2 Configure the Docker container for the app.
3 Define a script to start the app (in package.json).
4 Make a couple of tweaks to the software itself.
5 Commit and push to GitHub.
6 Give the app a public URL.

INITIALIZING A GIT REPOSITORY

First you need to establish a working area. Create a directory to contain the project (beagleweather, perhaps?) on your computer.

Inside of this directory, initialize a Git repository by running this command:

```
$ git init
```

To deploy your application, you need to be able to push your repository's master branch to resin.io. You'll need to add a resin.io-specific Git remote so that you can push to resin.io later. Resin.io conveniently shows you the exact command you need to run to get this remote set up: find it at the top right of the dashboard for your application. Execute the displayed command in your local repository (figure 12.7).

Figure 12.7   Detail of resin.io application dashboard showing where to find the command for adding your application's resin.io Git remote

You can see all of your repository's remotes by running this command:

```
$ git remote -v
```

You should see output something like this:

```
resin     <your resin username>@git.resin.io:<your resin username>/
➥ beagleweather.git (fetch)
resin     <your resin username>@git.resin.io:<your resin username>/
➥ beagleweather.git (push)
```

Next, copy the source files from the original BeagleBone weather application to your new working Git project directory—index.js, package.json, and the app directory and its contents.

DEFINING THE DOCKER APP CONTAINER

The base resin.io OS for your application that's now running on your BeagleBone Black consists of a stripped-down Linux and also contains some helpful, supporting tools. But you still need to create the Docker container that will run on your app's device(s) and tell it how to behave and what to do.

Create a file called Dockerfile.template in your project directory (the "template" extension allows the use of certain handy variables inside the file) and add the contents shown in the following listing. Most of the listing is boilerplate, sourced directly from resin.io's documentation.

Listing 12.1   Dockerfile.template

```
# base-image for node on any machine using a template variable
FROM resin/%%RESIN_MACHINE_NAME%%-node:6          ◁——  Uses a base image with
                                                        Node.js, version 6
# Defines our working directory in container
WORKDIR /usr/src/app

# Copies the package.json first for better cache on later pushes
COPY package.json package.json

# This install npm dependencies on the resin.io build server,
# making sure to clean up the artifacts it creates in order to reduce the
➥ image size.
RUN JOBS=MAX npm install --production --unsafe-perm && npm cache clean &&
➥ rm -rf /tmp/*

# This will copy all files in our root to the working  directory in the
➥ container
COPY . ./

# Enable systemd init system in container
ENV INITSYSTEM on

# server.js will run when container starts up on the device
CMD ["npm", "start"]          ◁——  You'll need to define an npm
                                    start script that starts your
                                    application.
```

MORE ABOUT RESIN.IO MACHINE NAMES, BASE IMAGES, AND TAGS Inside of resin.io Dockerfiles, you can specify a lot of details about devices, features, and Linux distributions and versions. There's too much to go into here, but if you're curious about this stuff, the resin.io documentation is thorough (https://docs.resin.io/raspberrypi/nodejs/getting-started/).

ADDING AN NPM START SCRIPT

This line appears at end of the Dockerfile.template configuration:

```
CMD ["npm", "start"]
```

This tells the builder to run the command npm start once the container is started. You don't have a start script yet, but you can easily add one by editing package.json.

Edit the scripts field in package.json so that it looks like the following listing.

Listing 12.2 Package.json scripts

```
"scripts": {
  "start": "node index.js",
  "test": "echo \"Error: no test specified\" && exit 1"
},
```

Now when the build process runs the command npm start, it will have the same effect as executing node index.js—it will start up your weather application.

TWEAKING THE APP CODE

There are two small changes to make to index.js before you're done.

Johnny-Five's REPL and resin.io don't get along. You can disable the REPL easily, by adding a property to the board-instantiation options object (repl: false).

Listing 12.3 Disable Johnny-Five REPL

```
const board = new five.Board({
  io: new BeagleBone(),
  repl: false
});
```

The existing port defined for the web server (4000) in server.listen() would work fine, but there's a really nifty trick you're going to pull off momentarily, so change the port to 80.

Listing 12.4 Change web server port to 80

```
server.listen(80, () => {
  console.log(`http://${os.networkInterfaces().eth0[0].address}:80`);
});
```

COMMITTING AND PUSHING

Add and commit the project files to Git (make sure you're in the project's top-level directory):

```
$ git add index.js package.json Dockerfile.template app/
$ git commit -m "first commit"
```

Now push to trigger the deployment to your BeagleBone Black:

```
$ git push resin master
```

The first time you do this, it will take several minutes (it's faster subsequently). You can track the progress on your resin.io dashboard (figure 12.8). You'll be able to view the app in a browser on your computer at its local IP address.

Figure 12.8   Resin.io application dashboard during deployment

To iterate on your app, you can make changes in your local repository, commit, and push as often as you need to.

GIVING YOUR APP A PUBLIC URL

You've been building a lot of web-based interfaces for your gadgets, but so far you've only been able to visit your web applications from the same network. Resin.io has a nifty feature that will generate a public URL for a device, allowing external access to port 80 on that device (now you know why you changed the port number!).

To enable public URLs for the application as a whole, head to the Actions section from your application's dashboard (figure 12.9).

Figure 12.9   Enable public URLs for your application from the application's Actions tab.

Next, get into a device-specific view by navigating to the Devices section and clicking on the name of the device you'd like to manage—*red-night* in my case (figure 12.10).

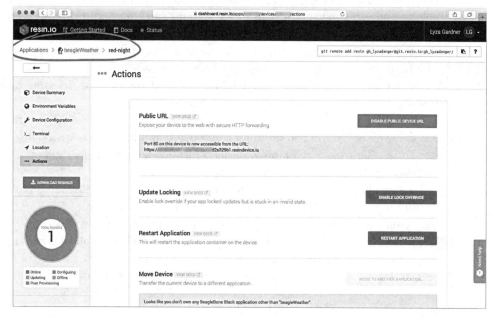

Figure 12.10   See the public URL for a device by navigating to the device-specific Actions tab.

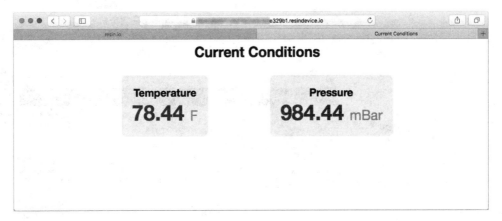

Figure 12.11   The weather station app, running on a BeagleBone Black, accessed by a resin .io-generated public URL

Head to the Actions section again—these are actions for just this device instead of the whole application. You should be able to see—and, helpfully, click on—the public URL for your application running on your BeagleBone Black (figure 12.11).

12.3 *Hardware and the web browser*

The weather station application takes advantage of a relatively modern web API, Web-Sockets (more accurately, it uses `socket.IO`, which uses the WebSockets API in browsers that support it). This API is used to maintain a connection between the client (browser) and server (running on the BeagleBone Black, in this case). The server is able to emit updated sensor data that the client can "hear" and process accordingly. But that's still indirect—the browser relies on the server to handle the actual interaction with the BeagleBone Black's I/O and attached sensor. Is it possible to interact with hardware, directly, from within the browser itself?

The answer is complex—a combination of "it depends" and "in some browsers," with a hefty dose of "wait and see just a bit longer."

The web is, without doubt, a much more physically capable platform than it was just a few years ago. It wasn't that long ago that you'd have to create a native application to be able to access a mobile device's location services or its camera, or to send push notifications. Now all of that can be done in the browser.

The web platform is a (vast) collection of technologies and APIs. Sure, there are the headlining stars—HTML, ECMAScript, and CSS (though, technically, CSS isn't one thing but a collection of *modules*)—but there are also dozens and dozens of other pieces: Web Workers, WebGL, XMLHttpRequest, Web Audio, WebSocket, WebRTC (I could go on all day). Different technologies and APIs are at different stages in the standardization process, and some aren't technically on the standards track at all, yet.

12.3.1 *The Web Bluetooth API*

The Web Bluetooth API allows for interaction with Bluetooth Low Energy (BLE) devices via the Generic Attribute Profile (GATT). There's an active community group for Web Bluetooth on the W3C (the World Wide Web Consortium, the main body that develops web standards), and it's implemented in some versions of Chrome, Opera, and the Android browser. But it's neither a standard nor even on the standards track yet (though it is headed in that general direction). It's complicated.

Web Bluetooth has also hit a snag typical of web-hardware APIs: security concerns. It doesn't take a genius to conjure up a few visions of how physical devices exposed to the web could pose a security nightmare. At this point, Mozilla (Firefox) isn't pursuing Web Bluetooth implementation because it's dissatisfied with the (current) security model.

But lest this sound bleak, these struggles are't atypical of proposed standards. It's just hard to predict where Web Bluetooth will be in six months or two years. And you can—and will—use it today in Chrome.

12.3.2 *The Generic Sensor API*

Web Bluetooth isn't the only nascent, hardware-related web API in town (though it does have the most complete browser implementations at this point). The W3C's Device and Sensors Working Group (https://www.w3.org/2009/dap/) is tasked with creating APIs that "interact with device hardware, sensors, services and applications such as the camera, microphone, proximity sensors, native address books, calendars and native messaging applications."

The group's Generic Sensor API (https://www.w3.org/TR/generic-sensor/), currently in draft stage, defines an abstract `Sensor` base class, which does nothing on its own but is intended to be extended by component-specific APIs. An example of this is the Ambient Light Sensor API (also a draft, https://www.w3.org/TR/ambient-light/), which defines an interface—based on `Sensor`—for interacting with ambient light sensors. If you review the specs' details, it may come as no surprise that one of the editors of the generic and other sensor APIs is Rick Waldron—the inventor of Johnny-Five. There are certainly aspects of the API's component-behavior encapsulation that are in harmony with how Johnny-Five abstracts behavior.

These APIs aren't concerned with the nuts and bolts of how hardware is detected and connected to so much as defining a higher-level API for interacting with components. As such, early implementations of Ambient Light Sensor rely on the presence of built-in hardware (typically a device's camera), and on the browser exposing that hardware accordingly. Ambient Light Sensor is available (behind a flag—you have to explicitly enable it within the browser's settings) in Chrome and in Microsoft Edge.

12.3.3 *The Physical Web*

The Physical Web is a discovery service that greatly simplifies interacting with objects via simple Bluetooth LE beacons, taking advantage of one of the greatest gifts the web gives us: the URL.

We looked at the Physical Web briefly way back in chapter 1. The scenario envisioned there was of a beacon-enabled bus stop. The beacon constantly broadcasts a URL that corresponds to a page where the next bus arrivals can be tracked (figure 12.12).

Or say you're walking through a sculpture garden. Some of the works have a beacon near or on them, broadcasting a URL to a web page with information about that piece and its artist. As you wander, you can see the beacons near you and opt to interact with one of them, visiting the URL it's advertising.

Google is championing the Physical Web and the related open BLE protocol, Eddystone. Because the technical demands are so straightforward—a BLE device merely needs to advertise a URL using a certain protocol—the hardware needs are minimal and beacon batteries can last a long, long, long time. Apps, available now for Android and iOS, allow you to find any beacons near you.

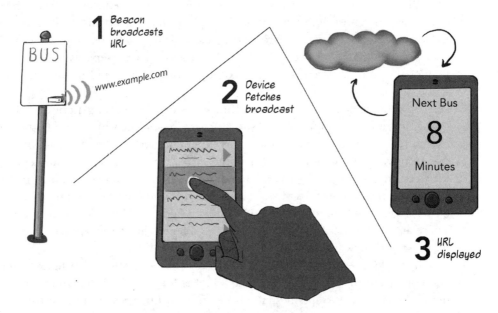

Figure 12.12   With the Physical Web, Bluetooth Low Energy (BLE) beacons attached to or embedded in a physical object broadcast a URL pertinent to interacting with that device. Nearby users can detect and engage with devices, opening their associated web pages in a browser.

12.4 Exploring Bluetooth LE with Puck.js

Espruino makes a device that allows you to experiment—today! right now!—with Web Bluetooth and the Physical Web. The Puck.js is a button-shaped device that runs the Espruino interpreter and communicates using BLE (figure 12.13). You'll harness that to get hands-on with both Web Bluetooth and the Physical Web.

Puck.js has a flexible silicone cover.

The Puck.js board fits into a case.

Figure 12.13　Puck.js is a BLE beacon device that—like the Pico—runs the Espruino JavaScript interpreter.

12.4.1 Core features

Puck.js is built around an ultra-low-power Nordic Semiconductor SoC (system on a chip) that includes Bluetooth LE and NFC support as well as an ARM Cortex M4 CPU that's not too dissimilar from the Pico's. Although both the Pico and Puck.js run the same underlying Espruino software, Puck.js differs from the Pico in the way that you communicate with it: over BLE versus the Pico's direct USB connection.

Puck.js's onboard components include a built-in magnetometer, thermometer, and three LEDs (red, green, blue). The red LED can also be used as an ambient light sensor.

The Puck.js is a 3.3 V device powered by a coin-cell battery. It's roughly comparable to a Pico, though somewhat more constrained: slower clock speed, a little less memory, and fewer I/O pins (figure 12.14).

Puck.js has a flexible silicone cover. The whole thing can operate as a big button, making a tactile click as you press down on it (and activate its built-in button).

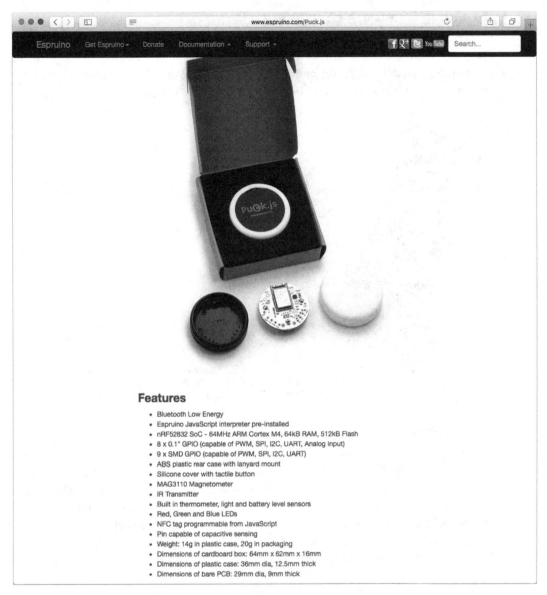

Features

- Bluetooth Low Energy
- Espruino JavaScript interpreter pre-installed
- nRF52832 SoC - 64MHz ARM Cortex M4, 64kB RAM, 512kB Flash
- 8 x 0.1" GPIO (capable of PWM, SPI, I2C, UART, Analog Input)
- 9 x SMD GPIO (capable of PWM, SPI, I2C, UART)
- ABS plastic rear case with lanyard mount
- Silicone cover with tactile button
- MAG3110 Magnetometer
- IR Transmitter
- Built in thermometer, light and battery level sensors
- Red, Green and Blue LEDs
- NFC tag programmable from JavaScript
- Pin capable of capacitive sensing
- Weight: 14g in plastic case, 20g in packaging
- Dimensions of cardboard box: 64mm x 62mm x 16mm
- Dimensions of plastic case: 36mm dia, 12.5mm thick
- Dimensions of bare PCB: 29mm dia, 9mm thick

Figure 12.14   Some of Puck.js's features, as listed on Espruino's website

12.4.2 *GPIO features and pinouts*

Puck.js has various GPIO capabilities, including I²C, PWM, SPI, and ADC (figure 12.15). You'll make use of its onboard hardware (only) in these experiments.

Figure 12.15 A detail of the Puck.js pinout from Espruino.com. Pin D11 can sense capacitive input. I²C, SPI, and USART support is available on any pin (there's support for one hardware interface each, but unlimited software support for I²C and SPI).

12.4.3 Configuration and workflow

Head on over to Espruino's Puck.js Getting Started Guide: http://www.espruino .com/Puck.js+Quick+Start. You'll need to disassemble the device to remove a protective battery tab.

What happens after that depends on your development platform OS and the state of Web Bluetooth at the moment. Chrome on Mac OS supports it—that's easy. Linux users may have an extra step and may need to enable a flag or two in Chrome. Web Bluetooth support in Windows (in Chrome) is potentially imminent (mid-2017). Refer to the Getting Started Guide for up-to-date information.

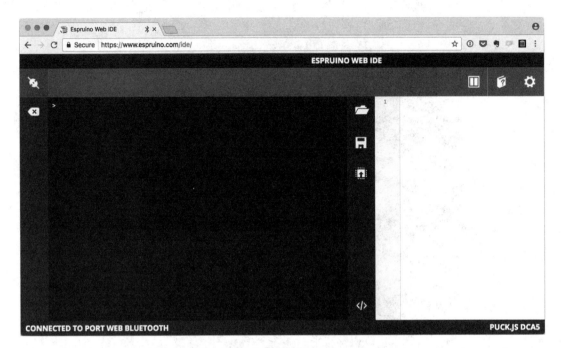

Figure 12.16   Espruino's web-based IDE

If you followed along with the Pico experiments in chapter 11, you may have already installed the Espruino Chrome app IDE. If not, don't worry, because you can actually work with Puck.js using the web-based IDE at https://www.espruino.com/ide (no installation required). The Web IDE (figure 12.16) is a spittin' image of the Chrome app IDE.

> **IF YOU CAN'T GET WEB BLUETOOTH SUPPORT...**   A browser that supports Web Bluetooth is required for the web-controlled LED and remote doorbell experiments later in the chapter. You don't need Web Bluetooth support for the basic Hello World LED blinking, nor for the Physical Web example—Puck.js can be controlled from within the IDE for those.
>
> You won't be able to use the web-based IDE at https://www.espruino.com/ide if you don't have Web Bluetooth support. Instead, you'll need to install the Web IDE (see Puck.js's Getting Started Guide for details: http://www.espruino .com/Puck.js+Quick+Start).

Recall also from chapter 11 that Espruino code authoring involves the use of Espruino modules—encapsulated behavior and support that can be imported into Espruino scripts.

There are three main ways to get Puck.js to do something:

- Once it's connected, Puck.js will execute any commands typed into the left side of the IDE interface, similar to a REPL or console.

- Code written in the right side of the IDE can be uploaded using the send-to-Espruino icon.
- Data and commands can be sent to and received from Puck.js over Web Bluetooth. This is done within the browser execution context, relying on a small client-side JavaScript library provided by Espruino. (This method is unique to Puck.js, unlike other Espruino boards.)

12.4.4 Examples, tutorials, and API documentation

Fire up the IDE and connect to your Puck.js so you can try out a Hello World LED blink and poke at a few of Puck.js's features.

Try typing some of the following commands into the left side of the IDE. After you press Enter, the command will sent over BLE to Puck.js and be executed there:

- Turn the red onboard LED on with `LED1.set()`.
- Turn the red onboard LED off with `LED1.reset()`.
- Try the preceding commands with the other two LEDs: `LED2` (green) and `LED3` (blue).
- The red LED also serves as an ambient light sensor. Make sure that all of the LEDs are off (`LEDx.reset()`), and then try `Puck.light()` to return an ambient light reading. Try covering up Puck.js with your hand and sending the `Puck.light()` command a second time to see the difference.
- Try `E.getTemperature()` to get a temperature reading. `E` is Espruino's utility class. The temperature should be accurate to about +/-1 degree (Celsius).

Espruino's API documentation (http://www.espruino.com/Reference) covers the API available to all Espruino devices, as well as the Puck-specific capabilities exposed on the `Puck` global object.

12.4.5 Controlling the LED from a web page

What you'll need
- 1 Puck.js
- 1 Web Bluetooth–enabled web browser

As you've seen, you can control Puck.js by using the IDE: sending it commands or writing a script and deploying it to the device. This is a similar workflow to the Espruino Pico.

But there's another way: you can control Puck.js from your own code within the browser. In this experiment, you'll build a web page that allows a user to turn Puck.js's red LED on and off by clicking buttons in the browser (figure 12.17).

The page's JavaScript will need to pair with Puck.js and communicate with it (send it commands) using Web Bluetooth.

Espruino makes this part easy for you by providing a small client-side library (a JavaScript file) that you can use in our page. The library abstracts away the details of the Web Bluetooth API, giving you a simple interface you can use to pair and interact with Puck.js.

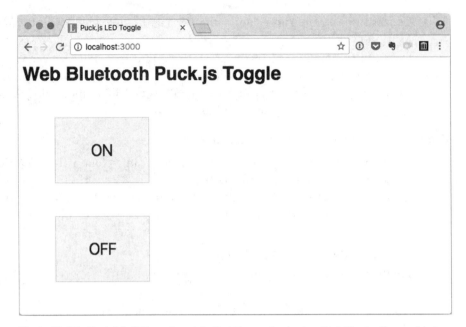

Figure 12.17   Puck.js's LED can be controlled via a web page in a Web Bluetooth–capable browser.

That client-side library can be found at https://www.puck-js.com/puck.js. You'll include it in the index.html page of the project.

> **WEB BLUETOOTH: STILL CURIOUS?**   If you're curious about how Web Bluetooth works under the covers, you can read the source of the puck.js JavaScript file, which is well-commented: https://www.puck-js.com/puck.js.

The JavaScript library from puck-js.com gives you utilities for connecting to and communicating with Puck.js, but you'll still need to write your own specific logic for handling button clicks and sending commands to Puck.js to turn the LED on and off.

SETTING UP THE PROJECT STRUCTURE

First you need to establish a working area—make a directory called led-toggle. Then, inside of that directory, run this command:

```
$ npm install express
```

That's the only project dependency.

Next, create an application entry point in index.js, which spins up a super-basic static web server for assets in app/, as shown in the next listing.

Listing 12.5   index.js

```
const express = require('express');
const path    = require('path');
const http    = require('http');
```

```
const app    = new express();
const server = new http.Server(app);

app.use(express.static(path.join(__dirname, '/app')));
server.listen(3000);
```

Now it's time to create the application's HTML page. To do so, create an app directory in the project and add index.html with the contents shown in the following listing.

Listing 12.6   index.html

```
<html>
 <head>
  <title>Puck.js LED Toggle</title>
  <style>
    h1 {
       font-family: "Helvetica";
    }
    button {
      display: block;
      width: 6em;
      height: 4em;
      margin: 2em;
      background-color: #eee;
      border: 1px solid #ccc;
      font-size: 1.75em;
    }
  </style>
 </head>
  <body>
  <h1>Web Bluetooth Puck.js Toggle</h1>
  <div id="message"></div>            ◁────  Container to hold messaging if
                                             Web Bluetooth isn't supported
  <button id="onButton">ON</button>
  <button id="offButton">OFF</button>
  <script src="https://www.puck-js.com/puck.js"></script>   ◁──┐  Provides a Puck object
  <script>          ◁──┐                                         for communicating
    // ... TBD         │  The application's client-side           with Puck.js using
  </script>           │  logic: you need to write it!             Web Bluetooth
  </body>
</html>
```

The HTML page doesn't do anything on its own: it has some CSS and includes the script from the puck-js.com site that allows you to communicate with Puck.js using Web Bluetooth. It also has the markup for the ON and OFF buttons, but they don't do anything yet.

CREATING THE LED-TOGGLING LOGIC

Let's talk about click handlers for the ON and OFF buttons. When a button is clicked, you need to send a command to the Puck to turn its red LED on or off. As you saw in section 12.4.4, this is the command that Puck.js needs to execute to turn on the red LED:

```
LED1.set();
```

That's the command that you need to send to Puck.js from the browser, using the puck.js client-side library as a messenger. The command needs to be sent to Puck.js as a string, including the \n (line break) character. This is the resulting command string:

```
'LED1.set();\n'
```

To send this to Puck.js, you'll use the `write()` method on the `Puck` object, which is globally available in your page's JavaScript because you included the client-side puck.js library (figure 12.18).

```
Puck.write('LED1.set();\n');
```

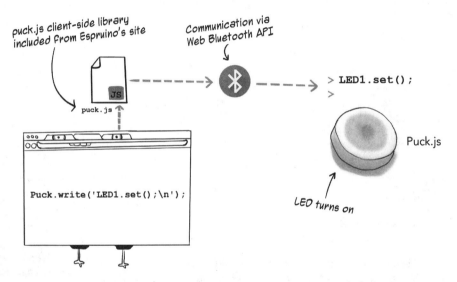

Figure 12.18 Your browser-executed JavaScript invokes the `write()` method on the `Puck` object provided by the `puck.js` library. That library uses Web Bluetooth to send the string to the physical Puck.js, which evaluates it. The \n at the end of the string command lets Puck.js know the command is complete; it's almost like typing into a virtual REPL and hitting Enter.

What does Puck.js even mean?

There's a `Puck` object in the browser, a different `Puck` object you can send commands to in the Puck.js IDE, and Puck.js and `puck.js` are totally different things. Yikes!

The naming conventions are admittedly a tad brain-melting. Here's a summary:

- Puck.js—The Puck.js physical device itself
- `puck.js`—A client-side JavaScript library, provided by Espruino, used in the browser for communicating with a Puck.js device via Web Bluetooth (BLE)

- Puck object—Confusingly, this is one of two (totally different) things depending on where the code is executing:
  - In the IDE or scripts running on Puck.js directly—It's the Espruino `Puck` global class (http://www.espruino.com/Reference#Puck), which adds some hardware-interaction functionality specific to Puck.js—that is, functionality that's not available on other Espruino boards (such as using `Puck.light()` to get a reading from Puck.js's ambient light sensor)
  - In a browser, assuming the inclusion of the `puck.js` client-side library— Provides access to some methods for communicating with Puck.js over Web Bluetooth (such as `Puck.write()` and `Puck.connect()`). Keep in mind that any commands sent are evaluated on Puck.js itself, in the Espruino interpreter.

This means that in a browser script—assuming the `puck.js` client library is included—the following statement is valid:

```
Puck.write('Puck.light();\n');
```

`Puck.write()` is executed in the browser's context, which means it refers to the object provided by the included `puck.js` library. But the command it sends via `write()` is evaluated on Puck.js itself: the `Puck` object in `Puck.light()` is a reference to the global Espruino `Puck` object. Whew!

The following listing defines what goes between the `<script>` tags in index.html: the click event listeners and the commands sent to Puck.js.

Listing 12.7 Event listeners for toggling LEDs

```
window.addEventListener('load', () => {
  if ('bluetooth' in window.navigator) {
    const onButton = window.document.getElementById('onButton');
    const offButton = window.document.getElementById('offButton');
    onButton.addEventListener('click', () => Puck.write('LED1.set();\n'));
    offButton.addEventListener('click', () => Puck.write('LED1.reset();\n'));
  } else {
    const mEl = window.document.getElementById('message');
    mEl.innerHTML = "Looks like your browser doesn't support Bluetooth!";
  }
});
```

The ersatz feature detection in listing 12.7—if (`'bluetooth'` in `window.navigator`)— is admittedly ham-fisted and naive. Just because a browser exposes `navigator.bluetooth` doesn't mean it correctly implements what's needed for Puck.js. There's a more correct and thorough check for browser support in a function called `checkIf-Supported()`, inside of the JavaScript code that gives you the `Puck` object. Unfortunately, that function isn't exposed to the Puck object—it's not in any scope you have access to—so you can't invoke it directly.

Try it out! Start the web server using node index.js, and open a Web Bluetooth–capable browser to localhost:3000.

When you first click on a button, you'll see a pairing request pop up, similar to figure 12.19. Once the pairing is complete, you should be able to click ON and OFF and see Puck.js's red LED turn on and off.

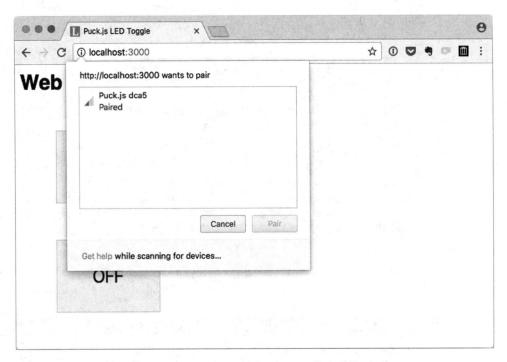

Figure 12.19   You'll be prompted to pair with Puck.js when you first click a button.

12.4.6 *The Physical Web and Puck.js*

What you'll need
- 1 Puck.js
- 1 mobile device running Android or iOS

The Physical Web is composed of beacons using a specific format—Eddystone—to broadcast an associated URL, and these broadcasts can be picked up by apps running on mobile devices.

Puck.js can serve as a Physical Web–compatible beacon quite easily. To get this going, you'll need to do the following:

- Install a Physical Web discovery utility application, or enable this feature in Chrome, on a mobile device.

- Determine what URL you'd like Puck.js to broadcast.
- Make Puck.js start advertising itself as a compatible beacon.

THE EDDYSTONE PROTOCOL

Eddystone is an open BLE beacon protocol created by Google. Physical Web beacons use this format to broadcast their associated URL, and client applications detect these Eddystone beacons.

Eddystone is straightforward. There are only a few kinds of information—*frame types*—that an Eddystone-speaking beacon can send, the most pertinent one being `Eddystone-URL`.

Length constraints of `Eddystone-URL`

The maximum length of an `Eddystone-URL` URL is 17. That's tight. But it's not as restrictive as it sounds. A separate byte is also used to hold a representation of the URL's *scheme* prefix, (https://www., http://, and so on)—those characters don't count against the 17. Also, common top-level domains (.com, .org, and the like) can be represented with a single character, leaving 16 characters free. It's assumed that developers will use URL shorteners (such as https://goo.gl) to minimize URL lengths.

The URL https://www.lyza.com is 20 characters long in its normal form, but it only requires 5 of the available 17 bytes.

CONFIGURING THE PUCK.JS AS A BEACON

Setting up Puck.js as an Eddystone-compatible Physical Web beacon is almost breathtakingly easy. There's a `ble_eddystone` Espruino module just waiting for you! Fire up the Web IDE, connect to your Puck.js, and enter the following command on the left side of the IDE:

```
require("ble_eddystone").advertise("https://www.lyza.com");
```

(Feel free, of course, to replace my domain's URL with any you like.)

Disconnect the IDE from your Puck.js so that it can start broadcasting in Eddystone format.

ENABLING PHYSICAL WEB DISCOVERY ON YOUR MOBILE DEVICE

You can detect your Puck.js Physical Web beacon with devices that run Android or iOS (figure 12.20); instructions can be found on the Physical Web website (https://google.github.io/physical-web/try-physical-web). Once it's configured, your mobile device should be able to see your Puck.js beacon.

It's time to go out with a bang (well, a ding, anyway). Our last experiment will combine Web Bluetooth, Web Audio, and data sent from Puck.js.

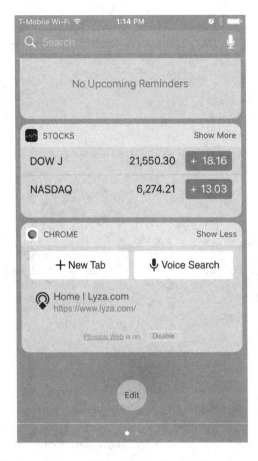

Figure 12.20   Physical Web support via the Chrome widget on iOS. Puck.js is configured to broadcast the URL https://www.lyza.com using the Eddystone protocol.

12.4.7   A web-based Bluetooth doorbell

What you'll need

- 1 Puck.js
- 1 Web Bluetooth–enabled web browser

This experiment plays a (high-quality) sound and displays a visual alert in a browser whenever the paired Puck.js button is pressed. Think of it as a web-based doorbell. It takes advantage of the Web Audio API—yet another handsome web API—to load and play a (public-domain) chime sound.

The application logic uses the client-side `puck.js` library to connect to Puck.js over Web Bluetooth, configures the Puck.js to monitor its onboard button, and parses data—string output that will signify button presses—emitted by Puck.js.

SETTING UP THE PROJECT STRUCTURE

Start by establishing a working area. Make a directory ("doorbell") and install `express` as a dependency in that directory:

```
$ npm install express
```

Create index.js, the static web server. You can reuse the code in listing 12.5, which will run a static web server on port 3000.

CREATING THE HTML AND EVENT LISTENERS

Create an app directory inside of doorbell. Add an index.html file with the following content.

Listing 12.8   index.html

```html
<html>
 <head>
  <title>Puck.js Remote Chime</title>
  <style>
    body {
      max-width: 90%;
      font-family: "Times New Roman";
      margin: 1em auto;
      color: #111;
      background-color: transparent;
      transition: background-color 0.5s ease-in-out;
    }
    .ding {
      background-color: #e60a62;
      transition: all 0.1s ease-in-out;
    }
    button {
      width: 100%;
      height: 100%;
      border: 5px solid #e60a62;
      font-family: "Times New Roman";
      text-transform: lowercase;
      font-variant: small-caps;
      background-color: transparent;
      font-size: 3em;
      font-weight: 600;
      cursor: pointer;
    }
    button:hover {
      color: #fff;
      border-color: #b5084d;
      background-color: #f62c7d;
    }
    .active {
      opacity: 0;
      transition: all 1s;
    }
  </style>
 </head>
 <body>
    <button id="goButton">Turn it on</button>
    <script src="https://www.puck-js.com/puck.js"></script>
    <script src="PuckChime.js"></script>
    <script>
      // ... add event listeners
```

```
      </script>
    </body>
</html>
```

If you were to view index.html in a browser now, you'd see what's shown in figure 12.21, but it wouldn't do anything yet.

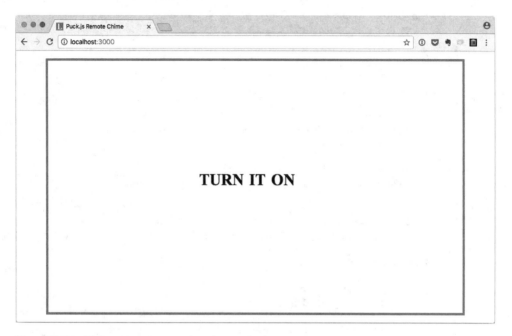

Figure 12.21   Right now, index.html shows a really big button, but it doesn't have any functionality.

The button (`#goButton`) will ultimately have a click-event handler that will enable the doorbell. You may be wondering why this extra click step is needed—why not just activate the doorbell on page load? For privacy and permissions reasons, there needs to be an explicit user interface action before Bluetooth pairing is allowed by the browser—if you tried to do this without active user input, you'd get an error.

The index.html file contains a chunk of CSS. Some of the styling is to format the big Turn It On button, but there are also styles to make the screen flash when the doorbell chimes and to fade out the Turn It On button (the `.active` class) once the doorbell is activated.

You can now fill in the `<script>` content with the code in the following listing. This code assumes the existence of a `PuckChime` class, whose creation we'll get to next.

Listing 12.9   Click handler for the Turn It On button

```
window.addEventListener('load', () => {
  const onButton = window.document.getElementById('goButton');
  onButton.addEventListener('click', function () {
```

```
      var chime = new PuckChime();
      chime.init().then(() => {
        onButton.classList.add('active');
      });
    });
  });
```

> Once the chime.init() Promise resolves, you'll know the BLE Puck.js chime has been set up successfully.

> You don't need the button anymore, so you can add the active class to make it fade out.

CODING THE PUCKCHIME CLASS

The logic for the BLE doorbell is more involved than dispatching one-line commands to Puck.js in click event handlers, as in the previous LED-controlling web page.

It makes sense to encapsulate the code in a class, PuckChime, inside a new file, app/PuckChime.js. The API surface for PuckChime is shown in the following listing. You'll fill it out in the next few steps.

Listing 12.10   The API surface for PuckChime

```
class PuckChime {
  constructor () {

  }

  init () {
    /**
     * - establish connection to Puck.js
     * - reset Puck.js
     * - send command to Puck.js: observe builtin button for presses
     * - invoke `chime()` as aural/visual confirm when successful
     */
  }

  connect () {
    /**
     * - connect to Puck.js with BLE
     * - add an event handler for Puck.js `data` events
     */
  }

  send (cmd) {
    // format and send `cmd` to Puck.js
  }

  reset () {
    // send a `reset` command to Puck.js and wait 1.5 seconds for it to "take"
  }

  watchButton () {
    /**
     * send a command to Puck.js to watch its button for presses
     * and log (over Bluetooth) a string when button is pressed
     */
  }

  parseData (data) {
    /**
```

```
 *   `data` event handler for incoming data chunks from Puck.js
 *   - append `data` to buffer
 *   - parse buffer into lines (split on `\n`)
 *   - send each line (`cmd`) to `parseCommand()`
 */
  }

  parseCommand (cmd) {
    // if `cmd` is `CHIME`, invoke `chime()`
  }

  chime () {
    // play a chime sound and make visual chime
  }
}
```

Let's look at how the constructor and `init()` methods can be implemented in the next listing.

Listing 12.11   `PuckChime`: constructor and initialization methods

Holds the connection to Puck.js; it's initially null until connected

```
constructor () {
  this.connection = null;        ◄
  this.dataBuffer = '';          ◄
  this.sound = new Sound('/chime.mp3');   ◄
}

init () {
  return this.connect().then(() => {
    return new Promise((resolve, reject) => {
      this.reset()
        .then(this.watchButton.bind(this))
        .then(() => {
          this.chime();       ◄
          resolve();
        });
    });
  });
}
```

A buffer for holding and parsing incoming data from Puck.js

Sound is a convenience class for loading and playing a sound with the Web Audio API.

After init's work is complete, invokes chime() once

The `constructor` readies a sound—chime.mp3—by instantiating a `Sound` object. If `Sound` seems like a magical class that came out of nowhere, and chime.mp3 a file of mysterious origin, you're right! Hang tight; more details on them in a little bit.

The `init` method returns a `Promise` that resolves when the following steps are complete:

1 A connection is established with Puck.js
2 Puck.js is reset
3 Puck.js is instructed to watch its button for presses

Only when those things are all done does the Promise returned by init() resolve; chime() is also invoked as a confirmation (the doorbell will ring once when it's ready to go).

Moving along, the methods connect(), send(cmd), reset(), and watchButton() communicate with Puck.js, each returning a Promise. These methods rely on the client-side puck.js communication code provided by Espruino:

- connect()—Connects to Puck.js and adds an event handler (parseData) for Puck.js data events
- send(cmd)—Formats the string cmd appropriately and sends it to Puck.js, wrapping the callback-oriented connection.write() method with a Promise for consistency
- reset()—Sends a reset command to Puck.js and also waits 1.5 s for Puck.js to be ready again before resolving the Promise it returns
- watchButton()—Sends a more complex command to Puck.js to set up a watch on its built-in button

These methods are fleshed out in the following listing.

Listing 12.12   Methods for communicating with Puck.js

```
connect () {
  return new Promise ((resolve, reject) => {
    Puck.connect(connection => {
      this.connection = connection;
      this.connection.on('data', this.parseData.bind(this));
      resolve(this.connection);
    });
  });
}

send (cmd) {
  cmd = `\x10${cmd}\n`;
  return new Promise ((resolve, reject) => {
    this.connection.write(cmd, () => { resolve(cmd); });
  });
}

reset () {
  return new Promise((resolve, reject) => {
    this.send('reset()').then(() => { setTimeout(resolve, 1500); });
  });
}

watchButton () {
  const cb = "function() { Bluetooth.println('CHIME'); LED1.set();
➥ setTimeout(() => LED1.reset(), 250);}";
  const opts = "{repeat:true,debounce:250,edge:'rising'}";
  const cmd = `setWatch(${cb},BTN,${opts});`;
  return this.send(cmd);
}
```

Let's zoom in on the command sent by watchButton()—it's a bit of a doozy as formatted—and get a better understanding of what's going on with sending and receiving Puck.js data and commands.

As you saw in the web-controlled LED example in section 12.4.5, commands need to be formatted as strings before sending them to Puck.js from the browser. In the simpler LED experiment, this was done with individual calls to Puck.write() (see figure 12.18).

In this more complex case, where data is going in both directions, you're instead establishing a persistent connection (in the connect() method). Once the connection is established, commands are sent to Puck.js using connection.write(). Data is received from Puck.js via emitted data events on the connection (figure 12.22), which are handled by the registered data event handler, parseData(). We'll get to that in a moment.

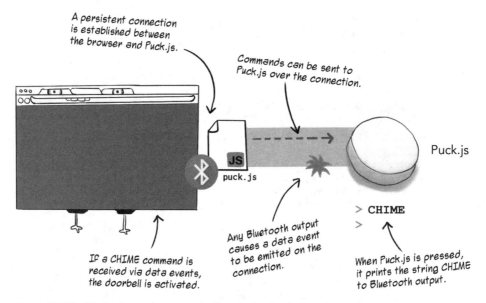

Figure 12.22 For the two-way communications in the doorbell example, the puck.js client library is used to establish a persistent connection between the browser and Puck.js. Commands can be sent to Puck.js over the connection, and any output to Bluetooth by Puck.js triggers a data event on the connection.

PuckChime objects send two commands to Puck.js: a reset() command during the init phase to clear any cobwebs or oddities out of Puck.js, and then a more complex command in watchButton(). The command constructed in that method, disabused of all its stringiness and ignoring line-break constraints, is shown expanded in the following listing. It makes use of the Espruino global setWatch(<callback>, <pin>, [<options>]) function.

Listing 12.13 Puck.js command, expanded

```
                    The first argument to
             setWatch(): a callback function
                   setWatch(
                     function () {                          Logs the string CHIME
                       Bluetooth.println('CHIME');          over Bluetooth; this will
   Turns the                                                trigger a data event
   red LED on          LED1.set();
                       setTimeout(() => {                   Turns the red LED off
                         LED1.reset();                      again after 250 ms
                       }, 250);
     The pin         },
     to watch        BTN,
                     {                                      Debounces the pin (button) to 250
                                                            ms to avoid triggering multiple
     Keeps             repeat: true,                        times per press or interfering with
  watching this        debounce: 250,                       previous presses
  pin repeatedly       edge: 'rising'
                     }                                      Triggers on a rising edge—the
                   );                                       transition from LOW to HIGH
```

The callback registered on Puck.js for button presses logs out a string via Bluetooth and also lights up the onboard red LED briefly as visual feedback.

Data is emitted from Puck.js any time something is output on Bluetooth. This happens when `Bluetooth.println('CHIME')` is executed in the button-watching callback, but not everything that comes from the Puck.js will be a `CHIME` command. For instance, several lines of debugging and version output are generated (automatically) right after a connection is established. Those lines aren't relevant to your logic, so the `parseCommand(cmd)` makes sure you have an actual match for the string `CHIME`.

Before you can feed the commands into `parseCommand()`, though, you have to parse out the "commands" from the other incoming data. Data comes in chunks, so it's up to the `parseData()` handler to keep a simple buffer and break the incoming string data into lines—delimited by `\n` (line-break) characters. Those lines are each passed to `parseCommand()` to see if they do, in fact, represent a valid command—`CHIME` being your only valid command. See the following listing.

Listing 12.14 Parsing data from Puck.js

-1 is the only value that will produce 0 (false) in the face of the bitwise NOT (~) operator.

Strips any non-alphanumeric characters in case a control character got crammed in

```
parseData (data) {
  this.dataBuffer += data;
  var cmdEndIndex = this.dataBuffer.indexOf('\n');
  while (~cmdEndIndex) {
    var cmd = this.dataBuffer.substr(0, cmdEndIndex).replace(/\W/g, '');
    this.parseCommand(cmd);
    this.dataBuffer = this.dataBuffer.substr(cmdEndIndex + 1);
    cmdEndIndex = this.dataBuffer.indexOf('\n');
  }
}
```

Passes this line to parseCommand() to see if it means anything

Snips the current command off the front of the data buffer and sees if there are more lines

```
parseCommand (cmd) {
  if (cmd.match('CHIME')) {
    this.chime();
  }
}
```

The final method in the PuckChime class is the chime() itself. The Sound that was instantiated in the constructor gets played (with play()) and a class—.ding—gets added to the body element and is then removed after 500 ms, as shown in the following listing. The .ding class creates a visual chime in the browser by changing the background color of the entire page temporarily.

Listing 12.15 The chime itself

```
chime () {
  window.document.body.classList.add('ding');
  this.sound.play();
  window.setTimeout(() => {
    window.document.body.classList.remove('ding');
  }, 500);
}
```

WEB AUDIO AND THE SOUND CLASS

Sound is a JavaScript class that encapsulates the loading and playing of the sound file at the url passed to its constructor. It uses the Web Audio API. Its source is reproduced in listing 12.16; you can put it at the top of the PuckChime.js file. Alternatively, you can find the entire PuckChime.js source, including the Sound class, in the book's GitHub repository.

In the same directory as the hosted PuckChime.js source, you can also find the chime.mp3 sound file—or feel free to use your own sound file (don't forget to update the Sound instantiation in PuckChime's constructor if you give it a different filename).

Listing 12.16 The Sound class

```
class Sound {
  constructor (url) {
    // Context in which to do anything related to audio.
    // It is prefixed with `webkit` in some browsers
    const AudioContext = window.AudioContext || window.webkitAudioContext;
    this.url = url;
    this.context = new AudioContext();
    this.buffer = null;
  }
  /**
   * Using XMLHttpRequest, Load the audio file at this.url
   * decode and store it in this.buffer
   * @return Promise resolving to this.buffer
   */
  load () {
```

```
      return new Promise((resolve, reject) => {
        if (this.buffer) { resolve(this.buffer); }
        var request = new window.XMLHttpRequest();
        request.open('GET', this.url, true);
        request.responseType = 'arraybuffer';
        request.onload = () => {
          this.context.decodeAudioData(request.response, soundBuffer => {
            this.buffer = soundBuffer;
            resolve(this.buffer);
          });
        };
        request.send();
      });
    }
    /**
     * Load an AudioBuffer, then create an AudioBufferSourceNode to play it.
     * Connect the AudioBufferSourceNode to the destination (output)
     */
    play () {
      this.load().then(buffer => {
        // Create a new AudioBufferSourceNode which can play sound from
        // a buffer (AudioBuffer object)
        const source = this.context.createBufferSource();
        source.buffer = buffer;
        // Connect the AudioBufferSourceNode to the destination
        // (e.g. your laptop's speakers)
        source.connect(this.context.destination);
        source.start(0);
      });
    }
}
```

The Web Audio API is powerful, and it's correspondingly somewhat involved. MDN's Web Audio API documentation is comprehensive: https://developer.mozilla. org/en-US/docs/Web/API/Web_Audio_API.

TRYING OUT THE DOORBELL

To recap, the Puck.js doorbell project should contain the following files:

- index.js—A simple web server.
- app/index.html—Includes styling and markup for the big Turn It On button, as well as a click-event handler for the button to initialize the doorbell (Puck-Chime object). It also includes the Puck.js client JavaScript library for communicating with Puck.js, as well as PuckChime.js.
- app/PuckChime.js—Includes both the Sound and PuckChime classes.
- app/chime.mp3 (or another sound file of your choosing)—The sound played when the doorbell is pressed.

Start the web server:

```
$ node index.js
```

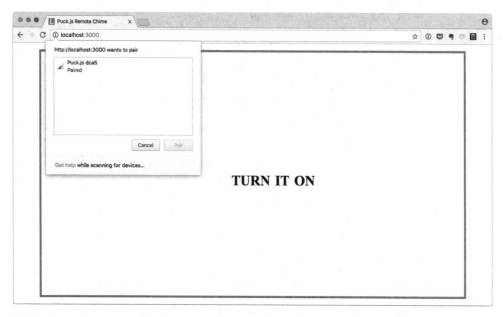

Figure 12.23   Clicking the Turn It On button will prompt for pairing to Puck.js.

Open up your browser to localhost:3000. It may help to also open up the Web Inspector's console in your browser to see any logged messages or errors. When you click the Turn It On button, you should see a pairing request pop up (figure 12.23).

After pairing, the initialization process takes a few seconds—you'll see some logging in the console. You'll know it's done and successful if you hear the doorbell sound play and see the screen flash pink briefly (figure 12.24).

Figure 12.24   When Puck.js's button is pressed, the chime sound plays and the screen flashes hot pink—one might even call it *pank*, it's so bright—momentarily.

12.5 Pushing the frontiers of JavaScript and hardware

This BLE doorbell experiment is a good illustration of where the frontiers are in the world of physical devices and JavaScript. Puck.js runs the Espruino interpreter, which is almost, but not quite, full JavaScript—optimizations are in place to make it possible to execute JavaScript on such constrained hardware. Web Bluetooth works in some browsers, but there are some shortcomings. At the time of writing, you have to re-pair on every page reload, which is a drag. And you may find it to be intermittently unreliable in tricky-to-debug ways.

But the very fact that Puck.js exists, and that Web Bluetooth is implemented in some browsers, is remarkable, and it's a huge leap from just 12 or 18 months ago. The continued popularity and I/O plugin growth of Johnny-Five, which turned five years old in 2017, is an indication that interest in these areas from JavaScript developers remains strong. This growing interest in the melding of JavaScript and other web technologies with physical devices is also echoed in the explosion of Node.js-capable cloud-managed options for IoT hardware, especially within the SBC class of devices that are capable of running Linux.

Building electronic-hacking competency doesn't mean planting a flag deeply and inflexibly. JavaScript doesn't have to be your hammer, your dogmatic single approach. Instead, it can serve as a paradigm for exploration, a familiar lens through which to examine the unfamiliar. JavaScript may indeed get you all the way to where you need to go. But for other cases, an open and curious mind is invaluable.

Thus, I encourage you not only to keep learning through JavaScript, but also, as you get more comfortable, to explore further. Read more about how different serial protocols work, dive deeper into bitwise manipulation, learn to write C-based firmware. And although it would be flip to say that C is easy, it's certainly approachable: Many have found the Arduino programming language (which, put very roughly, is basically C++ with some extra hardware-controlling goodies thrown in) a helpful gateway to C++ proficiency.

Tinker. Build. Ask questions. Read about technology. Break things on purpose. Know that, even if this is your very first time building circuits and working with physical I/O, you can figure out how to build the things you dream up. Happy hacking!

Summary

- There has been an explosion of cloud-based services for managing and deploying IoT applications, many targeted at the enterprise. Many of these services that are targeted at Linux-capable SBCs offer support for Node.js.
- Containerization is an approach that isolates applications and their dependencies from the vagaries of environment variations, and it's a popular choice for IoT application deployment.
- The Web Bluetooth API is not yet on the official web standards track, but implementations exist in several browsers. Some of its features aren't ironed out yet, and security and permissions models remain contentious.

- Espruino provides a small client-side JavaScript library that uses Web Bluetooth to communicate with Puck.js.
- The Generic Sensor API and further sensor APIs based on it, such as the Ambient Light Sensor API, are in their early days of standards definition, but they're under active development.
- To participate in the Physical Web, a BLE device can advertise a URL using the open Eddystone protocol. Nearby users with compatible discovery software can browse and interact with these beacons.

index